The World Bank Legal Review

Volume 7

Financing and Implementing the Post-2015 Development Agenda: The Role of Law and Justice Systems

AF817237

The World Bank Legal Review
Volume 7
Financing and Implementing the Post-2015 Development Agenda: The Role of Law and Justice Systems

The World Bank Legal Review is a publication for policy makers and their advisers, judges, attorneys, and other professionals engaged in the field of international development with a particular focus on law, justice, and development. It offers a combination of legal scholarship, lessons from experience, legal developments, and recent research on the many ways in which the application of the law and the improvement of justice systems promote poverty reduction, economic development, and rule of law.

Publication of Volume 7 of *The World Bank Legal Review* was made possible with the generous support of the OPEC Fund for International Development.

The World Bank Legal Review

Volume 7

Financing and Implementing the Post-2015 Development Agenda: The Role of Law and Justice Systems

Frank Fariello

Laurence Boisson de Chazournes

Kevin E. Davis

Editors

WORLD BANK GROUP

© 2016 International Bank for Reconstruction and Development / The World Bank
1818 H Street NW, Washington, DC 20433

Telephone: 202-473-1000; Internet: www.worldbank.org
Some rights reserved
1 2 3 4 19 18 17 16

This work is a product of the staff of The World Bank with external contributions. The findings, interpretations, and conclusions expressed in this work do not necessarily reflect the views of The World Bank, its Board of Executive Directors, or the governments they represent. The World Bank does not guarantee the accuracy of the data included in this work. The boundaries, colors, denominations, and other information shown on any map in this work do not imply any judgment on the part of The World Bank concerning the legal status of any territory or the endorsement or acceptance of such boundaries.

Nothing herein shall constitute or be considered to be a limitation upon or waiver of the privileges and immunities of The World Bank, all of which are specifically reserved.

Rights and Permissions

This work is available under the Creative Commons Attribution 3.0 IGO license (CC BY 3.0 IGO) http://creativecommons.org/licenses/by/3.0/igo. Under the Creative Commons Attribution license, you are free to copy, distribute, transmit, and adapt this work, including for commercial purposes, under the following conditions:

Attribution—Please cite the work as follows: Fariello, Frank, Laurence Boisson de Chazournes, and Kevin E. Davis, eds. 2016. *The World Bank Legal Review, Volume 7. Financing and Implementing the Post-2015 Development Agenda: The Role of Law and Justice Systems*. Washington, DC: World Bank. doi:10.1596/978-1-4648-0545-5 License: Creative Commons Attribution CC BY 3.0 IGO

Translations—If you create a translation of this work, please add the following disclaimer along with the attribution: *This translation was not created by The World Bank and should not be considered an official World Bank translation. The World Bank shall not be liable for any content or error in this translation.*

Adaptations—If you create an adaptation of this work, please add the following disclaimer along with the attribution: *This is an adaptation of an original work by The World Bank. Views and opinions expressed in the adaptation are the sole responsibility of the author or authors of the adaptation and are not endorsed by The World Bank.*

Third-party content—The World Bank does not necessarily own each component of the content contained within the work. The World Bank therefore does not warrant that the use of any third-party-owned individual component or part contained in the work will not infringe on the rights of those third parties. The risk of claims resulting from such infringement rests solely with you. If you wish to re-use a component of the work, it is your responsibility to determine whether permission is needed for that re-use and to obtain permission from the copyright owner. Examples of components can include, but are not limited to, tables, figures, or images.

All queries on rights and licenses should be addressed to the Publishing and Knowledge Division, The World Bank, 1818 H Street NW, Washington, DC 20433, USA; fax: 202-522-2625; e-mail: pubrights@worldbank.org.

ISBN (paper): 978-1-4648-0545-5

ISBN (electronic): 10.1596/978-1-4648-0546-2

DOI: 10.1596/978-1-4648-0545-5

Cover photo: © Arne Hoel / World Bank. Further permission required for reuse.

Cover design: Nigel Quinney

Library of Congress Cataloging-in-Publication Data has been requested.

The World Bank Legal Review

Volume 7

Financing and Implementing the Post-2015 Development Agenda: The Role of Law and Justice Systems

EDITOR IN CHIEF

Frank Fariello
Lead Counsel, World Bank

EDITORS

Laurence Boisson de Chazournes
Professor of Law, University of Geneva

Kevin E. Davis
Vice Dean, Beller Family Professor of Business Law, New York University School of Law

PRODUCTION EDITOR

Samuel V. P. Lucas
Legal Consultant, Legal Vice Presidency, World Bank

Contents

Foreword

Mahmoud Mohieldin
Senior Vice President for the 2030 Development Agenda, United Nations Relations, and Partnerships
The World Bank Group

With the adoption of the 2030 Agenda for Sustainable Development, which includes a set of 17 Sustainable Development Goals (SDGs), world leaders signed onto a global compact to end poverty and fight inequality and injustice, with a pledge to leave no one behind. The new goals, along with the broader sustainability agenda, seek to address the root causes of poverty and the universal need for development. This will necessitate a revitalized global partnership for sustainable development, with broad, multistakeholder participation.

The World Bank Group is fully committed to supporting the SDGs and the 2030 Agenda. In 2013, the World Bank Group established clear goals to guide its work: to end extreme poverty by 2030 and to promote shared prosperity in every country, in a sustainable manner. These goals are, conceptually and in practice, fully aligned with the SDGs.

In support of the SDGs and in collaboration with the United Nations and other development partners, the World Bank Group has identified three areas of focus and work: data, finance, and implementation. Addressing these challenges will be a significant task, but steps are already under way on all three fronts.

We are off to a good start with our work on data, commencing with a Memorandum of Understanding and its associated action program with other Multilateral Development Banks (MDBs) and the United Nations, as well as the creation of our own Data Council and the ongoing work on the data revolution. On finance, we are building on the success of the Addis Ababa Action Agenda (AAAA), agreed upon at the Third International Conference on Financing for Development, and we continue to strengthen our work as a financial institution with highly effective and innovative financing mechanisms and tools. On implementation, the World Bank Group is working to promote and support the global public goods agenda and help clients achieve the SDGs in accordance with national priorities.

During the Millennium Development Goals (MDGs) period, a lot was achieved through legal reform. But there is widespread recognition that some countries faced challenges that impeded progress, including weak governance and a lack of institutional capacity—sometimes exacerbated by the absence of peace and stability.

Rule of law is both an enabler and a facilitator of development. The ability of countries to implement the SDGs will hinge on improving rule of law, building strong institutions, and facilitating good governance, as well as introducing legal reforms. In line with the Rio+20 outcome document, *The Future We Want,* and the statement on Justice, Governance and Law for Environmental Sustainability, efforts such as these afford us an opportunity to explore the linkages between rule of law and good governance to reinforce the SDGs.

To address these challenges, Goal 16 of the SDGs was incorporated into the new agenda. This goal promotes "just, peaceful and inclusive societies" by building "effective, accountable and inclusive institutions at all levels." It includes targets relating to rule of law, reduction of illicit financial and arms flows, and citizens' participation in decision making, as well as transparency and equal access to justice for all. These goals require national action, as well as transboundary cooperation.

Strong governance is good not just for its own sake; it is a key enabler of development. The achievement of Goal 16, as well as the other SDGs, will depend in large part on legal means. Many of the targets underpinning the SDGs refer explicitly to legal concepts, such as property rights, as well as legal reforms, such as eliminating discriminatory laws. Others implicitly require the existence or adoption of regulatory measures or enforcing institutions to ensure access to services or resources.

The enabling role of justice and rule of law in supporting growth and poverty reduction must be fully realized. Ineffective private sector and business laws impede poverty reduction efforts (or increase poverty rates) in many nations. Without the legal institutions that allow innovation and entrepreneurship to thrive, other attempts to spur growth are more likely to fail. Sustained growth is nurtured through innovative business ventures. A challenge to such growth is a lack of trust between innovators with new ideas and financiers with capital. Property, contracts, and corporate law provide the legal framework to overcome distrust and allow innovative business ventures to flourish. This will be especially important for delivering the 2030 Agenda.

Yet efforts to deliver on these goals will face implementation challenges, including effective measurement and collection of data, incorporation of the goals and targets into national priorities and diverse cultural contexts, and balancing national priorities within an inclusive international framework.

In the implementation of this ambitious and transformative agenda, the World Bank Group—through knowledge sharing, technical assistance, and financial support—will be working alongside the United Nations, MDBs, and other partners to support governments in translating these global goals to the national level. In addition to providing traditional loans, the World Bank Group uses financial instruments to maximize available funds, including adding, pooling, and enabling instruments to generate new flows; debt-based/right-timing instruments that match flows to when cash is needed; risk management instruments to manage or reduce risk for investors; and results-based financing where payments are made specifically for desired results. Financing solutions can be customized to solve specific issues, replicated, and taken to scale.

During the 15-year effort to reach the MDGs, MDB support grew from US$50 billion to US$127 billion annually in grants, concessional and non-concessional loans, risk-sharing instruments, guarantees, and equity investments. Going forward, the MDBs are working to continue increasing the level of financing available to support our partner countries' efforts to achieve the SDGs. During the first three years of the SDG period (2016 to 2018), the MDBs plan to provide financial support of more than US$400 billion. Even more important than the direct financial assistance provided by MDBs is knowledge on how this assistance can best be used to catalyze, mobilize, and crowd-in both public and private sources of funds for development.

The World Bank Group, through the Legal Vice Presidency and the Governance Global Practice, has been working very closely with partners for the past two years on goals, targets, and indicators that pertain to rule of law. We have encouraged adoption of a framework that allows countries to select issues that are relevant to their particular contexts and that strengthen ties between citizens and their governments. In November 2015, as the keynote speaker for the World Bank's annual Law, Justice and Development Week, I had the opportunity to speak on the importance of rule of law, justice, and good governance in achieving the 2030 Agenda. The materials compiled here in this volume of *The World Bank Legal Review* expound the role that law and legal institutions can play in achieving the SDGs.

Rule of law, good governance, and robust institutions are indispensable for the achievement of the SDGs. New and existing partnerships will support this agenda, but most important, this vision requires all of us to take immediate action. As members of the global community, each of us can make a contribution to help millions lift themselves out of poverty—and ensure that no one is left behind.

Preface

ANNE-MARIE LEROY
SENIOR VICE PRESIDENT AND GROUP GENERAL COUNSEL
THE WORLD BANK

Since the publication of its first volume in 2003, *The World Bank Legal Review* has been a collaborative effort among legal scholars and development practitioners, whose work involves a range of disciplines, including law, economics, sociology, and other social sciences. Individually and collectively, they seek to inform policy makers and their advisers, judges, attorneys, and other professionals engaged in the field of international development, with a particular focus on law, justice, and development. *The World Bank Legal Review* offers a unique combination of legal scholarship, lessons from the field, reports on legal developments, and research on the many ways in which the law and justice systems help promote poverty reduction, economic development, and rule of law.

In past years, *The World Bank Legal Review* has delved into the relationship among law, equity, and development; the role of international financial institutions in global governance; legal innovation and empowerment for development; and the role of voice, accountability, and social contract in development. This year's volume, the seventh in the series, focuses on the role of law and justice in the post-2015 development agenda, with a special emphasis on how law will facilitate the implementation of the Sustainable Development Goals. The post-2015 development agenda was a central theme of the 2014 Law, Justice and Development Week held at the World Bank Headquarters in Washington, DC, on October 20–24, 2014; a number of chapters in this volume grew out of discussions during that week. This volume also includes contributions that address the broader theme of law and development, as well as the law of international organizations.

This volume has been shaped by the insightful and carefully researched contributions of various law and development experts, and the invaluable guidance provided by our distinguished team of editors: editor in chief Frank Fariello, Lead Counsel, Operations Policy Practice Group, World Bank Legal Vice Presidency; and his two coeditors—Laurence Boisson de Chazournes, Professor of Law, University of Geneva; and Kevin E. Davis, Vice Dean and Beller Family Professor of Business Law, New York University School of Law. I am grateful to them for directing this publication. My sincere appreciation also goes to Mahmoud Mohieldin, the World Bank's Senior Vice President for the 2030 Development Agenda, United Nations Relations, and Partnerships, who graciously wrote this volume's foreword, and to the authors of the chapters in the volume, which, we are confident, will make a valuable contribution to the global dialogue on the role of law and justice in the post-2015 development agenda.

Editors and Contributors

Editors

Laurence Boisson de Chazournes has been professor of international law and international organization at the University of Geneva's Faculty of Law since 1999. She has been invited as guest lecturer to numerous universities throughout the world. She is an adviser to various international organizations (the United Nations, the International Labour Organization, and the World Health Organization), governments, and law firms. In the area of dispute settlement, she has served as the chairperson of World Trade Organization arbitration panels on preshipment inspections, pleaded before the International Court of Justice, and been an arbitrator in investment arbitration for the International Centre for Settlement of Investment Disputes. She has authored and edited 20 books and has written more than 170 articles.

Kevin E. Davis is vice dean and Beller Family Professor of Business Law at New York University (NYU) School of Law. His research focuses on anticorruption law, contract law, and quantitative measures of the performance of legal institutions. His publications include "Transnational Anti-Corruption Law in Action: Cases from Argentina and Brazil," *Law and Social Inquiry*, volume 40 (2015) (with Guillermo Jorge and Maíra Machado); "Contracts as Technology," *NYU Law Review* (2013); "Indicators as a Technology of Global Governance," *Law and Society Review*, volume 46 (2012) (with Benedict Kingsbury and Sally Merry); and "The Relationship between Law and Development: Optimists versus Skeptics," *American Journal of Comparative Law* (2008) (with Michael Trebilcock). Before joining NYU, he was a member of the faculty of law at the University of Toronto, and held visiting positions at the University of Southern California, Cambridge University's Clare Hall, and the University of the West Indies.

Frank Fariello is a lead counsel with the Operations Policy Practice Group of the World Bank's Legal Vice Presidency. He is the Bank's primary legal focal point for its Governance and Anti-Corruption (GAC) strategy and legal adviser to the Bank's new Governance Global Practice. Mr. Fariello has played a major role in the Bank's sanctions system, having coordinated its 2009–10 reforms and in 2014 concluded a comprehensive review of the system. He heads a study on the drivers of corruption in international financial institution (IFI) operations, together with representatives from other IFIs, the Organisation for Economic Co-operation and Development, academia, and civil society. Mr. Fariello has been vice chair of the American Bar Association's International Anti-Corruption Committee since 2012. His publications include *The World Bank Sanctions System and Its Recent Reforms* (World Bank, 2012), "Coordinating the Fight Against Fraud and Corruption" (*The World Bank Legal Review*, vol. 3 [2012]; U.K. Serious Fraud Office [2011]); and

"Transforming Through Transparency: Opening Up the World Bank's Sanctions System" (*The World Bank Legal Review,* vol. 4 [2013]) as well as papers for the American Society for International Law on financial remedies in the context of World Bank sanctions and on the drivers of corruption. Engagements have included the Korean Institute of Criminology Anti-Corruption Forum (Seoul); Russia and CIS Anti-Corruption Summit (Moscow); Colloquia on Sanctions and Debarment (World Bank); Using History to Inform Development Policy (World Bank); Seminar on the International Fight against Corruption (George Washington School of Law); the ABA Section of International Law (New York); and the American Society of International Law. He has lectured at the Joint Vienna Institute, George Washington University, George Mason University, and New York University School of Law. Mr. Fariello holds a B.A. in history, magna cum laude, from Brown University (1980) and a J.D. from New York University Law School (1983). He is admitted to practice law in the State of New York.

Contributors

Marie-Anne Birken was appointed general counsel at the European Bank of Reconstruction and Development (EBRD) in June 2014. She is responsible for the Office of the General Counsel, which includes the Legal Department, the Operations and Administration Department, and the Procurement Department. Ms. Birken is a member of the Executive Committee and various other committees of the EBRD, such as the Operations Committee, Risk Committee, and Strategy Planning Committee. She joined EBRD from the Asian Development Bank, where she was the secretary; she previously served as deputy general counsel and as assistant general counsel responsible for private sector operations. Ms. Birken has extensive experience in emerging markets and lived and worked in Asia from 1995 until 2014. She was a partner in two international law firms and held the position of regional general counsel at Barclays Bank, where she supported corporate banking activities in Asia, the Middle East, and Africa. Ms. Birken is a Dutch national; she has a master's degree in law from the University of Utrecht and is qualified as a solicitor in England and Wales.

Megan Brewer is a governance, development, and foreign policy specialist at the Australian Department of Foreign Affairs and Trade. She is second secretary (political) in Timor-Leste and has worked across the Pacific, including in Papua New Guinea, Samoa, and Fiji. Prior to joining the Australian government, Ms. Brewer worked at the Research Institute for Asia and the Pacific at Sydney University and served in the Federal Court of Australia. She graduated from the University of Sydney with a master's in international law and undergraduate degrees in sociology and international relations.

Hassane Cissé is the director of Governance and Inclusive Institutions, Governance Global Practice, at the World Bank. In this capacity, he leads a department composed of teams of experts to support countries in building sustainable, inclusive, and trustworthy governance systems. Key areas of focus include citizen engagement and social accountability mechanisms, institutional reform and strengthening in respect of justice and rule of law institutions, legislatures, independent accountability mechanisms, centers of government, and other areas of public sector management. Mr. Cissé was deputy general counsel, Knowledge and Research, of the World Bank from 2009 to June 2014. In this capacity, he managed the Bank's advisory work on legal and justice reforms and led the Bank's knowledge activities on law, justice, and development. Prior to that role, he served for several years as chief counsel for Operations Policy, and as legal adviser on Governance and Anticorruption. Prior to joining the World Bank in 1997, Mr. Cissé worked at the International Monetary Fund, where he started his professional career in 1990. Mr. Cissé has lectured and published widely. He has in particular coedited several volumes of *The World Bank Legal Review*. He serves on several international boards and is a member of the World Economic Forum's Global Agenda Council on Justice and its Meta Council on Global Governance Architecture. Mr. Cissé holds an LL.B. from the Dakar University School of Law, in Senegal, and a Diplôme d'Etudes Approfondies (D.E.A.) in international law from the University of Paris II Panthéon-Assas. He received his D.E.A. in international economic law from the Sorbonne, where he also obtained a D.E.A. in African history. He also holds an LL.M. from Harvard University.

Samuel Cogolati is a Ph.D. fellow of the Research Foundation–Flanders at the Leuven Centre for Global Governance Studies, University of Leuven. His thesis is on the role of international law in the provision of global public goods in the field of development. He holds law degrees from the University of Leuven, King's College London, and Harvard Law School. He pursued an LL.M. in 2013–14 thanks to scholarships from the Belgian American Education Foundation, Fulbright Program, and Rotary. His main research interests are in international development law, international economic law, human rights, and refugee law.

Alan Colman is a partner at Corrs Chambers Westgarth, a leading Australian commercial law firm, where he practices in industrial and international law. He previously worked for the EBRD as senior counsel in charge of dispute resolution in the EBRD's Legal Transition Team, assisting governments in enhancing laws and institutions and improving the investment climate. While at the EBRD, he ran technical assistance projects in the Commonwealth of Independent States, the former Yugoslavia, and Mongolia, and led analytical studies on the quality of court decisions and the work of bailiffs. Mr. Colman also served as acting chief counsel in charge of the EBRD's Financial Law Unit. Early in his career, he worked for several years as a lawyer at the United Nations Office of the High Commissioner for Human Rights in Geneva. He is an Australian national.

Michele Forzley, J.D., M.P.H., is a practicing global health lawyer, a public health practitioner, and senior scholar at the O'Neill Institute for National and Global Health Law, Georgetown University Law Center. Her global practice is to align the ministry of health functioning with the national legal framework, to harmonize it with international obligations and best practices, and to revise the legal framework to support the achievement of national health system objectives. As a consultant for the USAID-funded Health Policy Project in Afghanistan from 2012 to 2015, she helped that country's health ministry improve its regulatory system, including designing a licensing department and procedures and forms, an inspection process, an internal review board, and sanctions guidelines for the private health sector. She is a graduate of New England School of Law, Boston, and Johns Hopkins Bloomberg School of Public Health.

Irene Khan is director general of the International Development Law Organization (IDLO). The first woman to hold this office, she was elected by the IDLO Assembly of Parties in November 2011 for a four-year term of office, starting on January 1, 2012. At the assembly's annual meeting in November 2015, she was reelected for a second four-year term. An international thought leader on human rights, gender, and social justice issues, Ms. Khan was secretary general of Amnesty International from 2001 to 2009. Prior to that, she worked for the United Nations High Commissioner for Refugees for 21 years, at headquarters and in various field operations. She was a visiting professor at the State University of New York Law School (Buffalo) in 2011. Ms. Khan sits on the boards of several international human rights and development organizations. She received the Sydney Peace Prize in 2006 for her work to end violence against women and girls. Her book *The Unheard Truth: Poverty and Human Rights* has been translated into seven languages. Born in Bangladesh, Ms. Khan studied law at the University of Manchester and at Harvard Law School.

Jasper Kim is a professor at the Graduate School of International Studies at Ewha Womans University in Seoul, Korea; founder of the Asia-Pacific Global Research Group; and senior fellow at Melbourne Law School. He was a visiting scholar at Stanford University (2014) and Harvard University (2011). He has worked for Barclays Capital, Credit Suisse, and Lehman Brothers. A member of the Washington, DC, Bar, Professor Kim received an M.Sc. from the London School of Economics, a J.D. from Rutgers University School of Law, and negotiation training at Harvard Law School's Program on Negotiation. He has published in numerous academic journals; his books include *International Economic Systems* and *American Law 101* (both published by the American Bar Association), and *Korean Business Law* (Carolina Academic Press). Professor Kim is also a contributor to various media, including the BBC, Bloomberg, CNN, and the *Wall Street Journal*.

Siobhán McInerney-Lankford is senior counsel at the World Bank Legal Vice Presidency and a recognized expert in international human rights law, advising the World Bank in this area since 2002. She serves as country lawyer for the Central African Republic, Comoros, Guinea, Mauritania, Mauritius, Namibia, and Syria. She regularly represents the World Bank in international human rights fora, including the United Nations, the European Union, and the Organisation for Economic Co-operation and Development (OECD). From 2006 to 2008, she served as chair of the OECD Development Assistance Committee's Human Rights Task Team. Dr. McInerney-Lankford has published widely on human rights law; she has taught at American University's Washington College of Law, the European Peacebuilding Liaison Office, the Venice Master's program, and the UN Summer Academy. She is cochair of the American Society of International Law Human Rights Interest Group; cochair of the Human Rights and Development Community of Practice under the Global Forum on Law, Justice and Development; and the Legal Vice Presidency adviser to the World Bank Governance and Health, Nutrition, and Population Global Practices. She holds an LL.B. (First-Class Honors) from Trinity College, Dublin, an LL.M. from Harvard Law School, and a B.C.L. and D.Phil. in EU human rights law from Oxford University. In 2010 and 2011, the *Irish Voice* newspaper named her among the Irish Legal 100. She is a member of the American Bar Association and admitted to practice law in the state of Rhode Island.

Anne-Marie Leroy is senior vice president and World Bank Group general counsel, a position to which she was appointed in March 2009. Prior to joining the Bank Group, she was a partner of the Paris office of Denton Wilde Sapte LLP, where she was in charge of the Department of Public Law. A French national, Ms. Leroy is a graduate of both the Paris Institute for Political Science and the National School for Public Administration, with a graduate degree in the sociology of organizations. In 1986, Leroy joined the Council of State (Conseil d'État), the highest court in France for public and administrative law, where she served as a judge for five years.

Nicholas Menzies is a senior governance specialist in the Governance Global Practice at the World Bank. He works on justice and governance issues in East Asia and the Pacific, Africa, and South Eastern Europe, and is a member of the Bank's Sexual Orientation and Gender Identity Task Force. Before his tenure at the World Bank, he worked as a land and natural resources lawyer for indigenous communities in Australia, on legal empowerment and access to justice issues in Cambodia, and as a policy adviser to the Papua New Guinean cabinet, providing advice on a range of matters, from participatory budgeting and microenterprise development to gender-based violence. Mr. Menzies has also worked in progressive political advocacy, building social movements for political, cultural, and environmental action.

Mahmoud Mohieldin is the World Bank Group senior vice president for the 2030 Development Agenda, United Nations Relations, and Partnerships. Before joining the World Bank, he held numerous senior positions in the government of the Arab Republic of Egypt, including Minister of Investment from 2004 to 2010. He also served on several boards of directors in the banking and corporate sector, including the Central Bank of Egypt. Dr. Mohieldin was a member of the Commission on Growth and Development and selected as a Young Global Leader of the World Economic Forum. He is a professor of economics and finance at Cairo University, an honorary professor at Durham University, and a member of the Advisory Board of the Durham Business

School. Dr. Mohieldin has also held leading positions in national and regional research centers and think tanks, and has authored numerous publications in both English and Arabic, including articles in leading journals in the fields of international finance, economics, and development. He received a Ph.D. in economics from the University of Warwick, an M.Sc. in economic and social policy analysis from the University of York, and a B.Sc. in economics, first in the order of merit, from Cairo University.

Anthony Molle is senior counsel in the Legal Special Operations Unit at the World Bank and assists with transformational operations in developing and frontier markets with innovative financial structures, including guarantees, aimed at leveraging private investment. He joined the World Bank in 2009 after a decade in private practice, including at top-tier U.S. law firms (White & Case and Latham & Watkins), specializing in structured and project finance; he represented sponsors, lenders, governments, and national utilities in connection with all phases of the development, financing, and acquisition of international infrastructure projects. Mr. Molle holds a law degree from the University of Montreal and an M.B.A. from the W. P. Carey School of Business at Arizona State University.

Hoda Atia Moustafa is senior counsel in the Legal and Claims Group at the Multilateral Investment Guarantee Agency (MIGA), World Bank Group. Since joining MIGA in 2007, she has worked closely with underwriters and political risk analysts to structure political risk guarantees in the context of international investments in developing member countries. Her sector focus is infrastructure and financial sector projects, with a regional focus on Africa and the Middle East. Before joining MIGA, Ms. Moustafa was assistant general counsel at the Overseas Private Investment Corporation (OPIC), a bilateral U.S. government agency providing financing and political risk insurance to private sector projects in emerging markets. Prior to joining OPIC, Ms. Moustafa was in private practice at two international law firms, Clifford Chance in Washington, DC, and Mayer Brown in Chicago. Ms. Moustafa holds a J.D. from Georgetown University Law Center and a master's degree in foreign service from Georgetown University. She is admitted to practice law in New York, Illinois, and Washington, DC.

Marino Perassi graduated in law from the University of Turin in 1984, qualified to practice law in 1986, and was admitted before the Supreme Court of Italy in 1998. He joined the legal department of the Bank of Italy in 1989. He has represented the Bank of Italy in numerous working groups of the European Monetary Institute, the European Commission, and the G10, and is currently a member of the Legal Committee at the European Central Bank. He is the author of various publications on commercial law, banking law, and payment systems. He is particularly interested in international issues, and has written on that subject in the law review *Euredia*. Mr. Perassi has lectured in banking law at the University of Florence and La Sapienza of Rome, and currently teaches at the Law Faculty of Libera Universtà Internazionale degli Studi Sociali in Rome. From 2006 to 2011, he was head of the Bank of Italy's

Legal Services Department. Since July 2011, he has been the bank's general counsel.

Michael Riegner is research associate at the Law and Society Institute of Humboldt University of Berlin. He specializes in international law, comparative public law, and law and development in the global South. His publications include articles in the *Yale Journal of International Law*, the *Journal of International Economic Law*, and the *International Organizations Law Review*, as well as a volume on comparative constitutionalism that he coedited. He served as a consultant for the German government and for UN agencies, and was a World Bank International Finance and Development fellow in 2014. He taught at universities in Germany, India, Brazil, and Kosovo, and was a research fellow at the Max Planck Institute for Comparative Public Law and International Law in Heidelberg. He studied law at Geneva University and at Passau Law School in Germany, and also holds an LL.M. from New York University School of Law.

Siniša Rodin is a judge of the Court of Justice of the European Union. He studied law at the University of Zagreb and at the University of Michigan Law School. He was a Fulbright fellow and visiting scholar at Harvard Law School. Judge Rodin is a tenured professor at the University of Zagreb, where he held the Jean Monnet Chair. He was a visiting professor at the Cornell Law School and was member of the Croatian Constitutional Amendment Committee and chairman of the working group on EU membership. He was also a member of the Croatian EU membership negotiating team.

Hans-Otto Sano is the acting research director of the Danish Institute for Human Rights. He worked for three years at the Nordic Trust Fund, the World Bank, as senior program officer, seconded by the Danish Ministry of Foreign Affairs. Dr. Sano is involved in research projects on poverty and human rights and is drafting a report on the economy of human rights. His recent publications span themes on human rights indicators, on the drivers of human rights change, on the methods of assessing the impact of social and economic rights, and on social accountability and human rights. Dr. Sano has also been involved in the European Union Framework Research Program: Fostering Human Rights among European Policies. He holds a Ph.D. in economic history.

Omarzaman Sayedi has worked for Palladium as a deputy chief of party and team leader on three USAID health projects in Afghanistan. He has overseen work with the Afghan government aimed at improving the private health sector environment through improving coordination and engagement, establishing policies and systems, and developing new areas of expertise in Afghanistan, such as large-scale hospital public-private partnerships. He has supported the Afghan Ministry of Public Health in undertaking several initiatives aimed at creating strong, sustainable health systems; increasing access to higher-quality secondary and tertiary health services; and promoting innovative health financing interventions, including domestic revenue generation. Dr. Sayedi received his medical degree from Kabul Medical University in 2003 and a diploma in business administration from the Kardan Institute of Business Administration, in Kabul, in 2005. He received a Fulbright scholarship in 2007 to study health policy and management at Emory University's Rollins School of Public Health, which awarded him a master's degree in public health, with honors, in 2009.

Jared Schott is a governance and justice specialist in the World Bank's Governance Global Practice, where his work focuses on inclusive governance, natural resources, and rights-sensitive development. Prior to joining the World Bank, Mr. Schott covered economic affairs, rule of law, and security portfolios as a special adviser to the Minister of Justice of Liberia, and subsequently with the United Nations Mission in Liberia's Office of the Deputy Special Representative of the Secretary General, Rule of Law. Previously, Mr. Schott practiced law at Latham & Watkins; served as a legal adviser to the Permanent Mission of Palau to the United Nations, focusing on human rights, development, and peacekeeping matters; and worked with NGOs in Kosovo on justice reform. Mr. Schott graduated from Stanford University in 2003 with distinction and interdisciplinary honors from its Center for International Security and Cooperation. He received his J.D. (2006) and LL.M. (2007) from New York University School of Law, where he was a dean's scholar and junior fellow at the Institute for International Law and Justice.

Kathleen Sears, B.A. M.S, has over 20 years of experience in international health and development, working primarily in Africa and Asia, including more than 6 years in Afghanistan. She has worked on and led four USAID projects in Afghanistan, collaborating closely with government and private sector entities. She helped establish the initial contracting mechanisms for outsourcing primary health care (implementing the basic package of health services) and the midwifery education programs. She has led initiatives in policy development, local capacity building, and systems strengthening, including projects dealing with private sector regulation, health management information systems, and the minimum required standards for private sector self-assessment. Based in Boston, she supports the USAID Health Sector Resiliency Project, which focuses on governance, health finance, and human resources for health, and which is implemented by Palladium.

Thomas Silberhorn was appointed as Germany's parliamentary state secretary to the Federal Minister for Economic Cooperation and Development in February 2014. Prior to that role, he was deputy chairman of the Christian Democratic Union/Christian Social Union (CDU/CSU) parliamentary group in the German parliament (Bundestag). The focus of his work as parliamentary state secretary is on core development issues for the future, including human rights and good governance, education, health, poverty reduction, water supply and sanitation, energy, and resources. He has been a member of the German Bundestag since 2002, representing the constituency of Bamberg-Forchheim. At the parliamentary elections in 2013, he won 52 percent of first votes in his constituency.

Julius Thaler is a senior counsel in the Environmental and International Law Practice Group of the World Bank Legal Vice Presidency.

Jan Wouters is full professor of international law and international organizations, Jean Monnet Chair Ad Personam EU and Global Governance, and founding director of the Institute for International Law and of the Leuven Centre for Global Governance Studies at the University of Leuven. He is an adjunct professor at Columbia University and a visiting professor at Sciences Po (Paris), Libera Universtà Internazionale degli Studi Sociali (Rome), and the College of Europe (Bruges). He is a member of the Royal Academy of Belgium for Sciences and Arts; president of the United Nations Association Flanders, Belgium; and Of Counsel at Linklaters, Brussels. Professor Wouters has published widely on international and EU law, international organizations, global governance, and financial law. He coordinates a number of major research projects, including FRAME (a large-scale FP7 Programme on human rights in EU Policies); advises various international organizations and governments; trains officials; and often comments on international events in the media.

The World Bank Legal Review

Volume 7

Financing and Implementing the Post-2015 Development Agenda: The Role of Law and Justice Systems

Introduction

Frank Fariello

The efforts of the international community to ensure the successful implementation of the 2030 Agenda for Sustainable Development are well under way.[1] The agenda's twin points of departure, the Millennium Development Goals (MDGs)[2] and the Rio+20 Principles,[3] have been synthesized and further developed, culminating in the UN secretary-general's report "The Road to Dignity by 2030: Ending Poverty, Transforming All Lives and Protecting the Planet,"[4] which was presented to the United Nations General Assembly in December 2014. The financing framework for sustainable development was enshrined in the Addis Ababa Action Agenda,[5] adopted at the Third International Conference on Financing for Development in Addis Ababa, Ethiopia, in early 2015 and endorsed in General Assembly Resolution 69/313.[6] These efforts culminated in September 2015, when the General Assembly formally adopted the Sustainable Development Goals (SDGs), comprising 17 goals and 169 targets, as part of the 2030 Agenda for Sustainable Development.[7]

The SDGs present legal scholars and practitioners with unique challenges and opportunities. From the legal perspective, Goal 16—"Promote peaceful and inclusive societies for sustainable development, provide access to justice for all and build effective, accountable and inclusive institutions at all levels"[8]—has the potential to be truly transformative. The role of law as an enabler for development was excluded from the MDGs, but with Goal 16,

---

1 The 2030 Agenda for Sustainable Development was originally styled as the "post-2015 development agenda" and is referred to as such in a number of the articles included in this volume.

2 See United Nations General Assembly, Resolution 55/2, "United Nations Millennium Declaration," A/RES/55/2, September 18, 2000, http://www.undocs.org/A/RES/55/2.

3 UN General Assembly, Resolution 66/288, "The Future We Want," A/RES/66/288, September 11, 2012, http://www.undocs.org/A/RES/66/288.

4 "The Road to Dignity by 2030: Ending Poverty, Transforming All Lives and Protecting the Planet. Synthesis Report of the Secretary-General on the post-2015 Sustainable Development Agenda, " A/69/700, December 14, 2014, http://www.undocs.org/ A/69/700.

5 United Nations, *Addis Ababa Action Agenda of the Third International Conference on Financing for Development* (New York: United Nations, 2015), http://www.un.org/esa/ffd/wp-content/uploads/2015/08/AAAA_Outcome.pdf.

6 UN General Assembly, Resolution 69/313, "Addis Ababa Action Agenda of the Third International Conference on Financing for Development (Addis Ababa Action Agenda)," A/RES/69/313, July 27, 2015, http://www.undocs.org/A/RES/69/313.

7 UN General Assembly, Resolution 70/1, "Transforming Our World: The 2030 Agenda for Sustainable Development," A/RES/70/1, September 25, 2015, http://www.undocs.org/A/RES/70/1.

8 Ibid., 26.

along with 12 related targets, good governance and rule of law are now recognized as key elements in achieving sustainable development and shared prosperity.[9]

In addition to informing the SDGs, law and justice systems will play a key role in ensuring that the SDGs are successfully implemented, including through the design of policy frameworks; the development of financing instruments, as described in Addis Ababa; and the making of data and governance arrangements for monitoring global, regional, and national indicators.

The objective of this seventh volume of *The World Bank Legal Review* is to contribute intellectually to the global discussion surrounding the 2030 Agenda for Sustainable Development, focusing on the ways in which law and justice systems can help further and promote the agenda.

As has become customary for the *Review*, this volume draws inspiration from the 2014 Law, Justice and Development (LJD) Week, held October 20–24, 2014, at the World Bank Headquarters. LJD Week is an annual conference on law and development issues that brings together World Bank Group staff, senior officials from other international financial institutions, international development practitioners, government officials, lawyers, judges, scholars, and representatives from nongovernmental organizations and other elements of civil society. This volume focuses on three central themes of the 2014 LJD Week: implementing the post-2015 development agenda (now more commonly known as the 2030 Agenda for Sustainable Development), financing the agenda, and the role of socioeconomic rights in the agenda. The contributors are distinguished international legal scholars and development practitioners. The 2014 LJD Week also included a day dedicated to legal, economic, and social developments in Europe, and this volume includes articles on some of the key themes discussed that day.

Implementation

Although Goal 16 explicitly refers to the promotion of rule of law and access to justice, implicit references to legal mechanisms and instruments can be found in the other goals, notably from the perspective of implementation. The SDGs embrace concepts such as inclusion, equity, rights, entitlements, and accountability, all of which are grounded, explicitly or implicitly, in law, and rely on law and justice systems for their implementation. Part I of this volume explores the legal dimensions of the SDGs, including the role of law in collecting data on SDG implementation, strengthening the governance of health sectors, and promoting legal and judicial reform.

In "Implementing the Data Revolution for the Post-2015 Sustainable Development Goals: Toward a Global Administrative Law of Information," Michael Riegner provides a comprehensive analysis of the "data revolution"

---

9 Ibid., 4.

in the transition from MDGs to SDGs. He examines the legal implications and challenges this transition poses for what he styles "the global administrative law of information"; his chapter pays particular attention to the opportunities for the multiple stakeholders of the SDGs to fully exploit the benefits of the data revolution.

Riegner contends that the SDGs will be a project of global information governance, requiring an evolution from reliance on statistics to reliance on indicators. He elaborates and defines the concept of the global administrative law of information and proposes an analytical framework focusing on norms governing the acquisition, processing, and distribution of data. These norms can be derived from the founding documents of international organizations, treaties, and other sources of international law to form a quasi-regulatory framework to guide SDG implementation. This framework is governed by the principles of informational cooperation, national ownership, and individual informational rights. Riegner analyzes the competences of international organizations in data collection and indicator monitoring, the requirements of human rights law for indicators and data disaggregation, and access to information norms at the national and international levels. The multilevel nature of this global administrative information law can be seen in discrepancies in access to data in development projects—for example, discrepancies between national freedom of information laws and the World Bank's access to information policy.

In "Internal Review Boards: An Innovation in Health Sector Governance," Michele Forzley explores the role of internal review boards (IRBs) in achieving SDG 3, "Ensure healthy lives and promote well-being for all at all ages."

Forzley contends that, with the transition from public to private health care provision, many countries are seeing their ministries of health evolving into health sector regulators. Most developing countries, however, lack adequate special-purpose mechanisms to address regulatory disputes in their respective health sectors. Moreover, the courts often lack the technical competence or resources to manage the regulatory matters unique to the health sector, and in the absence of health sector IRBs, there is no effective justice mechanism for dispute resolution or regulatory enforcement.

Forzley then looks at examples of IRBs—in Afghanistan and India, where IRBs are being progressively developed, and in Switzerland, which has a strong body of administrative law enforced by IRBs—to illustrate the key components of an effective IRBs, paying particular attention to what is effective in developing countries.

In "Law as a Guide to Regulatory System Design for the Health Sector: An Essential Tool for Regulating the Private Health Sector in Afghanistan and Other Developing Countries," Forzley, Kathleen Sears, and Omarzaman Sayedi depict the increasing proliferation of private sector health service providers in low- and medium-income countries (LMICs). Noting that there has been little research conducted on the subject from a legal perspective, the authors set out their vision for an optimal regulatory system design for these private health care providers.

The chapter draws on the expertise and experience of Forzley, especially her involvement in the Health Policy Project (HPP), which was undertaken in Afghanistan from 2012 through 2015 by the U.S. Agency for International Development. The HPP consisted of four key stages: assessing regulations and safety standards governing the private health sector; evaluating applicable laws in terms of substance, implementation, and conformity; addressing regulatory gaps and capacity needs with the Ministry of Public Health (MOPH); and defining the MOPH's roles and responsibilities, including creating a plan for an independent committee to review breaches and hear complaints against MOPHs.

Drawing on the HPP experience, the chapter prescribes three key elements of an effective regulatory system: incentives, self-regulation, and command and control. The authors note, however, that these three regulatory tools, on their own, do not seem to be effective in LMICs unless these laws are being adequately implemented and enforced. The authors note a lack of analysis of implementation and enforcement issues in academic literature, which the chapter aims to remedy through its approach to regulatory system design.

In "Between Transformation and Integration: The Regional Dimension of Legal Reform in Implementing the Sustainable Development Goals," Thomas Silberhorn, the parliamentary state secretary of Germany's Federal Ministry of Economic Cooperation and Development (BMZ), discusses the integral role that rule of law plays in the 2030 Agenda. Silberhorn identifies and distinguishes three aspects of law and justice in the SDGs that are relevant in implementing the 2030 Agenda. These are the standalone targets on rule of law, other goals and targets explicitly referring to rule of law, and targets that implicitly require legal measures. Referring to Germany's new Charter for the Future, he introduces the German approach to the promotion of rule of law in international cooperation. The 2030 Agenda is fully incorporated in the Charter for the Future, and it will also be an integral part of an upcoming BMZ policy paper on strengthening rule of law. Several case studies examine the regional dimensions of legal and justice reform programs in South East Europe and the South Caucasus as they relate to the SDGs. The conclusion highlights how regional dimensions can advance legal reforms in meeting the SDGs.

In "Mitigating Governance Risks in Identification Systems," Megan Brewer, Hassane Cissé, Nicholas Menzies, and Jared Schott provide an extensive overview of the benefits and drawbacks associated with universal legal identification, civil registration, and documentation systems, collectively referred to as "IRD systems," which are likely to be invested in heavily to achieve some of the targets on 2030 Agenda for Sustainable Development.

The chapter illustrates the wide-ranging appeal and potential development impact of IRD systems with examples from India and Nigeria. Both countries have been able to achieve annual savings of approximately $US1 billion through the introduction of such systems—in Nigeria, through the elimination of "ghost workers"; in India, through efficiency gains in cash transfers.

The authors posit that IRD systems make an important contribution to development, and provide six key recommendations to ensure that such systems have the maximum development impact. But a significant portion of the authors' analysis is dedicated to the shortcomings and risks associated with IRD systems. Numerous studies indicate that IRD systems depend on other systems to be effective, including a well-functioning judiciary as well as oversight agencies and redress mechanisms. Examples of the damage caused by poorly conceived IRD systems range from increased costs for election systems to outright discrimination and abuse of the most marginalized and vulnerable populations, including the blocking or limiting of access to basic services, such as health care and education, to those lacking proper identification.

Financing

In the aftermath of the global financial crisis, international development has had to deal with restricted aid budgets and rapidly escalating developmental challenges. International financial institutions face capital and other constraints on their ability to substantially increase lending, investment, and grant activities. At the same time, the complexities and urgency of delivering sustainable developmental assistance have increased. Faced with these challenges, the development community has been searching for innovative solutions to mobilize additional development capital and to increase the impact of development resources. Such solutions almost always involve significant legal issues and substantial legal involvement in structuring and implementation.

The two chapters in part II of this volume examine financial instruments deployed for development and the legal complexities surrounding these instruments, and how legal means can be used to help find innovative ways to scale up financing for the 2030 Agenda for Sustainable Development. One chapter focuses on the potential role of social impact bonds and development impact bonds in closing the "finance gap," the other on the evolving concept of sovereign immunity in contracts between states and private parties.

In "Education Financing: Utilizing Next-Generation Impact Bond Structures and Legal Agreements," Jasper Kim advocates a key role for social impact bonds (SIBs) and development impact bonds (DIBs) in financing SDGs—in particular Goal 4, which addresses quality education—in light of the significant decline in official development assistance for the education sector.

Kim explores the role that SIBs and DIBs could play in closing this financing gap by leveraging private sector sources of finance. Essentially, a form of "performance-based" financing, these mechanisms would enable a private sector entity to pay the full amount of an education project up front; the repayment of principal and payment of interest would depend on the achievement of objectives previously agreed on in a contract that featured a "success metric." Achievement of the objectives would be measured and evaluated by an independent third party.

This chapter provides a relevant case study that illustrates the practical applications and considerations of SIBs and DIBs in education financing, identifying the risks and benefits, as well as the contract law components involved. The chapter then recommends a set of improvements, including the use of plain language in contracts to ensure that contracts are understandable to all parties, and the use of alternative dispute resolution mechanisms to avoid lengthy and expensive litigation. The chapter also advocates the use of financial engineering tools to create so-called next-generation SIBs and DIBs, which would include instruments such as credit default swaps, credit ratings, tranched debt, alternative bonds, and financial guarantees.

In "Waivers of Sovereign Immunity: An Eroding Concept?" Hoda Atia Moustafa and Anthony Molle examine the history of and recent developments in the doctrine of sovereign immunity. This examination is made in the context of contractual relationships between states and private parties, with a focus on the application of sovereign immunity to state-owned entities and foreign state–owned assets in international project finance transactions.

The authors explore the recent body of case law in the enforcement of foreign arbitral awards, where state-owned entities and foreign state–owned assets have been increasingly subject to attachment. Some governments have reacted to this development by attempting to include "carve-outs" in contracts with private parties that exclude certain state assets from waivers of sovereign immunity. This stratagem raises important cost-benefit considerations as governments seek to balance their interests in, on the one hand, protecting their assets and entities with, on the other hand, guarding against potential adverse effects on market expectations and foreign direct investment.

Socioeconomic Rights

The UN secretary-general's report "The Road to Dignity by 2030" calls for ensuring that all actions taken to implement the post-2015 development agenda "respect and advance human rights, in full coherence with international standards." The report goes on to observe that "human development is also the respect of human rights" and that "laws and institutions must protect human rights and fundamental freedoms" to promote safe and peaceful societies and strong institutions.[10] In discussions leading up to the adoption of the SDGs, a broad consensus emerged that socioeconomic rights are important as enablers, strategies, and approaches for sustainable development, even if they are not enumerated as explicit goals.

The four chapters in part III of this volume explore the implications of an explicit-versus-implicit integration of rights into the SDGs, the concepts

---

10 Ibid., 15–19.

of universality and inalienability, and the extent to which the human rights–based approach (HRBA)[11] has been successfully integrated into the SDGs. In addition to focusing on the SDGs themselves, these chapters also discuss such social and economic issues as the evolving mandate of international institutions, such as the World Bank, for promoting global public goods, the role of law and justice systems in supporting minorities and vulnerable populations as they assert their rights, and the role of rule of law as an instrument of legal and social justice critical to the equity considerations at the heart of the post-2015 development agenda.

In "Human Rights and the Post-2015 Sustainable Development Goals: Reflections on Challenges and Opportunities," Siobhán McInerney-Lankford and Hans-Otto Sano explore the principal critiques of the MDGs and SDGs from a human rights perspective, emphasizing three principles: equality and nondiscrimination, participation and inclusion, and accountability.

McInerney-Lankford and Sano argue that there is a fundamental difference between the legally binding frameworks that enshrine human rights—notably, in international human rights treaties—and the nonbinding political commitments of the MDGs and SDGs. In this regard, the authors observe continuing weaknesses in the area of accountability of institutions and governments, both in achieving goals and in ensuring that policies do not infringe on human rights. Nevertheless, they note improvements in the SDGs over the MDGs, not least in the incorporation of equality and nondiscrimination as well as participation and inclusion.

In "Taking Sustainable Development Goal 17 Seriously: The World Bank's Legal Framework for Providing Global Public Goods," Jan Wouters and Samuel Cogolati contend that there has not been a thorough scholarly review of the legal framework within which the World Bank operates to provide public goods. The need for such a review is particularly pronounced in light of SDG 17 (which deals with strengthening global sustainable development) and the increased cooperation among international institutions necessary for its achievement.

Taking the definition of global public goods found in the World Bank's Development Committee staff report as a starting point, the authors note that the concept has evolved considerably over the years, moving away from a strictly economic view. Turning to the legal underpinnings of global public goods, the authors explore the Bank's Articles of Agreement, focusing on the Bank's interpretation of "productive purposes" and analyzing how they have evolved over the years. Drawing on an analysis of the Vienna Convention on the Law of Treaties, the opinions of the Bank's general counsel, and the authority of the Board of Executive Directors to interpret the Articles of Agreement under Article IX, the authors show that although the Bank faces certain

11 UNICEF, *State of the World's Children 2004*, Annex B, "The Human Rights–Based Approach" (New York: UNICEF, 2003), http://www.unicef.org/sowc04/files/AnnexB.pdf. See also the UN-sponsored website *HRBA Portal*, http://hrbaportal.org/the-un-and-hrba.

restrictions in its interpretation of what constitutes its mandate, there is still an inherent flexibility that makes the Articles of Agreement dynamic and living instruments.

Wouters and Cogolati then examine the various financial instruments, such as partnership programs and trust funds, that the Bank has devised to deliver global public goods. The authors observe that the Bank has found ways to collaborate with other international institutions on issues that lie beyond the strict scope of any one institution's charter, through the use of instruments such as trust funds that avoid the need to create new legal entities. Instruments involving cooperation arrangements with other international organizations—for example, the Global Environment Facility—need to be established through resolutions of both the Board of Executive Directors and the Board of Governors. The legal obligations of the Bank under these mechanisms vary widely, ranging from a mere trustee role, in which the Bank is responsible only for investing funds, to acting as an implementing agency, which is the case in 17 of the 21 financial intermediary funds in which the Bank participates. The authors conclude that the Bank is able to participate in the delivery of global public goods in both direct and indirect ways, using whichever of a variety of funds and facilities is most appropriate in the circumstances.

In "The Role of Law in Improving the Livelihoods of Indigenous Peoples under REDD+," Julius Thaler, drawing on the World Bank's experience in working with countries in Latin America, explores the various legal mechanisms and incentive structures used in reducing deforestation and forest degradation, which account for up to 20 percent of the world's greenhouse gas emissions; shows how these mechanisms impact indigenous peoples; and discusses the role the mechanisms are likely to play in future positive incentive structures.

Thaler focuses on the REDD+ initiative, which aims to reduce carbon emissions caused by deforestation and forest degradation and to foster conservation, sustainable forest management, and the enhancement of forest carbon stocks. This initiative consists of various multilateral initiatives, such as the World Bank's Forest Investment Program and the Forest Carbon Partnership Facility (FCPF).

The chapter examines the importance of land tenure as it relates to asserting carbon rights, notably the practical and legal challenges posed by informal forms of land tenure, and the absence of demarcation of indigenous lands. Thaler's review of recent legal decisions in Latin America finds that most countries do not have specific legislation for dealing with these challenges, and that an independent and remedial benefit-sharing mechanism is needed to enable indigenous people to participate fully and benefit under current and future schemes, such as REDD+ and the FCPF.

In "Shifting the Paradigm: Rule of Law and the 2030 Agenda for Sustainable Development," Irene Khan provides an extensive overview of the various ways in which rule of law advances the implementation of the SDGs. She contends that rule of law should be conceived as an instrument of legal and social justice encompassing political, civil, economic, social, and cultural rights. As such, rule of law is critical to meeting the equity considerations at the heart of the 2030 Agenda for Sustainable Development.

Using this concept, Khan analyzes the role of rule of law in achieving a host of SDGs, paying particular attention to the benefits of strengthening laws, building institutions, and improving access to justice. She provides practical examples from the International Development Law Organization's work program and other development work to illustrate the role of rule of law in promoting economic and social development and environmental sustainability, and reviews overarching challenges in the measurement of justice and rule of law.

Europe

Every year, LJD Week takes an in-depth look at the legal, economic, and social developments in a particular country or region. In 2014, LJD Week included a day dedicated to Europe. Participants included representatives of the European Commission, the European Parliament, the European Court of Justice, the European Central Bank in collaboration with the Italian Central Bank, the Council of Europe, the European Investment Bank, and the European Bank for Reconstruction and Development (EBRD).

The three chapters in part IV of this volume build on the LJD Week discussions and explore the EBRD's Legal Transition Programme, the unique legal and institutional features of the Court of Justice of the European Union, and the evolving financial architecture for addressing the ongoing financial crisis in Europe.

In "Enforcing Court Decisions: The Role of Enforcement Agents," Alan Colman and Marie-Anne Birken present the results of the EBRD's regional assessment of enforcement agents under the EBRD's Legal Transition Programme, as well as the legal and institutional challenges facing enforcement systems in the Commonwealth of Independent States region, South East Europe, Georgia, and Mongolia. The authors focus on the importance of legal reform—especially the establishment of legal certainty—in improving the investment climate, with reliable enforcement of judicial decisions being a key challenge in all countries surveyed.

In their analysis of the effectiveness of enforcement agents in the surveyed countries, three models emerge: public systems with enforcement agents working for the state, private systems that vest enforcement powers in companies, and hybrid systems, in which both systems coexist. The chapter shows that there is no consensus as to which model delivers the best results, but the authors do stress some of the benefits of the private system, including the ability to choose an enforcement agent. At the same time, Colman and Birken note certain drawbacks of the private model, including higher costs, the potential lack of service in nonlucrative cases, and reluctance to put state power in private hands. The authors also discuss the disruptive potential of external factors, such as the ability of debtors to frustrate court proceedings through spurious appeals, as well as the lack of effective deterrence for noncompliance with enforcement decisions in some jurisdictions.

In "Judicial Landmarks and Their Making at the Court of Justice of the European Union," Judge Siniša Rodin provides unique insights from the European Court of Justice, focusing on its procedural decision making and the intriguing question of what makes a court decision a "landmark."

Rodin discusses the question from four angles: the factors that turn a judicial decision into a landmark, the effect that the composition of the court may have on the creation of a landmark decision, examples of landmark decisions in the Court of Justice of the European Union (CJEU), and the evolution of the landmark-making capacity of the CJEU.

In "The New Pillars of the EU Financial Architecture and the Single Supervisory Mechanism," Marino Perassi provides an overview of the regulatory framework of the Euro Area in the aftermath of the 2008 financial crisis in Europe, focusing on how the framework can help solve the problems that caused the crisis. One of the key challenges was to break the link between sovereign debt and the banks that held such debt. There was also a need to harmonize the fragmented system of national regulators in a single economic and currency area.

Taking the recommendations made by the president of the European Council, Herman Van Rompuy, in a 2012 report titled "Towards a Genuine Economic and Monetary Union" as a starting point for analysis, Perassi outlines the so-called three pillars of the European Banking Union, two of which are already in place, and examines the principles of the functioning of European banking supervision.

The first pillar, the Single Supervisory Mechanism (SSM), is based on a single set of rules, the so-called single rulebook. The SSM entrusts the European Central Bank (ECB) with the direct supervision of 129 "significant" banks in the European Union, representing more than 82 percent of banking assets in the Euro Area. The SSM, which came into force in November 2014, ensures that all significant banks are directly supervised by a single regulator, with the remaining banking sector indirectly supervised by the ECB through national competent authorities.

The second pillar is the Single Resolution Mechanism (SRM), which came into force on January 1, 2016. The SRM, in addition to managing a backstop guarantee of €55 billion, ensures the orderly resolution of any bank failure in the Euro Area with minimum impact on public finance and establishes a permanent board, the Single Resolution Board, to work in close cooperation with national competent authorities, the ECB, and the European Commission.

The third pillar, the European Deposit Insurance Scheme (EDIS), is intended to provide common deposit guarantees across the Euro Area and complement the existing Common Deposit Guarantee Scheme (CDGS). The proposal for an EDIS is still being discussed among EU policy makers; it would entail the politically sensitive feature of common liability for deposits.

* * *

This introductory chapter is designed to give the reader a clear overview of this seventh volume of *The World Bank Legal Review*, and to inspire the reader to continue reading and delve into this extraordinarily rich and diverse collection of ideas and perspectives. Together, they provide a timely understanding of the challenges and opportunities involved in using law and justice systems to finance and implement the 2030 Agenda for Sustainable Development. Individually and collectively, these chapters make clear that the attainment of that agenda will require creativity, perseverance, and a readiness to learn from and apply the lessons of the past. We hope that, in some modest way, this volume will contribute to that attainment.

PART I

Implementation

1

Implementing the "Data Revolution" for the Post-2015 Sustainable Development Goals

Toward a Global Administrative Law of Information

MICHAEL RIEGNER

"You say you want a revolution / Well, you know we all wanna change the world," the Beatles sang about the political protests of the 1960s.[1] "Transforming our world" is also the ambition of the 2030 Agenda for Sustainable Development, adopted by the United Nations General Assembly in September 2015 ("the 2030 Agenda").[2] The 2030 Agenda contains 17 Sustainable Development Goals (SDGs) that apply to all member-states worldwide, developing and developed alike. A revolution is also involved: the "data revolution for sustainable development," proclaimed in two UN reports, is meant to drive implementation of the post-2015 Agenda.[3] Unlike the revolution set to music by the Beatles, however, the data revolution is an institutionalized one, and indeed a legal project. The report "A World That Counts" underscores the extent to which the data revolution will depend on legal frameworks: the report calls on international organizations to set standards, on governments to strengthen statistical systems and freedom of information, and on public, private, and civil society actors to share data, all while respecting privacy and human rights.[4]

This chapter analyzes the role of law in implementing the SDGs through the data revolution. The main argument is that existing legal norms form a patchy, multilevel framework for data governance based on actor-specific

I would like to thank Laurence Boisson de Chazournes and Maxim Bönnemann for valuable comments on an earlier version of this paper.

1 John Lennon and Paul McCartney, "Revolution," released August 26, 1968. Credit for this cultural reference goes to Enrico Giovannini and Eva Jespersen, "You Say You Want a Revolution," October 7, 2014, http://hdr.undp.org/en/content/you-say-you-want-revolution.

2 UN General Assembly, Resolution 70/1, "Transforming Our World: The 2030 Agenda for Sustainable Development," September 25, 2015 (hereafter 2030 Agenda), http://www.un.org/en/ga/70/resolutions.shtml.

3 UN Data Revolution Group, "A World That Counts: Mobilising the Data Revolution for Sustainable Development" (United Nations, New York, 2014); and United Nations, "A New Global Partnership: Report of the High-Level Panel of Eminent Persons on the Post-2015 Development Agenda" (United Nations, New York, 2013), 23.

4 UN Data Revolution Group, "A World That Counts," 18–23.

rules and cross-cutting general principles, such as informational cooperation, national ownership, and individual information rights. This framework is part of an emerging "global administrative law of information," which needs to be developed further to ensure that the data revolution is both effective and legitimate. International institutions, such as the World Bank, should contribute to this development by experimenting with and diffusing innovative legal solutions on global data governance.

This argument has practical legal implications for the implementation of the SDG data revolution: effective informational cooperation requires organizational reforms that legally ensure the independence of data collection in both national and international institutions. National ownership demands that political organs of international institutions have their say on policy questions that underlie the choice of globally applicable indicators, and that those global indicators not be imposed on national development planning and projects. Human rights indicators and data should inform SDG monitoring, and access to information rights should be used to empower citizens. There are deficits, however, in the SDG framework and in the global administrative law of information when it comes to privacy and data protection, for which international standards need to be improved and integrated into development operations, including those of the World Bank.

This chapter elaborates these arguments in three sections: the first outlines the genealogy and content of the SDGs and their implementation through the data revolution; the second develops the analytical framework and the concept of the global administrative law of information; and the third discusses the three general principles of informational cooperation, national ownership, and individual information rights and their practical implications. The analysis builds on literature on indicators in global governance,[5] transparency and freedom of information,[6] information law beyond the state,[7] Global Administrative Law, and the law of development cooperation.[8]

---

5 René Urueña, "Indicators as Political Spaces," *International Organizations Law Review* 12 (2015): 1–18; Kevin Davis, Angelina Fisher, Benedict Kingsbury, and Sally Merry, eds., *Governance by Indicators* (New York: Oxford University Press, 2012); and AnnJanette Rosga and Margaret L. Satterthwaite, "The Trust in Indicators: Measuring Human Rights," *Berkeley Journal of International Law* 27 (2008): 253–315.

6 Tarlach McGonagle and Yvonne Donders, eds., *The United Nations and Freedom of Expression and Information* (Cambridge: Cambridge University Press, 2015); and Andrea Bianchi and Anne Peters, eds., *Transparency in International Law* (Cambridge: Cambridge University Press, 2013).

7 Michael Riegner, "The International Institutional Law of Information," *International Organizations Law Review* 12 (2015): 50–80; Eberhard Schmidt-Aßmann, "Principles of an International Order of Information," in *Values in Global Administrative Law*, ed. G. Anthony (Oxford: Hart, 2011), 117–124; and Lee Bygrave, "Privacy Protection in a Global Context," *Scandinavian Studies in Law* 47 (2004): 319–348.

8 Philipp Dann, *The Law of Development Cooperation* (Cambridge: Cambridge University Press, 2013); and Benedict Kingsbury, Nico Krisch, and Richard B. Stewart, "The Emergence of Global Administrative Law," *Law and Contemporary Problems* 68 (2005): 15–61.

The Post-2015 Sustainable Development Goals and the Data Revolution

To understand the SDGs as a project of global information governance, one must understand that the SDGs are not a radical revolution but rather a step in a long-term historical evolution from using statistics as a governmental technique of the nation-state to using indicators as a technology of global governance. The following section traces this evolution and introduces the SDGs, their content, and implementation arrangements.

Genealogy and Content of the SDGs

The early use of official statistics for governance was closely associated with the formation of the modern nation and welfare state in the 19th and 20th centuries and supported both the consolidation of centralized state power and the emancipation of disadvantaged social groups.[9] Beyond the state, colonialism as an intellectual and administrative project relied significantly on statistics as a modality of knowledge.[10] After World War I, the League of Nations and the International Labour Organization (ILO) were given legal mandates to collect statistics and disseminate information, and states began to assume treaty obligations to report harmonized data.[11] This early marriage of international law and statistics laid the foundation for UN efforts on statistical governance and the ensuing process of "cognitive globalization" toward a common quantitative language and perception of the world.[12]

In the UN system, leadership for statistical activities was assigned to the UN Statistical Commission, which was established in 1946. The commission had a lasting impact through its System of National Accounts with economic indicators such as gross domestic product (GDP), but Cold War politics paralyzed the member-state-controlled body in fields such as social statistics. Statistical work thus shifted to more autonomous bureaucracies, such as the World Bank for development data, the International Monetary Fund (IMF) for financial statistics, the World Health Organization (WHO) for health data, and the United Nations Development Programme (UNDP) for its signature Human Development Index.[13] This division of labor and institutional fragmentation continue to shape contemporary global information governance, including the 2000 Millennium Development Goals (MDGs), the first global attempt to set time-bound, numerical goals and targets for development with an international

9 Alain Desrosières, *The Politics of Large Numbers* (Cambridge, MA: Harvard University Press, 1998).

10 Arjun Appadurai, "Number in the Colonial Imagination," in *Orientalism and the Postcolonial Predicament*, ed. C. Breckenridge (Philadelphia: University of Pennsylvania Press, 1993), 314–340.

11 Antony Anghie, *Imperialism, Sovereignty, and the Making of International Law* (Cambridge: Cambridge University Press, 2005), 150 et seq.

12 Michael Ward, *Quantifying the World* (Bloomington: Indiana University Press, 2004), 72.

13 Ibid., 76 et seq., 143 et seq.

follow-up process measuring progress based on quantitative indicators. Although the goals were based on a General Assembly resolution,[14] the final framework of 8 goals, 21 targets, and 60 indicators, which became known as the MDGs, was defined by technical experts from the World Bank, UNDP, the Organisation for Economic Co-operation and Development (OECD), and other international agencies, with little input from member-states, the UN Statistical Commission, or civil society.[15] Although the MDGs were nonbinding and mainly intended to be a global monitoring framework, they acquired considerable influence on development discourse, advocacy, policy priorities, and, to some extent, donors' and recipients' planning processes, resource allocation, and performance measurement.[16]

The SDGs adopted in September 2015 partly follow the model of the MDGs; in other respects, they break new ground. A difference at the outset was the process in which the SDGs were negotiated and the indicator framework was developed: the post-2015 process, as it is commonly called, is more politicized, open, and owned by national governments than the MDGs.[17] The outcome documents of the 2010 MDG summit and the 2012 Rio+20 conference laid down the political mandate and the process for the elaboration of new goals.[18] The task of preparing a proposal for the SDGs was delegated to a 30-member Open Working Group of the General Assembly, formed in 2013 through a constituency-based system of representation in which most seats were shared among several countries.[19] The UN system provided input in a 2013 report by the High-Level Panel of Eminent Persons on the Post-2015 Development Agenda and in a 2014 report by the secretary-general.[20] Various UN agencies organized multistakeholder consultations involving civil

---

14 UN General Assembly, Resolution 55/2, "United Nations Millennium Declaration," September 8, 2000.

15 The "MDG framework" was first published in UN Secretary-General, Doc. A/56/326, "Road Map Towards the Implementation of the United Nations Millennium Declaration," September 6, 2001. On the process, see Richard Manning, "Using Indicators to Encourage Development: Lessons from the Millennium Development Goals," *Danish Institute for International Studies Report*, Copenhagen (2009), 77 et seq.

16 Sakiko Fukuda-Parr, "Global Goals as a Policy Tool," *Journal of Human Development and Capabilities* 15 (2014), 118–131, at 122; and Manning, "Using Indicators," 24 et seq.

17 For an overview of the process, see United Nations, "UN Process for Coordinating the Post-2015 UN Development Agenda" (no date), http://www.un.org/womenwatch/daw/csw/csw57/panels/panel3-paper-amina-mohammed.pdf. For an early evaluation, see Andrea Ordóñez, "Perspectives from the Global South on Post-2015," *SAIS Review of International Affairs* 34 (2014), 121–128.

18 UN General Assembly, Resolution 66/288, annex, "The Future We Want," para. 248, September 11, 2012.

19 UN General Assembly, A/68/970, "Report of the Open Working Group of the General Assembly on Sustainable Development Goals," August 12, 2014. On this document, see Debapriya Bhattacharya, Towfiqul Islam Khan, and Umme Salma, "A Commentary on the Final Outcome Document of the Open Working Group on SDGs," *SAIS Review of International Affairs* 34 (2014), 165–177.

20 United Nations, "A New Global Partnership"; and UN Secretary-General, "The Road to Dignity by 2030," A/69/700 (United Nations, New York, 2014).

society, business, and academia as well as an online "vote" in which more than 7 million individuals participated.[21] These inputs led to a final phase of intergovernmental negotiations in the General Assembly, which concluded in August 2015.

The summit unanimously adopted the 2030 Agenda for Sustainable Development as General Assembly Resolution 70/1, which provides the legal basis for the SDG framework. Unlike the Millennium Declaration, Resolution 70/1 clearly distinguishes a "declaration" on values, principles, and basic features of the 2030 Agenda (paras. 1–53) from the enumeration of the actual SDGs in 17 goals and 169 targets (paras. 54–59). Two additional sections address "means of implementation" (paras. 60–71) and the indicator-based "follow-up and review" processes (paras. 72–91). The SDGs thus replicate the tripartite structure of goals, targets, and indicators but significantly exceed the MDGs in number, detail, and breadth. The SDGs cover the entire range of economic, social, and environmental sustainability, expanding pre-existing goals from the MDGs and adding new ones on energy, infrastructure, inequality within and among countries, cities, and sustainable consumption and production, as well as peaceful and inclusive societies. Each goal is concretized by several targets that are substantive ends in themselves or instrumental "means of implementation targets" (cf. 2030 Agenda, para. 40). Goal 17 is dedicated in its entirety to means of implementation and a global partnership for development, corresponding to MDG 8.

What distinguishes the SDGs from the MDGs and accounts for their breadth is their universal scope: whereas the MDGs focused on developing countries and development cooperation, the SDGs are explicitly addressed to all UN member-states and aim at transforming both developing and developed nations. This means that the European Union (EU), for instance, will have to adapt its sustainability reporting to the SDG framework.[22] To reconcile even greater disparities in country context and capacities, the 2030 Agenda distinguishes more clearly than the MDGs between targets to be achieved globally or nationally[23] and stipulates that "targets are defined as aspirational and global, with each government setting its own national targets guided by the global level of ambition but taking into account national circumstances" (para. 55). However, this compromise leaves important questions regarding the process of implementation and the formulation of indicators unanswered.

---

21 United Nations, "We the Peoples: Celebrating 7 Million Voices" (United Nations, New York, 2014). On the consultation processes, see United Nations, "UN Process"; and Daniel Esser and Yoonbin Ha, "Sustaining Development as We Know It," American University School of International Service Research Paper No. 2015-7, http://papers.ssrn.com/sol3/papers.cfm?abstract_id=2640297.

22 European Sustainable Development Network, "The Sustainable Development Goals (SDGs) and Their Impact on the European SD Governance Framework," ESDN Quarterly Report No. 35, January 2015.

23 Compare, for example, Targets 3.1 and 3.2 with Target 8.1; on the MDGs, see Fukuda-Parr, "Global Goals," 123–124.

Implementation, Indicators, and the Data Revolution

The 2030 Agenda makes detailed provisions for implementation[24] and for follow-up and review,[25] codifying some practices that evolved in MDG implementation. In the absence of a hard enforcement mechanism, the follow-up and review processes will not only fulfill monitoring functions but also serve as a governance structure.[26] Institutionally, follow-up and review will be organized as a multilevel system at the national, regional, and global levels (paras. 78–90). All levels will be governed by principles laid down in the 2030 Agenda, including voluntariness (i.e., its nonbinding nature), national ownership, inclusiveness and transparency, respect for human rights, and a basis in evidence and quality disaggregated data (para. 74).

The global review process consists of political and administrative components. A high-level political forum, formed in 2013 to replace the Commission on Sustainable Development, will carry out regular global and thematic reviews under the auspices of the Economic and Social Council (ECOSOC) and will provide political guidance when meeting in the General Assembly.[27] Political review will be informed by administrative processes in the UN system and two flagship reports: an annual progress report on the achievement of the SDGs, prepared by the secretary-general in cooperation with the UN system and modeled on MDG progress reports; and a global sustainable development report that will help "strengthen the science–policy interface" through a metareview of existing policy-relevant knowledge.[28]

The core of all review and reporting activities will be a framework of quantitative indicators that makes progress toward the goals and targets measurable over time and comparable across countries. This framework will be based on a set of global indicators, complemented by indicators at the regional and national levels chosen by member-states (2030 Agenda, paras. 48, 75). Some SDG targets, such as 1.1, formulate quantifiable measures, but most other indicators remain to be defined. The 2030 Agenda itself provides guidance on the criteria and process for the global indicator framework: it will be developed by an Inter-agency and Expert Group on SDG indicators (IAEG-SDGs), and then agreed upon by the UN Statistical Commission, and finally adopted

---

24 2030 Agenda, paras. 39–46, 60–71. These also incorporate the Addis Ababa Action Agenda, contained in UN General Assembly, Resolution 69/313, "Addis Ababa Action Agenda of the Third International Conference on Financing for Development," July 27, 2015.

25 2030 Agenda, paras. 47–48, 72–90. Cf. on MDG implementation; UN General Assembly Resolution 55/2, para. 31; and Manning, "Using Indicators," 25 et seq.

26 Manning, "Using Indicators," 24–42; Fukuda-Parr, "Global Goals"; Kerry Rittich, "Governing by Measuring," in *Select Proceedings of the European Society of International Law,* ed. H. Ruiz Fabri, R. Wolfrum, and J. Gogolin (Oxford: Hart, 2010), 463–487.

27 2030 Agenda, paras. 47, 82, 84–87; and UN General Assembly, Resolution 67/290, "Format and Organizational Aspects of the High-Level Political Forum on Sustainable Development," August 23, 2013.

28 2030 Agenda, para. 83; UN Secretary-General, E/2014/87, "Options for the Scope and Methodology for a Global Sustainable Development Report," June 12, 2014.

by ECOSOC and the General Assembly (para. 75). The UN Statistical Commission formed the IAEG-SDGs in March 2015; members consist of 28 representatives of national statistical offices and, as observers, international agency experts.[29] Unlike the MDG indicators, the SDG process thus takes place within the formal structures of the UN system and of member-state-driven political bodies. This procedural design can be seen as a requirement of the principle of national ownership and reflects the insight that the operationalization and simplification of complex concepts in a single indicator entails policy choices and political consequences.[30]

In addition to the indicators, the lifeblood of monitoring is the data that will feed into the review processes over the next 15 years. A weakness of MDG monitoring was that data were often years out of date, inaccurate, unavailable, or based on unreliable estimates.[31] Statistical capacities in many developing countries, namely in Sub-Saharan Africa, are insufficient to produce quality data.[32] The 2030 Agenda acknowledges these gaps and constraints (paras. 48, 57, 76) and formulates a means of implementation Target 17.18 on statistics, which functions as the textual basis for the data revolution. More concrete recommendations are elaborated in the 2014 report "A World That Counts" by the secretary-general's Independent Expert Advisory Group on a Data Revolution for Sustainable Development ("the Data Revolution Report").[33] These recommendations provide a reference point for efforts to implement the data revolution under the SDG framework. The report calls upon members of the United Nations to agree on basic principles related to the data revolution and to adopt standards for openness and exchange of data and for the protection of human rights. Recommendations on technology and innovation include the use of new data sources and big data analytics and the diffusion of information technologies, such as broadband Internet access and infrastructures for global data sharing. The report also assigns a leadership role to the United Nations to coordinate public and private, national and international data initiatives and institutions through a global partnership for sustainable development data that includes public-private partnerships.[34] Almost all aspects of the data revolution are touched in one way or another by international and/or domestic law. There is thus a need to pay attention to the legal infrastructure of the data revolution; the next section proposes an analytical framework.

---

29 UN Statistical Commission, "Terms of Reference for the Inter-agency Expert Group on Sustainable Development Goal Indicators," April 2015, http://unstats.un.org/files/IAEG-SDGs%20-%20Terms%20of%20Reference%20(April%202015).pdf.

30 Manning, "Using Indicators," 24–42; Fukuda-Parr, "Global Goals"; Rittich, "Governing by Measuring"; and Armin von Bogdandy and Matthias Goldmann, "Taming and Framing Indicators," in *Governance by Indicators*, ed. K. Davis, A. Fisher, B. Kingsbury, and S. Merry (New York: Oxford University Press, 2012), 52–85.

31 Jeffrey Sachs, "From Millennium Development Goals to Sustainable Development Goals," *The Lancet* 379 (2012), 2206–2211.

32 See generally Morten Jerven, *Poor Numbers* (Ithaca, NY: Cornell University Press, 2013).

33 UN Data Revolution Group, "A World That Counts."

34 Ibid., 21–27.

Analytical Framework: Toward a Global Administrative Law of Information

The SDGs are not a source of binding international law, and much of the indicator, measurement, and reporting activities in international institutions are not even captured by the uneasy category of soft law.[35] This raises the question of how we can legally conceptualize these activities and the rules applicable to them. The following section addresses this question.

Conceptual Focus: Information Governance and Informational Action

The fact that most SDG-related activities take the form of reports, statistics, and information lends support to the observation that "the major action modus of global governance has been collecting, processing, and forwarding information."[36] This modus of governance influences the way in which knowledge is produced, problems are perceived, public opinion is formed, policies are made, and resources are allocated. These effects have been described empirically for the MDGs and theorized in the literature on quantification and indicators. Empirical research confirms the (variable, but at times significant) impact of the MDG machinery on international discourse, advocacy, and public attention and on donor and recipient government policy and resource allocation.[37] More generally, indicators have been conceptualized as a "technology of global governance" that creates behavioral incentives in the relationship between an indicator user (e.g., the United Nations), an indicator target (e.g., a national government), and a third-party audience (the public, voters, donors, or markets that allocate political support or investments).[38] Sociological and anthropological approaches focus on quantification as an objectifying mode of knowledge production that shapes perceptions and preferences while empowering technically sophisticated actors and obscuring political questions lurking behind the numbers.[39] Ultimately, however, indicators can also function as political spaces and are appropriated and resisted in local contexts in diverse and often unpredictable ways.[40]

---

35 Roberto Virzo, "The Proliferation of Institutional Acts of International Organizations," in *Evolutions in the Law of International Organizations*, ed. I. Ingravallo (Leiden, Netherlands: Brill, 2015), 293–323; Joost Pauwelyn, Ramses Wessel, and Jan Wouters, eds., *Informal International Lawmaking* (Oxford: Oxford University Press, 2012); and Gregory Shaffer and Mark Pollack, "Hard vs. Soft Law," *Minnesota Law Review* 94 (2010): 706–799.

36 Schmidt-Aßmann, "International Order of Information," 118.

37 Manning, "Using Indicators," 24–42; Fukuda-Parr, "Global Goals"; Rittich, "Governing by Measuring"; and Liam Clegg, "Our Dream Is a World Full of Poverty Indicators: The US, the World Bank, and the Power of Numbers," *New Political Economy* 15 (2010): 473–492.

38 Kevin Davis, Benedict Kingsbury, and Sally Engle Merry, "Indicators as a Technology of Global Governance," *Law and Society Review* 46 (2012): 71–104, at 5.

39 Sally Merry, Richard Rottenburg, Johanna Mugler, and Sung-Joon Park, eds., *A World of Indicators* (Cambridge: Cambridge University Press, 2015); and Theodor Porter, *Trust in Numbers* (Princeton, NJ: Princeton University Press, 1995).

40 Urueña, "Indicators as Political Spaces."

Methodologically, these insights require legal analysis to place a conceptual focus on information governance, or, more precisely, governance *of* and governance *by* information. This focus is in line with an ongoing shift in doctrinal analysis away from formal sources of international law to the broader category of international public authority that can be exercised in legal or nonlegal forms.[41] Nonlegal forms include informational instruments, such as national policy assessments, that play an important role in cooperative problem solving but also require a legitimating legal framework.[42] In developing these approaches further, legal analysis should focus on more finely grained heuristic categories, namely three basic "modalities of informational action": acquisition, processing, and distribution of information. *Acquiring* occurs through the collection of data from primary or secondary sources. *Processing* involves the (re-)interpretation, harmonization, comparison, and aggregation of acquired data. *Distribution* makes the processed information available to specific recipients or to the general public, either proactively (as in open data or automatic information exchange) or at the request of external actors (as in access to information cases).[43] These three modalities capture activities that are central to the functioning of information systems in general and the SDG framework in particular. They also form the basis for processes of knowledge production, because acquired data become information only when they are processed and contextualized in the recipient's frame of reference; likewise, knowledge is generated only when cognitive expectations change in response to newly contextualized information. The same data can thus acquire very different meanings when they are distributed in different contexts, and a shared understanding requires not only harmonized statistical standards but also a certain convergence of interpretive contexts.[44]

The role of law in relation to informational action is twofold. First, legal systems can be the *object* of informational action. Since the 1990s, there have been attempts to measure rule of law, good governance, and the realization of human rights.[45] The SDGs formulate the first global goal on "peaceful and

---

41 Armin von Bogdandy, Philipp Dann, and Matthias Goldmann, "Developing the Publicness of Public International Law: Towards a Legal Framework for Global Governance Activities," *German Law Journal* 9 (2008): 1376–1400.

42 Armin von Bogdandy and Matthias Goldmann, "The Exercise of International Public Authority Through National Policy Assessment," *International Organizations Law Review* 5 (2008): 241–298.

43 For a detailed elaboration of this approach, see Riegner, "Institutional Law of Information," 59–63.

44 For the theoretical underpinnings of this approach, see Ino Augsberg, "Observing the Law: The 'Epistemological Turn' in Public Law and the Evolution of Global Administrative Law," in *Regulatory Hybridization in the Transnational Sphere*, ed. P. Jurcys et al. (Leiden, Netherlands: Nijhoff, 2013), 11–27.

45 Kevin Davis, Benedict Kingsbury, and Sally Merry, eds., *The Quiet Power of Indicators* (New York: Cambridge University Press, 2015); Kevin Davis, "Legal Indicators," in *Annual Review of Law and Social Science* 10 (2014): 37–52; Daniel Kaufmann, Aart Kraay, and Massimo Mastruzzi, "The Worldwide Governance Indicators," *Hague Journal on the Rule of Law* 3 (2011): 220–246; and Rosga and Satterthwaite, "The Trust in Indicators."

inclusive societies" (SDG 16), which covers key elements of the good governance agenda, such as the promotion of rule of law and equal access to justice (Target 16.3), the reduction of corruption (Target 16.5.), and public access to information and protection of fundamental freedoms (Target 16.10). The indicators chosen to measure these targets will have a standardizing effect on the acquisition, processing, and distribution of information about legal systems in the future.[46] The range of possible indicators remains large, as is illustrated by the diversity of proposals for measuring Target 16.10 alone: the IAEG-SDGs and the U.S. government proposed an indicator based on the number of killed or mistreated journalists, trade unionists, and human rights advocates; African IAEG-SDGs members favored the "percentage of the population who believe they can express political opinion without fear"; the World Bank sought to add the "level of implementation of legislative guarantees . . . for public access to information"; and Brazil simply suggested "percentage of population with Internet access."[47] Whatever the eventual choice, SDG implementation should avoid overreliance on quantitative measurements and their pitfalls, such as oversimplification of complex realities and concepts, abstraction from relevant contexts and local circumstances, marginalization of important qualitative and tacit knowledge, "expertification" of public debate, and exclusion of less data-literate citizens.[48]

A second role of law, relevant in all policy fields, is to provide a normative framework that governs the acquisition, processing, and distribution of information by governmental authorities, international organizations, companies, and individuals. This function as a legal infrastructure for the SDG data revolution is best described through the conceptual lens of an emerging global administrative law of information.

Global Administrative Law as a Framework for Multilevel Information Governance

If much of global governance can be understood and analyzed as administration, then the law applicable to such activities should be conceptualized as global administrative law.[49] Yet, if the major modus of global governance is

---

46 For a discussion of SDG 16, see David Hulme, Antonio Savoia, and Kunal Sen, "Governance as a Global Development Goal? Setting, Measuring and Monitoring the Post-2015 Development Agenda," *Global Policy Journal* 6 (2015): 85–96; and Martin S. Edwards and Sthelyn Romero, "Governance and the Sustainable Development Goals: Changing the Game or More of the Same?," *SAIS Review of International Affairs* 34 (2014): 141–150.

47 UN Statistics Division, "Summary of Comments: List of Indicator Proposals" (2015), 92, http://unstats.un.org/sdgs/files/open-consultation-iaeg/Summary%20of%20Comments%20on%20Indicator%20Proposals%2025-9-15.pdf.

48 Davis, "Legal Indicators"; Rittich, "Governing by Measuring"; Fukuda-Parr, "Global Goals"; Linn Hammergren, "Indices, Indicators, and Statistics: A View from the Project Side as to Their Utility and Pitfalls," *Hague Journal on the Rule of Law* 3 (2011): 305–316; and Robert Salais, "On the Correct (and Incorrect) Use of Indicators in Public Action," *Comparative Labor Law and Policy Journal* 27 (2006): 237–256.

49 Kingsbury, Krisch, and Stewart, "Global Administrative Law," 16–17.

informational action, then the applicable law should also be conceptualized as law of information. Global administrative law is less decision driven and court oriented than information based, and global administrative spaces are chiefly constituted by information flows that transcend institutions, nation-states, and levels of governance.[50] Such global spaces are formed by multilevel systems of governance, such as development cooperation and its law.[51] Monitoring projects, such as the MDGs and SDGs, deepen the global spaces in which data circulate among national and international institutions, transnational networks, and epistemic communities.[52] The norms that govern the acquisition, processing, and distribution of data in these global spaces and composite administrations constitute the emerging global administrative law of information.

The sources of these norms are principally those of classical international law, in particular treaty law and the founding documents of international organizations. In addition, secondary law and internal administrative rules, such as the World Bank Operational Policies, require states to report debt data, prescribe the use of indicators in allocation and loan agreements, grant individuals enforceable access to information rights, and install a quasi-judicial review body for access to information.[53] The nonbinding norms laid down for the SDG framework expand this body of administrative rules, blurring the boundary between "hard" and "soft" law, but in a way that could drive processes of incremental hardening and legalization, for example, through adoption in national law. Domestic law, although not formally part of a "global" administrative law, affects the acquisition, processing, and distribution of information in global administrative spaces through legal rules on statistical systems, performance monitoring, data protection, and freedom of information. Private contracts, general conditions, and codes of conduct can function as quasi-regulatory standards for information infrastructures, such as the Internet or mobile phone networks, important data sources for development.[54] The interplay of international, national, and private norms thus affects information governance on all levels. For instance, data unavailable under national freedom of information laws may be accessible under the World Bank's Access to Information Policy, or vice versa.

---

50 Schmidt Aßmann, "International Order of Information," 118.

51 See generally Dann, "Law of Development Cooperation," 12 et seq.; Laurence Boisson de Chazournes, *Partnerships, Emulation, and Coordination: Toward the Emergence of a Droit Commun in the Field of Development Finance*, in *The World Bank Legal Review*, vol. 3, *International Financial Institutions and Global Legal Governance*, ed. Hassane Cissé, David Bradlow, and Benedict Kingsbury (Washington, DC: World Bank, 2012), 173–187.

52 On information networks, see Anne-Marie Slaughter, "Global Government Networks, Global Information Agencies, and Disaggregated Democracy," in *Public Governance in the Age of Globalization*, ed. K.-H. Ladeur (Aldershot, U.K.: Ashgate, 2004), 121–155.

53 World Bank Policy: Access to Information 2010, as amended July 1, 2015; Operational Policy (OP) 13.60 on Monitoring and Evaluation (2005); and OP 14.10 on External Debt Reporting and Financial Statements (1999).

54 See generally, Tim Büthe and Walter Mattli, *The New Global Rulers* (Princeton, NJ: Princeton University Press, 2011). On legal innovation through contract law, see Kevin Davis, "Contracts as Technology," *New York University Law Review* 88 (2013): 83–127.

At this point it helps to clarify the regulatory modus of the emerging global administrative law of information to avoid the misconception that law is generally unable to regulate information. Legal rules may not be able to directly govern information as such, but they can impose obligations for institutional and individual action in relation to acquiring, processing, and distributing information. Law can thus have an enabling, limiting, or legitimating function for informational action, and it can fulfill these functions in a direct or indirect regulatory modus.[55] Reporting obligations and access to information rights enable information flows, and privacy protections limit the collection or distribution of certain sensitive data. Likewise, the regulation of information infrastructures, such as Internet services provided by the Internet Corporation for Assigned Names and Numbers (ICANN) or privately owned broadband and mobile phone networks, can be more or less enabling for information flows.[56] Institutional arrangements, organizational rules, and procedural rights indirectly affect cognitive processes because they form part of the context that determines what data are interpreted as relevant for whom. Research in administrative law shows that institutional mandates direct attention to specific subject matters and types of information, and that procedural norms about evidence and participation shape the administrative construction of reality that predetermines normative decisions.[57] Last but not least, law plays an important role in legitimating informational action and making it normatively acceptable to stakeholders on whose compliance and cooperation effective global governance depends. Law has the potential to translate debates on the legitimacy of governance into questions of legality and to provide organizational forms and procedures for deliberation, contestation, and democratic self-determination of those affected by informational action.[58]

General Principles of the Global Administrative Law of Information

The legal rules applicable to global information governance can be described and structured along the lines of three general principles of the emerging global administrative law of information: informational cooperation, national ownership, and individual information rights. These principles provide basic

---

55 See Riegner, "Institutional Law of Information," 63–66; and Georgios Dimitropoulos, "Global Administrative Law as Enabling Law," IRPA Working Paper 7/2012 (2012), http://www.irpa.eu/wp-content/uploads/2012/10/WP_7_2012_Dimitropoulos.pdf.

56 See Christian Tietje, "Global Information Law: Some Systemic Thoughts," Beiträge zum Transnationalen Wirtschaftsrecht 107 (2011): http://telc.jura.uni-halle.de/sites/default/files/BeitraegeTWR/Heft%20107.pdf.

57 Jochen von Bernstorff, "Procedures of Decision-Making and the Role of Law in International Organizations," *German Law Journal* 9 (2008): 1939–1964, at 1951; and Adrian Vermeule, "Local and Global Knowledge in the Administrative State," Harvard Public Law & Legal Theory Working Paper Series (2013).

58 Benedict Kingsbury and Megan Donaldson, "Global Administrative Law and Deliberative Democracy," in *Oxford Handbook of International Legal Theory*, ed. A. Orford and F. Hoffmann (Oxford: Oxford University Press, 2016); and Bogdandy, Dann, and Goldmann, "Publicness of International Law."

normative orientation to the field; serve to systematize, interpret, and evaluate specific rules; and guide further analysis and evolution *de lege ferenda* in the SDG data revolution. Methodologically, they can be reconstructed deductively from existing principles of binding international law, such as sovereignty in Article 2(1) of the UN Charter, or abstracted inductively from a comparison of individual rules from different sources that converge in substance.[59] This reconstruction can build on prior attempts to formulate general principles in soft law documents, regional instruments, and legal literature.[60] The 2030 Agenda and the recommendations on the data revolution reflect the three general principles and the normative tensions that can arise among them. This section thus offers a way of viewing the SDGs and the data revolution through the lens of general legal principles and posits some concrete implications for the internal law and legal operations of the World Bank.

Informational Cooperation

The principle of informational cooperation obliges states, international institutions, and other legal subjects to cooperate through and in relation to informational action. Such cooperation can take the form of data collection and exchange, harmonization of standards, and capacity-building support for statistical and monitoring systems, as envisaged in SDG Target 17.18. As international law has evolved from coexistence to a law of cooperation, the obligation of states to cooperate with each other has been fulfilled principally through the exchange of information.[61] Treaties impose reporting obligations on states, and institutionalized forms of cooperation transfer legal powers over informational action to international organizations.[62]

---

59 Armin von Bogdandy, "General Principles of International Public Authority," *German Law Journal* 9 (2008): 1909–1939. Principles in this sense are broader than the notion of general principles in Article 38(1) lit. c of the Statute of the International Court of Justice, cf. Martti Koskenniemi, *General Principles*, in *Sources in International Law*, ed. M. Koskenniemi (Aldershot, U.K.: Ashgate, 2000), 359–402, and more grounded in positive law than the "principles of Global Administrative Law," cf. Carol Harlow, "Global Administrative Law: The Quest for Principles and Values," *European Journal of International Law* 17 (2006): 187–214.

60 See UN General Assembly, Resolution 68/261, "Fundamental Principles of Official Statistics," March 3, 2014; UN Committee for the Coordination of Statistical Activities, SA/2013/08, "Principles Governing International Statistical Activities," August 30, 2013, http://unstats.un.org/unsd/accsub/2013docs-22nd/SA-2013-8-FP-UNSD.pdf; and Paris Declaration on Aid Effectiveness, 2005; Article 338(2) TFEU on principles of EU statistics. See also Schmidt-Aßmann, "International Order of Information" (reconstructing data protection and transparency as two "pillars" of a global order of information).

61 See generally Rüdiger Wolfrum, "Cooperation, International Law of," in *Max Planck Encyclopedia of Public International Law*, ed. R. Wolfrum (Oxford: Oxford University Press, 2010), www.mpepil.com; and Wolfgang Friedmann, *The Changing Structure of International Law* (London: Stevens, 1964).

62 Reporting obligations range from the 1928 International Convention Relating to Economic Statistics to IBRD General Conditions (2012), Sections 5.08 and 6.01, and to human rights monitoring duties. For informational powers, see, for example, IBRD Article V, Section 13; and ILO Constitution, Article 10.

The principle of informational cooperation finds expression in the SDGs and the data revolution recommendations in several ways. The SDGs set global goals and standards for collective informational action in fulfillment of the UN mandate for economic and social cooperation (UN Charter, Article 55), and they explicitly confer autonomous monitoring and reporting functions on the UN system in the context of the global review process (paras. 55, 75, and 82 et seq.). Specialized agencies are designated as the scorekeepers for specific indicators and will report to the UN secretariat and a high-level panel for the global follow-up process. One open question is to what extent international institutions must rely on official country data or can use, independent of member-states, new sources and technologies of data acquisition, such as big data techniques and private satellite imaging.[63] The answer will depend on the interpretation of individual institutional mandates, which are generally construed broadly to comprise implied powers to acquire, process, and distribute information necessary to fulfill their respective purposes.[64] In the SDG framework, such a broad interpretation seems warranted, at least in the case of the types of standardized and comparable data that qualify as a global public good, which individual states and the private sector have limited incentives or capacity to provide.[65]

If one follows such functionalist reasoning, effective informational cooperation also demands that an international institution's internal organization be functionally adequate. The Data Revolution Report touches on organizational law when it declares the independence of statistical offices to be a basic principle of the data revolution.[66] But data collection and statistical research in international institutions and under the MDGs have not always been separated from policy and operational functions or been insulated from political interference.[67] Although statistical work does require overall political guidance, there is a need for legal guarantees against political interference and conflicts of interest, which can render institutionalized informational cooperation dysfunctional.[68] The SDG framework should provide impetus to reassess and,

---

63 Jennifer Shkabatur, "A Global Panopticon? The Changing Role of International Organizations in the Information Age," *Michigan Journal of International Law* 33 (2011–2012): 159–214.

64 See Riegner, "Institutional Law of Information," 66–68, 74–75.

65 World Bank, *World Development Report: Knowledge for Development* (Washington, DC: World Bank, 1999); and Joseph Stiglitz, "Knowledge as a Global Public Good," in *Global Public Goods*, ed. I. Kaul, I. Grunberg, and M. Stern (New York: Oxford University Press, 1999), 308–325. On global public goods in international law, see generally F. Cafaggi and D. D. Caron, "Global Public Goods Amidst a Plurality of Legal Orders: A Symposium," *European Journal of International Law* 23 (2012): 643–649.

66 UN Data Revolution Group, "A World That Counts," 23.

67 Marie Guimezanes, "An Inquiry into the Life and Death of Indicators," *International Organizations Law Review* 12 (2015): 116–145; Heinrich Brüngger and Svein Longva, "International Principles Governing Official Statistics at the National Level: Are They Relevant for the Statistical Work of International Organisations as Well?," *Statistical Journal of the United Nations European Economic Commission* 15 (1998): 221–235.

68 On such guarantees, see generally Anne Peters and Lukas Handschin, eds., *Conflict of Interest in Global, Public, and Corporate Governance* (Cambridge: Cambridge University Press, 2013);

where necessary, bolster institutional independence and legal guarantees for impartial data collection and objective statistical work at the national and the international levels. An example of such an organizational reform comes from the World Bank Group: one if its most influential data and research projects, the Doing Business project, started as an operational unit of the International Finance Corporation (IFC) but was moved to the Bank's research department in the Development Economics Vice Presidency in order to bolster independence and quality control.[69]

Another field of informational cooperation concerns the private sector. The SDGs envisage public-private cooperation in data collection and stipulate targets for multistakeholder partnerships (para. 76; Goals 17.16, 17.17). Private sector infrastructures and technologies provide new data sources, analytics, and communication channels, which are increasingly harnessed for public policy, including sustainable development.[70] International law generally does not impose direct obligations of cooperation on private companies in this regard.[71] In contrast, national law can play an enabling role in governing Internet access or can require corporations to collect, retain, and report specific data to fulfill a public purpose. To highlight one example, corporate sustainability reporting is legally required under the U.S. Dodd-Frank Act and the EU Accounting Directive as amended in 2014, which obliges large companies to disclose information on policies, risks, and outcomes regarding environmental matters, social aspects, respect for human rights, and anticorruption efforts.[72] Such corporate sustainability reporting is an important field for public-private data partnerships envisaged in the global partnership for sustainable development in SDG 17.[73] The World Bank can help expand existing public-private initiatives, such as the IFC-informed Equator Principles, in

---

and Matthias Ruffert and Matthias Steinecke, *The Global Administrative Law of Science* (Heidelberg: Springer, 2011).

69 World Bank, "Independent Panel Review of the Doing Business Report" (World Bank, Washington, DC, 2013); World Bank Independent Evaluation Group, "Doing Business: An Independent Evaluation" (World Bank, Washington, DC, 2008). This move may refocus questions on the independence of the Bank's research department, cf. Robin Broad, "Research, Knowledge, and the Art of 'Paradigm Maintenance': The World Bank's Development Economics Vice-Presidency (DEC)," *Review of International Political Economy* 13 (2006): 387–419.

70 Patrick Meier, *Digital Humanitarians* (Boca Raton, FL: CRC, 2015); World Bank, "Big Data in Action for Development" (World Bank, Washington, DC, 2014); and Emmanuel Letouzé, "Big Data for Development: Challenges and Opportunities," UN Global Pulse Paper (2012).

71 Jan Klabbers, "Of Round Pegs and Square Holes: International Law and the Private Sector," in *Regulatory Hybridization in the Transnational Sphere,* ed. P. Jurcys et al. (Leiden, Netherlands: Nijhoff, 2013), 29–48. But see Molly Land, "Toward an International Law of the Internet," *Harvard International Law Journal* 54 (2013): 393–458 (arguing that ICCPR Article 19 imposes obligations on dominant private actors with regard to Internet access).

72 See EU Directive 2014/95/EU of October 22, 2014, on the disclosure of nonfinancial and diversity information by certain large undertakings and groups, amending Accounting Directive 2013/34/EU. On the U.S. approach, see David M. Lynn, "The Dodd-Frank Act's Specialized Corporate Disclosure: Using the Securities Laws to Address Public Policy Issues," *Journal of Business and Technology Law* 6 (2011): 327–355.

73 See also UN High-Level Panel, "A New Global Partnership," 24.

this direction.[74] However, such initiatives must take into account the limits of corporate reporting as a governance tool[75] and should include safeguards against undue corporate influence and greenwashing for mere public relations purposes.[76]

National Ownership

States remain the primary source of development data and the primary organizational form for regulating and monitoring statistical systems in line with demands for political accountability and collective informational self-determination. National ownership is thus an important general principle of global information governance. The 2030 Agenda conceives of ownership as a principle that guides the implementation of the SDGs in general and the monitoring and review processes at all levels in particular (paras. 46, 66, 74(a), 76). Member-states will formulate their own national indicators, and the national review processes will be the foundation for regional and global follow-up (paras. 74(a), 75, 78–79).

Ownership has a hard legal core derived from the principle of sovereignty, as enshrined in Article 2(1) of the UN Charter.[77] Informational sovereignty denotes the idea that states retain a measure of control over how data and information about themselves are produced. This notion informed early institutional decisions and legal debates at the United Nations, in which the principle of nonintervention in Article 2(7) of the UN Charter was interpreted as a principle of noninquiry into domestic affairs.[78] Such arguments have lost traction today in a world in which international law leaves few exclusive *domaines réservés* to states and in which governments have accepted informational cooperation in broad monitoring regimes, such as the MDGs and human rights indicators. Hence, the political prohibition in its Articles of Agreement does not bar the World Bank from acquiring information about the political situation in a member country,[79] but it does require the Bank to take organizational measures to ensure that its informational action and knowledge production are impartial and objective.[80]

---

74 See generally Michael Riegner, "The Equator Principles on Sustainable Finance Assessed from a Critical Development and Third World Perspective," *Transnational Legal Theory* 5 (2014): 489–510.

75 Galit Sarfaty, "Regulating Through Numbers: A Case Study of Corporate Sustainability Reporting," *Virginia Journal of International Law* 53 (2013): 575–621.

76 Cf. World Bank Independent Evaluation Group, "World Bank Group Support to Public-Private Partnerships," (World Bank, Washington, DC, 2014); and Lou Pingeot, "Corporate Influence in the Post-2015 Process," Misereor/Brot für die Welt/Global Policy Institute Working Paper (2014), https://www.globalpolicy.org/images/pdfs/GPFEurope/Corporate_influence_in_the_Post-2015_process_web.pdf.

77 Dann, *Law of Development Cooperation*, 241–244.

78 Ward, *Quantifying the World*, 37 et seq., 143 et seq.

79 Ibrahim Shihata, "Issues of 'Governance' in Borrowing Members," in *World Bank Legal Papers*, ed. I. Shihata (The Hague: Martinus Nijhoff, 2000), 245–282, at 269–270.

80 On impartiality of knowledge activities, see Hassane Cissé, "Should the Political Prohibition

The main contemporary significance of informational sovereignty thus lies in the organizational and procedural consequences for global cooperation. One such consequence is arguably that the mandate and the basic political direction for international indicator frameworks entailing an exercise of international public authority must be decided by the political organs representative of member-states, not by the secretariats or administrative organs of international institutions.[81] In this respect, national political ownership and the functional independence of international statistics must be balanced and applied differentially to the process of indicator formulation, on the one hand, and indicator application, on the other. The SDG process, led by the IAEG-SDGs, places emphasis on national ownership in the formulation of indicators, whereas MDG indicator drafting tended to favor independent international expertise with little input from states.[82] Ownership played even less of a role in the World Bank's flagship indicator project, the Doing Business project; considered a research project, the initial design and economic policy orientation of Doing Business was not subject to member-state participation or public consultation and thus met with significant criticism.[83]

Another aspect of national ownership concerns the issue of to what extent the SDG indicators can and should be used in financing operations at country and project level, be it as monitoring tools or as disbursement-linked indicators and triggers.[84] It may be tempting to align results-based monitoring and disbursements at the operational level with universal indicators in the SDG framework to enable aggregation of results on the global level. But this alignment would not necessarily be in accordance with national ownership. The 2005 Paris Declaration on Aid Effectiveness calls on donors to refrain "from requesting the introduction of performance indicators that are not consistent with partners' national development strategies" and to link funding "to a single framework of conditions and/or a manageable set of indicators

---

in Charters of International Financial Institutions Be Revisited?," in *The World Bank Legal Review*, vol. 3, *International Financial Institutions and Global Legal Governance*, ed. Cissé, Bradlow, and Kingsbury, 59–92, at 91.

81 Armin von Bogdandy and Matthias Goldmann, "Taming and Framing Indicators," in *Governance by Indicators*, ed. K. Davis, A. Fisher, B. Kingsbury, and S. Merry (New York: Oxford University Press, 2012), 52–85, at 80 et seq.

82 United Nations, "Road Map Towards the Implementation of the United Nations Millennium Declaration"; Manning, "Using Indicators to Encourage Development"; United Nations, "UN Process for Coordinating the Post-2015 UN Development Agenda"; and Ordóñez, "Perspectives from the Global South on Post-2015."

83 Cf. Timothy Besley, "Law, Regulation, and the Business Climate: The Nature and Influence of the World Bank Doing Business Project," *Journal of Economic Perspectives* 29 (2015): 99–120, at 106–112; Peter Bakvis, "The World Bank's Doing Business Report," *European Review of Labour and Research* 29 (2009): 419–438.

84 In World Bank operations, this concerns indicators in monitoring and evaluation pursuant to OP 13.60; triggers in programmatic development policy lending under OP/BP 8.60; and disbursement-linked indicators in the new Program for Results Financing pursuant to OP/BP 9.00.

derived from the national development strategy."[85] This call for ownership is reinforced by an argument concerned with effective informational cooperation: the MDG experience indicates that targets and indicators need to be adapted to local contexts to be useful monitoring tools at the country and project levels.[86] Hence, the complementary national SDG indicators developed by member-states will likely be a useful starting point for negotiations about operational monitoring tools. Even then, the risk remains that national SDG monitoring becomes "tainted" by operations because indicators that become targets can distort incentives and cease to be good measures.[87] Disbursement-linked indicators in particular require strong, independent third-party verification protocols.[88] These must be complemented by qualitative feedback channels and grievance mechanisms for citizens and project-affected individuals, as envisaged by the Bank's proposed Environmental and Social Standard 10 on Stakeholder Engagement and Information Disclosure.[89]

Individual Information Rights

Citizens are not only passive sources of data and objects of informational action, but subjects with individual rights and legal agency over the collection, processing, and distribution of information. The fundamental legal position of individuals in global information governance is defined by international human rights law and constitutional guarantees, complemented and concretized by a host of administrative rules at the national and international levels. It is beyond the scope of this chapter to provide a comprehensive analysis, but I will sketch three types of individual information rights relevant to the implementation of the SDGs. These rights revolve around international obligations to collect and report on human rights data, access to information, and privacy and data protection.

Interestingly, the 2030 Agenda declares itself to be "an Agenda of the people, by the people, and for the people" (para. 52) but does not contemplate the role of individual citizens in any detail. Accountability to citizens is mentioned as the purpose of review and follow-up processes but not elaborated further (paras. 47, 73). Human rights appear in 11 mostly generic references in the text of the resolution (cf. paras. 3, 8, 10, 20, 29, 35). The goals themselves contain direct or indirect references to human rights, somewhat obscure at the target level, namely in Target 4.7 on human rights education, in Target 16.10 on access to information and fundamental freedoms, and in relation to women's rights, including reproductive rights (e.g., Targets 1.4 and 4.5,

85 Paris Declaration on Aid Effectiveness, 2005, paras. 45, 16. On indicators in the aid effectiveness framework, see Guimezanes, "An Inquiry."

86 Fukuda-Parr, "Global Goals," 123 et seq.; and Manning, "Using Indicators to Encourage Development," 43–44.

87 Cf. Besley, "World Bank Doing Business Project," 117; and Rosga and Satterthwaite, "The Trust in Indicators," 285.

88 This requires making full use of the possibilities foreseen in BP 9.00 para. 12(3), note 9.

89 World Bank, *Environmental and Social Framework, 2nd Draft,* July 1, 2015.

Goal 5, and Target 5.6). Finally, follow-up and review processes must respect human rights, besides being participatory, people centered, gender sensitive, and focused on the poor and vulnerable (paras. 73(d), 73(e)).

If development and human rights appear like "ships passing in the night" under the MDGs,[90] the SDGs provide textual ground for a human rights–based approach—at least, the ships now pass in daylight. One strategy to further integrate development and human rights is the use of data and indicators as a shared quantitative language and methodology.[91] Certain human rights explicitly entitle individuals to compel their government to collect data, for instance, the right to birth registration in Article 24(2) of the International Covenant on Civil and Political Rights (ICCPR), Article 7 of the Convention on the Rights of the Child (CRC), and SDG Target 16.9. Beyond such explicit entitlements, UN treaty bodies have interpreted human rights treaties, in particular the Covenant on Economic, Social, and Cultural Rights (CESCR), as imposing obligations on governments to collect data and use indicators to monitor the progressive and nondiscriminatory realization of rights.[92]

The SDGs can rely on these obligations, indicators, and data from the human rights system when monitoring explicit rights targets, such as "protecting fundamental freedoms" (Target 16.10), and also when measuring social targets on health (Target 3) and education (Target 4.1) that correlate with the rights to health and education under the CESCR.[93] Furthermore, SDG targets that require disaggregation of data according to gender, race, disability, and other status[94] are underpinned by human rights obligations for nondiscrimination, which are interpreted as giving rise to a duty to disaggregate data accordingly.[95] International aid agencies can make a contribution

---

90 Philip Alston, "Ships Passing in the Night: The Current State of the Human Rights and Development Debate Seen through the Lens of the Millennium Development Goals," *Human Rights Quarterly* 27 (2005): 755–829.

91 Siobhan Airey, "The Taming of the Shrill: From Indicators to Indicatorisation," *International Organizations Law Review* 12 (2015): 81–115; and Siobhan McInerney-Lankford and Hans-Otto Sano, *Human Rights Indicators in Development* (Washington, DC: World Bank, 2010).

92 Rosga and Satterthwaite, "The Trust in Indicators," 269 et seq.; and OHCHR, "Human Rights Indicators: A Guide to Measurement and Implementation," HR/PUB/12/5 (OHCHR, New York, Geneva, 2013).

93 See generally Sital Kalantry, Jocelyn Getgen, and Steven Koh, "Enhancing Enforcement of Economic, Social, and Cultural Rights Using Indicators," *Human Rights Quarterly* 32 (2010): 253–310. On SDG monitoring, see Center for Economic and Social Rights, "Submission to the UN Secretary-General's Independent Expert Advisory Group on the Data Revolution for Sustainable Development" (New York, 2014), http://www.cesr.org/downloads/CESR_Submission_to_IEAG_data_revolution.pdf; and OHCHR, "Who Will Be Accountable? Human Rights and the Post-2015 Development Agenda," HR/PUB/13/1 (New York, Geneva, 2013).

94 2030 Agenda, para. 73(g), Goals 1.4, 4.1–4.6, 5.1, 5.5, 10.2, 11.2, 16.3, 17.18.

95 Kalantry et al., "Enhancing Enforcement," 288–299. See also UN Convention on the Rights of Persons with Disabilities, Article 31; and Eliza Varney, "Convention on the Rights of Persons with Disabilities: Ensuring Full and Equal Access to Information," in *The United Nations and Freedom of Expression and Information*, ed. T. McGonagle and Y. Donders (Cambridge: Cambridge University Press, 2015), 171–207.

in this regard by disaggregating monitoring data in their operations, as envisaged by social safeguards in internal World Bank and UNDP administrative law.[96] Harnessing these synergies, however, requires overcoming the persistent institutional, cultural, and epistemic barriers between the development and human rights systems.[97] Even more important, new ways must be found in which human rights information can empower individual rights holders, rather than the institutions that administer such information.[98]

Access to information has been championed as one such empowerment and accountability tool because it decentralizes control over the distribution of information and partly hands it over to individual citizens. This approach is reflected in SDG Target 16.10, which places access to information at the same level of prominence as other, unspecified, "fundamental freedoms" in the same target.[99] The legal background to this newfound prominence is the "explosion" of national freedom-of-information legislation, which is also used to promote development objectives.[100] International law guarantees access to information held by public bodies based on the human right to information, international environmental law, and other sources.[101] In this context, international aid institutions, such as the World Bank and the UNDP, have granted enforceable access to information rights to individuals.[102] They could go even further through open data initiatives and practices of open contracting in

96 For example, World Bank OP/BP 4.10 and Environmental and Social Standard 10, 2nd draft, July 1, 2015, para. 11; and UNDP Social and Environmental Standards (2014), para. 24.

97 See, for example, Mac Darrow and Louise Arbour, "The Pillar of Glass: Human Rights in the Development Operations of the United Nations," *American Journal of International Law* 103 (2009): 446–501; Galit Sarfaty, "Why Culture Matters in International Institutions: The Marginality of Human Rights at the World Bank," *American Journal of International Law* 103 (2009): 647–683; and Samuli Seppänen, *Possibilities and Challenges of the Human Rights–Based Approach to Development* (Helsinki: Erik Castrén Institute, 2005).

98 Cf. Martti Koskenniemi, "Human Rights Mainstreaming as a Strategy for Institutional Power," *Humanity* 1 (2010): 47–58; and Sundhya Pahuja, "Rights as Regulation," in *The Intersection of Rights and Regulation*, ed. B. Morgan (Aldershot, U.K.: Ashgate, 2007), 167–191.

99 See SDG 12.18 on access to environmental information. Besides the goal's legal dimension, access to information has a technological and infrastructural aspect to it, which is addressed in Target 9.c. on access to information technology and the Internet; this in turn has regulatory and legal prerequisites, as discussed, for example, by Land, "International Law of the Internet."

100 Sean Fraser, "The Role of Access to Information in Promoting Development," in *The World Bank Legal Review*, vol. 5, *Fostering Development through Opportunity, Inclusion, and Equity*, ed. H. Cissé, M. Menon, and M.-C. Cordonier Segger (Washington, DC: World Bank, 2014), 189–209; John Ackerman and Irma Sandoval-Ballesteros, "The Global Explosion of Freedom of Information Laws," *Administrative Law Review* 58 (2006): 85–130.

101 See UN Human Rights Committee, General Comment 34, CCPR/C/GC/34, September 12, 2012, paras. 18–19; Michael O'Flaherty, "International Covenant on Civil and Political Rights," in *The United Nations and Freedom of Expression and Information*, ed. T. McGonagle and Y. Donders (Cambridge: Cambridge University Press, 2015), 55–88; and Bianchi and Peters, *Transparency*.

102 For example, World Bank Policy: Access to Information 2010, as amended July 1, 2015; Megan Donaldson and Benedict Kingsbury, "The Adoption of Transparency Policies in Global Governance Institutions," *Annual Review of Law and Social Science* 9 (2013), 119–147.

their own operations.[103] Still, the potential of access to information as a tool for social change depends on complex enabling conditions and on assumptions about individual agency and public opinion that require careful scrutiny.[104]

One aspect that is conspicuously absent from the 2030 Agenda is privacy and data protection. The 2030 Agenda states that follow-up should "respect human rights" (para. 74(e)), and the Data Revolution Report mentions data protection, privacy, and data rights as principles, but neither refers to existing international norms.[105] This abstinence may be due to the lack of universally agreed-upon international standards and due to diverging national conceptions of privacy and data protection.[106] Yet, such differences can become obstacles to the free flow of data, as illustrated by the European Court of Justice's holding that the transfer of personal Facebook data to U.S. servers, subject to government surveillance, violates the EU fundamental right to private life.[107] Not least because of the revelations about U.S. National Security Agency (NSA) surveillance, there is a growing resistance to interference with digital privacy. This resistance could affect the perceived legitimacy and the effectiveness of the SDG data revolution. To protect both privacy and necessary data flows, there is a need for international minimum standards of privacy and data protection. These standards can be informed by interpretations and case law derived from the human right to privacy in Article 12 of the Universal Declaration of Human Rights, Article 17 of the ICCPR, and regional instruments that have recently been affirmed and adapted for the digital context.[108] Beyond individual privacy, data that are anonymized but otherwise sensitive are legally protected, mainly in regional instruments and national law.[109] These protections react to specific experiences of abuse and are thus

---

103 See, for example, World Bank, "Open Data for Sustainable Development" (World Bank, Washington, DC, 2015); and Open Contracting Partnership, http://www.open-contracting.org/. This also requires negotiating transparency clauses into loan agreements with governments and private actors to avoid that such information is deemed as provided in confidence under the Bank's Access to Information Policy, cf. Case AI2623: Emission Reduction Purchase Agreement (Access to Information Appeals Board, June 19, 2013).

104 Sina Odugbemi and Taeku Lee, eds., *Accountability through Public Opinion* (Washington, DC: World Bank, 2011); and Amitai Etzioni, "Is Transparency the Best Disinfectant?," *Journal of Political Philosophy* 18 (2010): 389–404. Critical to the assumptions underlying this approach is Boaventura de Sousa Santos, "Public Sphere and Epistemologies of the South," *African Development* 37 (2012): 43–67.

105 UN Data Revolution Group, "A World That Counts," 23.

106 Lee Bygrave, "Privacy Protection in a Global Context."

107 ECJ Case 362/14: *Schrems v Data Protection Commissioner*, judgment of October 6, 2015.

108 UN Human Rights Committee, "General Comment No. 16" (1988), UN Doc. HRI/GEN/1/Rev.9 (vol. I) pp. 191 et seq.; UN General Assembly, Resolution 68/167, "The Right to Privacy in the Digital Age," December 18, 2013; and Sarah Joseph and Melissa Castan, *The International Covenant on Civil and Political Rights*, 3rd ed. (Oxford: Oxford University Press, 2013), 533 et seq.

109 Cf. Peter Malanczuk, "Data, Transboundary Flow, International Protection," in *Max Planck Encyclopedia of Public International Law*, ed. R. Wolfrum (Oxford: Oxford University Press, 2009), www.mpepil.com; and Schmidt-Aßmann, "International Order of Information," 119–123.

important.[110] Yet they can also lead to conflicts with other information rights, namely obligations to disaggregate data; the collection of data on the basis of race, for instance, is considered unconstitutional in countries such as France.[111]

These problems affect the implementation of the SDGs in the operations of development organizations. National limitations on sensitive data collection can conflict with the social safeguards of international donors prescribing a disaggregated census of project-affected indigenous peoples or other vulnerable groups.[112] International access to information policies do not always contain explicit third-party privacy protections. This deficit was at issue in one of the first cases before the World Bank Access to Information Appeals Board.[113] The Bank lacks formal safeguards for privacy and data protection in its projects and programs, even though its operations increasingly use sensitive big data techniques and are progressively expanding to the security sector and law enforcement.[114] If the SDGs are to respect human rights, they need to take the informational self-determination of their ultimate beneficiaries seriously and give citizens a say in the processes through which data about them are acquired, processed, and distributed.

Conclusion: On Solutions

The legal problems arising in the implementation of the SDG data revolution indicate that the global administrative law of information is not a fully coherent system of rules. Rather, the law applicable to SDG implementation follows three different principles and normative logics that sometimes reinforce and sometimes contradict each other. This is not necessarily a bad thing; multiple constituencies and stakeholders can thus frame their arguments in legal terms, and disputes and contestation can be channeled into shared frames of reference and institutional venues. International institutions can offer such venues if they seize the occasion presented by the SDGs to develop international law and standards regulating global information governance. Hence, the World Bank's aspiration to be a "solutions bank" should not focus narrowly on technological innovations but encompass the experimentalist search for legal solutions and standards that balance the needs of informational cooperation,

---

110 William Seltzer and Margo Anderson, "The Dark Side of Numbers: The Role of Population Data Systems in Human Rights Abuses," *Social Research* 68 (2001): 481–513.

111 *Décision n° 2007-557 DC* (Conseil Constitutionnel), November 15, 2007.

112 For a differentiated proposal to resolve such conflicts, see World Bank Environmental and Social Safeguard 1, 1st draft of July 30, 2014, para. 28 (proposing to give precedence to constitutional, but not legislative or administrative norms against a census based on indigenous status).

113 *Case No. AI3127: Public Access Requests Received by the World Bank in October 2013 and Related Information* (World Bank Access to Information Appeals Board, June 11, 2014). See, in contrast, UNDP Information Disclosure Policy, para. 11(b).

114 World Bank, "Big Data in Action"; World Bank Legal Vice Presidency, "Annual Report FY2014: Legal Aspects of the World Bank's Involvement in the Security Sector" (World Bank, Washington, DC, 2014).

national ownership, and individual information rights in diverse contexts.[115] For now, the general conclusion is that all stakeholders have homework to do before the data revolution can change the world. Or, as the Beatles would have it, "You say you got a real solution / Well, you know we'd all love to see the plan, oh yeah."

---

115 On experimentalism, see Gráinne de Búrca, Robert Keohane, and Charles Sabel, "Global Experimentalist Governance," *British Journal of Political Science* 44 (2014): 477–486. On legal innovation, see Kevin Davis, "Contracts as Technology."

2
Internal Review Boards
An Innovation in Health Sector Governance

MICHELE FORZLEY

Recently, when the head of law enforcement in a developing country's health ministry was asked, "What happens when a hospital, restaurant, laboratory, or other entity does not agree when your inspectors claim there is a violation of a health standard?" his reply was, "I invite him to my office and convince him."

A global comparative legal analysis, done to prepare this chapter, shows that many developing countries either lack a mechanism to resolve regulatory disputes in the health sector or fail to use one. Without such a mechanism—referred to here as an "internal review board" (IRB) but also known as an "appeals board" or an "administrative law panel"—citizens have no way to review a health ministry's regulatory decisions fairly and objectively.

According to our global analysis, some countries—India and Afghanistan, for example—are creating such mechanisms. One city, Dubai Health Care City, created an appeals board and named its members in 2014. The analysis, however, uncovered little guidance of a theoretical or practical nature to help these and other governments, as well as development practitioners, design and operate a mechanism for regulatory appeal.

Although many regulatory matters might be adjudicated in the courts or with the intervention of an attorney general, or, in the case of a crime, be addressed by a prosecutor, traditional or formal legal systems in developing countries are not known to be efficient, sufficient, or expeditious. Nor do they have the technical competence or resources to manage the numerous regulatory matters that can arise within a health sector for attention by a ministry of health (MOH). Common examples are disputes around public-private partnerships, procurement performance, health insurance coverage claims, licensing, marketing authorization, medicines manufacturing and distribution, and compliance with health facility safety and quality standards. Many health facility support services and concessions—for example, ambulance, laboratory, and food services and other nonmedical activities with potential health consequences, such as barber shops, restaurants, cosmetics companies, food and beverage companies, and funeral services—are or can be under the regulatory jurisdiction of an MOH. Thus, a ministry's decisions have consequences not only for health but for the economy, too.

As so clearly expressed by the United Nations secretary-general in the synthesis report on the post-2015 global development agenda, an enabling environment must be developed and maintained to achieve justice.[1] However, how can justice be enabled in the developing world's health sector in the absence of laws or other mechanisms for enforcement? Can Sustainable Development Goal (SDG) 3, for health—or any SDG—be achieved if Goal 16, for justice,[2] is not? To create the enabling environment for health envisioned in the synthesis report, developing countries must design and develop justice mechanisms in the midst of severe human and financial resource constraints so that matters needing fairness, objectivity, immediate resolution, and health expertise are resolved properly. Is this possible? This chapter contends that it is, even without comprehensive legislative reform, and even in a war zone such as Afghanistan.

This chapter is the first on the topic of IRBs. After a theoretical explanation of how IRBs in any regulatory agency contribute to building effective and accountable institutions and provide access to justice (SDG 16), the chapter addresses how such a body within an MOH builds rule of law into a health system and how this supports SDG 3 (ensuring healthy lives). Finally, the chapter provides practical guidance on how to create IRBs. It discusses their legal authority, title, scope, grounds for use, membership, procedures, decisions, and operations. This guidance is based on the field experience of the author (a health development expert and lawyer), an international comparative legal analysis of such boards in developed and undeveloped countries, and quantitative evidence on the relationship of rule of law to health. It may be useful to health development practitioners, government lawyers, health ministries (or any ministry, for that matter), and donors.

The Internal Review Board in Administrative Law and Its Legal Authorization and Structure

This section explains the relationship of health law to administrative law and to the concept of rule of law.

Health Law Is Administrative Law Applied by Administrative Entities

Administrative law is the body of law that establishes the ministry of health and any other government office and authorizes them to function. It has been said that health law is actually administrative law,[3] hence the importance of understanding its scope and dimensions. This understanding is particularly

---

1 United Nations, *The Road to Dignity by 2030: Ending Poverty, Transforming All Lives and Protecting the Planet; Synthesis Report of the Secretary-General on the Post-2015 Agenda*, http://www.un.org/disabilities/documents/reports/SG_Synthesis_Report_Road_to_Dignity_by_2030.pdf.

2 United Nations, *Transforming Our World: The 2030 Agenda for Sustainable Development*, https://sustainabledevelopment.un.org/post2015/transformingourworld.

3 Timothy S. Jost, "Health Law and Administrative Law: A Marriage Most Convenient," *Saint Louis University Law Journal* 49, no. 1 (2004–2005), http://scholarlycommons.law.wlu.edu/wlufac/90/.

relevant today, because many ministries of health are currently transitioning from the role of health care services provider to that of a health sector regulator, a transition that has accelerated as the private health sector has emerged and is maturing and as health insurance coverage expands.

Government agencies (notably health ministries but also ministries of finance and insurance offices) are administrative entities central to health sector regulation. Legislatures, courts, and private organizations also establish rules and resolve some conflicts for health sectors. The health ministry plays the central regulatory role because it has the necessary expertise in health that can be focused on the public interest and is less influenced by politics. The MOH and other relevant administrative entities also have a flexibility not characteristic of the legislative or judicial branches, and the capacity to attend to a variety of determinations that no other branch of government could easily perform, such as licensing health facilities, contracting with qualified private entities—such as insurers and data processors—to make coverage and insurance payment decisions, and deferring to private accreditation bodies.

A fuller understanding of how administrative law defines the health sector and the use of its mechanisms is worthwhile for several reasons. Administrative law defines the details, roles, and responsibilities of an MOH in making rules, conducting administrative processes, and adjudicating certain types of cases within its quasi-judicial powers.[4] Because ministries have these powers, courts defer to their rulings. Often, exhausting ministry procedures is a requirement that must be fulfilled (a "condition precedent") before bringing a case in court. Administrative law is concerned with procedure and the interaction of the public with administrative bodies.[5] It adds fairness to these procedures—to licensing, for example. For this reason, informal agency action (such as licensing) can be said not to settle disputes but, rather, to keep disputes from happening.

The scope of administrative law also encompasses all the other forms of regulatory activities, including those by private or quasi-public entities that carry out government functions. An example is the commercially operated external review body MAXIMUS Health Care Services (MAXIMUS), which administers the second level of appeals for Medicare, the health insurance system for the elderly in the United States.[6] Some countries—Switzerland, for example—have a comprehensive body of administrative law. Having a body

---

4 William F. Fox, Jr., *Understanding Administrative Law*, 4th ed. (Albany, NY: Matthew Bender and Company, 2000).

5 U.S. Agency for International Development (USAID), "Using Administrative Law Tools and Concepts to Strengthen USAID Programming: A Guide for USAID Democracy and Governance Officers," http://pdf.usaid.gov/pdf_docs/PNADK999.pdf.

6 See generally Lester M. Salamon, ed., *The Tools of Government: A Guide to the New Governance* (New York: Oxford University Press, 2002). This book describes many of the administrative tools used by government. See also MAXIMUS Federal Services, Inc., "Medicare Managed Care Appeals," http://www.medicareappeal.com/Medicare-Enrollees/Medicare-Appeals-and-Your-Rights.aspx.

of administrative law does not preclude the creation of an IRB but instead informs the board's structure, giving an MOH a starting point for many of the details the ministry needs to address. If there is no administrative law, a full-scale administrative law reform effort is not necessary; instead, an IRB, a more modest mechanism, can be introduced as a stand-alone intervention. Creating one increases transparency, opportunities for public participation, and challenges to administrative decision making.[7]

Rule of Law

Rule of law as a construct for development has been at the forefront of many political, legal, economics, and development discussions over the past 20 years.[8] This has not been the case, however, in the health sector. Only recently has rule of law been mentioned in terms of health sector performance, and even then there has been a dearth of detail on what mechanisms of rule of law serve the health sector. To help correct this lack of attention, this section explores the relevance of rule of law and administrative law to the functioning of an MOH.

The principle of rule of law, supported by widespread consensus, is that no one, including a king or minister, is above the law.[9] At regional levels, such as within the Council of Europe, the idea of rule of law is that of a law-governed state.[10] Strengthening rule of law is a mandate of the African Union Commission's Department of Political Affairs, an element of the African Union constitution, and the subject of high-level discussions.[11] The same is true in the Association of South East Asian Nations,[12] in Latin America,[13] and, at the global level, in the United Nations.[14] Some authors consider regulators

---

7 USAID, "Guide for USAID Democracy and Governance Officers."

8 Thomas Carothers, "The Rule of Law Revival," *Foreign Affairs*, 1998, https://www.foreignaffairs.com/articles/1998-03-01/rule-law-revival.

9 Brian Z. Tamanaha, "The History and Elements of the Rule of Law," *Singapore Journal of Legal Studies* (2012): 232–247. See also USAID, "Guide for USAID Democracy and Governance Officers," 5.

10 Council of Europe, "The Principle of the Rule of Law, Report, Committee on Legal Affairs and Human Rights," Doc. 11343, Rapporteur: Erik Jurgens, July 6, 2007, http://assembly.coe.int/nw/xml/XRef/X2H-Xref-ViewHTML.asp?FileID=11593&lang=EN.

11 Aisha Abdullahi, statement presented at the Constitutive Conference of the African Political Parties, Khartoum, Sudan, April 27, 2013, http://au.int/en/sites/default/files/speeches/h_e_commissioner_for_pa_ccoapp.pdf.

12 Association of Southeast Asian Nations (ASEAN), "The Rule of Law: A Fundamental Feature of ASEAN since Its Inception," http://www.asean.org/news/asean-secretariat-news/item/the-rule-of-law-a-fundamental-feature-of-asean-since-its-inception.

13 United States (U.S.) Government House of Representatives, Subcommittee on the Western Hemisphere, "Subcommittee Hearing: Building Prosperity in Latin America: Investor Confidence in the Rule of Law," July 30, 2014, http://foreignaffairs.house.gov/hearing/subcommittee-hearing-building-prosperity-latin-america-investor-confidence-rule-law.

14 Helen Clark, "Opening Remarks at Rule of Law and Post-2015 Global Dialogue" (statement presented at the UN meeting on Global Dialogue on the Rule of Law and the post-2015

Figure 1. Rule of law and infant mortality

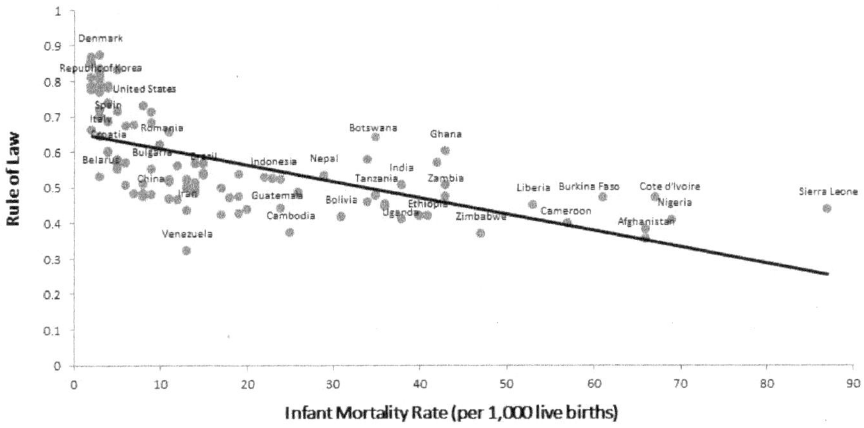

Source: WJP Rule of Law Index 2015 and World Bank 2015 Data (http://data.worldbank.org/indicator/SP.DYN.IMRT.IN). The figure is titled "Public Health and the Rule of Law."

part of the justice sector when they express their power to operate administrative review procedures such as IRBs.[15] Created as a separate institution with a law-related function within a ministry, an IRB demonstrates a government's commitment to *the rule of law, not man.* Legal restrictions, even when not fully honored, do matter.[16]

With so much focus on the value of rule of law, it is timely and fitting that rule of law should now be a critical dimension of health sector reform. Health statistics, such as immunization rates and infant mortality (see figure 1), show that where rule of law is respected, public health is better.[17] This chapter posits that the structure and use of an IRB within an MOH are an exact demonstration of rule of law and also show how important rule of law is to the health sector.

For this chapter's purposes, the following elements are sufficient to describe rule of law:

Development Agenda, New York, September 26, 2013), http://www.undp.org/content/undp/en/home/presscenter/speeches/2013/09/26/helen-clark-opening-speech-on-the-occasion-of-the-rule-of-law-and-post-2015-global-dialogue.html.

15 USAID, "Guide for USAID Democracy and Governance Officers."

16 See Stephen Holmes, "Lineages of the Rule of Law," *Democracy and the Rule of Law* 19 (2003): 25.

17 A. M. Pinzon-Rondon et al., "Association of Rule of Law and Health Outcomes: An Ecological Study," *BMJ Open* 5 (2015), e007004. doi:10.1136/bmjopen-2014-007004, http://bmjopen.bmj.com/content/5/10/e007004.full.pdf+html; and Lourdes de la Peza and Cary Peabody Perry, "Promoting Good Governance in Public and Private Health Organizations," in *Health Systems in Action: An eHandbook for Leaders and Managers*, ed. Management Sciences for Health (Cambridge, MA: Management Sciences for Health), 3:2–3:44, http://www.aidstar-two.org/CBHR/upload/msh_eHandbook_ch03_governance.pdf.

- A country is governed by a system of rules to which the government and its agents are accountable.
- The laws are clear, publicized, stable, and just and protect fundamental rights.
- The laws are enacted, administered, and enforced in a fair manner.
- Justice is delivered by a sufficient number of independent representatives and neutrals who have adequate resources.[18]

Essential Design of an IRB

For the design of an IRB, only justice (or fairness) is relevant and the only point on which there must be complete agreement. At least four aspects of justice guide the design of an IRB: there is a board to deliver justice, the board hears only certain kinds of cases, its officers are independent, and legal formality is in place.

Justice Is Delivered by an Internal Review Board

It would certainly be a solution for courts to review ministry actions and impose sanctions for regulatory violations. Unfortunately, court procedures are commonly expensive propositions that can take years to conclude. And in many countries, corruption, cronyism, overloaded calendars, and other barriers stand in the way of the ability of courts to redress public grievances. In a health system, where lives are at risk, stakeholders cannot afford to wait years for a court resolution or to rely on rulings made by judges who lack the knowledge to understand health cases fully. Without a review system, power is concentrated in the branch, institution, or level of government where decisions are made. Sadly, when there is no check or balance on the actions of government, power can be exercised in an arbitrary or abusive manner. An IRB differentiates or separates regulatory powers and provides a check and balance to keep governments contained within the law, thus providing a forum for justice. In short, having an IRB builds justice.

Depending on a minister to hear appeals, as some countries do, is like having a fox guard the chicken coop; it was the minister or a subordinate that made the objectionable decision in the first instance, and thus that decision is unlikely to be changed. The simple alternative is to create a body of some kind, even if it is only skeletal in the beginning. Having some form of review immediately makes the law a two-way street. People can know what will happen if they step out of bounds and do not act fairly. Private citizens will have a place to go where the government must answer for its actions.

---

18 World Justice Project, "What Is the Rule of Law?" (http://worldjusticeproject.org/what-rule-law).

Internal Review Boards Hear Only Certain Kinds of Cases

Ultimately, an IRB must answer only one basic question: Did the ministry or its representative (inspector, technical staff, etc.) or the entity in question act according to established rules, standards, or protocols? This question is the concern of regulatory enforcement, and the IRB is the institution that answers it. The board will not hear cases of medical negligence or crimes. A typical case is when an inspector claims to observe a condition that does not meet or comply with set standards and the operator disagrees with the inspector's judgment. In the absence of an IRB, the operator has no recourse. Either the inspector imposes a sanction or the operator succumbs and bribes the inspector in some way to avoid the sanction. And if the operator succumbs, the system is primed for continued corrupt behavior; the finding is never corrected, putting patients at risk; and the legitimacy of the regulator erodes. This loss of legitimacy will discourage the entrance of new and correct operators into the system. Other subjects within an IRB's scope are listed in box 1.

Box 1. Suitable subjects for IRBs to address

- Conflicts on procurement performance
- Contracts with nongovernmental organizations to deliver services in public facilities
- Review of reimbursement decisions in health insurance
- Public-private partnership disputes
- Failure by providers to comply with safety or quality standards

Independence of the Internal Review Board

To serve its function, an IRB must have a degree of independence from the ministry or other governmental apparatus that houses it. This means that the people who sit on the board, called "hearing officers," must be independent. Here, "independent" means that the hearing officers were not involved in the decision that is the subject of the review. It also means that the board has the legal authority to hold the ministry or complainant liable to its determination.[19] In some settings, "independent" means that participation by MOH staff is limited to administrative functions, such as scheduling meetings and recording proceedings; they may not sit on the IRB. (Medicare places highly trained specialized staff on its board but has safeguards to prevent interference in decisions by politicians or by those who make initial determinations.)

---

19 Albert Venn Dicey, *Introduction to the Study of the Law of the Constitution* (Indianapolis, IN: Liberty Fund Inc., 1982), 110–115.

Legal Formality: The Rules of the Game

"Legal formality" means that the IRB's procedures and the relevant substantive laws, regulations, and standards are written. "Transparent" means that these are publicly available, such as on a website or in a ministry's information office, and thus easy to find at no charge except perhaps for photocopying. Transparent legal formality provides predictability and informs everyone how things will proceed and on what basis a decision will be made. According to Friedrich Hayek, rule of law makes it "possible to foresee with fair certainty how the authority will use its coercive powers in given circumstances and to plan one's individual affairs on the basis of this knowledge."[20]

It seems only right and fair for both the government and the health actors to know in advance which actions expose them to the risk of sanction. In World Cup soccer, everyone knows the rules and the consequences, so why not in the health sector? At a minimum, this should be true of health sector regulation. Adding this legal certainty to the health sector avoids arbitrariness, reduces opportunity for corruption, and ensures consistent application of standards and rules to all similarly situated persons and entities. Here it is important to note that other health ministry responsibilities, such as adopting safety or quality standards or monitoring procedures, should be established with legal certainty. Although the form and design of these prescribed standards and procedures are outside the scope of this chapter, they bear mentioning, because it is during the implementation of standards and procedures that things can go awry, leading to cases for an IRB to decide.

Legal Authorization and Scope of Internal Review Boards

An IRB must have legal authorization, which can derive from several areas of the law, depending on the focus of the IRB. These options are described below, following a brief discussion of the different names given to IRBs and what those names do—or do not—signify.

Naming the Body

In this chapter, "internal review board" refers to any committee, tribunal, commission, or organized effort created to review the actions of an MOH and/or any of its divisions or to determine the consequences of noncompliance with regulatory standards or rules. In practice, such bodies go by many names.[21] The choice often reflects nothing significant about a body's grounds, scope, or legal authorization. When specific legal authorization creates a body, it also determines the name; otherwise, administrative law and practice and local practices will guide the naming. In Switzerland, Article 44-71 of the Administrative Procedure Act governs the appeal of actions or decisions by

---

20 Friedrich A. Hayek, *The Road to Serfdom* (Chicago: University of Chicago Press, 1944), 80.

21 Many legal materials were informally translated for this chapter. The reader is requested to excuse any imprecision.

administrative authorities through a body called an "administrative court." Australia calls its body the Administrative Appeals Tribunal.[22] In India, the body is called the First Appellate Authority; under the country's standards and rules for food safety, it is called the Food Safety Appellate Tribunal.[23] In Mexico, the name reflects the body's scope of work. Thus, an administrative court (the Judicio Contencisoso Administrativo) reviews any decision of the MOH, and a commission (the Comision Nacional de Arbitraje Medico) solves conflicts between users of medical services and providers.[24] Systems that do not establish an independent body use the term "appeal" to describe a review process, as in Uganda, for example, where the health minister hears appeals.[25]

Even in a well-developed system, the review body's name may merely reflect the size and participation of the private sector or the scope of review. Costa Rica, for example, has a private health sector but no private health insurance. Reviews for its public health insurance system are conducted by a constitutional court, with a designated room, Sala IV.[26] Private health providers with complaints against decisions or actions by the MOH have two options for appeal under Article 148 of the General Law of Public Administration: to the minister or to the head of the unit that made the decision.[27] The name may not even indicate the body's degree of authority; an example is Germany's Federal Joint Committee, which was created in 2004 as part of a health reform and which covers all the actors in the health system, public and private.[28] Review

---

22 Government of Australia. Administrative Appeals Tribunal website, http://www.aat.gov.au/StepsInAReview/ApplicationProcess.htm and http://www.aat.gov.au/ApplyingForAReview.htm.

23 Republic of India, Ministry of Health and Family Welfare [hereafter, India MHFW], Department of Health and Family Welfare, http://www.mohfw.gov.in/index1.php?lang=1&level=2&sublinkid=2526&lid=1810; and India MFHW, Food Safety and Standards Rules, *Gazette of India Extraordinary,* part II, sec.3(i), May 5, 2011, http://www.fssai.gov.in/Portals/0/Pdf/Gazetteenglish(08-04-2013).pdf.

24 Government of Mexico, Ley Federal de Procedimiento Contencioso Administrativo, Camara de Diputados del H. Congreso de la Unión, Secretaría General, Secretaria de Servicios Parlamentarios, Última Reforma DOF 24-12-2013, Secretaria de Salud, Comisión Nacional de Arbitraje Médico, http://www.conamed.gob.mx/conocenos/english.php.

25 Republic of Uganda, Public Health Act of 1935, http://health.go.ug/mohweb.

26 Jean-Pierre Unger, René Buitrón, and Werner Soors, "Costa Rica: Achievements of a Heterodox Health Policy." *American Journal of Public Health* 98, no. 4 (2008): 636–643; and María del Rocío Sáenz, Juan Luis Bermúdez, and Mónica Acosta, "Universal Coverage in a Middle Income Country: Costa Rica. Health Systems Financing the Path to Universal Coverage" (WHO Background Paper 11 for the "World Health Report" World Health Organization, 2010), http://www.who.int/healthsystems/topics/financing/healthreport/CostaRicaNo11.pdf.

27 Government of Costa Rica. arts. 59–63 of Ley Orgánica del Ministerio de Salud, http://www.pgrweb.go.cr/scij/Busqueda/Normativa/Normas/nrm_texto_completo.aspx?param1=NRTC&nValor1=1&nValor2=8204&nValor3=96263&strTipM=TC; and art. 148 of the General Law of Public Administration. Sistema Costarricense de Información Jurídica. Procuraduría General de la República, http://www.pgrweb.go.cr/scij/Busqueda/Normativa/Normas/nrm_texto_completo.aspx?param1=NRTC&nValor1=1&nValor2=57436&nValor3=96119&strTipM=TC.

28 Reinhard Busse and Mirial Blümel, "Germany: Health System Review," *Health Systems in Transition* 16, no. 2 (2014): 56.

bodies developed by organizations external to a ministry might be called "panels" or "committees," as is the case for accreditation awards.[29]

Legal Authorization

Regardless of the review body's name, what determines the scope and content of the work is the body's legal authorization. Particularly where an IRB is newly proposed, it is essential to understand the sources of its legal authority. An IRB must be authorized by some enabling legislation and cannot be created by a regulation. Generally speaking, there are several sources of legal authorization. These are not mutually exclusive and in fact can be cumulative: administrative law, health law (discussed below), laws specific to public and private health insurance, and laws regulating the private health sector and formal court procedures. Perhaps the most comprehensive source of an IRB's legal authority are the laws specific to public and private health insurance and those regarding the licensing, monitoring, and regulation of the private health sector. The organizing rules of a self-regulatory system might be considered another source; for example, the bylaws of a professional organization such as a medical council that can discipline its members. Even in an accreditation institution that accredits the accreditor, such as the International Society for Quality in Health Care (ISQua), there are review procedures.[30]

All ministries of health are created in some part of national law, generally starting with the constitution, which sets out the parts of the government. This constitutional outline is further delineated in national or enabling legislation often called "health law" or "public health law." Health law is either one comprehensive piece of legislation or several pieces that together comprise the "health law." The pieces of legislation can number more than 25, as is the case in Australia.[31] And as has been noted above, often much of the health law is actually the administrative law of the country.

The enabling laws authorize and direct the MOH to issue regulations, to manage the health sector, and to enforce its regulations. As the following examples from Mongolia, Afghanistan, and India show, these provisions do not specify all the details necessary to operate the ministry or an IRB. The details are left to further regulation or other subnational legal instruments, which are handled under the ministry's rule-making authority—a critical regulatory function in and of itself, not covered in this chapter.

---

29 The International Society for Quality in Health Care (ISQua), "Accreditation," sec. 4, http://www.isqua.org/accreditation/accreditation.

30 ISQua, http://www.isqua.org/.

31 Government of Australia, "A Listing of Legislation Administered by the Minister for Health," http://www.health.gov.au/internet/main/publishing.nsf/Content/health-eta2.htm.

Mongolia:

Article 8. Powers Of State Central Administrative Body Handling Health Matters

8.1. State Central Administrative Body handling health matters shall exercise following powers in order to protect and promote citizens' health:

8.1.1. Organise the implementation of the legislation on health at the national level;

8.1.2. Adopt rules on health protection and promotion of State Central Administrative Bodies, aimags [administrative subdivisions] and capital city and to ensure the enforcement . . .[32]

Afghanistan:

Article 33:

1. The Ministry of Public Health (MOPH) can prepare and process regulations to better implement the provisions of this law.

2. In case of violation of provisions of regulations mentioned in clause (1) of this article, the violators shall be dealt with according to the provisions of the respective regulations.[33]

India:

Art. 1 (1) This Act may be called the Clinical Establishments (Registration and Regulation) Act, 2010. Art. 52 (1) The Central government may, by notification, make rules for carrying out all or any part of Provisions of this Act.[34]

Administrative Law

This branch of legislation applies to every administrative agency across a government. It is the most rigid and least sensitive to the particulars of a sector. It can provide either the foundation of a review process or the exact terms. The Swiss and Mexican systems are examples of administrative law acts with appeal procedures whose details an MOH must use. Cases in any sector would follow these rules without allowance for the specific needs or technical aspects of the health sector. In contrast, the German, Indian,[35] and Australian

---

32 "HEALTH ACT of 1988, Government of Mongolia, Law of Mongolia, Ulaanbaatar, 7 May," 1998, http://www.sabin.org/sites/sabin.org/files/Mongolia%20Health%20Act%20and%20amendments%20%282006%29.pdf.

33 Government of Afghanistan, "Afghanistan Public Health Law," art. 33, on file with author.

34 Republic of India, The Clinical Establishments (Registrations and Regulation) Act, No. 23 of 2010 [hereafter, India Clinical Establishments Act], *Gazette of India*, August 19, 2010, http://clinicalestablishments.nic.in/WriteReadData/969.pdf.

35 India MHFW, Department of Health and Family Welfare.

systems[36] have an administrative procedure specifically for the health sector, and the types of cases are outlined with specificity.

The national health law itself may also provide for a review body, though its design may reflect any national administrative procedures acts. In Dubai, the rules of Dubai Health Care City and its appeals procedures were designed with a number of practices drawn from external influences.[37] Some older health laws, such as the 1935 Public Health Act of Uganda, allow appeals to the minister, a less modern approach.[38] Some of the guidance may derive from other parts of the law, as in India, where the Right to Information Act of 2005 established details of the appeal procedures and was amended in 2013 to add an online information portal.[39]

Public Health Insurance Laws

Within health insurance plans operated by governments (Costa Rica's, for example),[40] there are procedures to manage complaints of the insured and any private providers of health services and facilities. In Mongolia, the Social Insurance National Council discusses and decides corrective action in response to the petitions and complaints of citizens.[41] The United Kingdom's National Health Service operates with an internal review by the Parliamentary and Health Care Ombudsman, the final reviewer of complaints about the National Health Service.[42] Indicating the maturity of the U.K. system, there is a guide to good complaint handling and the office of the ombudsman reviews itself.

In federal systems, such as those of Germany and the United States, provincial or state review boards are authorized, and their decisions can be appealed to a national review body, such as the German Federal Joint Committee.[43] A national review process is useful to harmonize the regulatory system

---

36 Government of Australia, Administrative Appeals Tribunal.

37 Dubai Healthcare City Authority, Center for Healthcare Planning and Quality, http://dhca.gov.ae/microsite-cpq.php?page_url=cpq.

38 Republic of Uganda, Ministry of Health, http://health.go.ug/mohweb/node/76.

39 India MHFW, Department of Health and Family Welfare.

40 Jean-Pierre Unger, René Buitrón, and Werner Soors, "Costa Rica: Achievements of a Heterodox Health Policy," *American Journal of Public Health* 98, no. 4 (2008): 636–643; and Sáenz, Bermúdez, and Acosta, "Universal Coverage in a Middle Income Country."

41 Government of Mongolia, "Law of Mongolia on Social Insurance, 14 May 1994, Ulaanbaatar," art. 27, http://www.ilo.org/dyn/travail/docs/1705/Law%20on%20Social%20Insurance%201994%20-%20FIFTA.pdf.

42 Government of the United Kingdom, Department of Health, "Complaints Procedure," https://www.gov.uk/government/organisations/department-of-health/about/complaints-procedure. See also U.K. National Health Service, Parliamentary and Health Service Ombudsman, "The NHS Hospital Complaints System: A Case for Urgent Treatment," http://www.ombudsman.org.uk/__data/assets/pdf_file/0018/20682/The-NHS-hospital-complaints-system.-A-case-for-urgent-treatment-report_FINAL.pdf.

43 Government of the Federal Republic of Germany, Federal Joint Committee (G-BA), http://www.english.g-ba.de/.

across provinces. In the United States, private health services providers and insurers refer their disputes to state-operated boards, which may sit within the insurance commission or attorney general's office. Examples of these can be found in the U.S. state of Maryland[44] and in the Brazilian National Regulatory Agency for Private Health Insurance and Plans.[45]

In countries where health insurance is segmented by groups within the population—such as the elderly, veterans, the poor, the disabled, and the unemployed—there may be entirely distinct review systems for each group, as is the case for public and private insurance. It is sufficient to say these all fall under a combination of federal standards, state laws, and private health insurance review systems, which ultimately offer a review. Describing these alone could fill a book. They often mirror the appeal process of Medicare, as does the appeal process of the New York state Medicaid system.

Medicare has an extremely sophisticated five-level appeal process and only hears claims against it.[46] In it, the levels change if either party is unhappy with the result. The process begins with a simple request to the health plan for reconsideration of a decision. Next, the case is sent to MAXIMUS Federal Services, a private company that serves as an external review processor of claims. After that, the case goes to an administrative law judge in the Center for Medicare Services (CMS), the federal agency responsible for the program,[47] and then to the government-run Medicare Appeals Council (MAC),[48] which is also within CMS. The final stop is federal court if a case has a monetary value above a stated threshold ($1,430 as of 2014). An entire division of the U.S. Department of Health and Human Services contains the Departmental Appeals Board—specialized staff who serve as administrative law judges and members of the MAC. Effectively, the Medicare law provides several IRBs internal to Medicare, with a final appeal to court, as is typical for all administrative law review processes.

Private Health Insurance Laws

While technically not a source of legal authority for an IRB, private health insurance plans offer an appeal process that often is mandatory under insurance law. In this sense, the review process is legally authorized and the approach presents an opportunity for countries newly establishing health finance systems to mandate a review in any enabling laws. An internal review procedure is required in many states in the United States and in many

44 Maryland Insurance Administration, http://insurance.maryland.gov/Consumer/Pages/FileAComplaint.aspx.

45 Government of Brazil, National Regulatory Agency for Private Health Insurance and Plans (hereafter, Brazil NRAPHIP), http://www.ans.gov.br/the-ans/regulatory-agenda.

46 MAXIMUS, "Medicare Managed Care Appeals."

47 U.S. Department of Health and Human Services, Office of Medicare Hearings and Appeals, www.hhs.gov/omha.

48 http://www.cms.gov/Medicare/Appeals-and-Grievances/MedPrescriptDrugApplGriev/MedicareAppealsCouncil.html.

countries, such as Brazil, where private health insurance supplements the national plan. The procedure can be conducted within the health ministry, as in Brazil, or within the insurance company, as is the case in 47 of the 50 U.S. states (as of 2011).[49]

In New York, the insurance law is so detailed that the state insurance administration even provides model language on grievances, external appeals, and many other provisions for insurance contracts.[50] Massachusetts follows in degree of specificity, with an internal and external process outlined by its Department of Financial Services.[51] Internal appeal procedures, outlined in private insurance plan documents, tell the insured how to complain about an adverse decision on coverage, what steps to take for further review, and how to complain to the insurance commission. All U.S. carriers have such provisions.

Another level of appeal was added by "Obamacare," the Patient Protection and Affordable Care Act,[52] which gives consumers the right to appeal to an external panel. This requirement was introduced in response to data showing that nearly 2 million claims were denied each year, leaving private health insurance clients no recourse other than court. The external panels must comply with the Uniform Health Carrier External Review Model Act promulgated by the National Association of Insurance Commissioners, which sets model minimum standards for such consumer protection procedures.[53]

Private Health Sector Laws

Older public health laws have been inadequate to authorize an MOH to manage a private health sector. Many countries are therefore undergoing extensive regulatory and legislative reform. The need to support universal health coverage, whether public or private, will give this trend momentum. Among the systems regulating the private health sector that have undergone extensive reform in the past five years are those of Afghanistan, India, and the United Arab Emirates (UAE).

---

49 Brazil NRAPHIP; and National Conference of State Legislatures, "States Implement Health Reform, Right to Health Insurance Appeals Process," http://www.ncsl.org/research/health/right-to-health-insurance-appeals-in-aca.aspx.

50 New York State Department of Financial Services, "Health Insurance Checklists, Model Language & Guidance," http://dfs.ny.gov/insurance/ihealth.htm.

51 Commonwealth of Massachusetts, Executive Office for Administration and Finance, Office of Patient Protection (OPP), http://www.mass.gov/anf/budget-taxes-and-procurement/oversight-agencies/health-policy-commission/patient-protection. Formerly, the OPP was located in the Massachusetts Department of Public Health (DPH). Chap. 224 of the Acts of 2012 moved OPP from DPH to the Health Policy Commission. See also Session Laws of 2000, chap. 141, an act relative to managed care practices in the insurance industry; and Session Laws of 2012, chap. 224, an act improving the quality of healthcare and reducing costs through increased transparency, efficiency, and innovation.

52 U.S. Government, sec. 1001, as amended by sec. 10101, of the Patient Protection and Affordable Care Act (PPACA), Pub. L. 111-148 adds Section 2719 to the Public Health Service Act.

53 National Association of Insurance Commissioners, "Uniform Health Carrier External Review Model Act," http://www.naic.org/documents/committees_b_uniform_health_carrier_ext_rev_model_act.pdf.

A board to review the decisions of a ministry regarding a private health sector actor, such as a hospital, clinic, drug importer or manufacturer, food producer or importer, or health insurance company, can be found in many countries. A board's scope can encompass a variety of activities, as in Brazil, or be very limited, as in Uganda, where statutorily authorized appeals are limited to nursing home concerns, although other appeals to the minister are loosely authorized.[54] IRBs in Singapore, Spain, and the UAE are focused on those hospitals and clinics regulated by a licensing body. In the UAE, which drafted its governing regulations for Dubai Health Care City in 2013, the city's licensing board is responsible for clinical regulation and licensure of facilities and professionals, and has the authority to impose penalties on licensees.[55] Penalties may take the form of fines, the requirement of additional training, supervision, suspension, revocation, or the denial of renewal of a license. In September 2014, the government created a full appeals board to hear cases against facilities and the government, and by patients.[56] Singapore has a similar structure.[57] In Afghanistan, after assessing the health ministry's capacity to implement the 2012 Private Health Centers Regulation Act, the Health Policy Project—funded by the U.S. Agency for International Development (USAID)—worked with the government for several years to improve the private health sector regulatory system, streamlining the licensing of private hospitals and clinics and proposing both a sanctioning process for substandard safety and quality and an IRB. In late 2014, the health ministry approved the regulatory improvements, designed in consultation with the author, which included the new IRB.[58]

In recognition of the size of the private health sector in India, the Indian Parliament passed the Clinical Establishments (Registrations and Regulation) Act, No. 23 of 2010, which established a regulatory structure for states that adopted the act.[59] When any standard or requirement is contravened, the act

---

54 Republic of Uganda, Ministry of Health, "eHMIS," http://health.go.ug/mohweb/node/76.

55 Dubai Health Care City, Center for Healthcare Planning & Quality, "Regulations," http://www.cpq.dhcc.ae/cpq/regulations/; and Center for Healthcare Planning and Quality Boards and Councils, http://www.cpq.dhcc.ae/cpq/boards-and-councils/.

56 Dubai Health Care City, Appeals Board, http://www.dhcc.ae/Portal/en/media-center/news/15/9/2014/dubai-healthcare-city-regulator-introduces-appeals-board.aspx. Established in accordance with sec. 102 of the Governing Regulation No. 1 of 2013, this board is a milestone for Dubai Health Care City's regulatory framework.

57 Republic of Singapore, Private Hospitals and Medical Clinics Act, chap. 248, Attorney-General's Chambers, http://statutes.agc.gov.sg/aol/search/display/view.w3p;page=0;query=DocId%3A4fce9480-8295-4b7f-8b81-189f6a59fbd3%20Depth%3A0%20ValidTime%3A02%2F01%2F2011%20TransactionTime%3A30%2F12%2F1999%20Status%3Ainforce;rec=0;whole=yes.

58 Health Policy Project, "Building Public Private Partnerships to Improve Health Services in Afghanistan," http://www.healthpolicyproject.com/index.cfm?ID=AfghanistanPPPHealth; and Michele Forzley, "Capacity Assessment of the Afghan Ministry of Public Health to Implement a New Private Health Sector Regulation: A Legal Analysis and Design for Strengthening Regulatory Effectiveness," http://www.micheleforzley.com/uploads/3/5/5/3/3553263/forzley_moph_regulatory_capacity_assessment_final_report.pdf.

59 India Clinical Establishments Act.

has specific provisions for actions to be taken and identifies the licensing body to hear cases.[60] It also authorizes penalties for offenses under the act committed by any department of government or, in effect, through decisions by the ministry. The Indian constitution has an entire section devoted to administrative tribunals.[61]

India also has an extensive national regulatory system for food safety, a subject often within a health ministry's jurisdiction and thus mentioned here. An administrative tribunal is declared within the system and given an enforcement structure, appeal procedures, directions on sampling and testing, and model forms for the following procedures: seizure, notice to the operator of a nonconforming condition, appeal of a decision, notice of a hearing, and directions on the contents of orders by the tribunal.[62]

Especially noteworthy for resource-constrained environments, an IRB can hear any number of types of cases and need not be limited to matters involving private or public insurance or the private health sector. The same body can review a range of ministry decisions, perhaps by adjusting representation on the board to suit the type of case; for example, insurance, a private midwife clinic, accreditation, licensing, public-private partnerships, procurement, or a nongovernmental provider of health services. The same staff can manage the "back office" or serve as the "secretariat." An IRB's structure certainly can evolve into something as complex as the one under Medicare but need not be so elaborate to serve its purpose.

Formal Court Reviews and Other Special Legal Proceedings

Although review bodies exist within court systems, they are widely covered in legal literature. Moreover, their formation is dictated by national constitutions and parliaments, not health ministries, which are the focus here.

Specialized review boards or courts exist for some topics not covered by IRBs. One example is medical malpractice; in the U.S. state of New York, this is adjudicated through arbitration.[63] Another example is a constitutional right to health care, which in Brazil is enforced by a prosecutor. These and other kinds of cases, such as those for damages against an MOH or its staff, civil service cases, criminal prosecutions, bribery claims, and other nonregulatory matters, are neither addressed by IRBs nor should be, as these are covered by other legal procedures.

---

60 Ibid.

61 The constitution of India, part XIVA, Tribunals, http://lawmin.nic.in/olwing/coi/coi-english/coi-indexenglish.htm.

62 India MHFW, *Gazette of India Extraordinary*, Food Safety and Standard Rules, part II, sec. 3(i), May 5, 2011.

63 State of New York, New York Civil Practice Law and Rules, art. 75A—Health Care Arbitration, http://codes.lp.findlaw.com/nycode/CVP/75.

Generally, formal court procedures around health care are found in systems such as Costa Rica's, where health care services and insurance are predominantly public and where there is a lesser role for private providers and insurers. There may also be a law on the creation of review panels for government procurement, particularly in countries where procurement follows international models. Contracts with ministries commonly refer to dispute resolution options such as arbitration, and these will be especially relevant to public-private partnerships or other large investment projects.

Procedures: The Operation and Functioning of an Internal Review Board

There are a number of topics to consider when designing the procedures that govern the operation and functioning of an IRB. These are the levels of appeals; the staff and the composition of the board and the selection of its members; how a case is commenced; the evidence and procedures for cases; and the decision itself.

Levels of Appeals

IRBs serve the useful purpose of resolving problems before they get worse. A multilevel review process first allows those who make a decision to reconsider it and correct their own errors, as is the case with the Indian food safety system, Medicare, and private health insurance. After such an effort, if a concern remains, a series of steps is in place. A system of appeals that moves through increasingly higher levels of dispute resolution manifests the principles of a fair hearing and justice.[64] Courts will often defer to an IRB out of respect for a ministry's technical expertise and for the administrative law concept that all administrative (and, if applicable, customary) systems should be exhausted before going to court. The opportunity for the complainant to seek change creates an environment of fairness, in which ministry staff and citizens ultimately have equal power. Otherwise, the number of levels is limited only by a ministry's resources, but by the same token, no more than one level of review is necessary.

Staff and Board Members

Whether they are called "clerks," the "secretariat," the "back-office," or some other name, a staff is necessary for an IRB to manage the clerical work. There must also be persons who determine cases, who may be called "members," "administrative judges," "officers," "adjudicating officers," "authorities," "council members," "designated officers," or some other name. Deciding

---

64 Epiphany Azinge, "Restatement of Customary Law of Nigeria sections 1–67, As Adopted and Promulgated by the Nigerian Institute of Advanced Legal Studies at Abuja," Subchapter E Resolving Disputes in the Community (April 29, 2013), http://www.nials-nigeria.org/Editedbookcovers/1.%20Main%20Preliminary%20PagesRestatement%20of%20Customary%20Law.pdf.

how many there should be, their qualifications, what a quorum is, and who appoints the officers or members is best outlined in the law, and if not, in a regulation. Hearing officers may be civil servants, independent, or staff of a commercial entity, as in MAXIMUS. If their term is to be limited, like that of the Dubai Health Care City Appeals Board, then this, too, must be defined. Very often, the details of board membership are left to the ministry to finalize in a regulation.

The most effective systems have safeguards to ensure that the officers are neutral, that they have not participated in the objectionable decision or action and are not on the ministry's staff. Such systems also seek members with skills not only in the relevant technical area but also in adjudicating cases. Many boards are a mix of ministry staff and civil society. Ministries have a lot of flexibility on such matters as who should serve and whether and how much to pay them. For example, in Mongolia, the Parliament established the Social Insurance National Council, consisting of equal numbers of non-MOH staff and representatives of the rest of government, the insured, and employers. Enabling legislation in India directs a state government to set up a district registering authority, which serves both as the licensing agent and as the hearing body. The members are "the District Collector, District Health Officer, and three members with such qualifications and on such terms and conditions as may be prescribed by the Central Government."[65] In systems based on formal administrative law, like that of Switzerland, the members are trained as adjudicators. In the Medicare system, there is an entire department of highly specialized administrative law judges. In other systems, the officers may have only medical training or they may represent civil society or patients. None of the members of Dubai Health Care City's new appeals board are civil servants; one is a physician and two are in business.[66]

How a Case Is Commenced

Any number of formats can be used to register or start a case: a letter, a statement, or the filing of a form with designated information. The Australian system has a detailed form and list of grounds; other systems have fewer requirements. At a minimum, there is a need to know the complainant's contact information and the complaint's subject and date. There is usually a deadline by which a complaint must be filed and defined in the regulation or in the IRB's rules. Some countries have online systems for filing complaints.

---

65 India Clinical Establishments Act, arts. 2(a), 10.

66 Dubai Municipality, Governing Regulations, secs. 102, 103, http://www.cpq.dhcc.ae/uploads/regulations/1-Governing-Regulation-No-1-of-2013.pdf; and *Khaleej Times*, "Dubai Healthcare City appoints Appeals Board," September 17, 2014, http://www.khaleejtimes.com/nation/inside.asp?xfile=/data/nationgeneral/2014/September/nationgeneral_September144.xml&section=nationgeneral.

Evidence and Procedures for the Board to Hear a Case

At a minimum, there must be a designated date for the board to hear a case and for the complainant to be told that date, with sufficient notice to prepare. The board may be given the power to summon witnesses, to enforce attendance of any person who may have relevant testimony, and to produce documents or other evidence. The time and place of hearings should be announced and, for the sake of transparency, hearings should be open to the public. The complainant may also be given the ability to have the board compel witnesses and produce evidence on its behalf. Any information that may be confidential should be accorded reasonable protection.

Decisions

Perhaps the most important aspect of an IRB is its ability to render determinations, apply sanctions, and require remediation of a condition or other methods of enforcement. Board decisions take three forms: a factual determination that the health actor did or did not violate some standard; a determination that the ministry or its staff did or did not perform its duty in accordance with the stated procedures, a law, or a regulation; and a decision that states the consequence to be imposed on the health actor or the ministry.

Clearly, the board members must have access to the laws, regulations, standards, and procedures. Too often, the enabling legislation does not give a lot of guidance to an IRB on the permissible level of penalty or scope of a mandate that can be ordered in relation to the nature of the failure or error. For example, Article 28 of the Kenyan Public Health Act of 1921 refers to exposing others to infectious diseases and states the person "shall be guilty of an offence and liable to a fine not exceeding thirty thousand shillings or to imprisonment for a term not exceeding three years or to both." The statute does not offer guidance on what behaviors or circumstances justify the maximum punishment. Here, there is room for guidance by a regulation or some other document that board members would be required to follow. If the case is one of a ministry performing or not performing according to procedure, the board simply directs compliance, leaving the director or supervisor of the unit to impose any other penalties that the civil service commission may authorize.

Some laws also stipulate what should happen if a health actor does not comply with a decision of the board. In India, for example, a board may impose a financial penalty that is treated as an unpaid tax. If a ministry does not comply with a decision, a board's recourse might be to refer the case to the justice department.

An IRB's decisions should be public, both to deter improper behavior and to ensure that the board remains transparent and accountable.

Conclusion

Establishing a system to review the decisions of a health ministry and its stakeholders creates a forum for the rapid resolution of conflicts and a means to impose penalties for bad behavior. Although courts technically serve the function of resolving conflicts, they are often too busy and lack the relevant technical know-how. Rapid resolution is important to a health care system to avoid gaps in the delivery of care, promote constant improvement by means of immediate feedback to the ministry and stakeholders, and exploit the deterrent effect of sanctions. A well-designed IRB holds both the MOH and all health actors accountable and builds transparency and system integrity.

Generally, health development programs do not focus on administrative and health law reform, and traditional rule of law projects are disconnected from projects to strengthen the health sector. Nonetheless, adding a standalone administrative law mechanism, such as an IRB, is feasible, and full-on law reform is not needed to create one. Recognized for their value to rule of law, such boards are recent developments to manage the relationship between the private health sector and the ministries of health in Afghanistan, India, and the UAE. They are a long-standing component of the health systems in many other countries. The IRB is not a new idea, but it is an innovation in health sector governance and should be thoroughly integrated into all aspects of health sector regulation.

3

Law as a Guide to Regulatory System Design for the Health Sector

An Essential Tool for Regulating the Private Health Sector in Afghanistan and Other Developing Countries

MICHELE FORZLEY, KATHLEEN SEARS, AND OMARZAMAN SAYEDI

Millions of people use private health services every day.[1] In low- and middle-income countries (LMICs), a substantial portion of total health expenditures goes to the private health sector; in African countries, the share is half or more.[2] Poor and rich people alike use private health care, for such reasons as "better and more flexible access, shorter waiting time, greater confidentiality, and greater sensitivity to user needs."[3] In low-income countries, according to the World Bank's 2013 World Development Indicators, out-of-pocket expenses account for almost half of total health expenditures, in comparison

---

Work on this article was supported by the Health Policy Project, a five-year cooperative agreement funded by the U.S. Agency for International Development under Agreement No. AID-OAA-A-10-00067, beginning September 30, 2010. The project's HIV activities are supported by the U.S. President's Emergency Plan for AIDS Relief (PEPFAR). It is implemented by Futures Group, in collaboration with Plan International USA, Avenir Health (formerly Futures Institute), Partners in Population and Development, Africa Regional Office (PPD ARO), Population Reference Bureau (PRB), RTI International, and the White Ribbon Alliance for Safe Motherhood (WRA).

The authors thank Brenda Dvoskin, 2014 Abogada (JD equivalent), Universidad Torcuato Di Tella, for her significant contribution in the research and drafting of this chapter. We also thank Naina Ahluwalia, 2014 LLM, Georgetown University Law Center, and Lauren Archer, Health Policy Project, for their work on this chapter.

1 World Health Organization (WHO) Executive Board, "Capacity Building to Constructively Engage the Private Health Sector in Providing Essential Health Services" (WHO, Geneva, 2009), 124, http://www.who.int/iris/handle/10665/2134#sthash.ipafpmWV.dpuf.

2 Ramesh Bhat, "Regulation of the Private Health Sector in India," *The International Journal of Health Planning and Management* 11 (1996): 253–274; Lilani Kumaranayake, "The Role of Regulation: Influencing Private Sector Activity within Health Sector Reform," *Journal of International Development* 9, no. 4 (1996): 642–649; B. C. Forsberg, D. Montagu, and J. Sundewall, "Moving Towards In-Depth Knowledge on the Private Health Sector in Low- and Middle-Income Countries," *Health Policy and Planning*, supplement, 26 (2011): i1–i3; and Jane Doherty, "Regulating the For-Profit Private Health Sector in East and Southern Africa," Equinet Discussion Paper 99 (2013), http://www.equinetafrica.org/bibl/docs/Pol%2035%20finregs.pdf.

3 A. B. Zwi, R. Brugha, and E. Smith, "Private Health Care in Developing Countries," *The BMJ* 323 (2001): 463–464.

with the world average of 18 percent.[4] And in some very poor countries, the share, according to World Bank data, is even greater; for example, 70.1 percent in Azerbaijan and 80.7 percent in Myanmar. In Afghanistan, the most recent estimate puts the share at 73 percent.[5] Extensive services provided by the private sector match this extensive use. Although data vary considerably among countries, private hospitals represent as much as half of all health services in many Asian countries, such as Cambodia, Indonesia, the Lao People's Democratic Republic, Malaysia, Myanmar, the Philippines, Thailand, and Vietnam.[6]

There is no evidence to suggest that the private health sector in LMICs will shrink. In Africa, for example, the size of the private health sector was expected to double from 2006 through 2015.[7] The question is not whether the private health sector will or should operate, but how to regulate it to ensure safety, quality, affordability, and access, and at the same time enable an environment in which this sector can operate successfully and participate in meeting national health needs.

Some studies of private health sector regulation in developing countries have found these countries' laws and regulations to be either inadequate[8] or not implemented or enforced.[9] This is not surprising; to date, the scope of health reform programs, health system strengthening, and other initiatives related to the private sector has been narrow, such as examining the role of private providers in expanding access to care.[10] Less attention has been paid

---

4 World Bank Development Indicators 2013, http://data.worldbank.org/data-catalog/world-development-indicators.

5 Afghanistan Ministry of Public Health and Health Policy Project, "Afghanistan National Health Accounts with Subaccounts for Reproductive Health 2011–2012" [hereafter, "Afghanistan National Health Accounts"], http://www.healthpolicyproject.com/index.cfm?ID=publications&get=pubID&pubID=262.

6 R. Morgan and T. Ensor, "The Regulation of Private Hospitals in Asia," *International Journal of Health Planning and Management*, May 13, 2014, http://onlinelibrary.wiley.com/doi/10.1002/hpm.2257/abstract.

7 International Finance Corporation (IFC), "The Business of Health in Africa: Partnering with the Private Sector to Improve People's Lives," Working Paper 44143 (IFC, Washington, DC, n.d.), http://www.unido.org/fileadmin/user_media/Services/PSD/BEP/IFC_HealthinAfrica_Final.pdf.

8 Rich Feeley, Barbara O'Hanlon, Angela Stene, and Yuksel Segzin, "Finding Middle Ground: Making Better Use of the African Private Health Sector through More Effective Regulations" (Bethesda, MD: Private Sector Partnerships-One Project, Abt Associates Inc., 2009), http://pdf.usaid.gov/pdf_docs/Pnadp183.pdf; and Jane Doherty, "Regulating the For-Profit Private Health Sector in East and Southern Africa," Equinet discussion paper 99 (2013), http://www.equinetafrica.org/bibl/docs/Pol%2035%20finregs.pdf.

9 Charles Hongoro and Lilani Kumaranayake, "Do They Work? Regulating For-Profit Providers in Zimbabwe," *Health Policy and Planning* 15, no. 4 (2000): 368–377; and K. Sheikh, P. S. Saligram, and K. Hort, "What Explains Regulatory Failure? Analysing the Architecture of Health Care Regulation in Two Indian States," *Health Policy and Planning* (2013): 1–17.

10 Betty Ravenholt, Rich Feeley, Denise Averbug, and Barbara O'Hanlon, "Navigating Uncharted Waters: A Guide to the Legal and Regulatory Environment for Family Planning Services in the Private Sector," Technical Report no. 5, (Private Sector Partnerships-*One* project, Abt Associates, Bethesda, MD, 2006), http://www.shopsproject.org/sites/default/files/resources/3178_file_Technical_Report_005_Final4.pdf.

to enhancing the capacity of governments to define and enforce the mix of regulatory options.[11] Little to no work has been devoted to guiding regulatory design from the perspective of the law.

This was the focus of work by the U.S. Agency for International Development–funded Health Policy Project (HPP) in Afghanistan from 2012 through 2015. The project began with an assessment of the ministry's regulation of the private health sector and of the safety and quality standards in place. Next an analysis was conducted of the law (that is, the 2012 Private Health Centers Regulation [PHCR] Act), the extent to which the law was followed, and the capacity of the Ministry of Public Health (MOPH) to implement the law. With HPP's assistance, the MOPH started addressing the gaps and capacity needs that emerged, using the principles and steps of good regulatory design. As a result of this effort, the roles and responsibilities of the ministry were defined; the licensing process was streamlined, reducing 17 steps for the applicant to 6; and a plan was established for an independent committee to determine breaches of regulatory requirements, impose sanctions, and hear complaints against the MOPH. All of this was done and approved by the ministry's executive board within a two-year period.

Most of the studies just cited conclude with broad recommendations that encourage implementation and enforcement, and stop there, creating a "knowledge-implementation gap." Law cannot implement or enforce itself. This chapter's task is to help fill the knowledge-implementation gap by introducing relevant concepts, definitions, principles, and steps that together constitute *good regulatory design practice*. Our intention is to support the work of governments, policymakers, practitioners, and donors who are concerned with regulating every aspect of a developing country's health system, including the private health sector.

The guidance provided in this chapter on how to design a regulatory system is based on the principle that the law is the foundation of any regulatory system and essential to sustainable development. Respect for the rule of law is necessary to achieve sustainable development and is part of the global discourse.[12] Rule of law is a target of the sustainable development goals and is now recognized as having a significant relation to development.[13] No claim is made that law by itself is enough, but integrating the law has been largely absent from health reform work. Anyone engaging in health systems strengthening and health governance work needs to appreciate that a health

11 "Capacity Building to Engage the Private Health Sector."

12 Jan Eliasson, deputy secretary-general of the United Nations, "Remarks at Opening of High-Level Session of the Global Dialogue on Rule of Law and Post-2015 Development Agenda," New York, United Nations, September 26, 20 http://www.un.org/sg/dsg/statements/index.asp?nid=447. See also Goal 18 in the UN synthesis report on sustainable development goals, at https://sustainabledevelopment.un.org/majorgroups/post2015/synthesisreport.

13 Sustainable Development Goal 16: Promote just, peaceful and inclusive societies, http://www.un.org/sustainabledevelopment/peace-justice/.

system's regulatory mechanisms are vitally tied to the law.[14] Considering how to implement and enforce the law is a key task for this work to succeed.

This chapter begins with a review of the literature on regulating the private health sector and is followed by a summary of the three main categories of options to regulate the private health sector. One of the categories is discussed in depth: command and control, the name used in the public health literature for what the legal community refers to as rule of law. The relationship between rule of law and health outcomes and the implementation and enforcement of laws are presented as concepts and ideas fundamental to good regulatory design practice. The chapter concludes by describing steps and principles of good regulatory design practice. By following them, regulators can ensure that the law is successfully implemented and enforced and that command and control regulatory options function optimally.

This material is based on Michele Forzley's work with the health systems of a number of developing countries, including Albania, Morocco, Swaziland, and Uganda. Examples from Afghanistan, offered throughout this chapter, are of particular interest, for two reasons. First, Forzley's work there as an HPP consultant was unusual in that it directly assessed, designed, and facilitated the building of a health ministry's regulatory capacity from the standpoint of the legal infrastructure that authorizes a regulator to act. Much health systems–strengthening work, in contrast, focuses on building clinical capacity. Second, this approach merits documentation because HPP's work in Afghanistan demonstrates that making the law an integral part of health system assessment and fundamental to capacity-building plans is both possible and extremely effective. In fact, doing so is a necessary step for the field of health sector governance to mature.

Findings from the Literature Review

This chapter was conceived as a result of a literature review conducted during the course of development projects that aimed to establish effective regulatory structures in ministries of health. The regulatory challenges related to the implementation and enforcement of law in the health sector are noted here, followed by a discussion of the options available to regulate the health sector, with a particular focus on the private health sector. The finding that there are gaps between implementation and enforcement underscores the need for the guidance that this chapter provides.

---

14 In this chapter, "law" is defined to include every type of legal instrument, such as legislation, decrees, orders, contracts, and regulations or subnational legislation issued by a ministry. The term "regulation" has one meaning that indicates the activities of control, supervision, and government and that is often cause for confusion with the term when it is used to describe a law in the form of a regulation. A regulatory mechanism is an activity, process, procedure, requirement, standard, and so forth, that is used to regulate a targeted actor and/or activity.

Regulatory Challenges

In most developing countries, the entire private sector, encompassing all types of businesses, is responsible for the majority of employment and income-generating opportunities, and has become a driving force for poverty reduction.[15] The nature of business is to find niches to fill with a product or service or both. The private health sector thus has grown where public services are of poor quality, hard to access, or absent altogether.[16] In Afghanistan, the private sector has been growing since 2004, when it was authorized in the constitution.[17] Even though in 2003 the MOPH introduced a basic package of free health services to which roughly 60 percent of Afghans have access,[18] as of 2011, household out-of-pocket payments for services in the private sector accounted for 73 percent of total health expenditure.[19]

As the private health sector in LMICs grows, health ministries are challenged by this new target of regulation, whose dimensions are different from those of more familiar targets, such as clinical best practices. Although the issues covered in the literature on private health sector regulation vary, two themes—lack of adequate regulation and lack of enforcement of the laws—are constant. They point to the pressing need to build governmental capacity to implement and enforce the law as part of programs designed to strengthen the health systems of LMICs. Indeed, building that capacity is, and should be, a critical dimension not only of efforts to regulate the private health sector but also of any health systems–strengthening work.

In India, for example, the major concerns are the lack of quality standards for services,[20] price regulation of services, mechanisms to control unqualified providers, and consumer protections.[21] Researchers who studied the situation in Africa point out the lack of effective consumer protection and control over quantity, price, and distribution of private health services.[22] Some of the most pressing problems noted in Benin are the insufficiency of registration

---

15 "Private Sector Development and Partnership Strategy Policy," http://www.ifad.org/pub/policy/private/e.pdf. See also "Development through the Private Sector," http://www.miga.org/documents/IFI_report_09-13-11.pdf.

16 Kumaranayake, "The Role of Regulation," 642–649; and Rich Feeley and Barbara O'Hanlon, "Why Policy Matters: Regulatory Barriers to Better Primary Care in Africa—Two Private Sector Examples" (policy brief, U.S. Agency for International Development [USAID], 2007), http://pdf.usaid.gov/pdf_docs/pnadk717.pdf.

17 Art. 10, Constitution of the Islamic Republic of Afghanistan, 2004, http://www.afghanembassy.com.pl/afg/images/pliki/TheConstitution.pdf.

18 Ministry of Health, Transitional Islamic Government of Afghanistan, "A Basic Package of Health Services for Afghanistan" (Kabul: Transitional Islamic Government of Afghanistan, 2003), http://unpan1.un.org/intradoc/groups/public/documents/apcity/unpan018852.pdf.

19 "Afghanistan National Health Accounts."

20 Ramesh Bhat, "Regulation of the Private Health Sector in India."

21 Sheikh, Saligram, and Hort, "What Explains Regulatory Failure?"

22 Kumaranayake, "The Role of Regulation"; Feeley, O'Hanlon, Stene, and Segzin, "Finding Middle Ground."

and licensing processes;[23] in Dominica, the need for more regulation to ensure quality of services;[24] in Grenada, the lack of regulation governing health care facilities;[25] and in Malawi, the existence of multiple and confusing quality and accreditation standards for health facilities.[26] Another issue in Benin and other African countries is overregulation.[27] In Afghanistan, the government's "longstanding distrust" of the private sector and "the lack of a systematic mechanism for private sector engagement" hampered the MOPH's regulatory capacity. Because "the public sector's oversight and regulation of the private sector was weak," the health services delivered were of uneven quality.[28]

These findings across many LMICs that regulations are inadequate do not in themselves constitute a guide that policymakers can follow. Moreover, even in LMICs where regulations are deemed adequate (however "adequate" is defined; no consensus in the literature has emerged), they are enforced poorly or not at all.[29]

Many reasons are cited to explain lack of enforcement (another term for which a good definition is needed), varying with the social and economic context of each country. The obstacles cited are shortages in human and other resources;[30] the unclear role of professional institutions; the confusing organization of government departments;[31] poor communication of information to consumers, private providers, and even public regulators; the susceptibility of regulatory authorities to political influence;[32] the low priority that health ministries give to enforcement; weak mechanisms to eliminate corruption; and

---

23 Carlos Cuellar, Andrew Carmona, Andrea Harris, and Piotr Korynski, "Benin Private Health Sector Assessment" (Strengthening Health Outcomes through the Private Sector [SHOPS] Project, Abt Associates Inc., Bethesda, MD, 2013).

24 Strengthening Health Outcomes through the Private Sector and Health Systems 20/20, "Dominica Health Systems and Private Sector Assessment" (Health Systems 20/20 and SHOPS projects, Abt Associates Inc., Bethesda, MD, 2012).

25 Laurel Hatt et al. "Grenada Health Systems and Private Sector Assessment 2011" (Health Systems 20/20 and SHOPS projects, Abt Associates Inc., Bethesda, MD, 2012).

26 Ilana Ron Levey et al., "Malawi Private Health Sector Assessment" (Strengthening Health Outcomes through the Private Sector Project, Abt Associates Inc., Bethesda, MD, 2011).

27 Feeley and O'Hanlon, "Why Policy Matters."

28 M. Bishop, O. Sayedi, and Y. Jabarkhil, "Building Public-Private Partnerships to Improve Health Services in Afghanistan" (Health Policy Project, Washington, DC, 2014).

29 Hongoro and Kumaranayake, "Do They Work?"; D. Asiimwe and J. C. Lule, "The Public/Private Mix in Financing and Provision of Health Services in Uganda," in *Proceedings from the Workshop on the Public/Private Mix for Health Care in Developing Countries,* Health Policy Report, ed. S. Bennett and A. Mills (London: London School of Hygiene and Tropical Medicine, 1993); P. Mujinja, D. Urassa, and K. Mnyika, "The Tanzanian Public/Private Mix in National Health Care," in *Workshop on the Public/Private Mix for Health Care in Developing Countries,* ed. Bennett and Mills; C. A. K. Yesudian, "Behavior of the Private Health Sector in the Health Market of Bombay," *Health Policy and Planning* 9 (1993): 72–80; and Kumaranayake, "Role of Regulation."

30 USAID, "Health CLIR Pilot Diagnostic: The Philippines, Health Business Climate Legal and Institutional Reform," http://egateg.usaid.gov/sites/default/files/Philippines_Health.pdf.

31 Bhat, "Regulation of the Private Health Sector in India."

32 Hongoro and Kumaranayake, "Do They Work?"

weak procedures to enforce sanctions.[33] This chapter posits that the sheer lack of legal capacity in LMICs is the most important reason.

Options for Regulating the Private Health Sector

The options for regulating the private health sector can be grouped in three categories: incentives, self-regulation, and command and control.[34] Incentives are inducements to do or not to do something, such as a tax credit for locating a clinic in a rural area. Self-regulation is regulation by a professional association, as well as by internal influences, such as a desire to attract customers. Command and control consists of mechanisms established by law, such as a licensing requirement or the authority of a ministry to issue safety or quality standards and enforce compliance with them. (Chart 1 shows in more detail the tools that might be employed in these three categories.)

Incentives

Incentive regulatory tools or instruments are available to providers, but generally these are not legally binding. Nonfinancial incentives include credentials or certificates for achieving quality goals or completing training programs, which can be targeted both to hospitals and health professionals. In Afghanistan and elsewhere, professional associations representing midwives, pharmaceutical services, private hospitals, and social marketers have been established and, to greater or lesser extent, serve these functions, among others.

Financial incentives can be loans or other mechanisms that facilitate access to capital, direct subsidies (such as cash payments), or indirect subsidies (such as tax reductions, credits, exemptions, or deferrals). All such mechanisms have a legal component that allows them but does not mandate their uptake. They can be used to encourage expansion of the provision of private health services. Indeed, some of the strongest evidence on the effectiveness of regulatory options is on financial incentives, such as tax credits, subsidies, and loans, which have been shown to have a positive effect on the quality of health services, and to increase access to health services in rural and other underserved areas.[35] Such incentives are generally the purview of a ministry of finance, not the ministry of health—pointing to the importance of interagency cooperation. Moreover, the possibility of financial incentives hinges on a financial sector that is functioning and able to provide secured and unsecured loans,

---

33 Feeley, O'Hanlon, Stene, and Segzin, "Finding Middle Ground."

34 Morgan and Ensor, "The Regulation of Private Hospitals in Asia."

35 L. A. Petersen, "Does Pay-for-Performance Improve the Quality of Health Care?" *Annals of Internal Medicine: Journal* 145, no. 4 (2006) 265–272; I. P. Sempowski, "Effectiveness of Financial Incentives in Exchange for Rural and Underserviced Area Return-of-Service Commitments: Systematic Review of the Literature," *Canadian Journal of Rural Medicine* 9, no. 2 (2004); Robert Town, Robert Kane, Paul E. Johnson, and Mary Butler, "Economic Incentives and Physicians' Delivery of Preventive Care: A Systematic Review," *American Journal of Preventive Medicine* 28, no. 2 (2005): 234–240.

credit, microloans, debit cards, pay-by-phone systems, equipment leases, capital markets, and more.

Chart 1. Private health sector regulatory tools

Categories	Command and Control	Command and Control	Command and Control
Mandates/Command and Control Legal Mandates Policy Mandates Patient Perspective Self-Regulation Incentives Non-MOPH Options	*Legal mandates* Rational standards, pre-/post-license Licensing facilities/staff Monitor/inspect Procedures and sanctions for noncompliance Required data reporting	*Policy mandates* National Policies Encourage private sector economy Reduce corruption	*Policy mandates* MOH Policies Universal health care Meet post-2015 targets Transparency Stewardship Accountability Partner with private sector
Patient Perspective	**Self-Regulation**	**Incentives**	**Non-MOH Tools and Legal Mechanisms**
Increase demand for quality Insurance and vouchers Subsidies for targeted populations for high-impact interventions to increase supply by private sector and therefore demand Social marketing programs Educate and incentivize patients to demand the most beneficial services Citizen report cards/quality comparisons and complaint lines—educate consumers, regulate advertising, labels, BCC on healthy behavior Build civil society as advocate and watch-dog	*Strengthen ethics and self-accountability* Foster ethical behavior and create standards Accreditation Training and continuous provider education Franchises, networks, HMO model Professional associations Technology EHR and databases Telemedicine	*Align incentives with quality, affordability, and access* Purchasing and contracting Pay for performance Demand side financing insurance or vouchers, coupled with interventions known to succeed Right to operate Cooperation and collaboration with private sector	*Various goals* Contract law Medical malpractice laws Antitrust laws Consumer protection and patient rights Legal framework for health insurance and banking Investment incentives Respect for rule of law Tax holidays Waivers of import duties Land grants Banking system Power and telecom grid PPP Subsidies

Copyright Forzley 2014. All rights reserved.

Self-regulation

Self-regulatory tools are those employed by a professional association with its own internal governance structure, including bylaws and various other procedures, such as self-policing. Some self-regulatory activities, such as professional conferences offering training on new techniques, need no government cooperation. Other activities require legislative authorization for a ministry to delegate authority to a nongovernmental organization (NGO) that the ministry might previously have exercised itself. For self-regulatory activities to function within a larger regulatory system, they must be appropriate for a ministry to delegate and integrate with the relevant parts of the system that government operates. In essence, the NGO engages in activities that have the effect of regulating a target, such as a medical board's oversight of doctors, a professional association's standards for members, or an organization's criteria for granting the coveted status of accreditation to a hospital.

Self-regulation also entails a working relationship among stakeholders who have an opportunity for input, and a ministry's acceptance of and integration of that input—two of the four factors that make a regulatory system legitimate and sustainable.[36] Stakeholder representation in Afghanistan's health system began with the creation of the Afghanistan Private Hospitals Association (APHA). This association was actively involved in the health ministry's development of a set of minimum required standards for private hospitals,[37] which are now fundamental to the ministry's system for regulatory implementation and enforcement.

In mature health systems, a professional association may police its members for noncompliance with regulations on a health ministry's behalf. Self-policing requires a clear delegation of authority, establishing where an association's responsibility ends and where the health ministry or other government agency must take charge to impose civil penalties or refer for criminal prosecution. Hospital accreditation organizations, such as Joint Commission International, are an example of self-regulation. Accreditation is a special status, generally accorded by an NGO, and can be accompanied by benefits; for instance, when a hospital is accredited, it can participate in national health insurance schemes or the frequency of the Ministry of Health (MOH) inspections can be reduced. Self-regulation complements command and control but does not replace it entirely and cannot function without it. Some activities, such as licensing, cannot be delegated. Thus, no matter how mature a health system might be, a health ministry will always have the superior role and must maintain oversight of both the private and the public health sectors.

---

36 Wade Channell, "Practice Note Series 2: Business Environment Reforms in Conflict-Affected Contexts," http://www.international-alert.org/sites/default/files/publications/practice_note2_march2010.pdf.

37 Feeley and O'Hanlon, "Why Policy Matters."

Command and Control

Command and control regulatory tools are present in every country and legal system and are those most widely used in LMICs.[38] Command and control tools derive from the law, which a health ministry must implement and enforce. Examples are information and requirements related to the opening and operation of a health center; licensing or business registration; standards of operation; monitoring or inspections to determine compliance with standards and requirements; and a process for determining breaches of regulatory requirements and for imposing sanctions. Contracts are another command and control instrument widely used in health insurance schemes. Many but not all of these tools are easily recognized by their mandatory nature, expressed by the use of the word "shall." Chart 2 offers examples of Afghanistan's regulatory mandates.

Chart 2. Afghanistan legal mandates

▪ Article 3: MOPH "*shall* facilitate and monitor private sector" ▪ Article 6: MOPH "*shall* be responsible to manage, guide, control, evaluate, the provision of comprehensive and quality health services to all citizens" ▪ Article 8: MOPH "*shall* fix geographic location"	▪ Private Health Center Regulation (PHCR): MOPH *shall* license, set standards, monitor, enforce and sanction, collect information ▪ MOPH Stewardship Policy ▪ Principles: oversight, transparency, accountability, and legitimacy ▪ Strong leadership, administration, and management ▪ Effective regulation ▪ An environment conducive for the private sector to deliver good quality services in sufficient quantity

Copyright Forzley 2014. All rights reserved.

The Evidence Base for These Options

Unfortunately for the regulator, evidence of the relative effectiveness in LMICs of the regulatory options noted in chart 1 is extremely limited in the public health literature.[39] One reason is that such studies have tried to measure a regu-

---

38 Morgan and Ensor, "Regulation of Private Hospitals in Asia."

39 M. Chopra, "Effects of Policy Options for Human Resources for Health: An Analysis of Systematic Reviews," *Lancet* 37 (9613): 668–674. See also L. Kumaranayake, C. Hongoro, S. Lake,

lation's public health outcome when the regulatory system was not necessarily designed to support or remove a barrier to the health outcome of interest. This chapter proposes that regulators can confidently rely on command and control tools as the basis of regulatory design and need not wait for public health evidence, because, beyond the public health literature, a body of evidence does exist on the value and impact of command and control mechanisms.

Law Is a Proven Strategy to Achieve Health Goals

Success stories abound about law's role in achieving public health goals. Examples of these are presented below to show the power of the law to support positive health outcomes, including by providing the framework for the regulation of the health sector. Laws by themselves are not enough; they must be implemented and enforced. This chapter focuses on just one of the several ways in which laws are implemented and enforced, namely, the manner in which a government agency, the MOH, operates, performs its functions, and fulfills its mandates. Other ways include litigation, voluntary compliance, and private contracts, some of which are also available to the MOH but are neither the main activities of a regulator nor the foundation of effective regulation.

Law and Health Outcomes

For years, human rights, national constitutions, and other laws have been the basis for citizens to receive access to medicines[40] and to compel governments to provide and deliver health services.[41] Recently, bodies of international law made by the World Health Organization (WHO) Assembly have changed the way the world conducts surveillance and manages infectious disease outbreaks, such as Ebola,[42] and have altered the course of morbidity and mortality related to smoking.[43]

In Africa, for example, the shortage of human resources has been partly solved by laws allowing people with less training to perform duties previously undertaken only by doctors or nurses. Scope of practice studies show that when a physician is required by law to be the owner or director of a health facility, operating costs rise. Once such a law is amended to allow ownership

---

P. Mujinja, and R. Mpembeni, "Coping with Private Health Markets: Regulatory Effectiveness in Sub-Saharan Africa," in *The New Public-Private Mix in Health: Exploring the Changing Landscape*, ed. N. Söderlund and P. Mendoza-Arana (Geneva: Alliance for Health Policy and Systems Research, World Health Organization, 2003), http://researchonline.lshtm.ac.uk/19443/.

40 Hans V. Hogerzeil, M. Samson, J. V. Casanova, and L. Rahmani-Ocora, "Is Access to Essential Medicines as Part of the Fulfilment of the Right to Health Enforceable through the Courts?" *Lancet* 36 (9532).

41 "Readings in Comparative Health Law & Bioethics," chap. 1 in *The Right to Health and Its Implementation*, ed. Timothy S. Jost, 2nd ed. (Durham, NC: Carolina Academic Press, 2007).

42 International Health Regulations 2007, http://www.who.int/topics/international_health_regulations/en/.

43 Framework Convention on Tobacco Control 2003, http://www.who.int/fctc/about/en/.

by others and the change is integrated in licensing practice, a dramatic increase in primary and reproductive health and family planning service facilities has been observed.[44] Pooled procurement is used to reduce expenditures on medicines, and contracting in and out is widely used. Courts treat a health ministry's contracts with businesses to operate hospitals and clinics as the "law between the parties," and enforceable unless against *ordre publique*, or public policy. Chart 3 presents additional examples of successful solutions to public health problems that would not be possible without laws enabling them.[45]

Chart 3. What works and the critical role of law

Problem	Solution
Shortage of human resources	Less specialized personnel Resource-sharing initiatives
High prices	Cross-subsidization
Inconsistent quality	Outsourcing agreements with government for specific services
People do not "trust" public facilities	Creation of a reputation for quality through franchising
Large expenditures in pharmaceuticals and medical supplies	Procurement pooling

Source: IFC, "The Business of Health in Africa: Partnering with the Private Sector to Improve People's Lives," Working paper 44143 (IFC, Washington, DC, n.d.), http://documents.worldbank.org/curated/en/2008/01/9526453/business-health-africa-partnering-private-sector-improve-peoples-lives. Copyright Forzley 2014. All rights reserved.

Work over the past 20 years on the rule of law, governance, and transparency has demonstrated that when governments are stable and operate fairly and a body of law is in place, public health is better. Statistically significant and robust correlation between the rule of law and various health outcomes has been shown in a recent study, demonstrating, for example that infant mortality rates are lower in countries where the rule of law is respected (see figure 1).[46]

---

44 Ravenholt, Feeley, Averbug, and O'Hanlon, "Navigating Uncharted Waters."

45 IFC, "The Business of Health in Africa."

46 A. M. Pinzon-Rondon et al., "Association of Rule of Law and Health Outcomes: An Ecological Study," *BMJ Open* 5 (2015), 5: e007004. doi:10.1136/bmjopen-2014-007004; and William H. Neukom, "Rule of Law for All" (presentation at the World Justice Forum IV, The Hague, July 8–11, 2013), http://worldjusticeproject.org/sites/default/files/16x9_neukom_welcome_wjforum5_2.pdf.

Figure 1. Rule of law and infant mortality

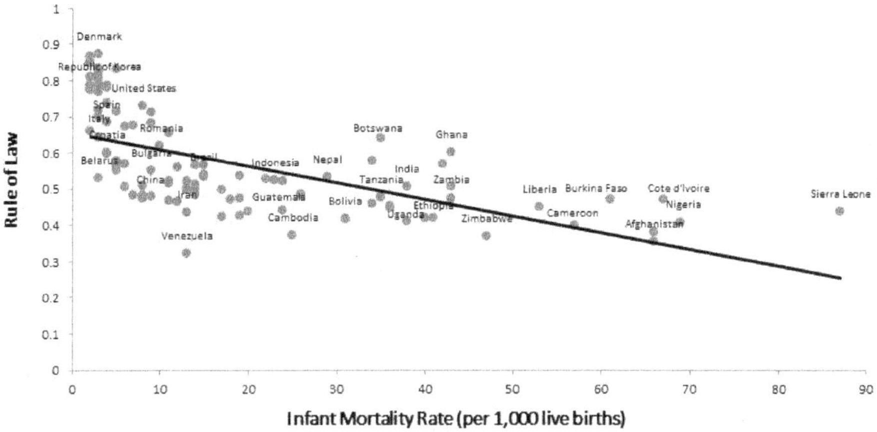

Source: WJP Rule of Law Index 2015 and World Bank 2015 Data (http://data.worldbank.org/indicator /SP.DYN.IMRT.IN). The figure is titled "Public Health and the Rule of Law."

Another compelling reason for regulators in LMICs to focus on command and control is that people generally respect the law, even though the level of respect does vary across and within countries.[47] A given law can be unclear, inadequate, or objectionable; nonetheless, a discernible faith in the body of law as a common language exists and represents a level of social agreement. And despite historical examples to the contrary, law can be a catalyst for change and a force to "knit healthcare together into a more effective system for everyone."[48] This is true even in a conflict zone such as Afghanistan, which in 2012 passed a law defining the MOPH's authority to improve the standards and quality of care in the private health sector: the PHCR Act.[49] Since then, MOPH regulators and the APHA have been working together to amend the act to make it a tool for both effective regulation and an environment that supports private sector investment in health facilities—further evidence of respect for the legal process and the growing regulatory legitimacy of the MOPH.

Implementation and Enforcement

Regulatory systems have two parts. One is rules of some sort: laws, administrative regulations, or standards against which a product, service, process, or operator is judged. The other is a process for assessing and assuring

---

47 W. K. Mariner and R. G. Feeley, "The Role of Law in Russian Health Reform" (2001), http://pdf.usaid.gov/pdf_docs/pnacq545.pdf.

48 Ibid. See also Rich Feeley, "Regulation of Private Health Providers: Tools for Improvement" (presentation at Boston University, School of Public Health Center for Global Health and Development, 2011), http://ps4h.org/docs_iheapdf/2B_Feeley.pdf.

49 Government of Afghanistan, Private Health Centers Regulation Act, on file with Michele Forzley.

conformity to the rules. This involves implementation and enforcement, which are distinct functions.

In regulatory system design, implementing the law means carrying out the day-to-day operational activities that the law mandates or describes. Implementation is part of governance, an essential function of a health system.[50] At ground level, implementing health system regulations means developing standards for the private health sector; ensuring that ministry staff understand and apply what the law requires; and establishing or reforming relevant units within a ministry, such as licensing or monitoring and evaluation, to align their operation with the law's provisions. Implementation also means informing actors in both the public and the private health sectors of the legal requirements to operate; monitoring the private sector and the health ministry itself to make sure both are in compliance; amending the law when appropriate; and developing and applying measurable indicators of the plan's performance and achievement of regulatory goals.

A regulatory system's fulcrum, where implementation and enforcement diverge, is monitoring.[51] Monitoring implements the law by observing whether an actor is in compliance. When noncompliance is observed, the monitor starts the process of enforcement, which another ministry of health (MOH) department or some other part of government completes, either by compelling compliance or punishing for failure to comply.

The separation of these tasks is important because legal rights and privileges—such as a license to operate a health facility—are at stake. For enforcement to have integrity, the requirements of legal systems—both the formal court system and the informal dispute resolution systems, such as administrative law mechanisms or mediation by tribal elders or *shura* councils—must be taken into account. Providing notice and having both an opportunity to be heard and an independent arbiter applying known rules according to transparent procedures legitimize the formal or informal enforcement and review process.[52] Only when the rules are known to all and the consequences for their violation is also known can sanctions (fines, suspension, or closure, for example) have the desired rehabilitative or deterrent effect on noncompliance in the

---

50 WHO, "Everybody's Business: Strengthening Health Systems to Improve Health Outcomes," http://www.who.int/healthsystems/strategy/everybodys_business.pdf.

51 For the purpose of this article, "monitoring" and "inspection" are used interchangeably, although in some systems the two terms are used to describe the activities of different MOH units, and in other systems completely different functions.

52 Z. Lai, "Administrative Hearing Procedures and Practice," *Clearinghouse Review: Journal of Poverty Law and Policy* 44, nos. 3–4 (July–August 2010), http://drupaldev.povertylaw.org/sites/default/files/files/training/adminhs/lai-admin%20hearings%20article.pdf; and USAID, Office of Democracy and Governance, Rule of Law Division, "Guide to Rule of Law Country Analysis: The Rule of Law Strategic Framework" (Office of Democracy and Governance, Rule of Law Division, USAID, Washington, DC, January 2010), http://pdf.usaid.gov/pdf_docs/Pnadt593.pdf.

future.[53] A full discussion of internal review boards can be found in another chapter in this volume.[54]

Good Regulatory Design Practice

Every effort to reform a health system is prompted by some circumstance. In Afghanistan, it was the growth of the private sector and the passage of the PHCR Act. In Albania, the aim to join the European Union and accede to its requirements prompted the rewriting of the country's entire body of health law. In Swaziland, a donor funded the assessment and revision of laws affecting the health sector to support new and old initiatives. No matter the motive for or target of regulation, good regulatory design practice is effective, efficient, and essential.

The steps and principles that guide the process of implementing and enforcing the law as part of good regulatory design practice are presented next. The outline draws from existing approaches to integrate law into programs, Michele Forzley's fieldwork in Afghanistan and elsewhere, the factors that contribute to successful institutional change, and the concepts and ideas already presented in this chapter.[55]

Steps to Implement and Enforce the Law

Step 1: Create a Team to Determine How to Implement and Enforce the Law

This step is really a management tool, but it is important for other reasons as well. A team can ensure that the ways in which the law is implemented and enforced support health goals. A team approach also builds support within a ministry to sustain institutional changes. The team's task is to design a regulatory system for the target, which may be the private health sector, a universal health insurance scheme, the pharmaceutical sector, or any other aspect of the health system. The team details what each department is going to do and how; sets up the forms, procedures, and guidelines necessary for the regulatory system to operate; and integrates capacity building, where necessary, and other changes, such as amending the law or issuing regulations, as needed. The scope of this work constitutes implementation and enforcement.

The team is a dynamic group comprising those who carry out day-to-day operations, such as line staff; senior leaders who approve proposals prepared

---

53 P. Robinson and J. Darley, "Does Criminal Law Deter? A Behavioral Science Investigation," *Oxford Journal of Legal Studies* 24, no. 2 (2004) 173–205, https://www.law.upenn.edu/live/files/1352-does-criminal-law-deter-robinson-and-darley-edited.

54 See chapter 2, "Internal Review Boards: An Innovation in Health Sector Governance," by Michele Forzley.

55 S. Fernandez and H. G. Rainey, "Managing Successful Organizational Change in the Public Sector," *Public Administration Review* 66, no. 2 (2006): 168–176.

by the team; and lawyers, who analyze and interpret the law and explain how to translate the law into operations. Other ministries may be asked to appoint team members, as needed. For example, if the health law states that an applicant for a license to operate a health facility must also have a business license, the government department that issues such a license should be represented. Doing so can save a health ministry's resources by harmonizing and coordinating procedures with the other ministries. In Afghanistan, the team's membership reflected the departments—identified in the PHCR Act—responsible for the key components outlined there: licensing, information, monitoring and evaluation, and law enforcement. A health ministry's senior leaders are also members. They need not attend every meeting but do need to be briefed and their input and concurrence sought frequently as plans and details emerge. They set the tone and direction of the work and assign tasks.

Lawyers—either on the ministry staff or assigned by the ministry of justice or the office of the attorney general—are essential. Although the ability to understand the legal implications of policy is considered a core competency of a public health professional, this does not ensure that the full utility and value of the law will be exploited to the benefit of the health sector. Moreover, law is a profession subject to licensure. In the modern world, where there are national and international laws and bilateral and regional arrangements to consider, the work of law requires lawyers to support the public health professionals.

Many health ministries either have no dedicated law office or lack lawyers with the requisite capacity or skills or access to the specialized legal education suitable for their role. Other health ministries do not employ enough lawyers to do all the work. When HPP's capacity assessment began in Afghanistan, the MOPH had just one lawyer on staff. Following the assessment, the ministry hired two more—better, but still not nearly enough.[56]

Until legal capacity exists within a country, international legal experts can be deployed for this mission, as they were in Afghanistan. The legal expert serves on the team. Once a health ministry establishes a legal office, the ministry must fund the office from the ministry's regular budget and pay the staff at appropriate salary grades. Nowhere in the health development plans of international donors is closing this gap in legal capacity addressed, even though plans aim to improve governance and address shortages of health professionals.[57] Donor and MOH budgets and staffing plans must improve legal capacity. Otherwise, health governance objectives will not be met on schedule, if at all. In recognition of the need for lawyers in health systems work, the WHO

---

56 For purposes of comparison, 400 lawyers work for the Office of the General Counsel of the U.S. Department of Health and Human Services, http://www.hhs.gov/ogc/.

57 N. Crisp and L. Chen, "Global Supply of Health Professionals," *New England Journal of Medicine* 370, no. 10 (2014): 950–957.

hired a lawyer in that unit in 2015 to establish normative guidance on law in health systems and to provide technical assistance to countries.

Step 2: Check Policy

Most countries have a national health plan or policy enumerating the targets of regulation. Some countries, including Afghanistan, have a specific strategy for the private health sector.[58] Plans for the pursuit of other national interests—such as an economic plan that identifies the importance of the private sector as a whole to national development—may also have implications for the health sector.

Policies set out goals, objectives, and principles to guide a ministry's actions in carrying out the national plan. The team must consider these policies in its decisions. For example, Afghanistan adopted a policy of collaboration to guide its approach to the private health sector. Thus, when the MOPH faces noncompliance with a regulation, a monitor's first response, according to policy, is to allow for and assist in remediation instead of punishment. A policy analysis also directs attention to the targets and goals of regulation, so that these may be taken into account in the design. Chart 4 suggests targets and tools to demonstrate how this policy analysis may be done.

Step 3: Conduct a Macroanalysis of the Law

The policy review phase of the team's process prepares the lawyers on the team to conduct a thorough review—that is, a macroanalysis—of relevant laws and determine whether or not they serve the country's policy objectives and principles and whether each law is adequate. Law is adequate when it supports the MOH to accomplish its policy goals, fulfill its functions, and protect patients and the right to health. The lawyers then present their analyses to the rest of the team for consideration in the design of the regulatory system and in the plan for implementation and enforcement. Where a law creates tension with health goals and policies and/or does or does not support the health ministry's functions, plans to amend it can be made.

58 Government of Afghanistan, Ministry of Public Health, "Strategic Plan to Support the National Policy for Private Health Sector 2009–2014," on file with Michele Forzley.

Chart 4. Targets and tools; goals and tools

Targets and Tools	
Hospitals	Licensing (facility standards) Inspections and sanctions Institutional transparency Staff credentials Accreditation Medical equipment and supply standards
Pharmaceuticals	Inspections and sanctions Quality standards Registration
Physicians and other health professionals	Professional liability Accreditation and certification Professional associations/coordination with MOH
Consumers	Consumer rights (the right to know information inserts)
Goals and Tools	
Pricing	Price controls Balance billing (billing in excess of insurance) Nondiscrimination Publish information on maximum permitted prices Subsidies and financial mechanisms Exemption schemes Restrictions on ownership
Patients' rights and benefits	Advertising Incentives to practice in specific geographic areas Informed consent and the right to refuse treatment Medical records and confidentiality Nondiscrimination Access
Externalities and overall goals	Reporting requirements Medical records
Quantity	Market entry Competitive practices/control of market organization

Copyright Forzley 2014. All rights reserved.

Of interest for the macroanalysis are laws, whether specific to the health sector or elsewhere in the legal system, that state some affirmative actions to be undertaken and define the boundaries of the health ministry's authority. Typical affirmative actions to regulate the private health sector require the

MOH to license hospitals, clinics, and other private actors; issue safety and quality standards of operation; assess compliance with requirements; impose sanctions for noncompliance; and collect health data. In Afghanistan, this step was crucially important, because staff at all levels of the MOPH were unfamiliar with the PHCR Act and the affirmative actions it requires. Even the lawyer on staff did not have a copy of it. This experience in Afghanistan, where there is little to no awareness of the laws that specifically apply to different aspects of the health sector and how they are to be implemented, is not isolated and has been reflected in the literature.[59]

These well-known elements of regulating the private health sector are complemented by other MOH powers and obligations found in the law. Laws that guide implementation and enforcement draw from one or more areas in the legal system: the constitution; national legislation, including health law and public health law;[60] laws specific to the private health sector, to administrative law, and to other domains, such as insurance, commerce, criminal, tax, finance, real estate, torts, commercial contracts, importation, anticorruption, or customs; and even some international laws, such as the International Health Regulations.[61] A full exploration of the breadth of the potentially applicable laws and a discussion of how they apply are beyond the scope of this chapter, but unless these are brought to bear on improving health outcomes, regulators operate without a full arsenal of available tools.

Step 4: Build the Plan, Enumerating the Functions of Each Department

This step creates the road map for operationalizing the law. It clarifies what each unit or department of the MOH must do for the requirements of the law to be discharged. This effort, plus the legal and policy reviews, will make clear what regulatory instruments (such as forms, applications, instructions, standards, guides, and procedures) are needed so that departments can carry out and document their work. In addition, the plan will address procedures shared by departments, as many of the steps in a regulatory plan involve multiple units of a ministry. The plan should identify the points where senior leadership must ensure interdepartmental coordination. The plan must also take into account the implicit powers of a regulator. For example, the right to revoke a permit is implicit in the power to issue a permit, but revocation is not always an explicit power. In Afghanistan, this step took five months over the course of two years to execute.

---

59 Feeley, O'Hanlon, Stene, and Segzin, "Finding Middle Ground"; Doherty, "Regulating the For-Profit Private Health Sector"; Hongoro and Kumaranayake, "Do They Work?"; Sheikh, Saligram, and Hort, "What Explains Regulatory Failure?"; Private Sector Development and Partnership Strategy Policy; Kumaranayake, "The Role of Regulation"; and Feeley and O'Hanlon, "Why Policy Matters."

60 Here public health law is not the same as health law. Public health laws are those that provide for population-level interventions, such as surveillance and quarantine, not health care in public and private hospitals and clinics.

61 "Afghanistan National Health Accounts."

Step 5: Conduct a Microanalysis of What the MOH Departments Are Actually Doing in Relation to the Law

This step is an assessment prepared by the lawyers on the team that compares the duties, functions, and procedures enumerated in the law outlined in step 4 with the ministry's current activities. With this information, the gaps between what should be done and what is being done and the changes that must occur will be clear. These gaps will be the focus of capacity building. This step may take a significant amount of time, because it will involve clarification, brokering, and decisions on the roles of departments and staff, which may change as conflicts and duplications among departments are identified.

Parts of this process will occur in workshops or staff meetings (see step 6); other parts may require intervention by senior leadership. Senior leadership must make clear to staff at all levels when the new plan will take effect and when prior procedures must cease.

Step 6: Hold Workshops and Meetings with Staff and Other Stakeholders to Inform, Train, Solicit Input, and Revise

This step is not a one-time task. Probably nothing is more important to the success and sustainability of change than developing and fostering support from stakeholders. Informing and training must be a dialogue, not a monologue. This step, critical for the plan's evolution, is an opportunity to solicit ideas from line staff and middle and senior managers on how they think operations should be conducted and to integrate this input in the plan. Ministry staff members know the working conditions and local context. Without their buy-in, which can occur only with their participation, success will be hard to achieve. The entire process of change must be transparent, and all parties must be included and accountable for the result. Multiple workshops and departmental meetings are the process by which day-to-day operations and staff performance become aligned with the new regulatory system and the plan to implement and enforce it.

Finally, each country must identify its key health system stakeholders and create opportunities for them to learn about the system, offer their input, and consider where they may have responsibility. A typical example is the role of the ministry of finance in many matters that affect the health sector, such as the payment of a licensing application fee. Particular attention should be paid to health insurers and accreditation bodies, which both have a strong influence on behavior. These stakeholders should be included in some of the meetings and their input taken into account. In Afghanistan, over a two-year period, numerous meetings and workshops were held at all levels of the MOPH, between MOPH and the APHA, and between MOPH and the heads of the provincial health departments. The time and resources required for this critical process must be anticipated and provided.

Step 7: Institutionalize Review

Review and oversight are indispensable parts of good governance and leadership. And governance and leadership involve ensuring that strategic policy frameworks exist and are combined with effective oversight, coalition building, the provision of appropriate regulations and incentives, attention to system design, and accountability. Without review and oversight, leadership has no systematic way to gather information on how the plan is working in order to make course corrections. The team has three dimensions of institutional review to consider and build into the plan: a supervisory review of staff performance; a periodic review by the senior leadership of progress on the regulatory design and plan of implementation and enforcement, as measured by useful indicators; and a mechanism for review and possible adjustment of the health ministry's decisions at the request of a private actor.

The importance of review in improving health system performance and health outcomes is demonstrated by strong evidence. Ultimately, no regulator works without staff, and staff function better when they have good leadership and management skills and all respect the principles of good governance. No matter how correct a plan is according to the law, if regular and periodic review of staff performance is absent, the plan is less likely to be properly implemented. Staff reviews can be conducted according to the best practices of human resources management. But critical to the review is, first, that it happens, and second, that supervisory staff actually look at the work of the line staff to determine if the line staff are following procedures and implementing them correctly. If not, the supervisory staff must take appropriate corrective actions.

Measuring implementation and enforcement of a regulatory system should be done periodically. Ensuring that timelines and steps are followed is just good practice, but unless the plan itself is reviewed from time to time, new conditions cannot be taken into account or problems corrected. In the business world, this is called "strategic planning." The plan itself can establish the frequency of this review. Just as the ministry monitors the performance of private actors, it must also monitor itself. "What gets measured gets done"—the adage of Margaret Chan, the director general of WHO—applies to system design and implementation.

Good indicators are needed, of course, to evaluate performance; these can also be part of the plan. Some are easy to define, such as whether a periodic review was conducted and whether any changes were made in response. By itself, the answer to a simple query—Was a review conducted?—would be a powerful indicator of good governance. Additional indicators can mirror or build on those designed by others, such as the World Bank's "Doing Business" index. More indicators of health system regulatory effectiveness need to be developed at the national, subnational, departmental, and staff levels.

Critically important to institutional review is a system to review the decisions of the MOH. Such a system may be called an "internal review board" (as noted above, internal review boards are the subject of another chapter in this volume).

In Afghanistan, the PHCR Act did not call for such a board, but establishing one is within the administrative power of any health ministry and is a critical good governance practice. The board approved by the Afghanistan MOPH consists of a representative of the health ministry, a representative of the private health sector, and an independent lawyer. It will be staffed by the ministry's law enforcement unit, which is not only approved but also welcomed by MOPH departments for such matters as medicines regulation.

Principles for Implementing and Enforcing the Law

Principle 1: Apply Good Governance and Make It Concrete

Many national health plans are now incorporating notions of good governance, such as transparency, accountability, participation, inclusion, and effective regulation. Some of these notions are expressed in laws—especially in global covenants against corruption, such as the United Nations Convention Against Corruption, and in international trade and human rights laws. Any system design must take into account these legal meanings in addition to the ideas now being generated in health development discussions.[62]

Too often, the ideas of good governance are theoretical instead of concrete and thus are neither understood nor implemented. Finding ways to make good governance concrete and operational is essential to achieving good governance. For example, lack of transparency is often cited as an element of poor governance. Concretely, if the health ministry's legal department and senior and line staff have copies of the relevant standards, laws, and regulations (in other words, "the rules") and these are available on paper and digitally on the MOH website, transparency is increased. Few health ministries in LMICs have a full collection of their own rules readily available. It took more than two years to collect the rules in Afghanistan, but now these are available in the new information center. Transparency also means teaching staff about the rules, so they can be expected to know those rules needed to do their jobs and know that compliance is mandatory.

Another important reason for practical application of transparency is that unless private health actors can find the relevant rules, expecting compliance is grossly unfair. If these rules are public, easily located, and, best of all, disseminated or promoted, not knowing them cannot be claimed as an excuse for failure to comply. Transparency also reduces information asymmetry, so that a monitor cannot claim that a condition is noncompliant without a rule to justify the claim. This gives the private actor a way to counter a corrupt or uninformed inspector. Most important, when there are standards for compliance, health facilities know what to aim for, so that in the end, the quality of health care is improved. This, after all, is the goal of regulation.

---

62 The UN Convention Against Corruption, https://www.unodc.org/unodc/en/treaties/CAC/.

In order for facilities to know the standards, not only must these be published somewhere, but also the private sector must be educated on their content. In Afghanistan, the APHA is undertaking this educational role and at the same time strengthening its capacity in self-regulation.

Principle 2: Seek Balance

As a general rule, it is advisable to avoid overly burdensome regulations. The challenge of all regulatory activity is to choose an approach that achieves a goal, such as quality of services, without causing an unbearably negative consequence, such as prohibitive cost. This is as true for the regulator, who will have to enforce any regulatory scheme, as it is for the private health sector actor, who must follow the scheme. Balance can be achieved through open dialogue with the private sector before a plan is final. It is normal and to be expected that a private health actor will push back on any regulation; such resistance should be welcomed as an opportunity to refine the regulatory approach. In Afghanistan, communication between the private sector and the health ministry has been open and active since the creation of a public-private dialogue forum. The forum gives the APHA a regular opportunity to meet directly with ministry officials and to voice concerns about regulations and their implementation.

Some basic questions should guide regulatory refinement, as follows. All components of a regulatory system should be related to a goal and be circumscribed by a standard or other legal requirement. For example, the goal of quality can be reasonably assured by standards of operation. Pushback on any quality-related requirement should raise the following questions: Is every aspect of a regulation related to quality? Can the standard be enforced? Can compliance be measured or otherwise objectively evaluated? Does the standard achieve the goal in the least intrusive manner? Is there any evidence this approach has worked in the country itself or elsewhere? There will always be tension between the regulator and the regulated. In the end, based on Michele Forzley's experience in the field and in her opinion, a good indication that balance has been achieved is that both sides—the regulator and the private health actors—are somewhat unhappy.

Principle 3: Be Strategic with Resources

Implementing and enforcing the law is not as resource-intensive as one might think. Countries with less regulatory experience will naturally have a learning curve, which will necessitate the allocation of extra human resources and staff. No more need be said about lack of legal capacity. It is a health ministry's duty to implement and enforce the law; if the ministry does not have staff or other resources for this, the parliament should allocate the appropriate budget and the MOH should request it. Donors should integrate funding for this important building block of health systems–strengthening when possible. If there is no budget, there is no commitment.

Regulating the private health sector can also generate resources, because the MOH has the authority to apply financial sanctions and to collect fees, though this should not be the purpose of regulation or inspection. A serious effort to demonstrate this revenue source to the legislature might bring more budget resources to the ministry. Moreover, the MOH can take advantage of and often defer to the work of other ministries, including justice and commerce, or anticorruption offices, which have resources that the MOH need not duplicate. Furthermore, because building external support is essential to institutional change, it is essential for the MOH to cooperate with its natural allies and partners. A good example is price controls, an unwelcome technique often attempted in plans to regulate the private health sector. A ministry of commerce and any chamber of commerce will have more relevant expertise than a health ministry when it comes to influencing the government on a decision about price controls. Other examples where the MOH is not the lead are taxes, access to capital markets, and credit, which are fundamental to the enabling environment for any business, including the private health sector. By building alliances, the MOH can shorten the learning curve while establishing a strong regulatory system. Clearly, some operational and other standards are unique and special to the health sector, but many others, such as those governing accounting, tax, and labor, are not. Duplication should be carefully avoided and the MOH should press for this support from other regulatory agencies of government.

Complicated regulatory systems demand human and financial resources often lacking in developing countries. For example, an MOH that adopts a quarterly inspection schedule will exhaust its own resources and probably the goodwill of the private health facilities, which must take time to manage the inspection process. Risk-based inspections are one example of a less-resource-intensive approach to monitoring, and a more effective one. With a risk-based approach, only those facilities that have repeatedly not met standards are monitored more frequently.

Regulating the private health sector need not be a stand-alone system with staff devoted to that task. A licensing department can be responsible for different types of licenses, registrations, and certifications with separate procedures. Or the licensing unit of another ministry—commerce, for example—can assume responsibility for private health sector licenses.

Nonmandated options can be used to supplement regulatory design and conserve resources when the command and control system is in place. Feedback loops, such as complaint lines, client satisfaction surveys, report cards, and the publication of sanctions against noncompliant operators, can serve to amplify the effects of the command and control–based system without MOH staff doing anything. In the end, a private health actor is a business that cannot operate without extensive financial investment in the establishment of an office, hospital, or clinic. When the right to operate is at risk, quality actors will comply to avoid financial loss, because patients learn of noncompliance and will try to avoid using services provided by noncompliant actors. Moreover, incentive systems—such as those limiting participation in insurance reimbursement or extending contracting opportunities to actors with a good monitoring history or accreditation by an external body—can encourage good behavior.

Command and control elements of any system to regulate the private health sector do take resources to implement, but it is not necessary to implement all elements all the time. In fact, what is most important to the success of command and control systems is for the system to be in place; to be known to function, because its proceedings are publicly available; and, at times, to be in the headlines, as when sanctions are levied for egregious wrongdoing. An MOH can count on self-regulatory and incentive options to reduce demands on its resources so long as the command and control system is in place as the ultimate safeguard and the exoskeleton of the entire system.

Principle 4: Use Good Rule-Making Practices

Ministries of health are part of the executive branch. Their role is broadly framed in constitutional language, and their structure, function, and mission are defined in national legislation. The defining language varies from country to country but should always contain particular powers. One is to issue regulations without approval by Parliament. This power is based on the idea that each ministry has the technical expertise to manage the aspect of society that is the focus of its mission—in the case of an MOH, the health sector's functions and actors. The scope of regulations (also known as "subnational legislation") is limited to the sector regulated. Regulations particularize national legislation or statutes, thereby providing more guidance to the public as well as to the ministry. The best practice is to allow the public to participate in the formulation of regulations, or rule-making.

Some best practices for rule-making include providing the opportunity for public comment within a given period before rules become final. Once issued, a rule will have an effective date. It is important to avoid overlapping or inconsistent regulation and to use plain language so that everyone can understand the content. Finally, the teaching of rule-making processes and other administrative powers and obligations should be integrated in educational programs in public administration, law, management, and business, and also in capacity-building initiatives provided to ministries. Public education through and to the media is also needed.

Conclusion

Evidence in the public health literature of the relative effectiveness in LMICs of the three categories of regulatory tools—incentives, self-regulation, and command and control (grounded in law)—is extremely limited. In its absence, the law—we argue—is the proper starting point for designing a system to regulate the private health sector (or any other regulatory target) and for introducing concepts, steps, and principles that a health ministry should follow to implement and enforce the law. A regulator may be confident in this approach, because law is a common language, adherence to the law is mandatory, and law is essential to other regulatory options that do not fall within command and control. Although there is popular interest in having incentives and self-governance mechanisms form the basis for regulation of the private health sector, the role of government cannot be usurped by these approaches. In the end, a government has the primary responsibility to protect the health and welfare of its citizens. Self-regulation and incentive options may be phased in after command and control is in place and functioning. Adding them will be easier once command and control—the regulatory system's exoskeleton—is in place.

It is not enough just to pass laws; they must be implemented and enforced. The details of how to do this have not been extensively investigated in the literature. To help remedy this lack of attention, this chapter explores good regulatory system design, which begins with the law and follows steps and principles drawn from existing approaches to integrate law into programs, fieldwork, and research on the factors that contribute to successful institutional change. The law is the most effective tool, framework, and guide for building an effective regulatory system that can be enforced within a ministry's existing capacity. A private health sector regulatory system that is based on the law will strengthen a ministry's regulatory effectiveness. As the examples from Afghanistan demonstrate, this work is possible even in a war zone.

4

Between Transformation and Integration

The Regional Dimension of Legal Reform in Implementing the Sustainable Development Goals

THOMAS SILBERHORN

Development and the Law

The relationship between development and the rule of law has long been the subject of international discussion. In the UN Millennium Declaration of 2000, around 150 heads of state and government resolved to "spare no effort to promote democracy and strengthen the rule of law, as well as respect for all internationally recognized human rights and fundamental freedoms, including the right to development."[1] Yet time-bound targets derived from this declaration—the Millennium Development Goals (MDGs)—did not include the topic of rule of law or other more political aspirations of the declaration.[2] This omission has been regarded by many observers as a missed opportunity to make explicit the relationship of the rule of law and governance to the achievement of development goals.[3]

Since then, the belief that development and the rule of law are interrelated and mutually reinforcing has grown. The 2030 Agenda for Sustainable Development, agreed to by UN member-states in September 2015, moved the more political aspirations back on the agenda. The aspects of peace and good governance are now enshrined in the 17 Sustainable Development Goals (SDGs).[4]

---

1 See UN General Assembly (UNGA), Resolution 55/2, "United Nations Millennium Declaration," para. 24, A/RES/55/2, September 18, 2000, undocs.org/A/RES/55/2. For further information on the UN Millennium Summit, see www.un.org/en/events/pastevents/millennium_summit.shtml.

2 For further information on the MDGs, see www.un.org/millenniumgoals.

3 See, for example, the Millennium Project, commissioned by the UN secretary-general, which identifies governance failures as one of four overarching reasons why the MDGs are not being achieved, at www.unmillenniumproject.org/reports/why8.htm. Furthermore, as pointed out by the UN Development Programme (UNDP), various country reports have emphasized the importance of elements of the rule of law in achieving development goals. See the UNDP issue brief "Rule of Law and Development—Integrating Rule of Law in the Post-2015 Development Framework," April 2013, www.undp.org/content/undp/en/home/presscenter/events/2013/september/26-27-september-global-dialogue-on-rule-of-law-and-post-2015-.html.

4 The text of the SDGs was passed by the General Assembly as the "Draft outcome document of the United Nations summit for the adoption of the post-2015 development agenda" (A/RES/69/315) on September 1, 2015. The final agreement, titled "Transforming Our World: The 2030 Agenda for Sustainable Development," was adopted unanimously by world leaders at

Facing the challenge of putting this new agenda into practice, the international community must reconsider its approaches to cooperation in the area of legal and judicial reform. This challenge poses an opportunity to strengthen the rule of law as well. For several decades, German development policy has attached paramount importance to engaging in rule of law promotion and to furthering law and justice systems as enablers of development across all sectors. Germany's rich experience in this field spans rule of law promotion not only locally but regionally.

This chapter discusses the role that rule of law plays in the new sustainable development agenda and the German perspective on the role of rule of law in international cooperation. Several case studies of legal and justice reform programs with distinct regional dimensions are presented and are related to the SDGs. The conclusion presents observations on how regional dimensions can benefit legal reforms in meeting the SDGs.

The Rule of Law in the 2030 Agenda

The rule of law and aspects of it form an integral part of the 2030 agenda. SDG 16, which deals with broad concepts of good governance and peace, is at the center of discussions.

The role of law and justice systems in the SDG catalog extends far beyond SDG 16: an analysis of the SDGs reveals that many contain targets involving legal instruments. Some targets refer to regulations, international legal obligations, individual entitlements, or legal concepts, while others presuppose the existence or adoption of regulatory measures or enforcing institutions.

This chapter distinguishes between three layers of law and justice that can be identified within the 2030 SDG agenda: the stand-alone target on the rule of law, other goals and targets explicitly referring to law and justice systems, and targets that implicitly require legal measures.

SDG 16 and Access to Justice and the Rule of Law

Discussions on drawing up a rule of law development goal began with the Rio+20 conference in 2012.[5] On September 25, 2015, the SDGs were unanimously adopted by world leaders at the UN Sustainable Development Summit.[6] Of the 17 goals, SDG 16 enshrines the political topics of governance and the rule of law. It reads:

---

the UN Sustainable Development Summit on September 25, 2015, http://sustainabledevelop-ment.un.org/content/documents/7891Transforming%20Our%20World.pdf.

5 The conference's outcome document, *The Future We Want*, mandates the establishment of an intergovernmental Open Working Group tasked with putting together a proposal on global sustainable development goals. The outcome document also reaffirms the importance of the rule of law for sustainable development.

6 UNGA, "Transforming Our World."

> Promote peaceful and inclusive societies for sustainable development, provide access to justice for all and build effective, accountable and inclusive institutions at all levels.

Yet a universally agreed-on definition of the rule of law is lacking. In one UN context, the rule of law has been defined as

> a principle of governance in which all persons, institutions and entities, public and private, including the State itself, are accountable to laws that are publicly promulgated, equally enforced and independently adjudicated, and which are consistent with international human rights norms and standards. It requires, as well, measures to ensure adherence to the principles of supremacy of law, equality before the law, accountability to the law, fairness in the application of the law, separation of powers, participation in decision-making, legal certainty, avoidance of arbitrariness and procedural and legal transparency.[7]

In other UN contexts, the rule of law is understood as a broader concept, encompassing access to justice as one of its core components.[8] Within the 2030 agenda, previous drafts of SDG 16 had used the term "rule of law" itself; however, due to the difficulty of agreeing on a common definition and to differing opinions about the scope of the Open Working Group's[9] mandate,[10] the final iteration of SDG 16 uses the term "access to justice" rather than "rule of law." Yet the very term "rule of law" resurfaces in Target 16.3, which asks those implementing the agenda to "promote the rule of law at the national and international levels, and ensure equal access to justice for all."

Similarly, Target 16.6 asks to "develop effective, accountable and transparent institutions at all levels," whereas Target 16.7 underlines the need to "ensure responsive, inclusive, participatory and representative decision-making at all levels."

The enshrining of the more political aspects of development in SDG 16 is a great accomplishment and an important step forward compared with the 1990s Millennium Development agenda. The new SDGs, which explicitly

---

7 See UN Security Council (UNSC), "The Rule of Law and Transitional Justice in Conflict and Post-conflict Societies," Report of the Secretary-General, para. 6, S/2004/616 (August 23, 2004), http://undocs.org/S/2004/616.

8 See UNGA, Resolution 67/1, "Declaration of the High-Level Meeting of the General Assembly on the Rule of Law at the National and International Levels," para. 14, A/RES/67/1, (September 24, 2012).

9 The Rio+20 conference's outcome document mandated the establishment of an intergovernmental Open Working Group tasked with putting together a proposal on global sustainable development goals.

10 See Julinda Beqiraj and Lawrence McNamara, "The Rule of Law and Access to Justice in the Post-2015 Development Agenda," Working Paper 2014/4 (Bingham Centre for the Rule of Law, London, August 4, 2014), http://www.biicl.org/documents/289_post-2015_bingham_centre_paper_2014-04.pdf.

refer to the rule of law, provide momentum to the discussion of a common understanding and definition of the rule of law.

Explicit Reference to Law and Justice Systems in Targets of the SDGs

In addition to SDG 16 and its targets, the targets of several other goals that cover the social, economic, and ecological aspects of sustainable development explicitly refer to law and justice systems or certain legal instruments or norms.

One such example can be found in the targets of SDG 14,[11] which asks to "conserve and sustainably use the oceans, seas and marine resources for sustainable development."

Despite its primary focus on ecological sustainability, the goal has four targets (14.4, 14.5, 14.6, and 14.c)[12] that refer to legal norms or other legal measures.

Thus, a goal primarily concerned with ecological issues has several targets explicitly referring to legal frameworks and their implementation. Indeed, justice systems are engaged in ensuring progress and attaining results.

SDG 1, on ending poverty, has targets demanding economic, social, and cultural (ESC) rights and foresees the utilization of legal concepts such as ownership, property, and inheritance. SDG 5, on gender empowerment, participation, and equality, contains a target on ensuring reproductive rights. SDG 8, on growth, employment, and decent work, has targets concerning the prohibition and eradication of child labor, as well as the protection of labor rights. SDG 10, on reducing inequality within and among countries, has targets demanding the elimination of discriminatory laws, the promotion of appropriate legislation, and the improvement of financial market regulation.

Implicit References to Law and Justice Systems

In addition to the spelling out of the rule of law in SDG 16 and other explicit references to law and justice systems, a third aspect of law and justice systems can be identified in the new development agenda.

---

11 UNGA, "Transforming Our World," 20.

12 Target 14.4 demands the effective regulation of harvesting and an end to overfishing; to illegal, unreported, and unregulated fishing; and to destructive fishing practices. Hence, it requires the creation of an adequate legal framework and its enforcement by competent institutions. Target 14.6 refers to the prohibition and elimination of certain forms of fisheries subsidies that contribute to illegal, unreported, and unregulated fishing. Target 14.5 concerns the conservation of coastal and marine areas consistent with national and international law; which means that existing national laws or international treaties are used as benchmarks for conservation standards. Target 14.c, which deals with how to implement goal 14, asks states to ensure the implementation of international law as reflected in the UN Convention on the Law of the Sea, which provides the legal framework for the conservation and sustainable use of oceans and their resources.

Similar to the MDG framework, a number of goals contain targets that implicitly refer to rule of law aspects, as they require regulatory or other procedural measures for their successful implementation.

In the 2030 SDG framework, many targets concern equal or universal access to services or resources, such as land, financial services, health care services, medicines, and vaccines. Alongside nonlegal actions, many targets require a legal framework when it comes to providing individual legal entitlements, creating accessible mechanisms for the enforcement of these entitlements, or working on legal empowerment.

One such example—under SDG 1, on ending poverty—is Target 1.3, which deals with the implementation of nationally appropriate social protection systems and measures.[13]

Another example is Target 2.3, under SDG 2, on ending hunger, which refers to secure and equal land access. This requires property rights and the regulation of land utilization and exploitation.

Other examples of this regulatory approach include SDG 3, on healthy lives and well-being (see Target 3.7); SDG 5, on gender equality and empowerment (see Target 5.1); SDG 6, on water and sanitation for all (see Targets 6.2 and 6.3); SDG 8, on economic growth and productive employment for all (see Target 8.5); SDG 10, on reducing inequality within and among countries (see Target 10.4.); and SDG 12, on sustainable consumption and production patterns (see Target 12.c).

The German Approach to the Rule of Law and Development

The various layers of law that play a role in the 2030 agenda are proof that the rule of law is of great importance to the implementation of the SDGs throughout all sectors. German development policy has prioritized good governance—and the rule of law as one of its core elements—as one of its key strategic areas. German development policy considers the rule of law a catalyst to reach other development outcomes. Germany's rich experience in supporting rule of law programs reaches back many decades. The German government shared some of its experience in case studies on legal and judicial reform programs at the World Bank's Law, Justice and Development Week 2014. This chapter places those case studies in a wider regional context and takes a fresh look at them in light of the new development agenda.

This section briefly describes the German approach to the promotion of the rule of law and shares the German experience of technical cooperation programs in this area and analyzes how these programs relate to the SDGs. The selected case studies reflect varying degrees of orientation toward the

13 Any social protection system requires a legal framework that articulates individual entitlements, sets out the conditions for receiving benefits, defines the competent authorities, and provides for legal remedies against erroneous decisions.

regional regime of the European Union and also toward bilateral and regional cooperation frameworks.

The Rule of Law in German Development Cooperation

The rule of law has been a topic of German development cooperation for a long time. One recent reconfirmation of the importance of the rule of law is the Charter for the Future entitled "Our Responsibility for This One World," launched by the German Federal Ministry for Economic Cooperation and Development (known by its German acronym, BMZ). This charter aims to contribute to the adoption and implementation of the 2030 SDG agenda and is the outcome document of a participatory process involving a range of state and nonstate actors.[14] Promoting and ensuring human rights and good governance[15] emerged as one of the charter's eight focal areas.

The charter is one of many examples of German development cooperation committing itself to fostering the basic conditions required for good governance and respect for human rights in collaboration with cooperating countries. In accordance with Germany's development policy, support provided must be closely aligned to country-owned reform strategies. Examples of such reform strategy areas are the development of functioning, transparent, and inclusive public institutions; the fight against corruption; and the promotion of freedom of the press and independent civil society. The Charter for the Future reaffirms the commitment to promote democracy and the rule of law.[16] At the same time, it suggests clear areas of responsibility for different groups of stakeholders—such as governments, the private sector, and civil society—both in Germany and around the globe, with a view to joining forces and achieving sustainable development.[17]

To operationalize the charter and guide the implementation of the SDGs, a BMZ policy paper on strengthening the rule of law in German development cooperation is being prepared and will be issued in 2016.

The German concept of the rule of law is fully in line with the definition framed by the UN secretary-general,[18] and it includes an emphasis on the prohibition of the arbitrary use of state power. Germany asks its cooperation partners to guarantee the freedom and personal safety of all citizens, to oblige all public authorities to comply with the law, and to provide orientation for institutional and procedural reforms in all state sectors. The German concept also includes an institution-building element; moreover, it highlights

---

14 Federal Ministry for Economic Cooperation and Development (BMZ), "Charter for the Future: One World—Our Responsibility" (November 2014), 2, https://www.zukunftscharta.de/files/upload/daten_bilder_zukunftscharta/Zukunftscharta-en.pdf.

15 Ibid., 9.

16 Ibid., 35.

17 Ibid., 3.

18 See UNSC, "Rule of Law and Transnational Justice."

the interdependence of democracy, the constitutional state, the welfare state, human rights, and access to justice.

The main objective of German development cooperation in the area of the rule of law is to contribute to the development of effective and democratically legitimate legal and judicial systems. The approach is shaped by a number of principles and by the recognition that rule of law promotion is a complex and often politically sensitive undertaking. For this reason, Germany's development policy sets out support for the rule of law, starting with the individual social, political, and economic contexts of cooperation countries. It respects the authority of the law as being both a product of a political process and a reflection of social and cultural values, history, and tradition. German development cooperation puts the issue of ownership center stage. Thus, German support is primarily directed at its partners' own efforts to establish and implement their own programs and strategies. Germany follows a human rights–based approach to development, which means that all activities supported by the government must comply with and promote human rights as defined in the United Nations' International Bill of Human Rights.

Support for transformation in the legal and judicial field mainly takes place in the form of capacity development; that is, by enhancing the capacities of individuals, organizations, and societies to steer and implement transformation processes. In that legal reform is a lengthy and ambitious process, policy dialogues and other supporting measures are planned and implemented on a long-term basis in order to enhance the sustainability of actions taken. German rule of law promotion addresses actors at both state and civil society levels. It seeks to promote constructive relations between state and society. In addition to bilateral technical cooperation programs, Germany actively engages in the promotion of the rule of law through multilateral processes and institutions.

Support for Legal Reform and Transformation in the Context of EU (Pre-) Accession

The case studies in this section showcase bilateral and regional law and justice reform programs supported by the German government in Serbia, Kosovo, and South East Europe. Serbia and Kosovo are aspiring to accede to the European Union, as are several countries in South East Europe.[19] Serbia holds the status of "candidate country," while Kosovo has been granted the status of "potential candidate." Their national reform programs are complemented by the BMZ Open Regional Fund, which fosters cooperation among a number of countries in the region, including with EU member states.

19 To check the current accession status of each country, visit http://ec.europa.eu/enlargement/countries/check-current-status/index_en.htm.

Case Study: Serbia

The Serbian Legal and Judicial Reform Program focuses on Serbia's relatively low levels of transparency, efficiency, and participation in lawmaking, as well as on the impediments to implementing laws and regulations. The judiciary and public administration are the main beneficiaries. The program also aims at increasing the country's capacities for EU membership negotiations, with particular regard to chapters 23 (judiciary and fundamental rights) and 24 (justice, freedom, and security) of the EU "acquis communautaire."[20]

The program has a collaborative, flexible, and responsive approach and works with a wide range of national partners to ensure that the needs and priorities of the national legal and judicial reform agenda are identified and met accordingly. One visible result of the improvements in judicial execution in Serbia is the reduction of the average time for claim enforcement—from 635 to 100 days.

One key element of the program is the provision of support for introducing new legal professions such as public notaries, enforcement agents, and insolvency administrators. The program draws on expertise from national, regional, and international expert networks and facilitates dialogue and the exchange of knowledge.

The fieldwork for introducing public notaries in Serbia has recently been completed. The professional development of notaries is on a solid track. The notaries help to ensure the legality of important legal acts, such as the transfer of land and inheritance, thereby strengthening legal reliability. Likewise, the efficiency of, stakeholder participation in and transparency of, and overall quality of legislation of the law-making process have improved in Serbia. With a view to EU accession, the Serbian authorities were prepared for the negotiations on legal and judicial reforms.

The Serbian reform program contributes to the aims outlined in the SDGs, in particular to SDG 16, in several ways. By addressing the legislative process in order to achieve the full participation of all stakeholders, including civil society and the private sector, the program relates to Target 16.7, which asks member states to ensure responsive, inclusive, participatory, and representative decision making at all levels.

Support for the introduction of new judicial professions such as public notaries, the enhancement of judiciary and public administrative capacities, and the establishment of an effective and sustainable system for the enforcement of court decisions contributes to the effective implementation of laws and regulations. These activities relate to Target 16.3, on promoting the rule of law at the national and international levels and ensuring equal access to

20 The EU acquis is the body of common rights and obligations that is binding on all the EU member states. Candidate countries must accept the acquis before they can join the EU and make EU law part of their own national legislation. For further information on the EU acquis, see http://ec.europa.eu/enlargement/policy/glossary/terms/acquis_en.htm.

justice for all, and to Target 16.6, on developing effective, accountable, and transparent institutions.

Case Study: Kosovo

Kosovo's government attaches remarkably high priority to the reform of the judicial and administrative structure, especially because it relates to the country's potential accession to the European Union. This makes it a highlight of the German cooperation. The education and training of administrative and judicial staff is a main focus of Kosovo Judiciary Strategic Plan 2014–19. Two institutions, the Kosovo Judicial Institute and the Kosovo Institute of Public Administration, are mandated to develop the decision-making capacities of administrators and courts. The German cooperation project focuses on enhancing the capacity of these two institutions at both the personnel and the institutional levels. It aims to enable both institutions to provide high-quality legal education programs and public administration training, and to establish platforms for professional exchange within the public sector.

After a conflict-sensitive context assessment by the German technical cooperation, the Kosovo Judicial Institute and the Kosovo Institute of Public Administration were both encouraged to systematically extend their training programs to the Serbian-speaking regions of Kosovo, which had previously been neglected due to the tensions spurred by the conflict in the 1990s. The project ensures that training is now accessible to Serbian-speaking staff. This development was implemented by, among other actions, making the national legal framework, training sessions, and working documents of governmental institutions available in both of Kosovo's official languages: Albanian and Serbian.

Further inclusion issues are tackled by the project's focus on gender-sensitive topics in public administration and the legal system. In cooperation with the training institutions and the Agency for Gender Equality, the project strengthens the national network of municipal gender officers.

The project's aim is that trained judges, prosecutors, and civil servants will eventually provide better and more effective services in their respective fields of work than in the past. This aim in turn follows the overall objective of enhancing public trust in Kosovo's legal and judicial institutions.

By addressing the training needs of Serbian-speaking lawyers and civil servants, and by thus integrating this minority group into the public system, a higher level of acceptance of the state institutions is expected. Furthermore, having all parts of the population represented in state institutions is expected to enhance social cohesion and to contribute to state development.

The objectives of the judicial and administrative reform program in Kosovo are related to SDG 16 and three of its targets, namely, access to justice (Target 16.3), transparency in public administration (Target 16.6), and inclusive and representative decision making (Target 16.7).

With regard to gender equality, training for judges, prosecutors, and civil servants supports the implementation of legal provisions, in particular in the field of property and inheritance, such as making sure that women inherit the properties to which they are legally entitled. Training, in tandem with awareness-raising campaigns in the municipalities, aims to encourage women to actively claim their rights through administrative and judicial institutions. If the objective is reached, it would contribute to progress toward Target 16.3's access to justice and to demanding an end to all forms of discrimination against all women and girls everywhere, as enshrined in SDG 5.

Case Study: Open Regional Fund on Legal Reform

The countries in South East Europe face similar challenges and share common needs and perspectives with respect to their potential future EU membership, as do Serbia and Kosovo. Therefore, the national reform programs in Serbia and Kosovo that are supported by German development cooperation are complemented by German development cooperation's regional reform program: the Open Regional Fund for South-East Europe–Legal Reform (ORF LR).

The ORF LR supports partners in Albania, Bosnia and Herzegovina, Kosovo, the former Yugoslav Republic of Macedonia, Montenegro, and Serbia with the introduction of legal framework conditions and reforms that comply with the EU acquis and other legal framework instruments. To increase mutual learning, the ORF LR supports the exchange of lessons learned between countries in South East Europe by creating and strengthening regional expert networks and peer-to-peer learning platforms. It aims to enable participating partner institutions to independently implement legal reforms. Furthermore, in its advisory work, the ORF LR, besides offering German and European know-how, provides expertise from neighboring countries, which may relate better to the specific challenges of transition.

With the support of the ORF LR, partner institutions are given the opportunity to develop their capacities for judicial cooperation in transboundary matters such as cross-border execution and enforcement, bankruptcy proceedings, and the development of corporate law. Thirteen universities from six countries in the region cooperate in the South-East European Law School (SEELS) Network to improve quality standards in vocational and higher education, organize regional law conferences, and offer regional educational and research programs—such as summer schools, training courses, and postdoctoral colloquia that focus primarily on EU law—to law students and academics. The SEELS Network also develops joint projects to identify ways of modernizing national legal frameworks and aligning them with the EU acquis. Recently introduced public notary chambers support each other with the aim of consolidating their functions and services. Alternative dispute resolution and mediation centers work together on the recognition of arbitration awards. Via the ORF LR, German development cooperation supported the inclusion of international purchasing rights in national legislation in cooperation with the UN Commission on International Trade Law (UNCITRAL) to facilitate commercial transactions in the region and thus promote economic exchange and growth. A regional network of experts is supporting national reform efforts in civil law and monitoring the implementation of international and European guidelines in national legal systems.

The EU acquis contains detailed provisions on the rule of law. The regional cooperation supported by the ORF LR therefore makes the process of EU accession more efficient. The regional cooperation program promotes exchange between countries and facilitates peer learning with regard to reforms in the context of EU accession. The countries are at different stages in the EU accession process, so the exchange of experiences not only promotes best practices but also helps some countries avoid mistakes. This, in turn, contributes to the attainment of Targets 16.3 and 16.6 of the SDGs. Moreover, being a regional project with long-term networks, including professional contacts in legal institutions and ministries, the ORF LR contributes to easing cross-border animosities in South East Europe. This dimension goes beyond the notion of rule of law and relates to SDG 16 on promoting peaceful and inclusive societies.

Support for Legal Reform and Transformation in the South Caucasus

The fourth case study is set in a region that is politically and geographically more distant from the European Union: the South Caucasus. In comparison with the first three cases, this one reflects a lesser degree of orientation toward the regional regime of the European Union. All three South Caucasian countries—Armenia, Azerbaijan, and Georgia—are part of the European Union's Eastern Partnership initiative,[21] which supports and encourages reforms in these countries and aims at strengthening their political and economic relations with the European Union, and the European Neighbourhood Policy,[22] which is chiefly a bilateral policy operating between the European Union and each partner country. Yet neither the Eastern Partnership or the European Neighbourhood Policy is directly related to an EU accession. As a result of the Eastern Partnership initiative, the three South Caucasian countries have committed to a common goal of strengthening the rule of law and approximating their respective legal frameworks to EU regulations. There are two main obstacles to achieving these aims. The first is the low level of institutional and human capacities required to undertake the complex legal and structural reforms involved. The second is tensions and conflicting interests among communities and countries in the subregion, which hinder cooperation within and between South Caucasian countries.

German development cooperation set up a comprehensive regional program, which aims to initiate and strengthen the change process. It aims primarily to foster the dialogue on the rule of law at the national, regional,

---

21 The Eastern Partnership is based on a commitment to the principles of international law and fundamental values, including democracy, the rule of law, and respect for human rights and fundamental freedoms, as well as to a market economy, sustainable development, and good governance. For further information, see http://eeas.europa.eu/eastern/index_en.htm.

22 For further information on the European Neighbourhood Policy, see http://eeas.europa.eu/enp/about-us/index_en.htm.

and international levels. It does so by providing advisory services, capacity development, and exchanges of best practices. The topics covered in dialogues include strategic planning of reforms, the design and revision of legal frameworks, the provision of integrated legal education by connecting initial and continuing education, and approaches for raising the public's awareness of legal matters. Most important, the cooperation program operates at the national level in all three countries and at the regional level, to ensure coherence and complementarity.

In recent years, the program has significantly contributed to the introduction of administrative justice, including specialized courts, in all three South Caucasian countries. As a result, citizens are now able to challenge administrative acts. The cooperation program has also initiated a change process with regard to legal education. Training institutions have scaled up their education programs and now base their curricula on the knowledge and skills actually required in legal practice.

The so-called Transformation Lawyers network represents a special approach to regional exchange and cooperation. International and regional conferences bring together young professionals working in courts, ministries, and other public authorities in order to engage in a regional dialogue process. This dialogue focuses on legal and judicial topics, but it also considers the issue of peace and conflict in the region. The conferences have helped create a regional alumni network that actively promotes peaceful cooperation and legal transformation in the region.

The results of legal and judicial reform in the three South Caucasian countries pertain largely to Targets 16.3 and 16.6.

The experience from this program shows that regional approaches complement and reinforce support for national reforms. As mentioned above, with respect to the ORF LR, the exchange of lessons learned and best practices has proved to be a very useful tool. The same holds true for the program in South Caucasus. External guidance frameworks, such as the EU acquis and specific legal models (including the German approach to administrative law), help inform reflections at the regional level and allow for a clearer understanding of differences and similarities in relation to both neighboring countries and external standards.

In the end, this result may lead to a certain level of regional harmonization of laws and standards. A regional approach helps to create a competitive situation among countries. Neighbors' achievements serve as incentives, as each country seeks to claim a leading role or to achieve quicker or better results in terms of higher-quality reform.

In addition, in cases where there is conflict between countries, cooperation must work to maintain dialogue and exchange. With regard to the SDGs, this aspect goes beyond the targets related to the rule of law; it touches on the dimension of peaceful societies of SDG 16 itself.

Conclusion

Germany has defined good governance and the rule of law as a priority and has rich experience with a number of related targets now enshrined in the SDGs. Regarding the rule of law, German development policy has chosen an approach that is context specific and puts cooperation partners' local, national, and regional capacities, systems, values, and national development plans at center stage. This is demonstrated in the case study of Kosovo, where German development cooperation supports education and training of administrative and judicial staff, which is a main focus of Kosovo's own Judiciary Strategic Plan 2014–19. Another example is the design of the program described in the South Caucasus case study. The fact that the regional program operates at the national level in all three countries allows it to work in a context-specific way and to accommodate national priorities and particularities.

The national and regional cooperation examples showcased in this chapter share a specificity: all are cases of cooperation partners that are highly motivated to reform their legal and judiciary systems by the EU's pull factor. Yet other factors might contribute to a similarly high motivation for reform in other contexts. From the German experience, the issue of willingness to reform is crucial to the ownership of the reform process.

Looking at the cases, two different regional dimensions in rule of law cooperation can be distinguished: the complementary use of bilateral and regional cooperation programs and the orientation of cooperation measures toward an existing or evolving regional legal regime, such as the European Union.

Complementary Bilateral and Regional Approaches

The German experience shows that there are differences in how bilateral and regional programs relate to the judicial and legal reform processes. The strengths of bilateral cooperation lie in supporting the effective implementation of reform processes. Regional approaches are stronger when it comes to exchanging experiences and motivating (political) interest in specific reforms, thus improving the framework conditions for change agents.

Support for national reform processes tends to lead to quicker results. Orienting these processes along national strategic frameworks facilitates the tasks of tracking impact and measuring results. Bilateral cooperation can develop tailor-made solutions to address the particular needs of institutions in countries undergoing rule of law reforms. Activities and cooperation agreements can be dealt with in a flexible way. Bilateral cooperation relies on close ties with different governmental institutions, because these strengthen the respective partner institutions and thus make it possible to implement potential reform agendas at all levels of the state apparatus. Methodologically speaking, the support addresses primarily the development of institutional and personnel capacities, and the provision of technical advice on specific aspects of the implementation process.

Although regional cooperation affects the implementation of reforms less directly, it still has an important role to play. It can indirectly reinforce implementation through the creation of professional networks, the development of peer learning, the exchange of best practices, and the evaluation of experiences. Even more important, however, is its potential to create reform incentives and to set national agendas through regional benchmarking and competition. In this way, regional cooperation is vital for the promotion and legitimization of reform policies. Regional exchange has particular advantages over both higher (international) and lower (national) levels of professional dialogue. Regional exchange widens the perspective on reforms beyond the borders of the national legal system and allows countries to learn from one another's transformation experiences. Such exchanges take place in an area defined by a shared history and similar political and social structures.

Regional cooperation offers partners the opportunity to set aside the technical aspects of reform and, instead, to tackle higher-level issues. It allows issues that might be politically sensitive at the national level, such as judicial independence to be addressed. Also, matters arising from regional conflicts can be discussed, which fosters regional dialogue and peace in the sense of SDG 16.

Yet international professional dialogue—for example, on rule of law issues in the context of EU enlargement or on implementing the SDGs—also serves an important function. It enables partners to reflect on how they react to global challenges. This reflection, in turn, serves to promote standard setting and to inspire new approaches to legal policy.

Germany's experience strongly suggests that development cooperation should address impacts at both levels—national and regional—and, in so doing, draw up cooperation programs in a complementary way.

Regional Regimes as Orientation for Cooperation in Promoting the Rule of Law

The prospect of EU accession has served as a driver for transformation in the cases presented. Yet the experiences of these countries may be transferable to other regional contexts where regional cooperation and integration offers benefits to individual countries.

Ever greater integration in politics and markets is a strong incentive for reform and can tip the balance toward more progressive policies. The German experience of supporting the implementation of law and justice reform programs in Kosovo and Serbia shows that the EU pre-accession process provides a framework with which various reform agendas can be aligned and accelerated. This context creates a common understanding of the content and of the importance of reform strategies among state institutions of the acceding country and with international partners. A common understanding, combined with a political consensus for integration, can help when it comes to agreeing on reform agendas and can accelerate implementation.

However, the prospect of accession to the European Union also risks provoking reforms that are not sufficiently embedded in national reform agendas. Reforms primarily undertaken as a formal requirement for EU accession might end up being superficial and lacking ownership of the institutions involved, as well as the population. EU pre-accession planning brings with it a certain risk of overambitious time frames that, given the capacities available in the public institutions of candidate countries, may ultimately be unrealistic.

Lessons learned when implementing the program in the South Caucasus reaffirm that regional legal regimes act as a powerful driver for rule of law reform, even in countries that do not have a concrete prospect of EU accession. In addition to being part of two EU instruments, the Eastern Partnership initiative and the European Neighbourhood Policy, the countries of the South Caucasus are member states of the Council of Europe—which is also set in the geographical region of Europe but is an international organization of its own—and state parties to its European Convention on Human Rights.[23] Under the convention, all three countries are bound to certain obligations with respect to due process and to certain judicial guarantees, creating a common framework for the orientation of national legal and judicial reforms.

The experience in the South Caucasus shows that the European Union is not the only legal regime with the potential to guide rule of law reforms. Other regional regimes, such as those on human rights, may assume a similar role with comparable effect. Clearly, this also applies beyond Europe's borders. Regional political and legal regimes and organizations are consolidating on all continents; the Inter-American and African human rights systems are examples that could provide orientation and incentives for change agents involved in rule of law reforms.

As outlined in "The 2030 Agenda for Sustainable Development," regional regimes are anticipated to play an important role in the review of and follow-up to the attainment of the SDGs. It is foreseen that review at the regional level can, where appropriate, provide useful opportunities for mutual learning, cooperation on transboundary issues, and discussions on shared targets. Regional reviews, including peer reviews, can draw on national-level reviews and contribute to follow-ups and reviews at the global level.[24] In Germany's experience, this is a very clear and realistic approach to the implementation of the SDGs and can be applied to various regional contexts around the globe.

Regional approaches and programs are crucial elements in complementing bilateral cooperation arrangements.

---

23 For further information on the member states of the Council of Europe, see http://www.coe.int/en/web/about-us/our-member-states and the 1950 Convention for the Protection of Human Rights and Fundamental Freedoms, http://www.echr.coe.int/Documents/Convention_ENG.pdf.

24 See "Transforming Our World: The 2030 Agenda for Sustainable Development," adopted unanimously by world leaders at the UN Sustainable Development Summit on September 25, 2015, paras. 80–81, at http://www.un.org/ga/search/view_doc.asp?symbol=A/RES/70/1&Lang=E.

Germany welcomes the fact that the rule of law assumes a central role within the framework of the SDGs and is considered instrumental in the realization of various of its goals and targets. Germany, with its international partners, will continue its efforts and strengthen law and justice systems as catalysts for the implementation of the SDGs in local, national, and regional contexts. Against the background of its rich experience in that field, Germany welcomes fruitful dialogues on the topic.

5

Mitigating Governance Risks in Identification Systems

MEGAN BREWER, HASSANE CISSÉ,
NICHOLAS MENZIES, AND JARED SCHOTT

More than 150 countries maintain mandatory civil registration systems. The number, variety, and functionality of these systems have expanded with the rise of the Internet, and, relatedly, delivery mechanisms for services and benefits are increasingly tied to registration.[1] Attracted by the promise of new technology-driven solutions, countries and development partners alike have invested heavily in identification, registration, and documentation (IRD) systems, in terms of both development funding and strategy. This strategic focus is reflected in no less preeminent a platform than the United Nations' post-2015 Sustainable Development Goals (SDGs), which include the proposed Target 16.9, which states that all countries should, "by 2030, provide legal identity for all, including birth registration," under the broader goal of fostering more peaceful and inclusive societies.[2]

IRD systems can assist governments to more effectively and efficiently deliver public services and entitlements. They can generate demographic data to inform policy, planning, and delivery processes. They can provide tangible means through which citizens can assert their legal identity. Further, they can open up new economic opportunities, such as banking and other private sector services, which otherwise would be inaccessible. Functional applications of such systems have catalyzed flood relief for 1.5 million families in Pakistan, generated millions in payroll savings through the identification of "ghost" public sector employees in Nigeria, and underpinned social protection programs ranging from old-age pension cash transfers in South Africa to food programs for the poor in Kenya.[3]

This article builds on the earlier Just Development Series Working Paper No. 8, "Making Identification Systems Work for the Bottom 40%" (Washington, DC: World Bank, 2015). The findings, interpretations, and conclusions expressed herein are those of the authors alone and do not necessarily reflect the views of the World Bank, its Executive Directors, or the governments they represent.

1 World Bank, *Identification for Development (ID4D) Global Indicators: Data Collection and Analysis* (Washington, DC: World Bank, forthcoming).

2 United Nations General Assembly, "Transforming Our World: The 2030 Agenda for Sustainable Development," Resolution 70/1, September 18, 2015, http://www.un.org/ga/search/view_doc.asp?symbol=A/70/L.1&Lang=E.

3 A. Gelb and J. Clark, "Identification for Development: The Biometrics Revolution," Working Paper 315 (Washington, DC: Center for Global Development, 2013).

For all of their important development benefits, though, IRD systems may also pose risks, especially with regard to vulnerable populations. This chapter explores the prospects, challenges, and risks of pinning inclusive development ambitions on IRD systems. Much of the current discourse on IRD-related issues is framed from a state-centered perspective; that is to say, it primarily speaks to improving the functioning of government agencies and enhancing the collection of data for planning and policy. This chapter suggests complementing this vernacular and orientation with a stronger focus on the impacts of IRD systems on society's poorest and most marginalized people. This shift in emphasis reveals that, in many circumstances, these systems may not be serving the development needs of the poor, and the systems may in fact risk frustrating efforts to meet those needs. There is, therefore, a need to more clearly and critically articulate in IRD strategies the implied benefits and costs of alternative approaches. At the country-specific and subnational levels, strategy and implementation need to incorporate due diligence in assessing a broader, nontechnical spectrum of governance[4] and implementation risks. Toward this end, this chapter contends that dialogue and practice around identification and registration should be enhanced by

- clarifying the difference between the terms "identity," "registration," and "documentation";
- expanding the focus of dialogue from technical solutions to the development problems that IRD systems seek to address, and investing in ways to better understand how IRD systems are linked to development impacts; and
- understanding that IRD systems may result in *increased exclusion* of the poor and marginalized if underlying legal, social, and political contexts are not properly analyzed, and investing in mitigation strategies.

A First Point of Order: Disentangling Identity, Registration, and Documentation

Policy and operational dialogue around identification systems are hampered by the conflation of several important concepts, including "identity," "registration," and "documentation" (or "certification"). This confusion is not simply a matter of terminology. Delving into the distinctions between these terms is key to understanding their contrasting means and ends, which may even at times run at cross-purposes. A shared and clear definition of what is meant is important.

Legal identity is generally defined as a status ascribing rights and duties to people[5] based on certain characteristics. Legal identity can emerge from sources in both national and international law—one's citizenship, say,

---

4 Including legal, institutional, sociological, and political economy analyses.

5 Although organizations such as corporations and nongovernmental organizations may also possess legal identities, this chapter focuses on the identities of individual persons.

compared with one's refugee status. Often overlooked in identification[6] discussions but critical from a rights perspective is that *legal identity exists whether or not it is registered* (and whether or not documentation of such registration exists). When legal identity *is* recognized by a state, it can enhance a person's ability to enjoy that state's protection, using it to enforce his or her rights and to demand redress within the state by gainig access to courts and other law enforcement organizations.[7] At the same time, many aspects of one's legal identity do not require registration. For example, in many jurisdictions, a person who is arrested on suspicion of committing a crime has rights that attach to his or her identity as a criminal suspect (e.g., the right to remain silent). These rights are inherent to him or her as a person and a suspect and are not contingent upon registration or documentation.

People also have *multiple legal identities*. Depending on the factual circumstances, an individual person can have the identity of "citizen," "resident," "spouse," "voter," "driver," and/or "eligible claimant for services/benefits," among many others. Each of these identities can be used to further different development outcomes at personal and societal levels. An understanding that legal identity exists in many forms leads to the question of which legal identity (or identities) is being sought for recognition, and for what developmental ends.

Registration refers to the systems and processes by which a state (or other authority) recognizes and records certain aspects of an individual's legal identity. Registration systems may be broad-based (foundational), such as national ID cards, or deployed for particular purposes (functional), such as for securing driver's licenses, paying taxes, or receiving social security benefits.

As there are multiple legal identities, one register (and associated document) will likely not cover all dimensions of identification; indeed, multiple registration systems exist in most countries. This is the case even in countries that have a primary IRD system, such as those countries in which individuals use a national ID card. A single registry system is not necessarily a prerequisite to development; some developed countries (such as the United States, the United Kingdom, and Australia) have made the conscious choice *not* to have a national ID system.

Documentation (or *certification*) refers to the proof of registration, which traditionally has taken a physical form (a card, paper, or certificate) but in some circumstances may now be electronic. This proof of registration facilitates the holder's assertion of his or her legal identity in different locations. Increasingly, this documentation may also be a requirement if a person seeks

---

6 Used herein, the term "identification," in contrast to the term "identity," typically refers to the state process of discerning and officially recognizing legal identity—often, but not necessarily always, by way of registration.

7 See C. Vandenabeele, "To Register or Not to Register?" in *Children without a State: A Global Human Rights Challenge*, ed. Jacqueline Bhabha (Cambridge, MA: MIT Press, 2011), 307–330.

to gain access to essential services, obtain employment, vote, transfer property, drive a car, or open a bank account.[8]

Although registration and documentation are linked, it is nevertheless important to keep them functionally and conceptually distinct, for reasons that can be illustrated by global birth data. As recently as 2012, the births of 230 million children under five were not *registered*; in that same cohort, 70 million *registered* births went *undocumented*.[9] Registration and documentation may entail different processes and have different legal or programmatic implications. For example, a child's birth may be *automatically* registered by a hospital, though obtaining documentation may require a proactive application process. Registration may be sufficient to establish a person's eligibility under the law to, say, inherit land, but documentation may be required to actually effect the deed transfer.

The differences between identity (a rights- and status-based concept), registration (a system for recognizing and recording rights and status), and documentation (an instrument of proof) become more pronounced when considering how identity and registration serve cross-cutting development objectives. Legal identity is the intrinsic source of an individual's standing, and of his or her claim for inclusion and access. Registration, in contrast, can improve a system's ability to deliver services to identified claimants by recognizing and recording identities, but it is not always premised on inclusion. In fact, the rights and status bound up in legal identity are not inherently dependent on being recognized via a registration system. Understanding these conceptual distinctions is an essential first step in understanding how to tackle the distinct personal and societal development problems they seek to address. Moreover, although this conceptual clarity has important programmatic and welfare consequences, the need for such clarity is sometimes overlooked.[10] Applying the "legal identity" label to registration systems may unintentionally validate a priori their rights-based bona fides rather than open them up to appropriate scrutiny and standards. This is problematic because in practice, the very function of registration systems may in some cases contribute to the exclusion of certain individuals' identities, as discussed in the section

---

8 World Bank, "By Counting Every Life, Every Life Counts," June 23, 2014, http://www.worldbank.org/en/news/feature/2014/06/23/by-counting-every-life-every-life-counts; and World Bank and World Health Organization (WHO), "Global Civil Registration and Vital Statistics Scaling Up Investment Plan, 2015–2024" (World Bank, Washington, DC, 2014).

9 C. Dunning, A. Gelb, and S. Raghavan, *Birth Registration, Legal Identity, and the Post-2015 Agenda,* CGD Policy Paper 046 (Washington, DC: Center for Global Development, 2014).

10 In this regard, contemporary institutional definitions fall short. The formulation of proposed SDG Target 16.9, as previously noted, suggests that birth registration is equivalent to legal identity. The Inter-American Development Bank's *Civil Registration and Identification Glossary* (New York: Inter-American Bank, 2010) defines legal identity as "legal civil status obtained through birth registration and civil identification that recognizes the individual as a subject of law and protection of the state." The glossary is available at https://publications.iadb.org/bitstream/handle/11319/402/Civil%20Registration%20and%20Identification%20Glossary.pdf?sequence=2.

"Prioritizing Risk Analysis and Mitigation Measures to Address Exclusion and Disparate Impacts."

Deepening the IRD Evidence Base for Better Development Results

Since the turn of the century, the global proliferation of IRD systems has accelerated, as mobile connectivity, digitization, and biometric technology have become less costly and more widespread. All high-income countries have achieved civil registration completeness, and the world average coverage of birth registration for children under five has grown significantly, from 58 percent in 2000 to 72 percent in 2015.[11] The World Bank alone has supported more than 120 IRD-related investment projects in 70 countries during the past 10 years, more than half of which are ongoing. Not long into their lifespan, IRD systems are estimated to have saved Nigeria and India each US$1 billion per year—in Nigeria, by eliminating approximately 62,000 "ghost workers" from government payrolls; in India, by identifying recipients for a targeted cash transfer system, which realized significant efficiency gains over the fuel subsidy program it replaced.[12] More broadly, IRD systems can enable a country's progress toward a number of sustainable development goals in areas including social protection, disaster relief, fiscal policy and revenue mobilization, access to finance, women's empowerment, improvements in maternal and child health (including vaccine coverage), energy efficiency, child protection, and remittance cost reduction, as well as the fight against corruption, crime, and terrorism.[13]

Projections point to a continuing push toward digitization and universality. An oft-cited 2012 Boston Consulting Group study estimated global taxpayer savings of up to US$50 billion per year by 2020 deriving from the efficiency gains of digital IRD systems.[14] With an estimated 1.8 billion people still lacking registration or documentation and 625 million children not registered at birth, there is a concerted push among countries and development

---

11 Hague Colloquium Collective on the Future of Legal Identity, "Challenges in Measuring SDG 16.9: Legal Identity and Birth Registration," provisional position paper (The Hague, April 21–24, 2015); and United Nations Children's Fund (UNICEF), *A Passport to Protection: A Guide to Birth Registration Programming* (New York: UNICEF, 2013).

12 World Bank, "Internet for Development, WDR 2016: Spotlight on Digital Identity," *World Development Report* (Washington, DC: World Bank, May 2015), http://pubdocs.worldbank.org/pubdocs/publicdoc/2015/6/959381434483205387/WDR16-Spotlight-on-Digital-ID-May-2015-Mariana-Dahan.pdf; and P. Barnwal, "Curbing Leakage in Public Programs with Biometric Identification Systems: Evidence from India's Fuel Subsidies," job market paper (Columbia University, New York, 2015).

13 For further discussion of these contributions, see A. Gelb and M. Dahan, "Role of Identification in the Post-2015 Agenda," Center for Global Development–World Bank Group Working Paper (World Bank, Washington, DC, forthcoming).

14 J. Rose, O. Rehse, and B. Rober, "The Value of Our Digital Identity," *BCG Perspectives* (Boston Consulting Group, November 20, 2012), https://www.bcgperspectives.com/content/articles/digital_economy_consumer_insight_value_of_our_digital_identity/.

partners alike to invest in expanding IRD systems toward "legal identity for all."[15]

At the same time, IRD systems are expensive, in terms of both absolute outlay (with some budgets in the hundreds of millions of dollars) as well as the opportunity costs of forgone investments elsewhere. IRD systems can also pose both economic and noneconomic risks, ranging from procurement missteps to rights violations. These considerations point to the importance of understanding, for balancing purposes, the nature and likelihood of realizing the benefits of IRD. How do the costs and impacts of a digital integrated system compare with those of several overlapping low-tech functional registries? In order to balance these competing considerations and fortify the case for investing in high-cost systems, development partners should work together to develop a more robust evidence base for IRD systems. This is particularly the case for the two main instrumental benefits often ascribed to IRD systems by proponents: targeting services and benefits, and enhancing statistical data, which are discussed next.

Registration as a means of targeting public and private sector services and benefits is a core argument underpinning many IRD activities. The notion is that registration enhances access by allowing governments to expand the reach and efficiency of their programs, and by providing documentary proof of the validity of a person's claim to an entitlement or service.

The development benefits of identification systems are perhaps most clearly established in the realm of antipoverty cash transfers. A typical data point is the example of the Indian state of Andhra Pradesh, where a large-scale randomized control trial on the use of "smartcards" found that such cards delivered faster, more predictable, and less corrupt payment procedures for beneficiaries without adversely affecting program access.[16] Outside of this kind of social protection programming, however, the evidence is more limited, and even proponents of identification systems acknowledge the need for more rigorous empirical evaluation.[17]

Indeed, several pieces of research present a more mixed perspective about the overall development effect of registration and documentation. For example, a 2007 review conducted by the Asian Development Bank in Bangladesh, Cambodia, and Nepal examined the impact of documentation programs by comparing the quality of life of people with formal identity documents with those in similar circumstances without them. The research found the reality of IRD systems to be "far more complex and challenging" than that suggested by their conceptual appeal, and the beneficial impact of increasing the number of people with legal identity documents was, "at least for the most

---

15 Gelb and Dahan, "Identification in the Post-2015 Agenda."

16 K. Muralidharan, P. Niehaus, and S. Sukhtankar, *Building State Capacity: Evidence from Biometric Smartcards in India* (Boston: Poverty Action Lab, 2014), http://www.povertyactionlab.org/publication/building-state-capacity-evidence-biometric-smartcards-india.

17 Gelb and Clark, *Identification for Development.*

vulnerable communities, often . . . speculative and remote."[18] A 2014 report by Plan International expounded on the "complex and context-specific" relationship between birth registration and access to services with a mixed-methods study in India, Kenya, Sierra Leone, and Vietnam.[19] The study included qualitative interviews alongside a multivariate analysis of selected demographic and health survey datasets, in addition to Plan's own sponsorship datasets. Both the Plan and the Asian Development Bank (ADB) studies found that the purported benefits of birth registration for child protection were overstated, with little perceived impact on, for example, child labor or marriage.

Both studies also highlighted how the "concrete value" of IRD was limited by other "fundamental obstacles."[20] The ADB study found that even if documentation was required and people had obtained it, the majority of the populations evaluated were not able to access the linked services and opportunities due to other physical, political, economic, and social obstacles. And although the Plan study's quantitative analysis found positive correlations (to varying degrees of statistical significance) between birth registration and access to health and education services, contradictory qualitative research and questions about the causal mechanisms at work led the study authors to conclude that the development impacts were more significantly determined by other correlated but untested determinants.

One notable application of IRD systems is in elections, where biometric voting systems have been promoted as vote enablers and solutions to attendant inefficiencies, irregularities, and fraud. At least 25 countries in Africa have deployed biometric voter ID systems, although with mixed results.[21] Several countries, among them Ghana, Kenya, and Nigeria, have seen technical problems with biometric kits and electronic tally systems; they have also been stymied by power shortages in remote areas, disproportionately disenfranchising already marginalized rural constituencies, or have simply run into problems with distribution or political contestation over voter lists.[22] Although the data here are too limited and subject to too many uncontrolled variables to support a broad conclusion about biometric voting systems, the research does raise questions about whether they are the panacea that their substantial

---

18 Asian Development Bank (ADB), *Legal Identity for Inclusive Development*, Law and Policy Reform at the Asian Development Bank (Manila: ADB, 2007).

19 K. Apland et al., *Birth Registration and Children's Rights: A Complex Story* (Woking, England: Plan International, 2014), http://plan-international.org/about-plan/resources/publications/campaigns/birth-registration-research.

20 Ibid.

21 M. Wrong, "Africa's Election Aid Fiasco," *Spectator*, April 20, 2013, http://www.spectator.co.uk/features/8890471/the-technological-fix/; and C. Mungai, "Dirty Hands: Why Biometric Voting Fails in Africa—And It Doesn't Matter in the End," *Mail & Guardian Africa*, March 30, 2015, http://mgafrica.com/article/2015-03-30-why-biometric-voting-fails-in-africa-and-why-it-doesnt-matter.

22 Ibid.; and R. King, "Nigerian Election Successful Despite Biometric Voting Hiccups," *Biometric Update*, April 7, 2015, http://www.biometricupdate.com/201504/nigerian-election-successful-despite-biometric-voting-hiccups.

price tags would suggest. In the Democratic Republic of Congo, for example, the biometric voter IRD system for the 2011 election cost US$58 million out of a total election budget of US$360 million. In 2012, Ghana had a lower election budget (US$124 million) but spent a larger proportion on biometric kits (US$76 million). In Kenya and Côte d'Ivoire, recent elections utilizing biometric systems cost US$20 and US$44 per voter, respectively, compared with estimates of average election costs in established democracies of US$1–$3 per voter.[23]

Augmenting and enhancing statistical data for policy and planning purposes is another stated benefit of IRD systems. Civil registration can generate valuable demographic statistics to inform policy, planning, and delivery processes.[24] Although these systems can provide information on anything from where people live to important health and other vital statistics, the benefits of such data are invariably linked to the comprehensiveness and functionality of the underlying registration system.

Birth registration is the most common process through which states record key aspects of people's legal identity. Yet for the period 1995–2004, only 54 percent of countries reported complete coverage for births, and 52 percent reported complete information for deaths.[25] Current data highlight the coverage gap further. The total population of the 152 countries using mandatory birth and civil registration systems is 5.9 billion people; of these 5.9 billion, almost 1.5 billion people remain unregistered.[26] The data are particularly striking in low-income countries; in Ethiopia and Somalia, for example, birth registration systems capture only 6.6 percent and 3 percent of births, respectively.[27] It is fair to say that in most developing countries, registration has not yet reached a level of universality, accuracy, and reliability sufficient to be used for planning purposes.[28] Moreover, because registration among certain vulnerable or marginalized populations—such as minority ethnic groups, the rural poor, or

---

23 Wrong, "Africa's Election Aid Fiasco."

24 ADB, *Legal Identity for Inclusive Development.*

25 K. Wallman and S. Evinger, "International Standards for Compilation of Statistics: The Gap between Standards Adoption and Standards Implementation" (Paris: Organisation for Economic Co-operation and Development, 2006).

26 World Bank, *Identification for Development (ID4D) Global Indicators.*

27 Ibid., 35.

28 Apland et al., *Birth Registration and Children's Rights.* The World Bank and WHO have developed a Global Civil Registration and Vital Statistics Scaling Up Investment Plan with the goal of universal civil registration of births, deaths, marriages, and other vital events, including reporting the cause of death, and access to legal proof of registration for all individuals, by 2030. The cost of bridging the gap in the 73 low- and middle-income countries is estimated to be US$2.3 billion (2014). This is an important initiative, but until it is more fully realized, pragmatism is in order in tempering expectations as to the value of registry-generated data. In the absence of reliable registry data, alternative data sources, including household or population surveys, have proven to be effective tools for monitoring certain demographic indicators and trends (including birth registration—see UNICEF, *The "Rights" Start to Life: A Statistical Analysis of Birth Registration* [New York: UNICEF, 2005]), without the additional costs attendant to instituting comprehensive civil registries.

the LGBTI community[29]—can be significantly lower than national averages,[30] using registration data for development planning may lead to distorted information that does not reflect the needs of already vulnerable groups.

Proponents of IRD systems also raise noninstrumental arguments related to empowerment that elicit their own evidentiary challenges. Perception surveys highlight the intrinsic value of having one's legal identity recognized and affirmed by tangible documentation, especially in those populations historically marginalized by the state.[31] This is complemented by the value of empowering individuals to assert and protect their rights. Measuring these impacts, though, is challenging. It is difficult, for example, to untangle the often contradictory effects of the need to present documentation to protect rights, versus the effective implementation and enforcement of applicable law, versus the risks of individual rights being deprived on the basis of one's failure to present documentation.[32] It has also been difficult to generate a clear picture of the narrower empowerment effects of IRD. For example, the Data 2X partnership's 2014 *Mapping Gender Data Gaps* report, which looks at key domains of women's empowerment, identifies the impact of national identification documentation as one of 28 priority gender data gaps demanding additional research.[33]

In sum, the existing evidence evaluating the links among registration, documentation, and inclusive development reveal both complexity and uncertainty. Although new evidence is emerging, there is an overarching need to invest further in filling continuing evidentiary gaps.

Prioritizing Risk Analysis and Mitigation Measures to Address Exclusion and Disparate Impacts

Strengthening IRD systems without critically assessing and responding to the broader governance context can lead to a number of consequences that actually serve to undermine development gains. Registry systems may result in exclusion, for example, when underlying law does not recognize certain

---

29 LGBTI refers to people who are lesbian, gay, bisexual, transgender, or intersex.

30 D. Ladner, E. Jensen, and S. Saunders, "A Critical Assessment of Legal Identity: What It Promises and What It Delivers," *Hague Journal on the Rule of Law* 6 (2014): 47–74; Suzanne Duryea et al., *The Under-Registration of Births in Latin America,* Working Paper 551 (Washington, DC: Inter-American Development Bank, 2006), 14–18; Mia Harbitz and Maria del Carmen Tamargo, *The Significance of Legal Identity in Situations of Poverty and Social Exclusion: The Link between Gender, Ethnicity, and Legal Identity,* Technical Note (Washington, DC: Inter-American Development Bank, 2009), 10–16; and UNICEF, *"Rights" Start to Life,* 5–23.

31 Commission on Legal Empowerment of the Poor, *Making the Law Work for Everyone,* vol. 2: *Report of the Commission on Legal Empowerment of the Poor* (New York: United Nations Development Programme, 2008).

32 Apland et al., *Birth Registration and Children's Rights.*

33 M. Buvinic, R. Furst-Nichols, and G. Koolwal, *Mapping Gender Data Gaps* (Washington, DC: Data 2X, 2014).

identities. Exclusion can also come from refusing rights to those who might legally be entitled to register but who, for a variety of reasons, have not done so or do not have the required documentation. Lastly, exclusion may result from information that is disclosed in the documents and registration systems themselves. In order to ensure that IRD systems serve rather than impede *all* groups' development interests, the design and implementation of these systems need to incorporate mitigation strategies, ranging from legal and regulatory reform to grievance-redress mechanisms.

Exclusion from Registration Systems and Discrimination on the Basis of Law

Rights and statuses that make up legal identity are to a large degree determined by underlying law, which may be exclusionary or discriminatory prima facie, or, when translated into registry systems, may produce such a result. Minimizing the risks posed by registration and documentation requires going beyond the immediate systems to understand the broader legal framework and how it operates in the existing social and political context. Thus the promotion of IRD systems cannot be discussed without also examining the laws that convey or deny rights, as such systems will likely reinforce underlying legal (and social) frameworks.

One fundamental right is citizenship, which is determined by law. Citizenship laws are by their nature exclusionary, but some prove to be more arbitrary or inequitable than others. In some countries, as a matter of law, a child can be registered only by his or her father. In these countries, a woman who is not married or is married to a nonnational may be unable to register her child as a citizen. This may also be the case if the father refuses to acknowledge paternity. In addition to individuals, entire groups may be denied citizenship and relegated to statelessness by IRD systems overlaid on exclusionary legal-political frameworks, as the following examples show.

- In China, *heihaizi* ("black children") born in violation of the one-child policy are unable to obtain a *hukou* (household identity registration record) and are thus denied access to education, health care, and even legal standing to be heard in court. Migrant workers registered in their place of birth are unable to register in their place of employment and are therefore unable to access health care and other rights.[34]

34 In Shenzhen and other large Chinese cities at the height of the AIDS pandemic, rural migrants to urban areas who were unable to secure urban *hukous* were treated as "biological noncitizens." See K. Mason, "Mobile Migrants, Mobile Germs: Migration, Contagion and Boundary-Building in Shenzhen, China after SARS," *Medical Anthropology: Cross-Cultural Studies in Health and Illness* 31, no. 2 (2011): 113–131. Also ineligible for health care, rural migrants contributed to the transmission and spread of the virus both within and outside migrant communities. See K. W. Todrys and J. Amon, "Within but Without: Human Rights and Access to HIV Prevention and Treatment for Internal Migrants," *Globalization and Health* 5, no. 17 (2009).

- The Dominican Republic is moving forward to deport thousands of long-standing residents of Haitian descent after a 2013 court ruling stripped children of Haitian migrants of nationality, birth certificates, and other documents. A 2014 law providing two-year temporary status (upon furnishing a birth certificate) was passed in response to international outcry, but only a small percentage of eligible individuals were able to take advantage of this provision, raising important issues concerning documentation.
- In Myanmar, authorities view the Muslim Rohingya as illegal immigrants despite the fact that most have lived in the Buddhist-majority country for generations. Around 800,000 stateless Rohingya in Myanmar are currently denied citizenship rights (officially since 1982) and face severe restrictions on marriage, employment, health care, and education. Approximately 30,000 Rohingya refugees currently housed in Bangladeshi refugee camps are being resettled to a barren, 10-year-old sedimentary island in the Bay of Bengal, Thengar Char. It is symbolic that the island, prone to flooding, does not appear on most maps.[35]

Discriminatory effects may also occur within the intersections of IRD systems, law, and national policy. Transgender and intersex individuals compose particularly vulnerable populations whose standing and access to entitlements are put at risk by the uncertain treatment of their legal identity by some IRD systems. A 2011 U.S. National Transgender Discrimination Survey of more than 6,400 transgender and gender-nonconforming people revealed that fully one third of individuals in the United States who had transitioned gender had not successfully updated any of their identification documents or records, and only 21 percent of such individuals were able to update all of their records.[36] In all, 41 percent live with driver's licenses that do not match their gender identity. In addition to harassment—40 percent of those required to present non-gender-matching IDs report harassment—transgender and intersex individuals who have not updated their documents may be denied basic rights and economic opportunities. For example, they may be unable to fly in the United States if their driver's license (or other identifying document) is refused by an airport Transportation Safety Administration officer, or may be unable to secure a car loan.

On the positive side, global law reform trends (including a notable push in South America and Europe) demonstrate a concerted effort to address prior legal lacunae and ensure that IRD systems do not contravene individual gender identity.[37] Laws and court rulings in Uruguay, Ecuador, and Peru, among

---

35 "Exile Islands," *Economist*, July 25, 2015.

36 National Center for Transgender Equality, "National Transgender Discrimination Survey" (2011), http://transequality.org/issues/national-transgender-discrimination-survey.

37 P. Dunne, "Respecting Trans* Identities: Recent Movements for the Legal Recognition of Gender Identity in Latin America," *LGBTQ Policy Journal* (October 21, 2013), http://www.hkslgbtq.com/respecting-trans-identities-recent-movements-for-the-legal-recognition-of-gender-identity-in-latin-america.

other countries, have expressly enabled individuals to amend their name and gender in registries and documents.[38] Argentina's 2012 Gender Identity and Health Comprehensive Care for Transgender People Act has since established a progressive standard of self-identification akin to several European models.[39] In other jurisdictions yet to embrace the self-identification approach, statutorily established limits on, or requirements for, gender reidentification endure, including the mandatory intervention of a medical officer, a gender dysphoria diagnosis or evidence of a sex change operation, and limits on name changes to those falling within traditional gender categories.[40]

The examples do not speak to any intrinsic perniciousness in IRD systems. Rather, they serve as a reminder that IRD systems are at their core "mirror[s] on society."[41] As with many other systems with ostensibly technical functions and technological credentials, they can, for better or worse, reinforce existing patterns, norms, and vulnerabilities. There is a corresponding need for governments and development partners to rigorously assess these underlying frameworks or risk inadvertently undermining the development prospects of certain populations.

Exclusion from Services and Discrimination in the Absence of Registration and/or Documentation

The push for enhanced IRD systems is often accompanied by new rules mandating registration and/or documentation to gain access to basic entitlements, including health care and education. One motivation for tying services to registration is to make large-scale service delivery more manageable and less subject to abuse; another is to incentivize people to get registered. But if entitlements are inflexibly tied to untested IRD systems, there is a risk of excluding vulnerable populations from essential services. For example, in Kenya a policy was introduced requiring students to provide a birth certificate in order to take exams as a means of increasing the number of children with documentation. As a result, Nubian children born in Kenya, who are less likely to have their births registered (owing to stringent requirements and discretionary

---

38 Ibid.; Ley No 18.620, "Derecho a la Identidad de Genero y al Cambio de Nombre y Sexo en Documentos Identificatorios," November 17, 2009 (Uruguay, No. 27858), http://www.parlamento.gub.uy/leyes/AccesoTextoLey.asp?Ley=18620&Anchor=; "Justicia admitió pedido de Fiorella Cava para cambiar legalmente de nombre y de sexo," *El Comercio,* August 4, 2012, http://elcomercio.pe/luces/musica/poder-judicial-admitio-pedido-fiorella-cava-cambiar-nombre-sexo-noticia-1450987; and "Transgéneros, con nueva identidad," *El Universo,* March 7, 2009, http://www.eluniverso.com/2009/03/07/1/1445/57F0EA89F0B1405185AAE883673D4C24.html.

39 "The Argentinean Gender Identity and Health Comprehensive Care for Transgender People Act," (Decree No. 773/12, of Gender Identity Act No. 26.743), http://www.infoleg.gov.ar/infolegInternet/anexos/195000-199999/197860/norma.htm (English translation: http://globaltransaction.files.wordpress.com/2012/05/argentina-gender-identity-law.pdf).

40 Dunne, "Respecting Trans* Identities."

41 C. Cummings and T. O'Neil, *Do Digital Information and Communications Technologies Increase the Voice and Influence of Women and Girls? A Rapid Review of the Evidence* (London: Overseas Development Institute, 2015), http://www.odi.org/publications/9499-women-icts.

implementation), were denied educational access and advancement.[42] In this and similar scenarios, what is particularly troubling is that those who cannot register or obtain documents are likely to be the same people who already have difficulty accessing basic rights and essential services. Consider, for example, Indonesia, where possession of a birth certificate varies considerably with household income; 46 percent of children from families in the poorest quintile do not have a birth certificate, compared with 10.6 percent in the richest quintile.[43] There is no significant difference between girls and boys, but the percentage of children without a certificate in rural areas is double that in urban areas, and children are less likely to have a certificate if they are disabled or if their parents and grandparents also did not have a birth certificate.

In other words, the "tied" deployment of IRD systems, which aims to extend service and benefit delivery to previously underserved individuals, may perpetuate the exclusion of these individuals unless corresponding mitigation measures are put in place. In Vietnam, access to social services is closely linked to civil registration. This has exposed nonregistered individuals, particularly children and individuals from migrant families, to "multiple institutionalised vulnerabilities and risks."[44] In all, 70 percent of spontaneous migrants who approached employers in the formal sector were rejected because they did not have *hokhau* (household registration) in the city, leaving the vast majority of migrant workers in precarious and temporary jobs.[45] Even in high-income countries with high registration levels, marginalized populations (such as Australia's Aborigines) have significantly lower registration rates, which may frustrate access to education and other basic services.[46]

---

42 Apland et al., *Birth Registration and Children's Rights*; and NAMATI, "Implementation of Nubian Minors v. Kenya" (NAMATI, Washington, DC, 2014). By contrast, in Indonesia, despite policies mandating the presentation of a birth certificate for school enrollment, most schools will accept students who can submit an alternative form of identification. Research found that 74 percent of children who have never attended school do not have a birth certificate, but very few respondents reported the lack of a birth certificate as the reason for the child not attending school (0.8 percent) or having been enrolled previously but not currently (2 percent). See Australian Indonesia Partnership for Justice (AIPJ), *AIPJ Baseline Study on Legal Identity: Indonesia's Missing Millions* (Jakarta: AIPJ, 2014), http://www.aipj.or.id/uploads/reports_publication/8_f_20140227-011003_FA_baseline_report_english.pdf). In Bangladesh, although birth certificates are required for access to health care and education, health workers are trained not to deny services to unregistered children but instead to link them to the local registrar. See M. Muzzi, *UNICEF Good Practices in Integrating Birth Registration into Health Systems (2000–2009): Case Studies: Bangladesh, Brazil, The Gambia and Delhi, India,* working paper (UNICEF, New York, 2010).

43 AIPJ, *AIPJ Baseline Study on Legal Identity.*

44 L. Duong, T. Linh, and N. Thao, *Social Protection for Rural-Urban Migrants in Vietnam: Current Situation, Challenges and Opportunities,* CSP Research Report 08 (Brighton, England: Centre for Social Protection/Institute of Development Studies, 2011), http://www.ids.ac.uk/publication/social-protection-for-rural-urban-migrants-in-vietnam-current-situation-challenges-and-opportunities.

45 Ibid.

46 J. Topsfield. "Aborigines Lack Proof of Identity." *Sydney Morning Herald,* January 23, 2009, http://www.smh.com.au/national/aborigines-lack-proof-of-identity-20090122-7nx3.html.

There are any number of reasons why citizens may not possess documentation. Citizen distrust of government is one. Exclusion from registry systems, whether due to discrimination or otherwise, is another. Administration and informal fees can also pose a prohibitive financial barrier to participation. Residents of remote rural areas may have particular difficulty physically accessing or contacting intake centers. Papua New Guinea, for example, has one birth registration center to cover some 600 islands and 7 million people.[47] Complex procedures or inconsistent information may also preclude participation, and mundane reasons, such as an inability to replace lost, stolen, or damaged documents, contribute as well. There are also instances in which governments or nongovernmental organizations (NGOs) have advocated an increase in the number of people with identity documents, but underresourced government departments have been unable to sufficiently respond to increased demand, resulting in significant backlogs.[48] Elsewhere, poorly kept or inaccessible records can preclude registration, and, in particular, frustrate digitization. Depending on the country, gender-differentiated procedures may serve to amplify or mitigate disparate documentation rates and the related vulnerability and development impacts.[49]

Without documentation, individuals may face long-term hurdles to service provision, protection, and inclusion. Lacking documentation can also lead to a more immediate and seemingly absurd denial of such services. For example, the April 2015 earthquake that shook Nepal registered a 7.8 on the Richter scale, killed more than 9,000 people, and injured more than 23,000. Thousands of houses were destroyed, with possessions buried in the rubble. The government provided earthquake relief compensation for those whose houses had been destroyed beyond repair, as well as for those who had lost family members. This relief, though, was conditioned on applicants furnishing identification documents—documents that for many poor applicants seeking assistance were understandably buried under the rubble or otherwise lost, destroyed, or inaccessible.[50] In this chaotic scenario, many of Nepal's poorest

---

47 M. Dahan and L. Hanmer, "The Identification for Development (ID4D) Agenda: Its Potential for Empowering Women and Girls" (World Bank, Washington, DC, forthcoming), 11.

48 Muzzi, *UNICEF Good Practices*; and J. Miller, "Birth Registration and the Rights of the Child" (European Parliament Directorate-General for External Policies of the Union Policy Department, Brussels, 2007).

49 Dahan and Hanmer highlight examples of countries in which married women and married men face different procedural and/or substantive requirements to obtain a national identity card (in this case, in 9 countries: Benin, Cameroon, the Arab Republic of Egypt, Mauritius, Oman, Pakistan, Saudi Arabia, Senegal, and Togo); to confer citizenship on children (in 16 countries); and to apply for a passport (in 19 countries). They also make reference to a number of positive safeguards to address gender-specific vulnerabilities, ranging from Pakistan instituting "women only" registration days for voter IDs, to biometric authentication banking requirements in Malawi precluding male relatives from seizing control of a widow's assets on the death of the husband. See Dahan and Hanmer, "Identification for Development (ID4D) Agenda."

50 D. Tiwary, "Papers Lost, Earthquake Victims Unable to Claim Relief," *Times of India*, May 6, 2015, http://timesofindia.indiatimes.com/world/south-asia/Papers-lost-earthquake-victims-unable-to-claim-relief/articleshow/47169007.cms.

and most vulnerable families were unable to avail themselves of the social safety net intended to catch them because of this rigid conditioning of benefits on documentation.

For the foreseeable future and for a range of reasons, registration and documentation systems are unlikely to achieve universal population coverage. A push under the SDGs for universalization focusing on registering new births alone will exclude children and adults who have not already had their births registered; there are currently 750 million people younger than 16 without birth registration[51] and just as many (if not more) unregistered people 16 or older. Under these conditions, a push for universal birth registration for those younger than 5, when coupled with conditioning access to services on documentation, may *intensify exclusion* from basic rights and essential services. Governments and development partners confronting this possibility need to consider flexible protocols, including means of alternative identification and other strategies with which to mitigate exclusionary impacts.

Documentation Itself as Grounds for Exclusion

Even once registered and in possession of documentation, individuals face the risk that information contained in documents or the underlying registries may be used for discriminatory ends. This is especially the case when technical criteria (such as accuracy or efficiency) are not adequately balanced against rights principles (such as privacy or necessity). Registers and accompanying documentation may designate nationality, ethnicity, race, religion, place of birth, and other special statuses.[52] Ethnic classification on identity cards in Rwanda (first instituted by the Belgian colonial government) and the introduction of the "J stamp" on the identity cards of Jewish citizens of Germany in the 1930s are some of the most notorious reminders of how documentation may expose individuals to discrimination—and worse.

Today, although perhaps less insidiously, identity documents continue to contain information that may be used for discriminatory purposes. Identification cards highlighting nonindigenous origin may facilitate employment discrimination, as in the case of Ethiopian identity cards that point to the "previous [Eritrean] nationality" of Ethiopian citizens.[53] Even in more innocuous cases, such as when a person must provide documentation revealing his or her age to a potential employer or service provider, the resulting treatment of that person can be affected. Because of such risks, there is a need to determine whether the collection and disclosure of personal information inherent

---

51 Dunning, Gelb, and Raghavan, *Birth Registration, Legal Identity, and the Post-2015 Agenda.*

52 J. Fussell, "Group Classification on National ID Cards as a Factor in Genocide and Ethnic Cleansing" (paper presented to the Seminar Series of the Yale University Genocide Studies Program, New Haven, CT, November 15, 2001), http://www.genocidewatch.org/images/AboutGen_Group_Classification_on_National_ID_Cards.pdf.

53 Refugees International, "Ethiopia-Eritrea: Stalemate Takes Toll on Eritreans and Ethiopians of Eritrean Origin," *Refugees International Bulletin*, May 30, 2008, http://www.refugeesinternational.org/sites/default/files/Ethiopia_stateless0530.pdf.

in registration and documentation systems such as these are narrowly tailored to a clearly defined development end. This in turn raises important issues of personal information protection.

Securing Data and Privacy Rights

Another risk involved in expanding registration systems is that governments, authorized third parties, and unauthorized individuals may use them for surveillance, private data harvesting, or other functions (licit and illicit alike), violating individual rights. The increased collection of personal data also risks implicit or explicit "function creep," where data collected for one purpose are gradually used for others to which the individual has not consented.[54] In the United States, for example, citizens in the 1930s were once assured that social security numbers would be used only to track eligibility and contributions, yet these numbers are now used for a wide range of purposes by both public and private entities. Of equal concern are security breaches and unauthorized intrusions on private data.

These concerns—and the potential for harm—are heightened by the so-called aggregation effect. In combination, otherwise innocuous individual pieces of information may paint a portrait of personalities, physical and health characteristics, preferred activities, and individual attributes, greatly increasing an individual's vulnerability to dangers, such as targeted discrimination (both public and private), intrusive surveillance, identity fraud, stalking, or harassment.[55] Such system aggregation and integration make it more difficult for IRD systems to implement fair information principles, such as purpose specification or collection and use limitation. At the same time, *private* aggregation of a range of public and private data can be equally, if not more, problematic, having been used, for instance, to deny or limit the provision of health services to the neediest in private insurance–based systems. Elsewhere, police and civil liberties groups debate the constitutionality of facial recognition programs, which rely on passport and driver's license photos and are used in nonconsensual public video surveillance.

Particularly where trust between citizens and the state is weak, concerns regarding privacy and good faith use may seriously curtail the ability of the government to promote the use of IRD systems. Citizen-state distrust may also contribute to the decision of citizens to "opt out," that is, withhold information or intentionally misrepresent information, further undermining the ability of the IRD systems to deliver on their development promise.

In designing and strengthening IRD systems, steps must be taken to mitigate these risks and to safeguard personal information. Beyond committing to privacy and data security standards, due diligence (including politically

---

54 World Bank and WHO, "Global Civil Registration and Vital Statistics," 51.

55 To the extent that online digital data may be easier to manipulate or are stored in extraterritorial cloud platform data centers, digitization may create additional vulnerabilities.

astute privacy impact assessments) is an essential process for understanding and addressing the interaction of an IRD system with a country's broader legal-regulatory framework. Can police resort to biometric registry data in lieu of observing due process in criminal investigations? Might registration unintentionally entrench or amplify the discriminatory effects of previously unconsidered statutes, regulations, or jurisprudence? Although basic principles, such as those contained in the Fair Information Practice Principles of the Organisation for Economic Co-operation and Development and in the position paper "The Right to Privacy in the Digital Age"[56] by the United Nations Office of the High Commissioner for Human Rights (OHCHR), are an important starting point, their effective interpretation and application rest on an understanding of a country's underlying laws, institutions, politics, and socioeconomic dynamics.

Conclusion: Maximizing Development Benefits from Identification

IRD systems are important contributors to development, but they can also risk increasing or entrenching exclusion and discrimination for certain populations, especially those already vulnerable and marginalized. Far from amounting to a cry to abandon IRD expansion efforts, these concerns simply highlight the significant development improvements that attention, at low cost, to underlying dynamics and impacts can yield. These concerns also point to the need for both broader and deeper diligence in assessing the benefits and costs of IRD alternatives in a given context and in mitigating design and implementation risks. The performance and impact of IRD systems rest on the functioning of a series of other institutions—the law, implementing and oversight agencies, and grievance-redress channels, just to name a few. Investing in a more thorough understanding of the interplay between these institutions can yield as much, if not more, than spending on cutting-edge technology. This is especially true in fragile and low-income states where technological literacy is low and access to electricity and Internet connectivity is unreliable.

Beyond this need for initial diligence, the analysis suggests several other principles to enhance the development impacts of IRD programs:

- Be clear about the particular development outcomes that an enhanced IRD system seeks to address, and ensure that impact evaluations are undertaken to determine whether such benefits—or any unintended negative outcomes—ensue.
- Beginning with a political analysis of the legal framework and its application, forecast the likely impacts of enhanced IRD systems on the poorest and most marginalized, and establish measures to include those most

56 Office of the High Commissioner for Human Rights (OHCHR), "The Right to Privacy in the Digital Age" (OHCHR, Geneva, 2014), http://www.ohchr.org/EN/Issues/DigitalAge/Pages/DigitalAgeIndex.aspx.

likely to be otherwise excluded and to mitigate against them being made worse off.

- Weigh seriously the risks of exclusion if considering mandatory requirements for registration or documentation to gain access to essential services (such as health care and education).
- Conduct a "privacy (data protection) impact assessment"[57] to assess what, how, and why personally identifiable information is to be collected, used, accessed, shared, and stored. Narrowly tailor information collection and management protocols to development objectives, and, as warranted, apply additional restrictions on special categories of data, such as health, national origin, race, or other affiliations.
- Supplement registration data with population or household data to ensure that planning and policy do not "doubly exclude" by overlooking the needs of those who have not been able to register.
- Ensure that grievance-redress systems (and legal advice for using such systems) are in place to challenge cases in which registration is improperly denied, the lack of registration or documentation is unjustifiably or arbitrarily used to block or limit basic services, or registration data are used inappropriately.

---

57 R. Gellman, *Privacy and Biometric ID Systems: An Approach Using Fair Information Practices for Developing Countries,* Policy Paper 028 (Washington, DC: Center for Global Development, 2013).

PART II

Financing

6

Education Financing

Utilizing Next-Generation Impact Bond Structures and Legal Agreements

JASPER KIM

The United Nations Millennium Development Goals (MDGs) proclaim that universal primary education is a fundamentally important aspect of both individual and global development.[1] Basic education, as well as teacher training aimed at adults teaching children, has been reinforced through post-2015 development agenda efforts, including the United Nations' Education for All (EFA) initiative. Notable economists, such as Dani Rodrik, have commented on the recent development policy shift—away from promoting savings and capital accumulation and toward increasing human capital through better education—in answer to the policy problems surrounding improving education.[2] However, with budget constraints at both the national and the international levels, acquiring scarce funding for education projects has reached a critical stage, giving rise to questions about how to find innovative solutions to secure it.

The EFA Global Monitoring Report has demonstrated that basic education is underfunded by $26 million.[3] In most developing countries, the need

---

The author would like to thank Minjae Lee (Graduate School of International Studies, Ewha Womans University) for her invaluable research efforts relating to this chapter.

1 The United Nations' *Millennium Development Goals and Beyond 2015* states the following in "Goal 2: Achieve Universal Primary Education":

> Target 2.A: Ensure that, by 2015, children everywhere, boys and girls alike, will be able to complete a full course of primary schooling
>
> - Enrolment in primary education in developing regions reached 91 per cent in 2015, up from 83 per cent in 2000.
> - In 2015, 57 million children of primary school age were out of school.
> - Among youth aged 15 to 24, the literacy rate has improved globally from 83 per cent to 91 per cent between 1990 and 2015, and the gap between women and men has narrowed.
> - In the developing regions, children in the poorest households are four times as likely to be out of school as those in the richest households.
> - In countries affected by conflict, the proportion of out-of-school children increased from 30 per cent in 1999 to 36 per cent in 2012.

2 Ricardo Hausmann, Dani Rodrik, and Andres Velasco, "Getting the Diagnosis Right: A New Approach to Economic Reform," *Finance and Development (IMF)* 43, no. 1 (March 2006): http://www.imf.org/external/pubs/ft/fandd/2006/03/hausmann.htm.

3 UNESCO, *Teaching and Learning: Achieving Quality for All* (EFA Global Monitoring Report, 2013–2014, UNESCO, Paris, 2014). All dollar amounts in this chapter are given in U.S. dollars.

for basic education began to be more widely accepted only after the proclamation of the 1948 Universal Declaration of Human Rights.[4] A huge educational gap of approximately 100 years exists between developed and developing countries; more than 1.6 billion people in developing regions will need more than 85 years to reach the educational levels that the developed regions are at today.[5]

The lack of teachers and institutes to train teachers constitutes another impediment for developing regions. The total number of teachers needed by 2030 for the world's most populous countries—Bangladesh, Brazil, China, the Arab Republic of Egypt, India, Indonesia, Mexico, Nigeria, and Pakistan—is estimated at more than 7 million. Sub-Saharan Africa needs 6.2 million teachers to ensure that classroom sizes do not exceed 40 pupils per teacher.[6] Another challenge—teachers not sufficiently qualified to teach because of the lack of teacher training and resources—is related to the problem of students exceeding the number of available qualified teachers.

To meet such challenges, numerous intergovernmental organizations (IGOs), such as the United Nations Children's Fund (UNICEF) and the United Nations Educational, Scientific and Cultural Organization (UNESCO), are focusing their efforts squarely on children's education in developing regions. But it is estimated that at least $22–50 billion per year is needed to ensure

---

4 The United Nations Declaration of Human Rights Preamble states the following:

> Now, Therefore THE GENERAL ASSEMBLY proclaims THIS UNIVERSAL DECLARATION OF HUMAN RIGHTS as a common standard of achievement for all peoples and all nations, to the end that every individual and every organ of society, keeping this Declaration constantly in mind, shall strive by teaching and education to promote respect for these rights and freedoms and by progressive measures, national and international, to secure their universal and effective recognition and observance, both among the peoples of Member States themselves and among the peoples of territories under their jurisdiction.

Moreover, Article 26 states:

> (1) Everyone has the right to education. Education shall be free, at least in the elementary and fundamental stages. Elementary education shall be compulsory. Technical and professional education shall be made generally available and higher education shall be equally accessible to all on the basis of merit.
>
> (2) Education shall be directed to the full development of the human personality and to the strengthening of respect for human rights and fundamental freedoms. It shall promote understanding, tolerance and friendship among all nations, racial or religious groups, and shall further the activities of the United Nations for the maintenance of peace.
>
> (3) Parents have a prior right to choose the kind of education that shall be given to their children.

5 Rebecca Winthrop, "Global '100-Year Gap' in Education Standards," *Education Plus Development* (blog), Brookings Institution, Washington, DC, April 29, 2015.

6 UNESCO, Institute for Statistics, "Wanted: Trained Teachers to Ensure Every Child's Right to Primary Education," Policy Paper 15/Fact Sheet 30 (UNESCO, Paris, 2014), 2.

that every child receives a quality education at the preprimary, primary, and lower-secondary level by 2030.[7]

The need for innovative education financing is also based on recent macro-level data suggesting that, although in absolute terms aid increased in recent years, it failed to increase in *relative* terms. In 2001, for example, aid flows fell to 0.22 percent of gross national income (GNI) of member states of the Organisation for Economic Co-operation and Development (OECD), down from 0.33 percent in 1992.[8] Moreover, although aid to social sectors increased overall in the 2000s, the relevant share allocated to education *fell* from 10.2 percent in the 1990s to 8 percent in the 2000s. This drop occurred despite the fact that between 2001 and 2012 the share of total aid going to the least developed countries increased from 40 percent to 51 percent.[9]

The benefits of financing education projects include the following:

- *Reduction in unneeded deaths.* As of 2013, 40 percent of children in the developing world live in extreme poverty, and 10.5 million children under the age of five die from preventable diseases each year. By providing development and education financing, innumerable lives would be saved. Children living in poverty would then receive a chance to be educated and eventually join the workforce to further economic and social development.[10]
- *Economic growth in developing countries.* It is estimated that by increasing a specific metric, such as literacy rates for children, poverty in low-income countries would drop by 12 percent. Thus, the impact of increasing literacy rates in developing countries would be significant. Investing in education in disadvantaged countries could boost Sub-Saharan Africa agricultural output by 25 percent.[11]
- *Promotion of girls' and women's rights.* In Africa, 28 million girls do not attend school, and many will never enter a classroom.[12] Educating girls reduces youth marriage rates, which in turn lowers youth pregnancy, affording young girls a better chance to attend school and receive a basic education.[13]

To help developing countries and regions become more self-sustaining, a means of attracting alternative education funding is needed. Given the large

---

7 UNESCO, *Education for All 2000–2015: Achievements and Challenges* (EFA Global Monitoring Report, UNESCO, Paris, 2015), 296.

8 Ibid., 25.

9 Ibid.

10 Global Partnership for Education, "Strategic Plan, 2012–2015" (2013), 7, http://www.global partnership.org/content/strategic-plan-2012-2015.

11 Ibid.

12 UNESCO, "Girls' Education in Africa" (UNESCO, Paris, 2015), http://www.uis.unesco.org/_LAYOUTS/UNESCO/no-girl-left-behind/index.html#cover-intro-0.

13 UNESCO, "Girls' Education: The Facts" (UNESCO, Paris, 2013), http://en.unesco.org/gem-report/sites/gem-report/files/girls-factsheet-en.pdf.

populations of developing countries, education in those countries will have an immediate impact not only on individual countries but also on a global scale.

Providing education-based resources should not be the sole responsibility of the public sector. The private sector should also play a part in securing greater funding for education, which generates many positive economic and social spillover effects. But how can interested parties, such as states, non-profit organizations (NPOs), and IGOs, collaborate with private sector entities to secure scarce funding for education projects?

OECD data demonstrate a clear downward trend in total official development assistance (ODA) to the education sector from donors. For example, in 2009, education aid commitments amounted to $15.7 billion, compared with $13.1 billion in 2012, a $2.6 billion decrease in just three years.

Moreover, education ODA as a share of total aid has consistently lagged behind health and population programs, while also similarly reflecting a downward trend. For example, in 2009, ODA for health and population programs represented 12.2 percent of total aid, compared with 8.7 percent for education in the same year.[14] Although aid for health and population programs increased from 12.2 percent in 2009 to 12.9 percent in 2012 (increasing steadily every year), the opposite trend occurred in the area of education, which received 7.7 percent of total aid in 2012 as compared with 8.7 percent in 2009, the percentage decreasing steadily every year.[15]

If the targets for education in the post-2015 development agenda are to be met, more educational funding is needed, not less. Why not then simply issue bonds as a remedy? In short, bonds issued by sovereign issuers would increase debt to gross domestic product (GDP) ratios, which in turn could negatively impact credit ratings for the country in question, thus raising the price of financing overall for the sovereign issuer. Even at the IGO level, a crowding-out effect exists in which a critical issue arises: What sectors will be funded with scarce donor funds? If the OECD data pattern extends to bond issuances, education financing may again face relatively less funding as compared with other social programs.

This chapter proposes a solution that can be implemented through a market-based public-private partnership (PPP): social impact bonds (SIBs), also known as development impact bonds (DIBs),[16] which are a subset of the

---

14 UNESCO, "Domestic and External Financing for Education" (UNESCO 2012).

15 Ibid.

16 DIBs build on the current-generation (existing) SIB framework, typically by providing cross-border funding to projects, including education projects, in developing nations. In contrast to DIBs, SIBs thus far have been generally domestic in nature (case studies are provided later in this chapter). Because this chapter focuses on the *funding* of education projects, rather than the *use* of such funding, and because SIBs and DIBs overlap to such a large degree, the term "SIB/DIB" is used, while the author fully recognizes that subtle nuances may exist between the two entities.

social finance field as well as the finance, law, and development fields.[17] From a legal purview, SIBs and DIBs are a series of interrelated contracts that secure funding in an innovative, market-based manner. From a social finance purview, SIBs and DIBs are a bond-driven funding mechanism between public and private sector parties.[18] In the SIB/DIB structure, two parties take opposite positions in regard to "success metrics"—with one party providing education financing if the designated project is deemed successful, and a counterparty providing education financing if the project is deemed as not successful—for measuring the funding of a socially beneficial/development-oriented project.

Current-Generation Social and Development Impact Bonds

SIBs and DIBs (hereafter referred to as "SIB/DIB") can be utilized to secure funding for a particular education project.[19] In the SIB/DIB structure, the SIB/DIB investors (often referred to as "social impact investors" because both economic and societal returns are considered) provide complete up-front funding for a designated education project until the project is deemed either successful or not. If deemed successful, SIB/DIB social investors are typically repaid with principal and interest, thus making the education funding transaction a "performance-based" or "pay-for-success" education funding structure. In such a funding transaction, measurement and returns are based on one or more "success" metrics predetermined in a contractually binding agreement prior to the implementation of the chosen education project.[20] SIBs/DIBs have thus far been used in reducing homelessness and recidivism and in building infrastructure, including in Europe and the United States. However, and notably, the use of SIBs/DIBs can extend to other social benefits and causes, such as issues facing funding shortages within the education sector.[21]

SIB/DIB Transaction Components and Participants

In broad terms, the main legal SIB/DIB stakeholders (social and financial networks) include the following:

---

17 Nicholas Burnett, "Strategies for Financing of Education: A Global View" (paper presented at the International Working Group on Education [IWGE] conference held at UNESCO's International Institute for Educational Planning, Paris, June 7–9, 2010), http://www.resultsfordevelopment.org/sites/resultsfordevelopment.org/files/resources/Strategies%20for%20Financing%20of%20Education.pdf.

18 Scholars such as Kevin E. Davis have noted the importance of financial capital as a determinant in the field of development and growth. Davis argues for a more "holistic" approach, noting the significance of not drawing "sharp distinctions" between transactions involving public parties and those involving private parties. See Kevin E. Davis, "Financing Development as a Field of Practice, Study and Innovation," *Acta Juridica* 168 (2009): http://papers.ssrn.com/sol3/papers.cfm?abstract_id=1341291.

19 Mildred E. Warner, "Private Finance for Public Goods: Social Impact Bonds," *Journal of Economic Policy Reform* (2013): http://s3.amazonaws.com/mildredwarner.org/attachments/000/000/413/original/d116aef904347207d0dd8d5916616045.

20 Ibid.

21 Ibid.

- Social impact investors
- Intermediary
- Government (or IGO)
- Service provider
- Assessor/evaluator
- Constituents (assistance project, program, or persons)
- Local community/society at large
- Advisers

The project is initially funded by SIB/DIB *social impact investors*, who may be, but are not limited to being, individual philanthropists, philanthropic organizations, pension funds, mutual funds, high-net-worth individuals, insurance companies, or financial institution investors.[22] The government (or IGO) is a key SIB/DIB party, which repays principal and interest to the social impact investors if the education project is deemed unsuccessful.

Another key component is an *intermediary*, the entity that connects all the stakeholders involved. The intermediary issues structured bonds[23] to investors from contracts with the government and other funders and hires service providers to carry out the project.[24] The intermediary can be a special-purpose entity established by either a private or public sector[25] financially skilled institution (but a government entity can also serve as an intermediary).

If the project is successful, the *government* (or IGO) will step in and repay the social impact investors, with interest paid.

The *service provider* is the entity—often an NGO or NPO, but in some cases a state entity—that provides the relevant education facility or program.

An independent *evaluator* is also one of the parties within the SIB/DIB structure. The evaluator's mandate is to determine whether the SIB/DIB has met its stated objectives (i.e., whether the success metric was or was not achieved). If the independent evaluator's conclusion is that the stated

---

22 John Loder, "The Promise of Social Impact Bonds," *Social Space* (2011): 42–47, http://ink.library.smu.edu.sg/cgi/viewcontent.cgi?article=1087&context=lien_research.

23 The term "structured bonds" is used because social impact bonds are a form of structured (i.e., more complex) bond issuance. That is, a structured bond is typically a bond or stock that includes a derivative product, which alters the bond's risk/payout profile. In contrast, a "plain vanilla" bond typically features a plain bond, such as a five-year note yielding 5 percent annually, that does not include (embed) a derivative product altering its risk/payout.

24 Haley Sinklair, "Social Impact Bonds: A Public-Private Partnership That Benefits All?" (MacIver Institute, Madison, WI, 2013), http://www.maciverinstitute.com/2013/11/social-impact-bonds-a-public-private-partnership-that-benefits-all/.

25 The choice of public or private sector intermediaries is per the parties' agreement, as reflected in the relevant contractual arrangements.

objectives have been achieved, then the social impact investors are repaid the principal plus interest.[26]

The target group or groups for which the education project is being funded by SIBs/DIBs, often referred to as *constituents*, are key stakeholders in the SIB/DIB model, and play the role of an end-client for the SIB/DIB funding transaction.[27] The constituents are, in essence, the core concern of the stakeholders involved in the SIB/DIB program, because the constituents are the target audience for which financing is being sought for a particular education project. The constituents are a subset of the *local community*, which would also benefit from the education project being financed through SIBs/DIBs.

Advisers are also part of the SIB/DIB and smart social capital structure, providing guidance and advice relating to setting and implementing the SIB/DIB's performance criteria (metrics), particularly between the service provider and social impact investors. Unlike the evaluation advisers, who play a relatively active, hands-on role in day-to-day management, the independent evaluator's purpose is to be at an arm's length.

The following two diagrams illustrate how the SIB/DIB pieces fit together for the shared purpose of funding an education project. Figure 1 demonstrates how the intermediary, advisers, and evaluators work in conjunction with the

Figure 1. Current SIB/DIB structure

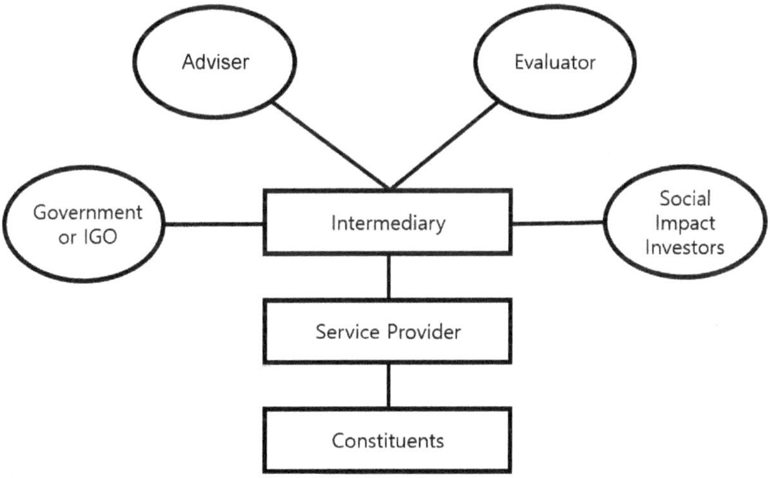

26 The SIB/DIB education-funding framework allows the government to save funds and provides a safety net for the private sector. The incentive- and performance-based SIB/DIB funding model allows social impact investors to receive a return that has both monetary and social value, while NGOs and other service providers gain efficiency and capacity in providing their services to constituents, which are then able to enhance the direct effects of the given educational project. The community is also able to benefit by receiving funding for higher quality education. The SIB/DIB model is evidence based and enhances transparency by using an external evaluator.

27 Ibid.

social impact investors and the government (or IGO). Figure 2 shows the shared interests of the SIB/DIB parties.

Figure 2. Shared interests (shaded) of stakeholders

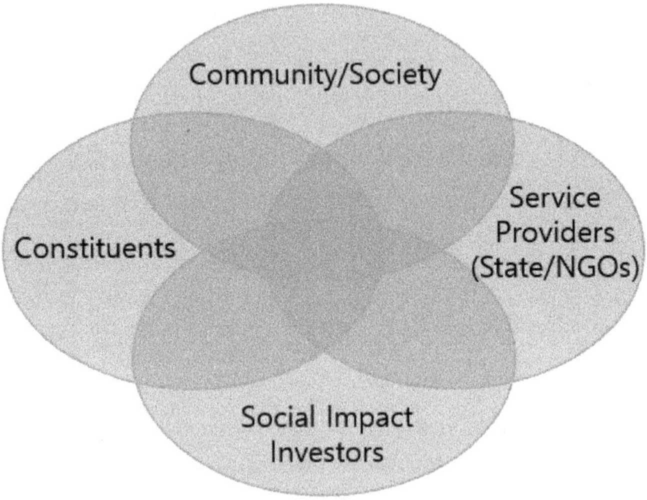

As an example of how the preceding SIB/DIB model might work for stakeholders, suppose a local government is willing to pay up to $1 million to increase graduation rates in girls' education in a fictional developing country, Alba. With all the stakeholders involved, a specific success metric is agreed on. Suppose the success metric is then further specified as $1 million in total payments to increase graduation rates to 80 percent by the year 2020 at the Girls' Generation Elementary School (GGES) in the country of Alba. The constituents are the girls attending GGES who will graduate in the year 2020. The service provider is the Ministry of Education of Alba. The social impact investor is an impact investment firm called Impact Investor. The intermediary could be Alba or an entity domiciled in Alba or elsewhere that is capable of issuing SIBs/DIBs. The adviser could be an organization, such as Social Finance, that has the requisite expertise for dealing with SIBs/DIBs. The evaluator could be a large accounting firm, such as KPMG. The local community and society at large would be the city and province in which GGES is located, and more broadly, Alba, and, most broadly, the international community, because a better educated population is beneficial at all levels.

As for the structure dynamics, let us suppose that the stakeholders agree that the SIBs/DIBs will be composed of $900,000 in principal and $100,000 in interest (the latter to be disbursed in a one-lump-sum payment at maturity in 2020). Upon issuance of the SIB/DIB, impact investor purchases all the SIBs/DIBs for $900,000 (the principal amount). This amount ($900,000, funded by impact investors) is then given directly to GGES for its graduate improvement rate program. Thus, the impact investor is the party that initially funds the entire education project. In 2020, the external evaluator, KPMG, in cooperation with all the stakeholders, but particularly GGES and the Ministry of Education (the service provider), gathers, verifies, and calculates the relevant data to determine the success metric (i.e., whether 80 percent or more of the class of has 2020 graduated). If the success metric has been met or exceeded, then the impact investors would receive $900,000 (principal) plus $100,000 (interest) for a total of $1 million. If the success metric has not been met, the impact investor could lose some or all of its investment amount (including principal and interest, based on the terms agreed on prior to the education project by the relevant stakeholders).

SIB/DIB Case Studies

The world's first global SIB project was implemented by the United Kingdom in fall 2010 as part of a program that aimed to reduce recidivism in Peterborough Prison.[28] According to Social Finance, experienced social organizations supported 3,000 short-term prisoners during a six-year period beginning inside the prison and extending to after release. The individuals were helped with transitioning back into society. The agreement involved a return for investors through a share of the government's savings if the program reduced reconviction rates by 7.5 percent or more. With reductions of reconviction rates greater than 7.5 percent, the project's social impact investors would receive an increasing return of up to 13 percent in correlation with the achieved success of the social outcome.[29] The results demonstrated a 6 percent decrease in the frequency of reconviction for 100 Peterborough prisoners in the time frame 2008–2010 to 2010–2012.[30] The overall decline was calculated to be 23 percent, making the project a notable instance of a successful use of SIBs/DIBs.[31]

In the United States, social impact bonds were used in 2012, when Goldman Sachs Bank invested $9.6 million in a social program project providing therapeutic services to 16-to-18-year-old youths incarcerated in Rikers Island Prison.[32] With the New York City Department of Corrections, Bloomberg Philanthropies, and social service providers, such as the Osborne Association and MDRC,[33] an SIB structure was created in the hope of reducing recidivism (i.e.,

---

28 Social Finance, "Peterborough Social Impact Bond Reduces Reoffending by 8.4%" (press release, August 7, 2014), http://www.socialfinance.org.uk/wp-content/uploads/2014/08/Peterborough-First-Cohort-Results.pdf.

29 Ibid.

30 U.K. Government Statistics, "Final Results for Cohorts 1 Payment-by-Results Prison Pilots" (Ministry of Justice, August 7, 2014), https://www.gov.uk/government/statistics/final-results-for-cohorts-1-payment-by-results-prison-pilots.

31 Ibid.

32 John Olson and Andrea Phillips, "Rikers Island: The First Social Impact Bond in the United States," *Community Development Investment Journal* (Federal Reserve Bank of San Francisco, April 2013), http://www.frbsf.org/community-development/publications/community-development-investment-review/2013/april/rikers-island-social-impact-bond/.

33 MDRC is a nonprofit organization that works to "improve programs and policies that affect the poor." See http://www.mdrc.org/about/about-mdrc-overview-0.

lessening the likelihood that formerly incarcerated individuals will be reincarcerated in the future). The loans would be repaid based on cost saving efforts. If recidivism fell by 10 percent, Goldman Sachs would earn as much as $2.6 million in premiums, whereas if the target rate was not met, Goldman Sachs would lose up to $2.4 million.[34] Thus, the private sector's pursuit of profit was converted to social good under the proposed SIB/DIB financing structure.[35] Other SIB/DIB projects have been undertaken in the U.S. states of California, Massachusetts, and Wisconsin.

In 2012 Instiglio, a nonprofit organization,[36] adapted the SIB framework to fund projects in developing regions, including an SIB funding program in Colombia to reduce school dropout rates.[37] In 2014 Instiglio, Educate Girls (an Indian NGO), the Children's Investment Fund Foundation (CIFF, an outcome payer), and the UBS Optimus Foundation (a DIB investor) launched the first DIB.[38] The objective was to increase girls' participation in school and in educational performance in rural India. The success metrics used are based on learning outcomes and enrollment, which will be assessed in 2017. If deemed successful, the UBS Optimus Foundation will receive its original investment amount (principal) plus interest. If deemed unsuccessful, it will, at a minimum, lose most or all of its interest payments on the DIBs.[39]

These and other examples illustrate the practical potential of SIBs/DIBs, but what do they look like when subject to a risk-benefit analysis?

SIB/DIB Structure: Risks vs. Benefits

How stakeholders determine whether to use SIBs/DIBs or other alternatives is a critical issue for practitioners, policy makers, and academics that raises the question of exactly what is meant by "other alternatives." Performance-based funding to a service provider that does not issue SIB/DIB bonds? Performance-based funding to a service provider that issues ordinary noncontingent (non-SIB/non-DIB) bonds? A fixed-price loan contract for the service provider (composed of principal and interest)? Or perhaps no education project whatsoever?

To simplify the analysis, the preceding funding options can be divided into three streams: (A) funding with SIBs/DIBs, (B) funding without SIBs/DIBs (e.g., noncontingent bonds and loans), and (C) no funding at all. Option A could arguably be viable if the following three minimum criteria are met:

---

34 Ibid.

35 Esma E. Deprez and Michelle Kaske, "Goldman Sachs Inmate Bet Fuels Social Impact Bonds: Muni Credit," *Bloomberg News*, August 21, 2012, http://www.bloomberg.com/news/2012-08-21/goldman-sachs-inmate-bet-fuels-social-impact-bonds-muni-credit.html.

36 Instiglio is a nonprofit based in Bogota, Colombia, that brings the SIB/DIB model to developing countries. See http://www.instiglio.org/en/our-mission/.

37 Instiglio, press release on development impact bonds, June 2014, http://www.instiglio.org/en/girls-education-india/.

38 Ibid.

39 Ibid.

(1) a minimum funding threshold amount of at least $1 million (ideally, substantially more, given the time, experience, and administrative costs involved); (2) the parties (stakeholders) are or can become familiar with structured bond issuances (such as those involved in a typical SIB/DIB) to understand the SIB/DIB structure's benefits and risks; and (3) the education project can provide verifiable data to the external evaluator and other related stakeholders to calculate and assess the relevant success metric.

In all other cases, options B and C may be more worth pursuing in terms of securing education financing when using a cost-benefit analysis. As discussed in the next section, notable risks involved in issuing SIBs/DIBs must be weighed against the potential benefits of using SIBs/DIBs.[40]

The following two sections—the first assessing the risks, the second assessing the benefits—are based on the assumption that these three criteria have been satisfied.

Potential Risks

Several potential risks exist with the SIB/DIB structure.[41]

First, financial and default risks exist. In the SIB/DIB structure, education project funding is initially provided entirely by the private sector SIB investor. The funding may later be repaid, plus interest, if the project is successful. But a risk exists for both the private and the public sector participants that a lack of funding prevents the transaction from proceeding. Such risk is mitigated in the financial marketplace by risk-shifting techniques, such as credit default swaps.

The intermediary, evaluator, and swap/guarantee[42] features (along with the other parties in a typical SIB/DIB transaction) could potentially involve substantial fees, including administrative costs,[43] for the services of the intermediary, adviser, and other related parties. Such fees should be weighed

---

40 One way of conducting the requisite analysis is by asking whether bonds have been issued in the past for a particular or similar education project. After all, not every project or entity has the scale and scope to issue bonds in the marketplace.

41 For an insightful overview of related intervention and execution risks, in addition to intermediary, political, financial, and reputation risks, see Deborah Burand, "Globalizing Social Finance: How Social Impact Bonds and Social Impact Performance Guarantees Can Scale Development," *NYU Journal of Law and Business* 9, no. 2 (2012): 447, http://www.nyujlb.org/wp-content/uploads/nyb_9-2_447-502_Burand.pdf.

42 A swap is a derivative financial contract in which parties exchange financial instruments, thus affecting future potential risks and payouts for the parties involved. A guarantee ensures that the liabilities of a designated debtor will be met by the guarantor in the event the debtor fails to meet certain payment events.

43 Related fees vary greatly, depending on the particular education project. In the case of financial engineering fees, and as mentioned in a subsequent section of this chapter, often such amounts are expressed and paid for as a percentage of the relevant funding (principal) amount. From another perspective, in terms of administrative fees for finance and development projects based in Sub-Saharan Africa, a Seoul-based IGO representative informed the author that a 7 percentage point fee (of the project amount) as a base rate is often initially assumed and then subsequently adjusted as needed.

against the possible SIB/DIB probability of savings gained by the public sector in relation to the education project. The decision-making calculus is as follows:

> EV = P x N, where EV = expected value, P = probability of success, and N = notional amount saved (as a function of budget savings minus related SIB/DIB fees)

Thus, the following decision-making calculus can be used:

> If EV (DIB/SIB) > EV (NBA), then the SIB/DIB education project should be considered

> If EV (DIB/SIB) < EV (NBA), then the NBA should be considered (as a relatively better alternative to SIBs/DIBs)

Second, a financial knowledge gap risk exists. Although all SIB/DIB parties must understand and be aware of the potential benefits and responsibilities of entering into an SIB/DIB transaction, it is likely that some parties, such as the constituents, may possess less financial knowledge than the other parties, such as the impact investors, advisers, and intermediary. To help remedy such a gap in financial knowledge, both the rights and responsibilities of the SIB/DIB transaction must be made explicit and be understood by all (not just most) of the SIB/DIB parties.[44]

Third, transactional risk exists. To date, relatively few SIB/DIB transactions have been completed. Therefore, little data on the viability of the model are publicly available. The risk to the SIB/DIB future pipeline is that the number of "successful" or "not successful" outcomes are highly lopsided (i.e., the outcome is extremely skewed to either successes or nonsuccesses).[45] To take a hypothetical example: If data suggest that nonsuccessful outcomes occur four out of every five times, future social impact investors may be disincentivized from participating in (i.e., funding) education projects. Thus, for the SIB/DIB structure to be sustainable, future potential social impact investors must anticipate that the end result is just as likely or more likely to be a success as a nonsuccess.

Fourth, intervention and execution risks exist. Such risks occur when the SIB/DIB structure is not suitable for a particular education project, such as

---

44 Thus, it is important for participants to understand minimum and maximum interest rates, as well as related payment payout schedules and conditions. This risk can be mitigated by full disclosure in written or oral form to all the related parties, or possibly by offering to provide such requisite financial knowledge to the needed parties or individuals. Whatever the form, plain language should be used.

45 Relatedly, in 2015, it was announced that the Rikers Island project did not meet the prespecified success metric, thus obligating Goldman Sachs to fund the entire program, which in effect saved the state of New York millions of dollars in potential budget losses. See Eduardo Porter, "Wall St. Money Meets Social Policy at Rikers Island," *New York Times*, July 28, 2015, http://www.nytimes.com/2015/07/29/business/economy/wall-st-money-meets-social-policy-at-rikers-island.html?_r=0. See also Development Impact Working Group, "Investing in Social Outcomes: Development Impact Bonds" (Social Finance, London; Center for Global Development, Washington, DC, 2013).

when needed data are lacking in order for the external evaluator to determine whether the success metric has been met. Even assuming that verifiable data exist, thus mitigating one type of execution risk, another type of execution risk could come in the form of a service provider's lack of capability to perform a stated education service, for example, meeting budgets or timelines for related education projects. However, this lack of capability risk can be mitigated by risk management and due diligence by the affected parties.

Potential, But Not Guaranteed, Benefits

Two potential (but not guaranteed) benefits exist with the SIB/DIB structure, which must be weighed against the potential risks described earlier.

The first benefit, which is associated with any performance-based funding, is the ability to potentially increase transparency.[46] Service providers, such as government (public) organizations, need to fund only projects (services) that are deemed "successful," based in large part on qualitative metrics. However, under the SIB/DIB social finance structure, clear, predesignated qualitative and quantitative success metrics are put in place, and verified by an external third-party evaluator. The SIB/DIB framework provides a very clear target for all parties involved—impact investors, intermediaries, service providers, advisers, outside assessors, and constituents—to analyze and conclude whether the particular project relating to the SIB/DIB investment was successful (as determined by the external evaluator/assessor).[47]

The second (but not guaranteed) benefit is the potential for cost savings.[48] With the SIB/DIB structure, the funders—most likely public entities and/or IGOs—generally pay only for services that have met the project's success metrics. The social finance impact investors provide (invest) the original funding amount in exchange for the possible SIB/DIB (but not guaranteed) economic benefit of a return on investment greater than its original investment amount.[49] Although the intermediary may pay additional costs in terms of interest payouts and administrative costs for successful education projects, such expense premiums can be weighed against those actual or potential SIB/DIB education

---

46 Jasper Kim and Sunghye Kang, "CSO-State Partnerships and Social Finance: Smart Social Capital and Shared Incentives towards Public-Private Partnership Efficiency Using Social Impact Bonds," *International Studies Review* 13, no. 2 (2012): 53–86.

47 Increasing transparency often assists in decreasing corruption, particularly in developing regions. For an insightful article on a strategic and philosophical approach to remedy corruption, see Morigiwa Yasutomo, "Making Delivery a Priority: A Philosophical Perspective on Corruption and a Strategy for Remedy," in *The World Bank Legal Review*, vol. 6, *Improving Development in Delivery: The Role of Voice, Social Contract, and Accountability*, ed. Jan Wouters, Alberto Ninio, Teresa Doherty, and Hassane Cissé (Washington, DC: World Bank, 2015), 437–456.

48 Ibid.

49 Mark J. Roe, "Shareholder Wealth Maximization Norm and Industrial Organization," *University of Pennsylvania Law Review* 149 (2001): 2063–2081, http://scholarship.law.upenn.edu/cgi/viewcontent.cgi?article=3331&context=penn_law_review.

projects in which the social impact investors financed the entire project, both initially and at the project's conclusion.[50]

A Contract Law Purview of SIB/DIB Contracts and Agreements

From a contract law purview, the following legal agreements and contracts typically fall within the range of agreements in a standard SIB/DIB transaction.[51] All of the following listed agreements are part of the current-generation SIB/DIB structure.

1. *Outcomes contract.* This contract details the relationship between the funders (from either the public or the private sector) and the intermediary (issuing the SIB/DIB), under which payment is contingent on achieving a predetermined quantitative and qualitative success metric. All related parties (described previously) should ideally be included in the negotiations leading to and including the final agreed-on contract.
2. *Investment agreement.* This is an agreement between the intermediary and investors that specifies how much investor capital will be drawn down (and the timeline for the drawdown), including the relevant terms and conditions under which payments are made to investors.
3. *Memorandum of understanding (MOU).* This memorandum relates to the general aspirations of the related parties. As with many MOUs, it may not be a binding contract but, at the very least, it is highly symbolic in nature.
4. *Advisory agreement.* This is an agreement between the adviser, the intermediary, the service providers, and other related parties that details the services to be supplied by the intermediary and the fee paid for these services. An advisory agreement is particularly related to performance management, data monitoring, or evaluation.
5. *Service provider agreement.* This is an agreement between the intermediary and the service provider(s) that specifies what services will be delivered, in addition to specifying, inter alia, payment and reporting schedules.
6. *Measurement/verification agreement.* This is an agreement between the funders and the external evaluator, which is the contracted entity that

---

50 A third potential benefit, somewhat related to the second potential benefit, would be a more optimal use of scarce resources due to a market-based incentive system incorporated into the SIB/DIB structure. Specifically, the resources for a typical education project embedded in the SIB/DIB structure can provide a more efficient way to allocate capital and ensure long-term measurable results because the stakeholders share the same goal: a successful education project, which is a function of an efficient use of SIB/DIB funding. Less taxpayer resources may also be needed because only those projects that do not meet certain predesignated standards related to the project are funded by the government (or by an IGO, as the case may be).

51 Although the term "standard" has been used in this section, an agreed-on, standardized contract for SIB/DIB transactions (akin to what the International Swaps and Derivatives Association has produced for contract derivatives) has yet to emerge, because to date relatively few such transactions have taken place.

independently measures outcomes or audits the reported results to determine whether the agreed-on success metric has been met.

7. *Swap agreement.* This agreement provides the terms and conditions related to any swap agreements between the parties, including any credit default swap (CDS) arrangements. The swap agreement includes specifics, such as the swap premium payment amounts (from the CDS premium payer to the CDS provider) and dates, as well as what "trigger events" will initiate a swap. (This agreement is not reflected in figure 3 because a wide variety of swap agreements and/or parties may be used.)
8. *Guarantee agreement.* This agreement sets forth the terms and conditions related to the guarantee features embedded in the next-generation SIB/DIB structure. (This agreement is not reflected in figure 3, because a wide variety of guarantee agreements or parties may be used.)

Within all of the preceding agreements, notwithstanding the current- or next-generation SIB/DIB structures, several SIB/DIB-specific features should be included. First, given that many of the SIB/DIB structures involve potentially disparate economic or geographic organizations, from both the public and the private sectors, the contract language must be understood by all involved parties. To achieve this, the agreements must be written in plain language to the greatest extent possible.[52]

Figure 3. Legal agreements for SIB/DIB structure

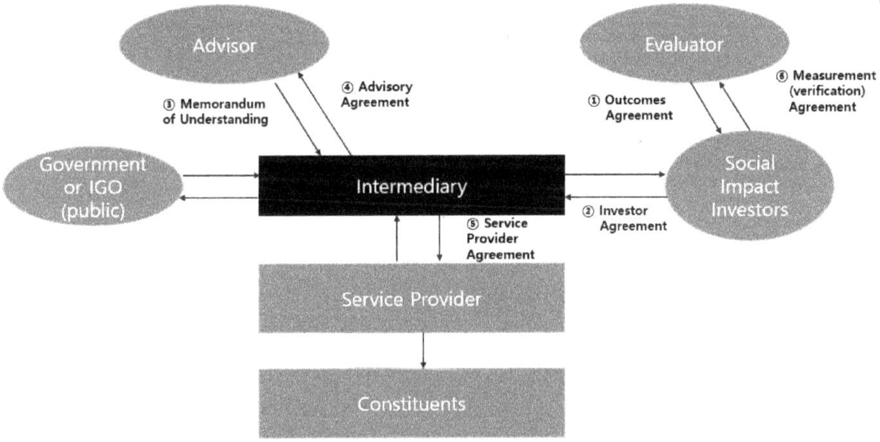

Key:
1. **Outcomes contract** between the DIP (a new corporate entity) and outcomes funder(s)
2. **Investor agreement** between the DIP and investors, specifying capital drawdown schedule
3. **Memorandum of understanding** between the developing country government and the DIP
4. **Advisory agreement** between the DIP and the intermediary
5. **Service provider agreement** between the DIP and the service provider
6. **Measurement/verification agreement** between the outcomes funder(s) and a selected external evaluator, who will measure or audit the results

---

52 United Kingdom Cabinet Office, "Guidance on the Template Contract for Social Impact

Second, clear roles and responsibilities must be defined in the legal agreements. This includes specifying the exact names and roles of the related parties, such as the investor, intermediary, and service provider, including references to each party's full legal entity name. Another area that requires specific focus and delineation is the discussion, negotiation, and agreement on a clear success metric.[53] To better achieve this, clear, specific qualitative and quantitative definitions of the success metric should be stipulated.[54] By making the success metric both qualitative and quantitative in nature, a higher degree of understanding is likely to be achieved among the disparate parties. Such a metric also allows the external evaluator to know what types of evidence and data are needed to determine whether an education project qualifies as a success. Having clear, specific qualitative and quantitative definitions of the success metric stipulated would provide substantial clarity, especially because the success metric would be the core contractual concern of the SIB/DIB parties. Indirectly, this level of specific qualitative and quantitative success metrics would be needed and benefit all the SIB/DIB agreements because the SIB/DIB transaction structure is a structured bond issuance involving a series of interrelated contracts, with terms and conditions cross-referenced throughout most or all such legal agreements.

Third, given the potentially disparate nature of SIB/DIB transactions, an alternative dispute resolution (ADR) clause could be used to avoid the potentially costly and lengthy process of litigation in the public court system. Many ADR options exist, but perhaps the most commercially viable would be the use of binding arbitration. If arbitration is chosen by the parties, issues that arise include the number of arbitrators that should be used and the specification of the exact steps relating to the arbitrator selection process. Generally, the more parties involved, the more likely that there will be a greater number of (an odd number of) arbitrators.

Next-Generation SIB/DIB Impact Bond Structure

SIBs/DIBs were a huge leap forward when first introduced, but they can, of course, be improved, not least by integrating elements of other financial products and technology. How, specifically, might the current-generation SIB/DIB model be further advanced?

Given that the public sector is typically the sector that finances public projects for education, the ability to increase the SIB/DIB marketplace arguably relates to the issue of how to incentivize greater private sector

---

Bonds and Payment by Results" (n.d.), https://www.gov.uk/government/uploads/system/uploads/attachment_data/file/199890/GUIDANCE_SIB_Template_Contract.pdf.

53 Ibid.

54 For example, rather than defining "success" as merely a "good outcome relating to high school literary rates," the definition could additionally be extended to include a quantitative dimension, such as ". . . which shall be construed to mean a literary rate of at least 80 percent at year 2020 for all students in grades 11 and 12."

participation. Determining how to achieve this involves paying attention to what motivated the private sector (and philanthropic organizations) to become SIB/DIB social investors: market-based incentives.[55]

This section presents five financial engineering techniques and tools that can incentivize greater participation and generate more capital funding for social projects by lessening or shifting risk.[56] Using one or more of these techniques would lead the way toward the next-generation SIB/DIB structure for education funding. Moreover, each of the techniques discussed already exists and has been used for years in the SIB/DIB financial marketplace[57] (which was part of the author's core legal responsibilities while working for various financial institutions on issues related to structured products and financial engineering).

1. *SIBs/DIBs plus credit default swaps.* The first financial technique that could be used in future SIB/DIB issuances would be CDSs.[58] CDSs essentially act as insurance policies in the event of certain predefined credit events, such as failure to pay owed obligations. In exchange for a CDS premium, the CDS provider assumes the risk of the CDS premium payer. By using a CDS, the SIB/DIB issuer can transfer its credit risk (e.g., failure to pay, bankruptcy, or a moratorium on owed obligations) to the CDS provider. This in turn lowers transaction funding–related risk, which benefits not just the SIB/DIB issuer (intermediary), but also the SIB/DIB social impact investors.[59] If an SIB/DIB in the notional amount of $10 million was protected using a CDS, the full notional amount ($10 million) would be repaid by the CDS provider.

---

55 Partisan perceptions relate to what motivates the public and private sector. Generally, public sector budgets must be used to the greatest extent possible for fear of receiving a smaller budget allocation for the next fiscal year. However, from the private sector purview, shareholders (and principals) are the "owner-funders" who demand "value for money" in most if not all transactions. From the perspective of potential future social impact investors, it is often challenging to provide economic justification to their shareholders when shareholder funds are being used with little or no financial quid pro quo. This may seem self-serving, but another term would be "rational" behavior. Not only is such "rational" pursuit desirable from an Anglo-American law purview, it is a fiduciary duty that, if not met, could lead to a shareholder derivative suit by shareholders against the entity itself.

56 This section is notably based on the author's practitioner experience in the legal and finance sectors relating to SIBs/DIBs. This section adds to the emerging literature in this related area, including leveraging complex derivative products to SIBs/DIBs in an effort to mitigate risk and thus improve SIB/DIB actual and potential market liquidity at the domestic and cross-border funding level.

57 Related costs for such financial engineering options vary tremendously. As a general matter, however, related fees are expressed as a percentage of the funding principal amount.

58 A credit default swap is one type of a derivative swap contract in which the credit risk exposure of a particular financial instrument is transferred from one party (the CDS protection buyer) to another party (the CDS protection seller).

59 Substantively, a CDS is not so different from car insurance, in which the car owner pays a monthly car insurance premium (comparable to a CDS premium payer) to the car insurance provider (a CDS protection provider). If the car is damaged, lost, or stolen, the car insurance provider normally pays an amount equal to the car's value. CDS products, like car owners, outsource their risk to the car insurance provider.

CDS premiums can roughly be equated to the payment of an insurance premium. CDS buyers (protection buyers) pay the CDS premium at a prespecified time (the provided example is a quarterly premium payment stream). Physical settlement occurs after a CDS "trigger event," in which the protected asset (or substitute asset) is delivered to the CDS protection seller, which keeps it under the assumption that it will increase in value in the future or be sold in the marketplace.

But from a practitioner's in-the-field perspective, why use CDS products? The short answer is that credit default swaps provide additional credit protection and thus would lower investment risk for SIB/DIB participants. As a result, CDS products would serve to increase the liquidity and scale of the SIB/DIB marketplace in the future. The use of CDS products can thus potentially change this landscape by incentivizing greater private sector SIB/DIB investment, because CDS products are presumed to lessen (but not completely mitigate) credit risk. This will be of particular interest to potential private sector SIB/DIB funders that have yet to fully participate in education projects. In using CDS products (or other swaps, such as foreign exchange or interest rate swaps), conducting due diligence on potential provider counterparties is critical.[60]

The term "credit default swap" may trigger trepidation, because of a lack of information about what exactly a CDS is and is not. The term can perhaps be better described by using plain English. Using alternative terms, such as "protection plan," "contingency contract," or "insurance initiative," might better convey the nature of the mechanism to many potential SIB/DIB participants, particularly constituents.[61] Conceivably, CDS providers can be public entities, not just private entities.

Figure 4 details how CDS products function and might be used for SIB/DIB transactions in the future. First, the CDS protection buyer pays the protection seller a CDS premium in exchange for protection of the notional amount of a particular SIB/DIB issuance. Second, in the event of default (e.g., nonpayment), the nominal amount of the SIB/DIB is recovered through one of two methods, either by "physical settlement" (in which the defaulted SIB/DIB is given to the CDS protection seller) or by "cash settlement" (in which the defaulted SIB/DIB is kept by the CDS protection buyer). In either case—physical or cash settlement—the CDS protection buyer is made whole for any loss incurred.

---

60 The costs of CDS products can vary greatly, depending on what entity or obligation is being protected (much like with insurance). The payment mechanism is typically a periodic CDS premium (e.g., quarterly, semiannually, yearly) paid to the CDS provider. Because the premium reflects risk, the higher the risk, the higher the CDS premium. However, features such as guarantees and credit ratings (discussed in this chapter) are generally a factor in lowering risk and lowering CDS premiums (fees).

61 Alternatively, a cash settlement can be chosen (in lieu of physical settlement), in which a cash amount is given by the CDS protection buyer to the protection seller to make the protection buyer "whole."

Figure 4. Credit default swap structure

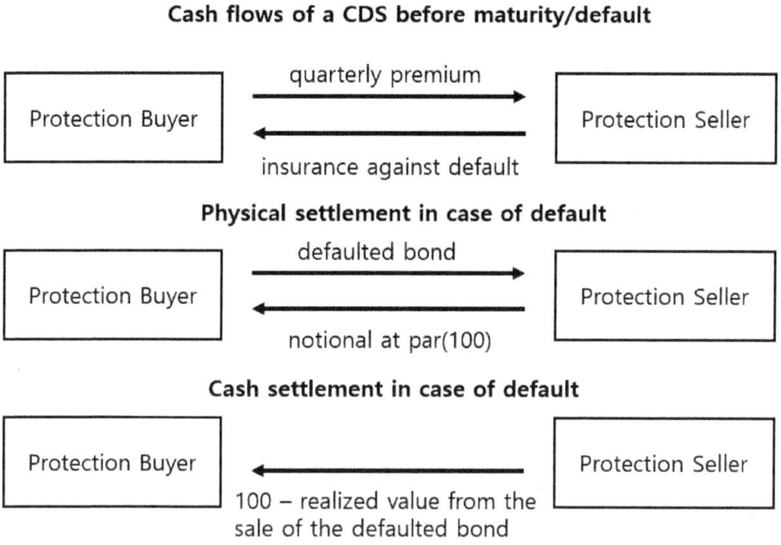

2. *SIBs/DIBs plus credit ratings.* The second financial feature that could be used in future SIB/DIB transactions is credit ratings. Credit ratings provide a market signal, indicating the quality of a particular asset. However, as the subprime crisis showed, even the most reputable credit ratings agencies, such as Standard & Poor's and Moody's, were far from perfect. Still, it is arguably better to have credit ratings than not, even if they are imperfect.[62] In the financial marketplace, credit ratings can be given to a wide variety of bonds, both plain and exotic. The social finance markets could thus be further improved if future SIB/DIB issuances came with credit ratings, especially given the relative infancy and thinness of the current SIB/DIB market.[63]

   When it comes to education financing, a broad array of credit rating agencies can be considered. Candidates can be from the public sector, including IGOs and NPOs, as well as the private sector, or from large, small, and medium entities, so long as the requisite level of expertise exists.

62 Credit ratings can be seen as working like grades given by an academic institution to a student. Although the grading process may vary from one faculty member to another, the grading system still sends an important signal to the markets as to the student's perceived quality. As an analogy, when employers look to hire, they generally prefer to select potential student candidates based on grades, at least as a starting point.

63 What types of entities can provide credit ratings when it comes to education financing? And how does an SIB/DIB deal receive a credit rating? In theory, almost any entity or qualified person(s) can qualify to provide a credit rating. The key issue is that the credit rating agency —whether a private firm, public sector entity, IGO, NGO, or NPO—has the relevant capacity and competency to provide such credit ratings for SIB/DIB issuances.

Typically, credit ratings agencies look at the degree of certainty of future promised cash flows, particularly from the SIB/DIB issuer to the SIB/DIB social investor. Moreover, high-grade collateral—including other financial engineering techniques such as CDSs and guarantees underlying an SIB/DIB issuance—would generally improve the likelihood of a higher credit rating, because collateral decreases the likelihood of SIB/DIB investors losing their principal or interest amount (also known as "default" or "credit" risk).

Overall, using credit ratings for certain SIB/DIB issuances would help increase transparency and lower risk, and thus lower the premium needed to incentivize social impact investors to buy SIBs/DIBs in the marketplace.

3. *SIBs/DIBs plus tranched debt.* The third financial feature of future SIB/DIB transactions is "tranching" of SIB/DIB debt paper. Tranching of debt paper is another common feature of debt markets, but it has yet to be widely incorporated with SIB/DIB issuances. A tranche of debt paper is simply a subportion of debt paper. The ranking of tranched debt normally runs from super-senior tranches (the least risky) to senior tranches, mezzanine tranches, and equity tranches (the most risky). The more senior (highly ranked) a particular tranche of debt paper, the higher the likelihood of recouping owed debt obligations in the event of liquidation. The financial technique of tranching (i.e., creating tranches of debt paper) would allow SIB/DIB issuers to create different subdivisions of debt, each reflecting different risk profiles, all in the same SIB/DIB issuance to investors.[64]

   Overall, tranched SIBs/DIBs would expand the potential social impact investor base because a wider array of risk profiles (and thus interest rates) would be offered in the same issuance, helping both the private and the public side of the SIB/DIB transaction.

4. *SIB/DIB using alternative bonds.* The fourth financial feature that could be used in future SIB/DIB transactions is advancing the current-generation SIB/DIB structure to incorporate an "alternative bond" SIB/DIB structure. One type of alternative bond structure is called SIB/DIB "mini-bonds," which would allow for the selling of SIBs/DIBS to retail (individual) investors. This has already begun in certain countries to high-net-worth (and relatively sophisticated) investors. One potential downside to issuances to retail investors would be the added disclosure and registration requirements typically associated with such issuances to noninstitutional

64 For example, let us say that Entity A issues SIB/DIB A, which is tranched into the categories explained on this page. Further, in the hypothetical SIB/DIB tranched debt paper issuance, the tranches could have the following returns (reflecting the cascading levels of risk profiles): super-senior tranche, 7 percent; senior tranche, 8 percent; mezzanine tranche, 9 percent; and equity tranche, 10 percent. In such a tranched SIB/DIB issuance, if Entity A is unable to pay owed obligations (interest payments) to the social impact investor, then the equity tranche debt paper holders would take the first loss. If such owed obligations continue, the mezzanine tranche debt paper holders would be the second loss group, and so on, up to the super-senior tranche debt holders. Note that the term "equity" in tranched debt paper is substantively different from equity (stock) paper.

investors. Still, assuming that some individuals have great interest in getting involved in impact bonds and social investments, SIB/DIB retail market issuances in the form of mini-SIB/DIB bonds could be a worthwhile endeavor, because it would bring individuals into the SIB/DIB markets.[65]

Another SIB/DIB alternative bond type could come in the form of an SIB/DIB index-linked bond, which would be somewhat similar to index-linked funds for general financial products. In lieu of a certain fixed return (interest) on the SIB/DIB, the note would have a variable, or floating, rate that directly or indirectly, depending on the parties, reflects the return of a particular index. For example, an S&P 500 index–linked SIB/DIB bond could be structured to be more amenable to certain potential SIB/DIB investors, thus broadening the SIB/DIB marketplace and providing greater liquidity (funding) for education-related public projects worldwide.

A "convertible bond" SIB/DIB structure could also be created as part of the next-generation SIB/DIB structural model. With a convertible bond structure, the SIB/DIB noteholder could have the option to convert a certain bond level (based on amount, percentage of ownership, or other contractual arrangement) to a certain level of equity in the education project. This financial technique would give potential social impact investors the option to own both bond and equity holdings, which would further incentivize SIB/DIB market participation.

5. *SIBs/DIBs plus guarantees.* Guarantees are another financial contract that could be part of the next-generation SIB/DIB model.[66] At its core, a guarantee contract is relatively simple and straightforward. It states that in the event that a particular party is unable to make one or more payments, the guarantor would step into the shoes of such a party and make the required payments.

   A legal guarantee is another means of lowering credit risk within the SIB/DIB framework. The guarantee essentially obligates more than one party to make payments on behalf of another party relating to an SIB/DIB. For example, a parent company could provide a guarantee contract on behalf of one of its subsidiaries or branches; that guarantee contract would legally obligate the parent company to make future payments on behalf of a subsidiary or branch under certain circumstances. But with SIBs/DIBs, either a private or public sector entity could be contractually obligated to make payments to the SIB/DIB investors (in the event that the SIB/DIB transaction failed to meet its predetermined and agreed-on success metric). As a matter of practice, a guarantee by an affiliated or more senior private/public sector entity could be incorporated into the SIB/DIB structure.

---

65 In offering such mini-bonds to the retail market, the requisite disclosures, approvals, and other related rules and regulations must be in place.

66 See Burand, "Globalizing Social Finance."

* * *

The preceding five SIB/DIB techniques, and their related legal agreements, have been used for years in the financial marketplace around the world, so why not apply them to the SIB/DIB markets (providing another avenue for possible education financing) to improve philanthropic investments based on market principles, converting greed into good in the 21st century in the process?

Overall, any of the preceding financial features used with SIBs/DIBs—CDSs, credit ratings, tranched debt, alternative bonds, and guarantees—would significantly improve the already innovative SIB/DIB funding framework. Furthermore, they can be used in combination to complement one another.

Conclusion

Impact bonds represent a relatively new market-based funding model whereby the public and private sectors collaborate to provide education financing for projects in developing regions. The impact bond education funding models described in this chapter provide shared stakeholder incentives within an innovative, market-based, public-private partnership framework.

Future SIB/DIB-related education financing contracts should incorporate plain yet definitive language that clearly sets forth the parties involved, each party's specific roles and responsibilities, the exact success metrics, and the possible arbitration clauses. Future contracts should also utilize financial engineering technology and tools, including swaps, credit ratings, tranched debt, guarantees, and alternative bond issuances. Integrating such key technologies and tools into contracts can create next-generation SIB/DIB funding structures for education projects and programs. These SIB/DIB funding structures can mitigate market risk, improve liquidity, and foster greater participation in both the public and private sectors for participants aspiring to provide education financing as part of the post-2015 development agenda.

7

Waivers of Sovereign Immunity

An Eroding Concept?

HODA ATIA MOUSTAFA AND ANTHONY MOLLE

In international project finance, when a host government enters into an agreement with a private-sector party, the government often provides a waiver of sovereign immunity to jurisdiction and from execution. This waiver ensures that if the host government breaches its contract with the private party, the government will not seek immunity from suit, execution, or enforcement by virtue of its status as a sovereign. Because the underlying documents are commercial in nature, such provisions are both appropriate and expected.

Recently, with respect to immunity from execution in particular, governments have attempted to negotiate "carve-outs" from the waiver of sovereign immunity in order to exclude certain assets—in particular, defense, diplomatic, and consular-related assets. Such carve-outs have largely been accepted, because these assets are generally immune under relevant local laws, such as the Foreign Sovereign Immunities Act (FSIA) in the United States, the State Immunity Act (SIA) in the United Kingdom, and various UN conventions. However, sovereigns have observed with alarm an increasing number of cases in which states' private contractual counterparties have attempted to attach government assets overseas in order to satisfy judgments or arbitral awards against the state. A famous example is the 2012 case of the Argentine naval vessel that was detained for ten weeks in Ghana, in which a local Ghanaian court ruled that its seizure by a U.S. hedge fund was legal.

Recent English case law suggests that although a government-owned entity or agency may be considered to be a separate legal entity, it may not necessarily be considered as separate from the sovereign in the enforcement of a judgment or an arbitral award against such sovereign. In certain circumstances, a contractual counterparty could successfully pierce the sovereign corporate veil, and a government's assets could potentially be attached in the United Kingdom when such counterparty enforces a judgment or an arbitral award against a government-owned entity or agency. Conversely, assets belonging to a legally distinct but government-owned entity or agency could be attached in the United Kingdom in order to enforce a judgment or an arbitral award against a government (known as "reverse veil-piercing").

Special thanks go to Pierre-Axel Aberg for his thorough research assistance on this chapter. Pierre-Axel will be joining Latham & Watkins in London, and aims to specialize his practice in project development and finance. He received his legal education in the United Kingdom (BPP University), the United States (Georgetown University, where he obtained an LL.M.), and France (Sciences Po Paris).

These developments have caused anxiety among governments that hold significant assets offshore, and some governments are exploring measures to curtail the risk of attachment. The question is whether these measures are—or can be—compatible with market expectations and project bankability requirements. This chapter explores these developments and their potential impact on foreign direct investment in developing countries.

Sovereign Immunity

An Overview of the Doctrine of Sovereign Immunity

According to the doctrine of sovereign immunity, a sovereign is immune from the jurisdiction of the courts of another state, and its assets are immune from execution or attachment.[1]

Sovereign immunity had long been considered as absolute and a mutual favor granted by sovereigns to one another. But the twentieth century saw an essential shift in the activities of states as they broadened the scope of their activities. Whereas states originally focused on providing essential government services (e.g., courts, public order, international defense), states now increasingly engaged in commercial ventures in certain sectors, including the exploration and exploitation of natural resources (e.g., oil and gas, minerals, metals); the construction, operation, and maintenance of various types of infrastructure (e.g., power, transportation, utilities, wastewater treatment, telecommunications); and the provision of financial services. States regularly act as commercial actors inasmuch as they purchase pens, Internet access, or photocopiers in order to perform their services. Over time, the increasingly commercial activity undertaken by sovereigns caused private contractual counterparties to voice concerns about a disadvantageous lack of judicial recourse as they risked that states might invoke sovereign immunity from suit, enforcement, or attachment. Several jurisdictions reacted by developing a new, more restrictive approach to sovereign immunity adapted to the shifting role played by sovereigns.

U.S. Law

In the United States, the concept of sovereign immunity was first articulated by the U.S. Supreme Court in *The Schooner Exchange v. McFaddon*.[2] The U.S. plaintiffs wanted a court to order the attachment of a French military ship formerly owned by them. In its landmark ruling, the Supreme Court found that a nation enjoys "exclusive and absolute" jurisdiction within its borders and that any limitation thereof could only derive from its explicit or implicit consent.[3]

---

1 The understanding of what constitutes a foreign sovereign is debated and the definition has often been extended beyond the state to incorporate the state's subdivisions, which may include regional entities, agencies, and state-owned enterprises. This chapter focuses on state-owned enterprises.

2 The Schooner Exchange v. McFaddon, 11 U.S. (7 Cranch) 116, 3 L. Ed. 287 (1812).

3 The U.S. Supreme Court found three situations in which a state might give its express con-

Implicit consent was considered to have been given by a state that allowed friendly warships to pass through its ports, and the Supreme Court thus considered that the United States had accepted to limit its jurisdiction over the French ship because of the critical importance of respecting the rights of a foreign sovereign that "conformed in all things to the law of nations and the laws of the United States." As such, a U.S. court did not have jurisdiction over a foreign warship, and the latter could not be attached in the suit of an individual.

An important shift occurred in 1952 when Jack B. Tate, acting legal adviser for the State Department, wrote the "Tate Letter," in which he announced the State Department's approach in handling requests for immunity presented by foreign sovereigns.[4] Where the State Department had previously advised U.S. courts to follow an absolute interpretation of the doctrine[5]—and courts tended to give "absolute deference to its suggestions"[6]—under the new policy, courts should do so only with regard to a foreign sovereign's public acts. As such, any private acts, including commercial, nongovernmental activities, could lead to suit. Tate says this:

> According to the newer or restrictive theory of sovereign immunity, the immunity of the sovereign is recognized with regard to sovereign or public acts (jure imperii) of a state, but not with respect to private acts (jure gestionis). There is agreement by proponents of both theories, supported by practice, that sovereign immunity should not be claimed or granted in actions with respect to real property (diplomatic and perhaps consular property excepted).[7]

Even though the Tate Letter was not binding on U.S. courts, it signaled a shift in policy that was instrumental in promoting a restrictive approach to sovereign immunity;[8] this policy was cemented in 1976 with the FSIA.

---

sent: immunity granted to a foreign sovereign in the person of a physical head of state; immunity granted to foreign ministers and ambassadors; and immunity granted to foreign troops that were authorized to enter the territory.

4 According to the Tate Letter, Belgian and Italian courts have always followed a restrictive approach to sovereign immunity; countries as diverse as Austria, the Arab Republic of Egypt, France, Greece, Peru, Romania, and Switzerland have also implemented this approach. German courts have been divided over the question but moved toward a more restrictive approach in the 1920s. The United States, the British Commonwealth, and the Soviet Union were among the latter proponents of an absolute theory of sovereign immunity.

5 William A. Dobrovir, "A Gloss on the Tate Letter's Restrictive Theory of Sovereign Immunity," *Virginia Law Review* 54, no. 1 (1968): 2.

6 Curtis A. Bradley and Laurence R. Helfer, "International Law and the U.S. Common Law of Foreign Official Immunity," *The Supreme Court Review* 2010, no. 1 (2010): 219.

7 The Tate Letter is included in full as appendix 2 to the opinion of the Supreme Court in Alfred Dunhill of London, Inc. v. Republic of Cuba, 425 U.S. 682 (1976).

8 The Tate Letter concludes, "It is realized that a shift in policy by the executive cannot control the courts, but it is felt that the courts are less likely to allow a plea of sovereign immunity where the executive has declined to do so. There have been indications that at least some Justices of the Supreme Court feel that, in this matter, courts should follow the branch of the Government charged with responsibility for the conduct of foreign relations."

The enforcement of judgment debts against assets belonging to foreign sovereigns is regulated in the United States by the FSIA of 1976, which defines the circumstances under which U.S. courts have jurisdiction over foreign states and under which execution may be levied on foreign states' property. The FSIA defines a "foreign state" to encompass its political subdivisions, agencies, and instrumentalities, including those with separate legal personalities.[9] A foreign state is immune from suit[10] unless it falls under one of the exceptions defined in sections 1605 to 1607, and once one party provides evidence of such an exception, the burden of proof falls on the sovereign claiming immunity to show why such exception should not apply.[11]

The most important exceptions[12] include situations in which the foreign state has explicitly or implicitly waived its immunity and in which it has carried out a commercial activity. The concept of "commercial activity" is determined by reference to the nature, rather than the purpose, of such acts, and includes those carried out in the United States by a foreign state, in the United States in connection with a commercial activity of a foreign state elsewhere, and outside the territory of the United States in connection with a commercial activity of a foreign state elsewhere but causing a direct effect in the United States. Generally, when a state performs "the type of actions by which a private party engages in trade and traffic or commerce," it will not benefit from sovereign immunity.[13]

Case law has brought some clarification to what may be construed as an implicit waiver, and in *Ipitrade International, S.A. v. Federal Republic of Nigeria,*[14] the court found that the foreign state had waived its immunity by agreeing to resolve all disputes under the contract by using Swiss law and through arbitration with the International Chamber of Commerce, adding that "the legislative history of [section 1605(a)(1)] expressly states that an agreement to arbitrate or to submit to the laws of another country constitutes an implicit waiver."[15]

With regard to the attachment of state assets, the FSIA provides that commercial assets[16] belonging to foreign states may be attached, with two notable limitations: property belonging to a central bank or monetary authority for its own account, unless the foreign sovereign has explicitly waived the immunity

---

9 28 U.S.C., sec. 1603.

10 Ibid., sec. 1604.

11 Saloni Kantaria, "The Challenges of Enforcing an Arbitral Award Against a Foreign State in the United States," *Journal of International Arbitration* 27, no. 1 (2010): 75–87, 77.

12 28 U.S.C. sec. 1605.

13 Republic of Argentina v. Weltover, 504 U.S. 607 (1992) at 614.

14 Ipitrade International, S.A. v. Federal Republic of Nigeria, 465 F. Supp. 824 (D.C.D.C. 1978).

15 Ibid., Supp. 826.

16 "Commercial assets" include property used for commercial purposes and property used by an entity engaged in commercial activity.

of that property; and property of a military character or under the control of a military authority.[17]

U.K. Law

The United Kingdom followed a similar path in the development of sovereign immunity. One case in particular, *Trendtex Trading Corporation v. Central Bank of Nigeria,*[18] was instrumental in the development of restrictive sovereign immunity in the United Kingdom and provided the case law on which the SIA was based one year later.[19]

In 1975, the Nigerian Ministry of Defense agreed to purchase a large quantity of cement from Pan-African Export and Import Co. Ltd. for delivery soon after, and it instructed the Central Bank of Nigeria (CBN) to open an irrevocable letter of credit to the company for more than $14 million as security for payment. This letter of credit was transferred to Trendtex Trading Corporation, a Swiss company, in order to cover the cost of delivering the cement and to fulfill the terms of the contract. A few months later, a new military government came to power in Nigeria and suspended the importation of cement in order to ease congestion at the country's ports and ascertain the economic viability of contracts entered into by its predecessor. Trendtex made several shipments of cement, but the new government refused to pay.

Trendtex sued the CBN before the High Court of England for the money owed under the letter of credit, but the court refused to exercise jurisdiction due to the CBN being "an emanation, an arm, and a department of the State of Nigeria . . . thus entitled to immunity from suit."[20] Trendtex appealed; in his ruling, Lord Denning noted that it was difficult to determine whether the CBN should be considered a government department. Lord Justice Shaw added that "whether a particular organization is to be accorded the status of a department of government or not must depend on its constitution, its powers and duties and its activities," and not solely on the opinion of that government."[21] This was no easy feat: although a legally separate body, the CBN has governmental functions[22] and is largely under governmental control (notably in determining its monetary, banking, and administrative policies). In the end, the court held that the CBN should not be considered a government body,[23] and it noted that because this conclusion had been particularly difficult to reach, the court was resting its "decision on the ground that there

---

17 28 U.S.C., sec. 1611.

18 Trendtex Trading Corporation v. Central Bank of Nigeria, Appeal decision [1977], QB 529.

19 Robin C. A. White, "State Immunity and International Law in English Courts," *International and Comparative Law Quarterly* 26, no. 3 (1977): 674.

20 *Trendtex,* QB 529 at F3.

21 Ibid., at 93.

22 These functions include issuing legal tender, safeguarding the international value of the currency, and acting as a banker and financial adviser to the government.

23 *Trendtex,* QB 529 at 55.

is no immunity in respect of commercial transactions, even for a government department."[24] As such, *Trendtex* represents a major evolution for the understanding of sovereign immunity by British courts by establishing that government bodies are not granted immunity from jurisdiction or attachment when a suit pertains to their commercial acts.

Marking the international relevance of the doctrine of sovereign immunity, Lord Denning drew inspiration from various sources, quoting Belgian, Dutch, and German court decisions, the Tate Letter, the European Convention on State Immunity,[25] and the Supreme Court of the United States in *Alfred Dunhill of London Inc. v. Republic of Cuba*.[26] Lord Denning incorporated this view of international law into English law,[27] famously noting that states should keep up with international law's evolution: "One country alone may start the process. Others may follow. At first a trickle, then a stream, last a flood. England should not be left behind on the bank. '. . . We must take the current when it serves, or lose our ventures.': *Julius Caesar*, Act IV, sc. III."[28]

The SIA came in *Trendtex*'s wake and, much like the FSIA, establishes a general principle of sovereign immunity[29] that is tempered by exceptions, including when a foreign state has submitted to the jurisdiction of U.K. courts,[30] when the suit is based on a state's commercial transaction,[31] and when a foreign state fails to perform a contractual obligation in whole or in part in the United Kingdom (such an obligation can be commercial or not).[32] However, the SIA overturned the particular conclusion reached in *Trendtex* regarding central banks, and specifically provides that property of a foreign state's central bank or other monetary authority shall not be considered as in use or intended to be used for commercial purposes.

---

24 Ibid., at 56.

25 The European Convention on State Immunity (CETS no. 74) was signed in Basel on May 16, 1972, and entered into force on June 11, 1976.

26 Alfred Dunhill of London, Inc. v. Republic of Cuba, 425 U.S. 682 (1976). In particular, Lord Denning cites the following: "Although it had other views in years gone by, in 1952, as evidenced by . . . [the Tate Letter] . . . the United States abandoned the absolute theory of sovereign immunity and embraced the restrictive view under which immunity in our courts should be granted only with respect to causes of action arising out of a foreign state's public or governmental actions and not with respect to those arising out of its commercial or proprietary actions. This has been the official policy of our government since that time, as the attached letter of November 25, 1975, confirms . . . 'Such adjudications are consistent with international law on sovereign immunity.'"

27 *Trendtex*, QB 529 at 28.

28 *Trendtex*, QB 529 at 34.

29 SIA 1978, part I, sec. 1(1).

30 Ibid., sec. 2(1).

31 Ibid., sec. 3(1)a.

32 Ibid., sec. 3(1)b.

For the purpose of the act, a "commercial transaction"[33] excludes employment contracts but includes agreements for the supply of goods or services; loans or other transactions for the provision of finance and any guarantee or indemnity in respect of such transaction or any other financial obligation; and any transaction or activity (notably commercial, industrial, or professional) into which a state enters or in which it engages other than in the exercise of its sovereign authority.

A "state" is understood as any foreign state, including the government of that state and any department of that government.[34] Unlike the FSIA, the SIA excludes "separate entities" (which are legally distinct from the executive organs of the government and capable of suing and being sued) and views them as private parties that do not benefit from immunity from suit or execution.[35] There are exceptions to this rule, however, and a separate entity will benefit from immunity if the proceedings relate to anything done by it in the exercise of sovereign authority and the circumstances are such that a state would have benefited from immunity.[36] Central banks are a specific exception to this rule. In making a determination as to whether a state-owned enterprise should benefit from immunity, a court will examine the common law, English law, and the foreign state's internal law.[37]

Recent Case Law

The ARA Libertad *in Ghana*

The doctrine of sovereign immunity as applied to warships has been the subject of more recent case law. In 2001 and 2002, the Republic of Argentina defaulted on its bonds, prompting U.S. hedge fund NML Capital Limited (NML) to initiate actions before U.S. and English courts. Argentina was ordered to pay sums in both jurisdictions but refused to settle its judgment debts, claiming that it enjoyed jurisdictional sovereign immunity and that the courts lacked jurisdiction. The Supreme Court of the United Kingdom disagreed with this argument, and rendered a judgment against Argentina.[38] Seeking to enforce this judgment and recover its debts, NML initiated proceedings in Ghana to seek the attachment of the *ARA Libertad*, a warship that belonged to Argentina and had docked in the country as part of a goodwill tour. Argentina claimed

33 Ibid., sec. 3(3).

34 Ibid., sec. 14(1).

35 Hazel Fox and Philippa Webb, *The Law of State Immunity*, 3rd ed. (Oxford: Oxford International Law Library, 2013), accessed online at Oxford Public International Law.

36 SIA, part I, sec. 14(2).

37 Fox and Webb, *The Law of State Immunity*. Further, in *Trendtex* the Court of Appeals found that there is "no satisfactory test" to determine whether an entity should be considered separate, and that it is thus necessary to "look to all the evidence to see whether the organization was under government control and exercised governmental functions" (*Trendtex*, QB 529 at 53). The questions of an entity's governmental control and functions are determined under English law primarily, and a court may use local law to inform its decision.

38 NML Capital Ltd. v. Republic of Argentina, Judgment (2011), UKSC 31.

sovereign immunity and argued that this immunity should be extended to the *ARA Libertad* as a military asset on the basis of relevant international conventions.[39] The Ghanaian High Court found that Argentina had explicitly waived its immunity under the initial bond agreement and ordered that the ship be detained, stopping short of calling for its seizure.

While the proceedings unfolded before Ghanaian courts and pending the constitution of an arbitral tribunal, Argentina initiated proceedings under the United Nations Convention on the Law of the Sea and filed an application before the International Tribunal for the Law of the Sea (ITLOS). The ITLOS subsequently ordered the government of Ghana to release the *ARA Libertad* on the grounds that "a warship is an expression of the sovereignty of the state whose flag it flies" and that "in accordance with international law, a warship enjoys immunity, including in internal waters."[40] The Ghanaian Supreme Court ruled in favor of Argentina, establishing the sovereign immunity of military assets under international and domestic Ghanaian law.

Kensington International Limited v. Republic of Congo

The more recent *Kensington* case, although decided at the court of first instance, has had an important impact on the doctrine of sovereign immunity, not least because the case played a part in triggering states' concerns with respect to waivers.[41] In 2002 and 2003, Kensington International Limited obtained four judgments against the Republic of Congo that remained unsatisfied. Seeking to recover funds, Kensington obtained debt orders and injunctions relating to funds owed to the Republic of Congo by third parties for the purchase of oil. Specifically, Kensington targeted the following chain of contracts: Cotrade SA, a wholly owned subsidiary of the Société Nationale des Pétroles du Congo (SNPC), the Congolese state-owned oil company, contracted with Africa Oil & Gas Corporation (AOGC) for the sale of oil; AOGC in turn sold the oil to Sphynx (BDA) Limited; Sphynx then sold the oil to Glencore Energy UK Limited; and finally, Glencore sold the oil to BP in a typical arm's-length commercial transaction.

Kensington wished to attach the purchase price payable by Glencore in order to enforce its judgments against the Republic of Congo and claimed that the court should "pierce the corporate veil" because Sphynx was "a mere device or façade"[42] used to hide the fact that funds received by it would in fact be received by the state. Several courts had previously come to the conclusion that SNPC "was part of the Congolese state and had no existence separate

---

39 Notably, the 2004 UN Convention on Jurisdictional Immunities of States and Their Property (which has yet to come into force), the 1982 UN Convention on the Law of the Sea, and the 1961 Vienna Convention on Diplomatic Relations.

40 International Tribunal for the Law of the Sea Order for Argentina v. Ghana (December 15, 2012), secs. 94–95.

41 *Kensington* (2005), EWHC 2684.

42 Ibid., at 6.

from it,"[43] notably the Commercial Court in an earlier *Kensington International Limited v. Republic of Congo* case[44] and the Paris Court of Appeals in two separate matters.[45]

The court held that the sale from Sphynx to Glencore had been genuine, but that the contracts between SNPC and Cotrade, Cotrade and AOGC, and AOGC and Sphynx could not be considered legitimate arm's-length transactions.[46] SNPC and Cotrade had no existence separate from the state,[47] and the transactions were "sham" because "they were devised to hide the reality of a sale by Cotrade, which is part of the State of the Congo, to Glencore." The structure of the corporations and the chain of contracts had been "put in place and employed by the [Republic of Congo]/SNPC/Cotrade with the object of evading enforcement of existing liabilities of the [Republic of Congo] by hiding its assets from view,"[48] thus allowing the court to reverse-pierce the corporate veil in order for Kensington to attach the purchase price of the oil from BP.

Ultimately, *Kensington* showed that U.K. courts were willing to conduct such reverse-piercing in order to permit the attachment of assets belonging to state-owned enterprises to satisfy the debts of a state. It also made clear that the courts would consider the underlying structure of a transaction to determine whether to do so. Finally, the case caused alarm among oil-producing countries concerned about the prospect of oil sales being used to satisfy sovereign debts.

Attaching Specific Types of Assets

Assets of State-Owned Enterprises

A state's creditor may seek to attach assets belonging to a state-owned enterprise (SOE) in order to satisfy the debt by "reverse-piercing the corporate veil." This tactic might not be simple, as statutes and courts will not easily set aside the privileges conferred by distinct legal personalities. As such, under the FSIA, an SOE may benefit from immunity if it meets certain criteria with respect to its relationship with the state.

U.S. courts were long reluctant to grant sovereign immunity to SOEs, especially before the shift from an absolute to a restrictive approach. They used tough criteria to counterbalance absolute immunity's "generosity" in not distinguishing between public and private acts, and followed a so-called

---

43 Ibid., at 10.

44 Kensington International Limited v. Republic of Congo (2003), EWHC 2331.

45 Court of Appeals of Paris, January 23, 2003, and July 3, 2003.

46 *Kensington* (2005) EWHC 2684, at 132.

47 *Kensington* (2005) EWHC 2684, at 193.

48 Ibid., at 200.

structural approach, focusing on an entity's incorporation rather than on its control or ownership structure. As a result, "foreign government–established, –owned, and –controlled corporations were denied immunity by U.S. courts precisely because they were corporations."[49] Under the FSIA, an SOE may benefit from immunity if it is legally separate from the state; is either an organ of a foreign state (or of a political subdivision) or is majority-owned by a foreign state; and is not a citizen of the United States.[50] In 2003, the Supreme Court ruled in *Dole Food Company v. Patrickson*[51] that "[a] foreign state must itself own a majority of a corporation's shares if the corporation is to be deemed an instrumentality of the state under the FSIA," establishing majority direct ownership as the rule. Consequently, a corporation that is indirectly owned by a foreign state would not be considered as an instrumentality of that state, would not benefit from sovereign immunity, and would not be able to use its assets to satisfy the debts of its indirect sovereign owner.

English courts tended to show more flexibility, and in *Baccus S.R.L. v. Servicio Nacional del Trigo,*[52] a Spanish corporation was granted immunity from suit despite being a separate legal entity that had the power to contract, sue, and be sued in its own name.

As the United Kingdom established a more restrictive approach, the courts broadened their criteria, and now they also take into account an SOE's activity, in particular because an entity found to be part of a state is subject to the commerciality exception.[53] Courts look at an SOE's past and current operations to "determine which factor—the extent of the foreign state's control or the functions of the entity in conformity with private law of the forum state—is to prevail."[54] At first blush, this approach seems favorable to private parties contracting with SOEs, as a court will adopt a holistic view of the matter before deciding to allow a suit against such an entity or the attachment of its assets. However, this approach has also led to inconsistencies, not least with regard to issues of sham and fraud and whether to order the reverse-piercing of the corporate veil.

The Privy Council tried to bring some clarification in *La Générale des Carrières et des Mines v. FG Hemisphere Associates LLC,*[55] in which the court departed from *Trendtex* by accepting that a separate legal entity capable of suing and

49 P. J. Kincaid, "Sovereign Immunity of Foreign State-Owned Corporations," *Journal of World Trade Law* 110, no. 10 (1976): 113.

50 28 U.S.C., sec. 1603.

51 Dole Food Company v. Patrickson, 538 U.S. 468 (2003).

52 Baccus S.R.L. v. Servicio Nacional del Trigo (1956), 3 W.L.R., 948.

53 Dhisadee Chamlongrasdr, "Defining a State for the Purposes of Immunity and Liability of a State and Its Entities," *European Business Law Review* 16 (2005), 1287–1324, 1290–1291.

54 Fox and Webb, *The Law of State Immunity*.

55 La Générale des Carrières et des Mines v. FG Hemisphere Associates LLC, appeal judgment (2012), UKPC 27, ILDC 2043 (UK 2012), Appeal No. 0061 of 2011, July 17, 2012, Privy Council [PC].

being sued could have a "hybrid status" with regard to "acts in the exercise of sovereign authority, identified with *acta jure imperii*."[56] However, to the extent that such an entity had been established for commercial purposes and had its own management and budget, there should be a "strong presumption . . . that its separate corporate status should be respected, and that it and the state forming it should not have to bear each other's liabilities."[57]

Hence, using the more restrictive approach, an English court would look at the incorporation, ownership, funding, and control structures of a legally separate entity in order to determine whether the corporate veil should be reverse-pierced and if the assets of the one should be available to satisfy a debt of the other. In *Gécamines*, the Privy Council concluded that because a Congolese SOE was a "real functioning corporate entity" that was "not an arm of the state," it was not liable for the judgment debt incurred by the Democratic Republic of Congo.[58] This ruling shifted the presumption against reverse-piercing and restricted the ability of counterparties to enforce judgments against sovereigns by attaching assets of SOEs. This 2012 ruling, which is the most recent on the topic of attaching SOE assets in satisfaction of a sovereign debt, seems to indicate that a legitimately created SOE functioning as a corporate entity separate from the state could not have its assets attached in satisfaction of a debt in an English court.

Central Bank Assets

Central banks and their assets benefit from a good degree of protection. In the United States, the relevant provision is Foreign Intelligence Surveillance Act, Section 1610(a)(1), which permits the attachment of property of a foreign state used for a commercial activity in the United States if that foreign state has explicitly or implicitly waived its immunity from attachment. Nevertheless, section 1611(b)(1) provides that, notwithstanding section 1610, property of a foreign central bank or monetary authority held for its own account is immune from attachment, unless that bank or authority has explicitly waived such immunity. In *EM Ltd. v. Republic of Argentina*,[59] the court held that waivers of the type described in section 1611(b)(1) must "clearly and unambiguously" waive a bank's immunity and that a general waiver provided by the parent government is inefficient.

In the United Kingdom, SIA section 13(2) provides immunity for the property of a foreign state, with the exception of property for which the foreign state has consented to attachment in writing[60] and property in use or intended to be used for commercial purposes.[61] However, section 14(4) specifically

56 Ibid., at 11.

57 Ibid., at 29.

58 Ibid., at H6–H9.

59 EM Ltd. v. Republic of Argentina, 473 F.3d 463 (2d Cir. 2007), note 22.

60 SIA, part I, sec. 13(3).

61 Ibid., sec.13(4).

provides that for the purposes of section 13(4), property of a foreign state's central bank or other monetary authority shall not be considered as in use or intended to be used for commercial purposes. As such, a central bank would benefit from immunity unless immunity is expressly waived as "the privilege against the English court's enforcement processes, conferred on a central bank which is a separate entity, is lost if and only if that entity gives its written consent."[62] The Bank of England noted in 2007 that "under U.K. law the assets of a foreign central bank or monetary authority are (other than with the written consent of the central bank or monetary authority concerned) immune from enforcement proceedings and cannot be seized in execution of judgment."[63] Hence, central bank property benefits from statutory protection in both the United Kingdom and the United States unless immunity is explicitly waived.

Military, Diplomatic, Consular, and Cultural Assets

State assets that have a military, diplomatic, or consular purpose are considered as being sovereign and noncommercial. These are generally granted sovereign immunity under international law and domestic legislation such as the FSIA.[64]

Assets that are typically immune from attachment include property used for a state's diplomatic and consular mission,[65] and property of a military character, such as warships, military aircraft, and other government ships and aircraft operated for noncommercial purposes.[66] In the case of the *ARA Libertad*, both the ITLOS and the Ghanaian Supreme Court ultimately found that the ship could not be attached due to its nature as a military asset.

Furthermore, a UN convention explicitly protects property forming part of the cultural heritage of a state or part of its archives and not placed or intended to be placed on sale, and property part of an exhibition of objects of scientific, cultural, or historical interest and not placed or intended to be placed on sale.[67]

---

62 Thai-Lao Ignite (Thailand) Co. Ltd. v. Lao People's Democratic Republic (2013), EWHC 2466. SIA secs. 13(2) and 13(3) specify that consent is necessary for the property of a state to be subject to attachment, and sec. 14(4) notes that for the purposes of these sections, "property of a State's central bank or other monetary authority shall not be regarded . . . as in use or intended for use for commercial purposes."

63 Bank of England, "Green Paper on Improving the Efficiency of the Enforcement of Judgments in the European Union: The Attachment of Bank Accounts," SEC (2006) 1341, at 1. http://ec.europa.eu/justice/news/consulting_public/judgements/contributions/other_authorities/bank_of_england_en.pdf.

64 28 U.S.C., sec. 1611.

65 UN Convention on Jurisdictional Immunities of States and Their Property, art. 21, "Specific Categories of Property."

66 Such assets are protected in UN Convention on Jurisdictional Immunities of States and Their Property, art. 21; UN Convention on the Law of the Sea, art. 32, "Immunities of Warships and Other Government Ships Operated for Non-Commercial Purposes"; and FSIA, sec. 1610(b)(2).

67 UN Convention on Jurisdictional Immunities of States and Their Property, art. 21.

Public versus Commercial Purpose Test

Many countries adhere to a restrictive understanding of sovereign immunity and use the commercial purpose test to determine whether a foreign state, one of its organs, or an SOE should be granted sovereign immunity. As the Tate Letter states, "the immunity of the sovereign is recognized with regard to sovereign or public acts (*jure imperii*) of a state, but not with respect to private acts (*jure gestionis*)." This shift was welcomed by private parties contracting with foreign states, because it grants the private parties judicial recourse with respect to private transactions in relation to which sovereign immunity should not have existed in the first place.

In the United States, a foreign state is immune from suit[68] unless it falls under one of several exceptions, notably by engaging in commercial acts whose commercial character is determined by reference to the nature, rather than the purpose, of such acts.[69] Commercial activities triggering the exception[70] include those carried out in the United States by a foreign state; those performed in the United States in connection with a commercial activity of a foreign state elsewhere; and those outside the territory of the United States in connection with a commercial activity of a foreign state elsewhere, but causing a direct effect in the United States. Ultimately, the Supreme Court stated in *Republic of Argentina v. Weltover*[71] that "when a foreign government acts, not as regulator of a market, but in the manner of a private player within it, the foreign sovereign's actions are 'commercial' within the meaning of the FSIA." Thus, when a state performs "the type of actions by which a private party engages in trade and traffic or commerce," it will not benefit from sovereign immunity.[72]

In the United Kingdom, a similar commercial activity exception[73] to general sovereign immunity exists,[74] with a "commercial transaction"[75] encompassing goods and services supply contracts, loans and other financing transactions, the provision of guarantees, and any transaction or activity (notably commercial, industrial, or professional) into which a state enters or in which it engages other than in the exercise of its sovereign authority. Ultimately, as the court held in *Trendtex*, "there is no [sovereign] immunity in respect of commercial transactions, even for a government department."[76]

---

68 28 U.S.C., sec. 1604.

69 Ibid., sec. 1603(d).

70 Ibid., sec. 1605.

71 Republic of Argentina v. Weltover, 504 U.S. 607 (1992).

72 *Weltover*, 504 U.S. at 614.

73 SIA, part I, sec. 3(1)a.

74 Ibid., sec. 1(1).

75 Ibid., sec. 3(3).

76 *Trendtex*, at 56.

Mixed/Hybrid Purpose

Although a line between the public and the commercial undoubtedly exists, it can be difficult to discern at times because assets or property belonging to a state can take on a mixed or hybrid nature and be used by a sovereign for both purposes. A prime example is that of an embassy's bank account, which might simultaneously be used to fulfill a diplomatic mission and to conduct purely commercial transactions. In such cases, courts have often taken the side of caution and given weight to an asset's public, rather than commercial, purpose, as in the English case *Taurus Petroleum Limited v. State Oil Company of the Ministry of Oil, Republic of Iraq,*[77] in which the Commercial Court found that the Iraqi Oil Proceeds Account benefited from immunity (even though, prior to being deposited into the account, the funds did not). The approach has been the same in the United States, and in *LETCO v. Government of the Republic of Liberia,*[78] the court did not allow execution against bank accounts owned by the Liberian embassy in the United States on the basis of FSIA section 1609.[79] Indeed, the court found that the accounts' primary purpose was not commercial and concluded that "the concept of 'commercial activity' should be defined narrowly because sovereign immunity remains the rule rather than the exception."[80]

Sovereign Immunity: Examples of the Concept in Other States

Turkey

Sovereign immunity as applied in Turkey differs somewhat from the commonly accepted concept under international law. With regard to immunity from suit, governmental entities do not enjoy immunity under Turkish law and can be sued by Turkish or foreign individuals and corporations before the country's administrative courts. Also, the Turkish state or its governmental entities may enter into arbitration agreements with private contractual counterparties when the matter at hand is considered "arbitrable," as concession agreements have been since 1999,[81] thus limiting the jurisdiction of

---

77 Taurus Petroleum Limited v. State Oil Company of the Ministry of Oil, Republic of Iraq (2015), EWCA Civ. 835.

78 Liberian Eastern Timber Corp. (LETCO) v. Government of the Republic of Liberia, 650 F. Supp. 73 (U.S. Dist. 1986).

79 28 U.S.C., sec. 1609: "Subject to existing international agreements to which the United States is a party at the time of enactment of this Act the property in the United States of a foreign state shall be immune from attachment arrest and execution except as provided in sections 1610 and 1611 of this chapter."

80 Mathew Saunders and Claudia Salomon, "Enforcement of Arbitral Awards Against States and State Entities," *Arbitration International London Court of International Arbitration* 23, no. 3 (2007): 471.

81 Art. 125 was added to the constitution on August 13, 1999, by act no. 4446, and states that "in concession . . . contracts concerning public services . . . national or international arbitration may be suggested to settle the disputes arising from them." However, "only those disputes involving an element of foreignness may be submitted to international arbitration."

administrative courts. As such, it is not necessary to seek a waiver of sovereign immunity from the state or its governmental entities for arbitration clauses, project agreements, or project documents.

With regard to enforcement, state assets are immune from seizure or attachment under articles 82 and 83(a) of the Execution and Bankruptcy Law,[82] and this immunity cannot be limited or waived under Turkish law.[83] Further, if the state or a governmental entity is a debtor under a contract, assets that are used to provide public services may not be used to satisfy a court judgment or arbitral award rendered in relation to a dispute arising under this contract.[84]

Iraq

A foreign investor in Iraq seeking to enforce an arbitral award against the government would face two possible scenarios. First, enforcement could be sought against state-owned assets located in the country; however, such an attempt would likely be unsuccessful because state-owned assets enjoy absolute immunity from execution under Iraqi law, which cannot be waived. As such, an Iraqi court would likely refuse to enforce a foreign award against the state. Moreover, the country is not party to the Convention on the Recognition and Enforcement of Foreign Arbitral Awards.[85] As an alternative, enforcement may be sought against state-owned assets located abroad. An investor would seek recognition and enforcement of the arbitral award in a country that has acceded to the New York Convention and where the government of Iraq has assets; likely examples are the United States and Turkey. As long as the government has provided a clean waiver of sovereign immunity, its commercial assets in the United States, for example, would be attachable in the United States.

Sovereign Immunity versus Asset Protection: The Sovereign's Dilemma

Waivers of Sovereign Immunity and Recent Limitations

With the development of international project finance in which private parties often contract with host governments, it is commonplace for the governments to contractually waive their right to claim immunity from suit, execution, or enforcement. In such a case, a counterparty can sue a sovereign before foreign courts and attach its assets if the sovereign country declines or fails to settle a judgment debt or arbitral award. However, recent developments indicate that

---

82 Law No. 2004, published in the *Official Gazette,* dated June 19, 1932, no. 2128.

83 Jeffrey Delmon and Victoria Rigby Delmon, *International Project Finance and PPPs: A Legal Guide to Key Growth Markets* (London: Kluwer Law International, 2010), 31.

84 This includes assets of municipalities and other public entities allocated to public use that fall under the Execution and Bankruptcy Law, art. 82.

85 The 1958 Convention on the Recognition and Enforcement of Foreign Arbitral Awards is often referred to as the "New York Convention."

certain governments in emerging countries wish to reverse this trend. States rarely categorically reject waivers and instead seek to carve out certain valuable assets in order to shield them from attachment, for instance, those of a national oil company, sovereign investment fund, or central bank.

In one case, a host government attempted to negotiate specific arrangements for carve-outs to sovereign immunity subject to certain security arrangements to offset additional risk.[86] The attempt, which was ultimately rejected, resulted in protracted negotiations regarding an otherwise standard clause. An approach such as this one could result in sovereign immunity waivers becoming one of many contractual clauses subject to commercial negotiation.

In the end, this type of arrangement would run counter to international best practice, disadvantage weaker project sponsors, make host countries unattractive for investment, complicate transactions, and heighten the risk of disputes. Although the risks and concerns expressed by governments wanting to protect certain assets can be appreciated, one must not lose sight of the more immediate and potentially significant developmental objectives of a country and how such protections can adversely impact the country's ability to meet such objectives. Sovereign immunity provisions are sacrosanct in the international investment community, and diminishing the ability to enforce a judgment or arbitral award against a defaulting government is likely to send a negative message to investors and thus curtail development. Specific examples are set forth in this section.

Nigeria

On August 11, 2014, the federal government of Nigeria released a circular to "provide additional protection for [the federal government of Nigeria]" and "[limit] the waiver of immunity from foreign proceedings against the [federal government of Nigeria] or any of [its] departments."[87] The document was released in part in reaction to the *Kensington* ruling, which the circular explicitly cites in mentioning that the Commercial Court of England and Wales had "[reverse]-pierced the corporate veil," and which found that the Congolese national oil company was a part of the Congolese state and had no existence separate from it.

Rather than rejecting waivers of sovereign immunity outright, the circular sought to limit the efficiency of waivers by mandating the insertion into all contracts and arbitration agreements entered into by the federal government

---

86 The proposal, which was ultimately not implemented, contemplated that, in the event of a dispute, the state would put in place a payment security to cover the claim. In exchange, the private counterparty would agree to limit the state's waiver of sovereign immunity and carve out certain assets from attachment. If the state failed to offer acceptable security, then the standard waiver of immunity would be reinstated, including over the protected assets.

87 "Protection of the Federal Government and Its Corporation from Foreign Enforcement Proceedings Arising from Contract or Arbitration in Foreign Jurisdictions," circular no. SGF/OP/1/S:3/X/737, does not appear to have the force of law, but it has proved to be a significant obstacle in concluding bankable project finance transactions in the country.

of Nigeria of a "specimen indemnity clause," which would qualify any waiver of sovereign immunity with respect to three entities whose assets would thus be ring-fenced and secured. The three entities, which are linked to, but legally separate from, the federal government of Nigeria, are the Nigerian National Petroleum Corporation, the Nigerian Sovereign Investment Authority, and the CBN.

Under the terms of the indemnity clause, a party that enters into an agreement with the federal government of Nigeria cannot bring suit against any of these three entities in foreign jurisdictions, nor seize or attach any of their assets in arbitration award enforcement proceedings taking place in foreign jurisdictions. Should a contract counterparty nevertheless succeed in doing so, it would have to indemnify the relevant entity.

As might be expected, the reaction from foreign investors, sponsors, lenders, and political risk insurers has been largely negative. In the context of project finance transactions, the insertion of such language significantly departs from established best practice and hampers projects' bankability, a serious drawback considering that project financings tend to be highly leveraged. The federal government of Nigeria's contract counterparties are unable to seek recourse abroad and are unlikely to rely on domestic procedures because attaching assets belonging to the three entities is either illegal under Nigerian law[88] or sufficiently impractical to deter attempts.[89] Further, Nigeria's economy is highly dependent on oil, which represents more than 90 percent of the value of the country's exports[90] and 75 percent of government revenue.[91] Because so much of the country's wealth stems from oil revenue and considering the Nigerian National Petroleum Corporation's track record with respect

---

88 For instance, the Nigerian National Petroleum Corporation Act (no. 33 of 1977, chap. 320, Law of the Federal Republic of Nigeria 1990), sec. 14, states that "in any action or suit against the Corporation no execution or attachment or process in the nature thereof shall be issued against the Corporation." Further, Sheriffs and Civil Process Act (June 1, 1945, chap. 407, Laws of the Federation of Nigeria 1990), sec. 84, provides that funds in the custody or control of a public officer may be attached only with the consent of the attorney general of the federation (or the attorney general of a Nigerian state, if the funds are under the control of a state officer). Under the Nigerian constitution, "public service of a state" is defined to include the "staff of any statutory corporation" (1999 constitution of the Federal Republic of Nigeria, part IV, sec. 318), and as such, the attorney general must grant consent for the attachment of assets belonging to statutory corporations, such as the Nigerian National Petroleum Corporation or the Nigerian Sovereign Investment Authority.

89 It is at times claimed that Nigerian state entities benefit from "tacit protection" in Nigerian courts and can "turn to nebulous public policy considerations as a basis for disallowing enforcement." See Templars, "Beating the System," *International Financial Law Review* (September 1, 2012), http://www.iflr.com/Article/3083700/Nigeria-Beating-the-system.html.

90 The value of Nigeria's petroleum exports stood at almost $77 billion in 2015, for total exports of just under $84 billion (Organization of the Petroleum Exporting Countries, Nigeria Facts and Figures, http://www.opec.org/opec_web/en/about_us/167.htm).

91 "Well Below Par: Over-reliance on Oil Spells Trouble for Nigeria," *The Economist* (November 29, 2014), http://www.economist.com/news/finance-and-economics/21635051-over-reliance-oil-spells-trouble-nigeria-well-below-par.

to transferring oil proceeds to the treasury,[92] ring-fencing the corporation's assets effectively precludes an investor from satisfying an arbitral award or judgment made in its favor. Ultimately, the federal government of Nigeria is seeking to limit its exposure and the effect of any waiver of sovereign immunity by restricting the judicial recourse available to contract counterparties. Recognizing that implementing this circular would deter foreign investors and financial institutions from investing in the country, the recently elected government has indicated that it will review the application of the circular so as to provide clean waivers to make transactions bankable.

Ghana

The Ghana Petroleum Revenue Management Act (PRMA)[93] laid down the framework for the collection and use of oil revenues by the government of Ghana and provides that three funds be created to manage various oil assets;[94] that petroleum assets may not be pledged as collateral;[95] and that a court may not order their attachment.[96] In recent transactions, the government of Ghana has sought to go beyond the PRMA's language by carving out a number of protected assets to shield them from attachment procedures, namely defense, diplomatic, and consular, but especially petroleum and assets, domestic and abroad.

Such a shift would have broadly negative consequences by increasing the risks associated with investments into the country, sending a negative message to the investment community and undermining the bankability of privately financed investments where the government is a direct or indirect party. Financiers in project finance transactions who are interested in investing in developing markets carefully consider the ability to enforce judgments and arbitral awards outside the host country when assessing the attractiveness of competing investment opportunities and do not view favorably jurisdictions where states' contract counterparties are denied the right to seek redress for investment disputes or to enforce judgments and arbitral awards.

---

92 William Wallis, "Nigeria Audit: State Oil Company Siphoning Oil Revenues," *Financial Times* (April 28, 2015), http://www.ft.com/intl/cms/s/0/5ebb5f3c-edb2-11e4-987e-00144feab7de.html#axzz3hlw9klxz. For a comprehensive analysis, refer to PWC's report "Auditor-General for the Federation: Investigative Forensic Audit into the Allegations of Unremitted Funds into the Federation Accounts by the NNPC" (February 2015), http://cloudflare.qurium.info/premiumtimesng.com/docs_download/Full%20report--20billion%20dollars%20missing%20oil%20money.pdf?cf=1.

93 Ghana Petroleum Revenue Management Act, no. 815 (April 11, 2011), http://www.mofep.gov.gh/sites/default/files/reports/Petroleum_Revenue_Management_Act_%202011.PDF.

94 The Petroleum Holding Fund, the Ghana Stabilization Fund, and the Ghana Heritage Fund were created by arts. 2, 9, and 10 respectively of the PRMA. The holding fund is an intermediate fund in which all oil revenue is deposited before being forwarded to other funds; the stabilization fund is used to mitigate the negative effects on the national budget of volatile oil prices; and the heritage fund is used to save oil revenues for future generations. The latter two are collectively known as the Ghana Petroleum Funds (PRMA, art. 11).

95 PRMA, art. 5(1)(b).

96 Ibid., art. 41.

Signs indicate that the government of Ghana might be less preoccupied with the attachment of its assets or those of the Ghana National Petroleum Corporation than it is with these assets risking attachment prior to an arbitral award having been rendered. As such, the government seems to be amenable to providing unconditional waivers of sovereign immunity in Ghana other than with respect to preaward attachment.[97] Ultimately, although protection for petroleum assets is not customary, investors could accept the carving out of military, diplomatic, and consular assets, especially because these benefit from a degree of protection under customary international law.

Conclusion

The doctrine of sovereign immunity has developed over recent decades under both international treaties and relevant domestic legislation, but clarity is needed on the application of these laws. In particular, the issue of whether the enforcement of commercial assets of a state abroad—whether belonging to an SOE or to the sovereign—should be allowed in all circumstances needs to be elucidated.

Although the risks and concerns expressed by governments wanting to limit waivers of sovereign immunity can be appreciated from a legal perspective, the more immediate and potentially significant adverse implications such waivers will have on investments in a country must be considered. Limiting a sovereign's waiver of immunity could be perceived as diminishing the counterparty's ability to enforce a judgment or arbitral award against a defaulting government and could send a negative message to the international investment community; increase the risks associated with investments in sectors that, given their current status of development, require government backstops; and undermine the "bankability" of privately financed investments in which the government is party to a crucial transaction document.

These concerns can be exacerbated when considering the economic challenges in certain emerging markets. For instance, a country highly dependent

---

97 Africa Centre for Energy Policy, "Ghana's New Petroleum Agreements Show Major Improvements as Risks [sic] Levels Reduce: The Cases of Ghana-AGM and Ghana-COLA/MEDEA Petroleum Agreements" (May 2014), http://www.aceplive.com/wp-content/uploads/2014/06/Comparative-Review-of-AGM-and-COLA-Contracts.pdf, 16. Note that in February 2014, an agreement for oil exploration, development, and production (between the government of Ghana, the Ghana National Petroleum Corporation, Camac Energy Ghana Limited, Base Energy Ghana Limited, and GNPC Exploration and Production Company Limited) was presented to the Parliament of Ghana in accordance with art. 268 of the 1992 constitution requiring that all agreements or leases involving natural resources be ratified by the legislature (session of February 27, 2014, regarding the Expanded Shallow Water, Tano Block Offshore). The agreement concluded that "an important feature of the Petroleum Agreement noted by the Committee was the prohibition against the attachment of Government assets in the case of a dispute prior to the final arbitral award" and "urged the Ministry to make this provision a permanent feature of Petroleum Agreements of the State" (Official Report for March 21, 2014, of the Select Committee on Mines and Energy. Elements can be found at http://www.parliament.gh/publications/30/812).

on oil can be vulnerable to commodity price volatility and thus may need to diversify its economy to achieve sustainable, inclusive growth. This diversification will require, among other policies, a thriving private sector and the attraction of large sums of local and foreign private investment. Achieving these objectives requires a climate that supports private sector investment. Any atypical limitation to the waiver of sovereign immunity may hinder progress in meeting these objectives.

Ultimately, it is up to each country to determine the balance between its interests in meeting commercial and developmental goals and objectives, which includes attracting investment and developing infrastructure, on the one hand, and the desire to protect public assets by instituting limitations to waivers of sovereign immunity, on the other.

PART III

Socioeconomic Rights

8

Human Rights and the Post-2015 Sustainable Development Goals

Reflections on Challenges and Opportunities

SIOBHÁN MCINERNEY-LANKFORD AND HANS-OTTO SANO

The debate about the relationship between human rights and the Millennium Development Goals (MDGs) is a well-known one, to which authoritative voices from both the development and human rights communities have contributed.[1] Scholars have pointed to the convergence of human rights and MDGs, citing as evidence the compatibility of their general aims and orientation. However, others have highlighted that MDGs and human rights operate in separate, parallel spheres, underscoring that the disconnects and divergences are more pervasive than the points of convergence, which arguably results in a lack of coherence and accountability, particularly in terms of legal obligations.[2] There are also important qualitative differences between the frameworks governing each: MDGs are couched essentially in terms of political commitments, while human rights are embedded in legal obligations underpinned by international treaties and transposed into domestic legal and regulatory frameworks. Human rights, by their nature, imply obligations, as reflected in the range of international human rights treaties.[3] By contrast, development activities have been undertaken under "looser" frameworks that are posited in terms of action plans, goals, and declarations; rarely invoking the notions of duty or obligations, whether of an international or a domestic sort.

The views expressed in this article are those of the authors and do not necessarily reflect the views of the Board of Executive Directors of the World Bank or the governments they represent. The authors thank Anna Chytla, Laurence Boisson de Chazournes, and Frank Fariello for comments on an earlier draft of this chapter. Responsibility for errors or omissions remains with the authors.

1 See, for example, Mac Darrow, "Master or Servant? Development Goals and Human Rights" (chap. 4), and Thomas Pogge, "Poverty, Hunger, and Cosmetic Progress" (chap. 8), in *The Millennium Development Goals and Human Rights: Past, Present and Future*, ed. Malcom Langford, Andy Sumner, and Alicia Ely Yamin (Cambridge: Cambridge University Press, 2013).

2 Siobhán McInerney-Lankford, "International Development Actors and Human Rights," in *Millennium Development Goals and Human Rights*, ed. Langford, Sumner, and Yamin, 160.

3 Such as the International Covenant on Civil and Political Rights (ICCPR) and the International Covenant on Economic, Social and Cultural Rights (ICESCR), as well as the regional human rights instruments, such as the European Convention on Human Rights (ECHR), the American Convention on Human Rights (ACHR), the African Charter on Human and Peoples' Rights (ACHPR), and the EU Charter of Fundamental Rights.

This chapter assesses human rights critiques of the MDGs and considers the extent to which the Sustainable Development Goals (SDGs)[4] respond to these. The human rights critiques of MDGs are analyzed along the vectors of three human rights principles: (1) equality and nondiscrimination, (2) participation and inclusion, and (3) accountability. These are among the key principles of a human rights–based approach (HRBA), proclaimed by the UN agencies in the 2003 "Human Rights–Based Approach—Statement of Common Understanding."[5]

These three principles are used in the chapter as a frame for the analysis of the SDGs to assess whether and how the latter respond to the human rights critiques of the MDGs, either explicitly or implicitly, acknowledging that if they do, it may also be fortuitous, and not the result of deliberate effort to respond to human rights critics of the MDGs. This chapter also considers the role and place of indicators in integrating human rights into the SDGs, and provides a preliminary "human rights assessment" of the proposed indicators under the SDGs. The assessment is organized according to the three foregoing substantive principles and along two structural dimensions: the SDG declaration and its goals and targets, and the SDG indicators.

The overall purpose of the chapter is to answer the question of whether, considering the human rights critiques of the MDGs, there has been an "effective integration" of human rights into the 2015 SDG framework.[6]

General Features of MDGs and SDGs

This section introduces both MDGs and SDGs. The discussion of MDGs focuses more on goals; the discussion of SDGs considers the SDG framework in more detail, with more in-depth analysis of its goals, as well as the accompanying targets and indicators of those goals.

---

4 The SDGs were formally adopted by the UN General Assembly on September 25, 2015, under Resolution 69/85 http://www.un.org/ga/search/view_doc.asp?symbol=A/69/L.85&Lang=E. The SDGs (also called the Global Goals) and accompanying targets have been endorsed by governments, but their indicators have yet to be elaborated. They were also presented in a document entitled *Transforming Our World: The 2030 Agenda for Sustainable Development* (August 1, 2015) [hereafter referred to as the "2015 SDG outcome document"].

5 "Annex B" in UNICEF's *State of the World's Children* (2004), http://www.unicef.org/sowc04/files/AnnexB.pdf. See also http://hrbaportal.org/the-un-and-hrba. Other human rights principles identified by the United Nations in an HRBA are universality and inalienability, indivisibility, interdependence, and interrelatedness. For a discussion of these human rights principles and the distinction between the substantive and structural principles among them, see Axel Marx, Siobhán McInerney-Lankford, Jan Wouters, and David D'Hollander, "Human Rights and Service Delivery: A Review of Current Policies, Practices, and Challenges," in *The World Bank Legal Review*, vol. 6, *Improving Delivery in Development: The Role of Voice, Social Contract and Accountability*, ed. Jan Wouters, Alberto Ninio, Teresa Doherty, and Hassane Cisse (Washington, DC: World Bank, 2015).

6 2015 SDG outcome document.

The MDGs

The MDGs are a set of eight goals elaborated in 2000 following the Millennium Summit and Millennium Declaration.[7] The MDGs comprise the following eight development goals, with corresponding targets and indicators (not included):

1. Eradicate extreme poverty and hunger
2. Achieve universal primary education
3. Promote gender equality and empower women
4. Reduce child mortality
5. Improve maternal health
6. Combat HIV/AIDS, malaria, and other diseases
7. Ensure environmental sustainability
8. Develop a global partnership for development

The significance of the goals can be understood in a variety of ways. For example, the goals represent a first global effort to reduce poverty by reference to a set of agreed-on goals supported by wide political consensus. Moreover, the goals are visible, easily communicated, and put numbers and targets behind otherwise potentially vague or inchoate goals. Despite some shortcomings of the MDGs, many observers acknowledge their influence on improved monitoring and in strengthened development-related data and statistics. However, even aside from human rights critiques, the goals were also criticized for focusing excessively on growth and poverty defined in relation to only income poverty, for failing to consider poverty in multidimensional terms, and for giving insufficient attention to gender, marginalized groups, the environment, employment and working conditions, and hunger and nutrition, as well as governance. The MDGs were the subject of a range of other critiques, such as for being insufficiently ambitious; undergirded by weak and inappropriate targets; incapable of registering discrimination and inequality, whether within or between countries; and unlikely to have their potential met, even as inequalities were growing. They were also viewed by some commentators as crowding out other priorities and as being reductionist;[8] the UN secretary-general's report "In Larger Freedom" made clear that the MDGs were a key component of the development agenda, but they did not account for the agenda in its entirety: "We need to see the MDGs as part of an even larger development agenda. While the goals have been the subject of an enormous amount of follow-up both inside and outside the UN, they clearly do not in themselves represent a complete development agenda" (para. 30). Indeed, of

---

7 UN General Assembly Resolution 55/2, "United Nations Millennium Declaration," http://www.un.org/millennium/declaration/ares552e.htm.

8 Sakiko Fukuda-Parr, Alicia Ely Yamin, and Joshua Greenstein. "Synthesis Paper – The Power of Numbers: A Critical Review of the MDG Targets for Human Development and Human Rights," Working Paper Series (Harvard School of Public Health, The New School, 2013).

the 48 goals enumerated in the Millennium Summit and the Millennium Declaration, the MDGs were distilled to just 8.

The SDGs

The SDGs emerge as a confluence of the post-2015 framework and Rio+20. It was also agreed that the SDG framework should be based on Agenda 21 and the Johannesburg Plan of Implementation. It was further agreed that the SDG framework should (1) fully respect all the Rio Principles; (2) be consistent with international law; (3) build upon commitments already made; (4) contribute to the full implementation of the outcomes of all major summits in the economic, social, and environmental fields; (5) focus on priority areas for the achievement of sustainable development, being guided by the outcome document; (6) address and incorporate in a balanced way all three dimensions of sustainable development and their interlinkages; (7) be coherent with and integrated into the UN development agenda beyond 2015; (8) not divert focus or effort from the achievement of the MDGs; and (9) include active involvement of all relevant stakeholders, as appropriate, in the process.[9] The Rio+20 outcome document also envisaged the establishment of an Open Working Group (OWG) which later became the focal point for formulating the new goals in a manner that was more participatory and transparent than the formulation of the MDGs was.[10]

The SDGs comprise the following 17 goals:

Goal 1: End poverty in all its forms everywhere

Goal 2: End hunger, achieve food security and improved nutrition and promote sustainable agriculture

Goal 3: Ensure healthy lives and promote well-being for all at all ages

Goal 4: Ensure inclusive and equitable quality education and promote lifelong learning opportunities for all

Goal 5: Achieve gender equality and empower all women and girls

Goal 6: Ensure availability and sustainable management of water and sanitation for all

Goal 7: Ensure access to affordable, reliable, sustainable and modern energy for all

Goal 8: Promote sustained, inclusive and sustainable economic growth, full and productive employment and decent work for all

---

9 See the Rio+20 outcome document, *The Future We Want*, http://www.uncsd2012.org/content/documents/727The%20Future%20We%20Want%2019%20June%201230pm.pdf.

10 Space does not permit a detailed account of the OWG processes. By July 2014, after 13 sessions, the OWG made proposals for the 17 goals, which were endorsed in July 2015 and confirmed at the UN General Assembly in September 2015.

Goal 9: Build resilient infrastructure, promote inclusive and sustainable industrialization and foster innovation

Goal 10: Reduce inequality within and among countries

Goal 11: Make cities and human settlements inclusive, safe, resilient and sustainable

Goal 12: Ensure sustainable consumption and production patterns

Goal 13: Take urgent action to combat climate change and its impacts[11]

Goal 14: Conserve and sustainably use the oceans, seas and marine resources for sustainable development

Goal 15: Protect, restore and promote sustainable use of terrestrial ecosystems, sustainably manage forests, combat desertification, and halt and reverse land degradation and halt biodiversity loss

Goal 16: Promote peaceful and inclusive societies for sustainable development, provide access to justice for all and build effective, accountable and inclusive institutions at all levels

Goal 17: Strengthen the means of implementation and revitalize the global partnership for sustainable development

The goals have also been synthesized by the UN secretary-general around six essential elements or themes:

1. Dignity: to end poverty and to fight inequalities (Goals 1 and 10)
2. Prosperity: to grow a strong, inclusive, and transformative economy (Goals 7, 8, 9, and 12)
3. Justice: to promote safe and peaceful societies, and strong institutions (Goal 16)
4. Partnership: to catalyse global solidarity for sustainable development (Goal 17)
5. Planet: to protect our ecosystems for all societies and for our children (Goals 2, 11, 13, 14, and 15)
6. People: to ensure healthy lives, knowledge, and the inclusion of women and children (Goals 3, 4, 5, and 6)[12]

The SDGs enumerated above have been fixed, along with a set of 169 targets, in a document titled "Transforming Our World: The 2030 Agenda for Sustainable Development" (August 1, 2015, accepted by the General Assembly September 2015).

---

11 Acknowledging that the UN Framework Convention on Climate Change is the primary international, intergovernmental forum for negotiating the global response to climate change.

12 United Nations, *The Road to Dignity by 2030: Ending Poverty, Transforming All Lives and Protecting the Planet*, Synthesis Report of the Secretary-General on the Post-2015 Agenda (New York: United Nations, 2014).

While the goals and targets set forth in that document are not expected to change at the time of going to press, the work on indicators accompanying them is still under way and not yet complete. At the 46th meeting of the UN Statistical Commission in March 2015, the Inter-agency and Expert Group on SDG Indicators (IAEG-SDGs) was established to elaborate a global indicator framework to monitor the goals and targets of the post-2015 agenda. The IAEG-SDGs is composed of member-states and includes representatives of regional and international agencies as observers. A list of proposed indicators consisting of approximately two indicators per target was prepared; altogether, 304 indicators were proposed relative to the 169 targets. The first meeting of the IAEG-SDGs on the proposed indicators was held in June 2015, in advance of which a first "Proposed Priority Indicator List" was circulated. A conclusion of the June 2015 meeting was that proposals from agencies had not been adequately taken into account. This led to the formulation of a new set of proposed indicators presented on July 7, 2015, incorporating inputs from statistical agencies and international organizations. A consultation on the current list of indicators among statistical agencies and major stakeholders closed on September 21, 2015, with a second meeting of the IAEG-SDGs held at the end of October 2015. On December 7, 2015, a document was submitted to the IAEG members in the process of preparing the UN Statistical Commission for its 47th session in March 2016.[13] It is therefore too early to make a final human rights assessment of the proposed indicators, but some preliminary observations are offered below.

Three Human Rights Critiques of the MDGs

Human rights critics of the MDGs often cite the lack of a freestanding human rights goal and the absence of an explicit mention of human rights in either the goals or targets. Even if the substance of a number of economic, social, and cultural rights can be identified in several of the goals, the civil and political rights content is almost entirely absent, as evidenced in the weak reflection of equality and nondiscrimination, participation and inclusion, and accountability.[14]

Equality and Nondiscrimination

Human rights law provides for the protection of particular vulnerable groups[15] (e.g., children, persons with disabilities, and migrant workers), and an HRBA, by definition, focuses on the poorest and most marginalized, which in turn may be seen to translate into concern for the bottom quintiles. Through equality

---

13 See IAEG-SDGs, http://unstats.un.org/sdgs/iaeg-sdgs/index.html.

14 See also the succinct analysis by Paul Nelson, "Human Rights, the Millennium Development Goals, and the Future of Development Cooperation," *World Development* 35, no. 12 (2007): 2041–2055.

15 The two main covenants on, respectively, civil and political rights and on economic, social, and cultural rights prohibit distinctions of any kind based on race, color, sex, language, religion, political or other opinion, national or social origin, property, birth, or other status. A human rights–based interpretation of vulnerable groups will depart from this understanding.

provisions and prohibitions on direct and especially indirect discrimination,[16] human rights tackle structural discrimination and barriers and intersecting forms of discrimination (e.g., gender and race). The MDGs, for their part, were focused on averages, not disaggregated data, and had the potential to overlook the bottom quintile and the most vulnerable.[17] Thus, interventions based on the MDGs could replicate embedded structures of exclusion and discrimination.

Participation and Inclusion

Human rights law places emphasis on *process*, on *how* entitlements are distributed, and on the *means* by which rights are respected, protected, and fulfilled. A critique related to participation and inclusion can be applied both to the content of the MDGs and SDGs, as well as to the process by which they were elaborated. Human rights–based approaches emphasize transparency, access to information, meaningful consultation, participation, inclusion, and redress, whether through courts and quasi-judicial bodies or more informal mechanisms such as ombuds. By doing so, HRBAs implicate a broad range of civil and political rights. Human rights augur the potential for transformative, inclusive processes, and they can help guide trade-offs and policy choices; critically, they view individuals and communities as both subjects and agents of development. It is noteworthy that the Millennium Declaration referred to the effective participation of all citizens in the political process, albeit only once.

MDG Content. The content of the MDGs does not reveal an emphasis on process or participation; there is no goal or target that speaks to a civil or political right. A single relevant exception is the proposed indicator measuring the proportion of seats held by women in national parliament.

MDG Process of Elaboration. Beyond content, a number of related criticisms can be leveled against the *process* of elaboration of the MDGs, which was widely perceived to be closed, veiled in secrecy, and run by technical experts. Some observers have noted that the process lacked transparency, that the criteria for

---

16 For example, ICCPR, article 26: "All persons are equal before the law and are entitled without any discrimination to the equal protection of the law. In this respect, the law shall prohibit any discrimination and guarantee to all persons equal and effective protection against discrimination on any ground such as race, colour, sex, language, religion, political or other opinion, national or social origin, property, birth or other status."; and ICESCR, article 2 (2) 2: "The States Parties to the present Covenant undertake to guarantee that the rights enunciated in the present Covenant will be exercised without discrimination of any kind as to race, colour, sex, language, religion, political or other opinion, national or social origin, property, birth or other status." The EU Charter of Fundamental Rights also contains equality provisions under chapter 3.

17 See UN System Task Team on the Post-2015 UN Development Agenda *Review of the Contributions of the MDG Agenda to Foster Development: Lessons for the Post-2015 UN Development Agenda. Discussion Note* (New York: United Nations, 2012), http://www.un.org/millennium-goals/pdf/mdg_assessment_Aug.pdf. From a human rights point of view, critiques have been raised against the MDG monitoring of national averages, namely, that these metrics mask significant differences with respect to ethnic or indigenous groups. See Office of the High Commissioner for Human Rights (OHCHR), UNICEF, and Norwegian Center for Human Rights (NCHR), *Human Rights and the MDGs in Practice: A Review of Country Strategies and Reporting* (New York: OHCHR and UNICEF, and Oslo: NCHR, 2010).

the selection of the eight goals was not debated or made clear, and that there was little discussion of the goals and targets in advance of their adoption. This overall set of circumstances has led some critics to challenge the participatory quality of the process of elaborating the MDGs.[18]

Accountability

A general problem identified in the MDGs is the ad hoc accountability framework underpinning them. Accountability can be understood as "answerability" of institutions, mandating justifications for rules or policies and reasoned decisions, and some consequences if states fail to live up to applicable standards through redress mechanisms and remedies.[19] At a foundational level, the MDGs represent soft commitments, with a weak monitoring mechanism (Global Monitoring), which is particularly evident with respect to MDG Goal 8. There is, moreover, no legal redress or recourse where the goals or targets are not met. If there is any legal accountability attaching to the MDGs, it is reflected only selectively at the national level, which, while not insignificant, is no substitute for binding international treaty obligations in the context of a global development pact.

The explicit incorporation of human rights would potentially have had important implications for the "accountability deficit" of the MDGs, because rights imply duties or obligations. Indeed, an increased focus on accountability is viewed by many as a key contribution that human rights can make in development.[20] By definition, rights and duties are about increased accountability. Put differently, "the principle of accountability asserts that people are active subjects or claim holders. To have a right is to have a claim against others, whether against other individuals or against organized social units like the family or the state."[21] Moreover, human rights treaties create a double compact, with obligations operating both horizontally (between states parties) and vertically (between governments and their citizens).[22] Invoking a right makes a significant difference to the nature of claims: it makes entitlements

---

18 See, for example, Roberto Bissio, "Civil Society and the MDGs," *Development Policy Journal*, 3 (2013): 151–160.

19 Jutta Brunnée, "International Legal Accountability through the Lens of the Law of State Responsibility," *Netherlands Yearbook of International Law* 36 (2005): 4; and P. Newell and J. Wheeler, eds., *Rights, Resources, and the Politics of Accountability* (London: Zed, 2006).

20 Siobhán McInerney-Lankford, "International Development Actors and Human Rights," 162; and Paul Gready, "Rights-Based Approaches to Development: What Is Value Added?" *Development in Practice* 18, no. 6 (2008): 735–747.

21 Lachlan Munro, "The Rights-Based Approach to Programming: A Contradiction in Terms?" in *Rights-Based Approaches to Development: Exploring the Potential and Pitfalls*, ed. Sam Hickey and Diana Matlin (Sterling, VA: Kumarian Press, 2009), 190.

22 "The double compact focuses on the 'network of rights and obligations underpinning the state's claim to sovereignty . . .' and refers first to the 'compact . . . between a state and its citizens . . . embedded in a coherent set of rules,' and second, 'between a state and the international community to ensure adherence to international norms and standards of accountability and transparency.'" See Ashraf Ghani and Clare Lockhart, *Fixing Failed States: A Framework for Rebuilding a Fractured World* (Oxford: Oxford University Press, 2008), 8.

(e.g., economic and social rights) the subject of legal obligation. Rights require effective accountability mechanisms, monitoring systems, and mechanisms of redress to enforce entitlements and respond to violations. These are necessary at both the national and the international level (both "upward" and "downward"), corresponding with the vertical and horizontal accountability mentioned above. Human rights require both peer review, such as the Universal Periodic Review (UPR) mechanism and complaints mechanisms (committees with protocols), and they imply judicial (courts) and nonlegal[23] (media and social accountability mechanisms, including budgets), quasi-judicial (e.g., national human rights institutions), and parliamentary bodies, as well as ombuds. In sum, had they been made an explicit part of the framework, human rights would have introduced some (legal) accountability for both the process and the outcomes of the MDGs.

A related consequence of the accountability deficit is that the MDGs have been critiqued for being charity-, not obligations-based; the absence of an explicit reference to human rights or human rights obligations can leave the goals without a binding (normative) standard against which to measure efforts or progress or generate implications where the goals or targets are not met. Furthermore, human rights law introduces a minimum value baseline, which is undergirded by a basic commitment not to undermine the prevailing standard of human rights enjoyment. Human rights law can provide a framework to balance competing interests and to assess reasonableness (e.g., through proportionality tests). The principle of "do no harm" requires making informed decisions, assessing risk, and mitigating it where possible. This may be important here, because some MDG-related policies have been argued to have the potential to violate human rights; for instance, in the construction of a large dam, which generates power to benefit an entire country, and hence may help achieve Goals 1 and 7, but which also displaces certain vulnerable communities, depriving them of property, livelihoods, and cultural heritage without due process and in violation of their rights.

Reflections on Human Rights in the SDGs

The following discussion offers reflections on the nature and extent of human rights integration in the SDGs with a focus on equality, participation, and accountability.

General Observations on Human Rights in the SDGs

The preamble of the declaration in the final text of the SDG framework, which was adopted during the September 2015 UN General Assembly,[24] contains a number of references to human rights.

---

23 United Nations Development Programme (UNDP), *Beyond the Midpoint: Accelerating Support for MDG Achievement* (New York: UNDP, 2009), 24.

24 Hereafter, the "2015 SDG outcome document."

The preamble proclaims, "The 17 Sustainable Development Goals and 169 targets . . . seek to realize the human rights of all and to achieve gender equality and the empowerment of all women and girls. They are integrated and indivisible and balance the three dimensions of sustainable development: the economic, social and environmental."

The introduction to the declaration states, "We resolve, between now and 2030, to end poverty and hunger everywhere; to combat inequalities within and among countries; to build peaceful, just and inclusive societies; to protect human rights and promote gender equality and the empowerment of women and girls; and to ensure the lasting protection of the planet and its natural resources."[25]

Elsewhere, the introduction reads, "we envisage a world of universal respect for human rights and human dignity, the rule of law, justice, equality and non-discrimination; of respect for race, ethnicity and cultural diversity; and of equal opportunity permitting the full realization of human potential and contributing to shared prosperity."[26]

The Millennium Declaration also mentioned human rights, but it emphasized that human rights and the MDG agenda were consistent with one another.[27] The SDG outcome document, for its part, observes that the goals and the targets "*are aimed at the realization of human rights*."

Under "shared principles and commitments," the document asserts, "The new Agenda is guided by the purposes and principles of the Charter of the United Nations, including full respect for international law. It is grounded in the Universal Declaration of Human Rights, international human rights treaties, the Millennium Declaration, and the 2005 World Summit Outcome Document. It is informed by other instruments such as the Declaration on the Right to Development."[28]

With respect to gender, the text provides, "Realizing gender equality and the empowerment of women and girls will make a crucial contribution to progress across all the Goals and targets. The achievement of full human potential and of sustainable development is not possible if one half of humanity continues to be denied its full human rights and opportunities."[29] Human rights are likewise invoked regarding migration.

The SDG outcome document affirms the link between sustainable development, peace, and security: "Sustainable development cannot be realized

---

25 "Introduction to the Declaration" of the 2015 SDG outcome document para. 3.

26 Ibid., para. 8.

27 UN General Assembly, "United Nations Millennium Declaration," Resolution 55/2, September 18, 2000. See also Langford, Sumner, and Yamin, eds., *Millennium Development Goals and Human Rights*; OHCHR, *Claiming the MDGs* (New York: OHCHR, 2010); OHCHR, *Who Will Be Accountable? Human Rights and the Post-2015 Development Agenda* (New York: OHCHR, 2014).

28 2015 SDG outcome document, para. 10.

29 Ibid., para. 20.

without peace and security; and peace and security will be at risk without sustainable development. The new Agenda recognizes the need to build peaceful, just and inclusive societies that provide equal access to justice and that are based on respect for human rights (including the right to development), on effective rule of law and good governance at all levels and on transparent, effective and accountable institutions."[30]

Human rights are referred to in connection with the follow-up and review process.[31] A number of key principles must guide the process at all levels, and the process must be "people-centred, gender-sensitive, respect human rights and have a particular focus on the poorest, most vulnerable and those furthest behind."[32]

Finally, in relation to the means of implementation and the global partnership, the text states, "We will foster a dynamic and well-functioning business sector, while protecting labor rights and environmental and health standards in accordance with relevant international standards and agreements and other on-going initiatives in this regard, such as the Guiding Principles on Business and Human Rights and the labour standards of ILO, the Convention on the Rights of the Child and key multilateral environmental agreements, for parties to those agreements."

Human Rights in the SDGs

The SDG goals and targets contain no general reference to human rights, nor is there a freestanding human rights goal. It is noteworthy that during the consultation process surrounding the SDGs, the official position of the UN Office of the High Commissioner for Human Rights (OHCHR) had not favored a freestanding human rights goal. Rather, the OHCHR had advocated for an effective mainstreaming or integration of human rights across the goals and targets. There are, moreover, no references to human rights treaty obligations, despite multiple human rights references in key preceding documents, namely, (1) the 2010 High-Level Panel Report (this report resulted from the secretary-general, not the intergovernmental process); (2) the Rio+20 outcome document; (3) *Realizing the Future We Want for All* (2012), *Delivering as One: Report of the Secretary-General's High-Level Panel on United Nations System-wide Coherence in the Areas of Development, Humanitarian Assistance and the Environment*; (4) the report of OWG cited above; and (5) paragraph 17 of the introduction to the 2015 SDG outcome document.

Equality and Nondiscrimination in the Content of the SDGs

There is a marked shift toward registering inequality and addressing discrimination in the SDGs, whether based on gender, racial or ethnic origin,

30 Ibid., para. 34.

31 Ibid., para. 74.

32 Ibid.

disabilities, or age. The SDGs, particularly in Goals 5 and 10, can be argued to reflect equality and nondiscrimination principles to a far greater extent than did the MDG framework; Goal 10 explicitly addresses inequality within and among nations, and Goal 5 calls for achieving gender equality and empowering all women and girls. Target 4.7 also explicitly addresses gender equality. Furthermore, the introduction to the proposed indicators states, "All indicators should be disaggregated by sex, age, residence and other characteristics, as relevant and possible." The need for disaggregated statistical documentation has found unequivocal endorsement in the SDG framework, and with that, preconditions for assessing inequality and equality of opportunity structures.

Participation and Inclusion in the SDGs

Proposed SDG Content. Proposed Goal 16 explicitly provides for inclusion and underscores participation implicitly in emphasizing access to justice and inclusive institutions. It calls on governments to "promote peaceful and inclusive societies for sustainable development, provide access to justice for all and build effective, accountable and inclusive institutions at all levels." With respect to SDG 16, the secretary-general himself has emphasized that "effective governance for sustainable development demands that public institutions in all countries and at all levels be inclusive, participatory, and accountable to the people."[33] Goal 4, on education, emphasizes inclusive and equitable quality education. Goal 8 aims to "promote sustained, inclusive and sustainable economic growth." Goal 9 will "build resilient infrastructure, promote inclusive and sustainable industrialization and foster innovation." Goal 11 intends to "make cities and human settlements inclusive." Inclusion has definitely become a strong feature of the goals, but it is also reflected in targets of Goals 4, 9, 10, and 11, in addition to the ones mentioned in Goal 16. In contrast, the outcome framework offers relatively few references to *participation*. Such references can only be found in the targets of Goals 5, 6, 11, and 16. The 2015 SDG outcome document contains a stronger reflection of the human rights principle of participation, but it does so primarily in its references to inclusion.

SDG Process of Elaboration. In terms of the process of elaborating the SDGs, a much more transparent process has been documented. In contrast to the process that yielded the MDGs, the process of elaborating the SDGs was far more inclusive, with over one hundred country consultations and the use of My World crowdsourcing. The deliberations of the OWG were relatively open, with divisions and points of contention disclosed promptly after meetings. At a more general level, the United Nations has ensured that interested parties have had access to relevant information and debates through the daily issuance of the *SDG Digest*.

---

33 United Nations, *Road to Dignity by 2030.*

Accountability in the SDGs

The human rights principle of accountability, as defined above, is reflected in Goal 16, on accountable institutions, and in one of the targets of Goal 10, which underscores the need for accountable institutions. Given the wording and the breadth of Goal 16, the foothold for accountability remains general and of a broad-based, political sort, relating either to global institutions and monitoring, or to national institutions and review practices. The accountability principle arguably reflected here is not one indexed to international legal commitments or treaty obligations, such that accountability emerges in the SDGs as a principle of a political rather than a legal nature.

A more systematic approach to human rights obligations of donors and partners in the goals themselves would, we argue, have resulted in a more legal anchoring of the principle of accountability. This in turn would have depended on a far greater commitment to international policy coherence and even systemic integration around international treaty obligations. The principle would have needed a more legally grounded understanding of "effective integration" of human rights into the goals, targets, and indicators. Thus, a more explicit incorporation of human rights and human rights obligations would have resulted in a more robust definition of accountability principles in the SDGs, because the link to duties and/or legal obligations would have been unavoidable.

Human Rights in the SDG Targets

Only one, relatively narrow, reference to human rights can be found in the targets. Target 4.7 ensures that "by 2030, all learners acquire knowledge and skills needed to promote sustainable development, including among others through education for sustainable development and sustainable lifestyles, human rights . . ." References simply to "rights" can be found in other targets, including Target 1.4, on women's equal rights to economic resources; Target 5.6, which ensures universal access to sexual and reproductive health and reproductive rights; Target 5.a, which undertakes reforms to give women equal rights to economic resources; and Target 8.8, which protects labor rights. These references are few and relatively limited in their formulation and spheres of application, such that it is difficult to see how they could be predicted to effect anything approximating an "effective integration" of human rights in the SDG framework.

However, assessed in broader terms, the targets draw on familiar HRBA language, with several references to "empowerment," such as in Goal 5 on gender equality. The targets refer to "accessible" institutions and to "available" and "affordable" services (e.g., water and sanitation, essential medicines, and energy), again familiar language from right-to-education and right-to-health discourses. Concepts and terminology historically associated with defining human rights targets and indicators have therefore been integrated in the SDG targets. At the level of discourse, and in terms of references to human rights–

related concepts, therefore, human rights are comparatively more prominent in the SDG targets than in the MDG targets.

Human Rights in the SDG Indicators

As noted by Merry, Davis, and Kingsbury, indicators are both a form of knowledge and a technology for knowledge and power. The formulation of indicators is influenced by governance structures, but indicators also exert a significant influence on governance in their conceptualization of problems and solutions.[34] In the case of the SDGs, the correspondence between the targets and the indicators merits attention, as some of the proposed indicators capture only certain aspects of the human rights content of the SDG targets. Put differently, the full extent of human rights content of the SDG targets is arguably not captured in the proposed SDG indicators. Target 10.2 (see box 1, below) may be a case in point, where the human rights "potential" of the target is significant, but its proposed indicator can be argued to be lacking ambition, at least from a human rights perspective.

Bearing in mind that the SDG indicators are still provisional and "proposed," the following analysis is based on the proposed 198 SDG priority indicators (at the time of going to press), which have been highlighted as the most relevant and measurable by the secretariat of the UN Statistical Commission.[35]

A first assessment is whether the proposed SDG indicators make reference to human rights. Altogether, 77 indicators include human rights references, some of them in an explicit manner; for instance, the indicator for Target 5.a, which refers to legal frameworks that guarantee women's equal rights; the indicator for Target 10.3, pertaining to the "percentage of population reporting having personally felt discriminated against or harassed within the last 12 months on the basis of a ground of discrimination prohibited under international human rights law"; the indicator for Target 16.b, which is formulated in the same way as the previous indicator for Target 10.3; and the indicator for Target 17.14, which refers to the number of countries that have ratified and implemented relevant international instruments, including environmental, human rights, and labor instruments.

Other SDG indicators refer to "vulnerable groups" and the need for disaggregation. These indicators are more implicit than explicit in their reflection of human rights, as can be seen in the SDG targets and their corresponding indicators, listed in box 1.

With respect to the human rights principles of participation, equality, and accountability, the proposed SDG indicators cannot be said to reflect them in an

34 Sally Engle Merry, Kevin Davis, and Benedict Kingsbury (eds.), *The Quiet Power of Indicators: Measuring Governance, Corruption and the Rule of Law* (Cambridge: Cambridge University Press, 2015), 1.

35 The analysis builds on the work of the Danish Institute for Human Rights. See its "Comments on the Proposed Global Priority Indicators for the 2030 Sustainable Development Goals (SDGs)," http://www.humanrights.dk/human-rights-guide-sdgs.

explicit way, other than in references cited above. Another exception is the indicator for Target 5.c, which reads, "Percentage of countries with systems to track and make public allocations for gender equality and women's empowerment."

With respect to human rights–related discourse, or terms associated with HRBAs or certain economic, social, or cultural rights, the assessment of the SDG indicators is far more positive compared to the MDGs, with numerous references to terms such as "empowerment," "access," "availability," "acceptability," and "affordability." In some cases, the proposed SDG indicators overlap in their formulations with the OHCHR illustrative indicators on health and education.[36] The most numerous human rights references in the SDG indicators are found under Goal 3, on healthy lives; Goal 4, on inclusive and equitable quality of education; Goal 5, on gender equality; Goal 8, on inclusive and sustainable economic growth and decent work for all; Goal 10, on reduction of inequality within and among nations; Goal 12, on ensuring sustainable production and consumption; and Goal 16, on peaceful and inclusive societies, including provision of access to justice for all and building effective, accountable, and inclusive institutions at all levels. Where human rights–related concepts are notably absent is in the context of Goal 13 related to climate change and the protection of sustainable use of ecosystems. A preliminary analysis of the proposed SDG indicators concludes that about 77 of the total 198 proposed SDG indicators include an explicit or implicit reflection of human rights and a reflection of HRBA-related concepts. With respect to

Box 1. Three SDG Targets and Indicators Reflecting Equality and Inclusion

Target 1.4: "All men and women, in particular the poor and the vulnerable, have equal rights to economic resources, as well as access to basic services."

Proposed indicator: "Proportion of the population living in households with access to basic services."

Target 10.2: "Empower and promote the social, economic and political inclusion of all, irrespective of age, sex, disability, race, ethnicity, origin, religion or economic or other status."

Proposed indicator: "Proportion of people living below 50% of median income disaggregated by age and sex."

Target 11.b: "The number of cities and human settlements adopting and implementing integrated policies and plans towards inclusion."

Proposed indicator: "Percentage of cities implementing risk reduction and resilience policies that include vulnerable and marginalized groups."

36 OHCHR, *Human Rights Indicators: A Guide to Measurement and Implementation* (New York: OHCHR, 2012), 88–102.

the proposed SDG indicators, they appear to bear a far stronger human rights imprint than do the MDGs, based on the human rights concepts they reflect and the specific human rights terminology they employ.

Conclusions

The assessment of whether the current proposed SDGs represent an effective integration of human rights in the SDG framework depends to some extent on how one defines "integration." The integration of human rights in development frameworks can be assessed in at least four ways. First, significant overlap exists between the economic and social content of the SDGs such that a greater *substantive overlap* can be said to exist between the SDGs and human rights than existed with the MDGs. Second, as this chapter emphasizes, the uptake of human rights *principles* in the SDGs is more discernible than it was in the MDGs, especially with respect to nondiscrimination and equality and to participation and inclusion. Third, at a discursive level, human rights concepts appear to have influenced the formulation of SDG *targets and indicators*. Fourth, however, there is no explicit reflection of human rights *obligations* in the text of the SDGs themselves, and in this respect, there is no departure from what prevailed in the MDGs.

The assessment of effective integration also depends on how broadly or narrowly the term "integration" is understood. If one assesses the integration of human rights in terms of explicit references to rights or to corresponding legal obligations, or in relation to legal accountability, the SDG outcome document and its goals and targets represent only a modest advance from the MDG framework; although, like the Millennium Declaration, the SDG Declaration reflects many important human rights priorities. On balance, however, it appears that member-states have again opted for a more diffuse form of political accountability, avoiding the specific language of human rights or legal obligations but still incorporating selected human rights principles and concepts.

By contrast, the human rights principles of nondiscrimination and equality and of participation and inclusion are much more integrated in the targets of the SDG framework than in those of the MDG framework.

Overall, based on the current SDGs, targets, and proposed indicators, as well as on the political process surrounding them, the prospects for the effective integration of human rights in the SDG framework remain uncertain but not without promise. The SDGs reflect human rights in some significant ways, and certainly to a greater extent than the MDGs. The SDGs do not, however, contain any human rights obligations. Therefore, whether human rights have been effectively integrated in the new SDG framework and whether it can help advance the full realization of human rights in development will depend on implementation and operational uptake. It will depend also on whether the use of human rights terms and obligations is essential or whether the implicit incorporation and/or mainstreaming of the SDGs is sufficient to ensure effective integration of human rights in the SDG framework. It will also depend on whether monitoring mechanisms are robust, and whether the final adopted indicators are explicit in reflecting human rights principles. Another question is whether any formulation of indicators will be able to compensate for the absence of explicit references to human rights in the goals. Significantly, outcomes will depend on the strength of commitments and implementation at the national level, on initiatives to support measurement, on resource availability and mobilization, and on the strength of human rights actors within member-states.

Ultimately, three questions need answers: Can human rights be realized without being explicitly grounded in (legal) obligations? Or will principles suffice? Do human rights indicators disconnected from human rights obligations make sense? The current SDG framework would have the effective integration of human rights rely to a great extent on the combination of targets and indicators, perhaps beyond what they are either intended for or capable of. The potential for targets and indicators to deliver on human rights challenges will emerge on a country-by-country basis, because national policy implementation and monitoring will be determinative of whether and how rights are respected, protected, and fulfilled in the context of the new development goals.

Thus, while the current content of the proposed indicators in combination with their proposed targets is promising, the true measure of their ability to bring about an effective integrating of human rights will hinge on implementation and operational uptake at both the global and national levels.

9

Taking Sustainable Development Goal 17 Seriously

The World Bank's Legal Framework for Providing Global Public Goods

JAN WOUTERS AND SAMUEL COGOLATI

Sustainable Development Goal (SDG) 17 aims to "strengthen the means of implementation and revitalize the global partnership for sustainable development."[1] Based on experience with the Millennium Development Goals (MDGs),[2] more and more practitioners believe that, to succeed, the renewed global partnership called for in SDG 17 will have to overcome collective action issues in the provision of "global public goods" (i.e., policy issues—such as climate change mitigation, the fight against corruption, and the control of communicable diseases—that transcend national boundaries and generations). Both the new global partnership for sustainable development and the global public goods agenda are actively supported by the World Bank, the world's foremost development agency, with near-global membership and with the single largest source of net income.[3] Yet although internal staff reports and other recent studies commissioned by the Bank have extensively analyzed the political, economic, and financial role the institution could play in providing global public goods, the legal dimension of the Bank's global public goods actions has attracted little attention. This chapter aims to put the Bank's policy discourse on global public goods on a more solid legal footing by analyzing the legal framework within which the Bank operates to deliver such goods.

The chapter starts with a short account of the link between the global partnership for sustainable development called for in SDG 17 and the concept of global public good. The aim of this explanation is to depict what is so distinctive about the legally underdeveloped notion of global public goods,

---

The authors would like to thank Laurence Boisson de Chazournes for her helpful comments on an earlier draft of this article. Any errors or omissions remain, of course, with the authors.

1 UN General Assembly (UNGA), Resolution A/RES/70/1, "Transforming Our World: The 2030 Agenda for Sustainable Development," October 21, 2015, 26, http://www.un.org/ga/search/view_doc.asp?symbol=A/RES/70/1&Lang=E.

2 UNGA, Resolution A/RES/55/2, "United Nations Millennium Declaration," September 8, 2000, http://www.un.org/millennium/declaration/ares552e.htm.

3 The World Bank Group consists of the International Bank for Reconstruction and Development (IBRD), the International Development Association (IDA), the International Finance Corporation (IFC), the Multilateral Investment Guarantee Agency (MIGA), and the International Centre for Settlement of Investment Disputes (ICSID). Together, IBRD and IDA make up the World Bank, hereafter referred to as the Bank.

particularly in the context of the post-2015 development agenda. The chapter then reviews how the Bank promotes the concept of global public goods in its development policies. This analysis is undertaken to show that a discussion of the concept of global public goods in the context of the Bank's operations is not an academic debate, but a policy discussion that has been under way since 2000. Finally, the chapter addresses the following questions: To what extent does the global public agenda fall within the Bank's legal mandate as laid down in the IBRD Articles of Agreement? What are (some of) the legal constraints that the Bank faces as it searches to reorient its programs toward the provision of global public goods? What are (some of) the innovative and distinct legal features of the Bank's financial mechanisms that address global public goods?

The Link between SDG 17 and Global Public Goods

The 2030 Agenda for Sustainable Development will be implemented through a revitalized global partnership for sustainable development called for in SDG 17 "with the participation of all countries, all stakeholders and all people."[4] The agenda, Target 16 of SDG 17, specifies that the goal is to "enhance the global partnership for sustainable development, complemented by multi-stakeholder partnerships that mobilize and share knowledge, expertise, technology and financial resources, to support the achievement of the [SDGs] in all countries, in particular developing countries."[5]

SDG 17 promotes a broad and holistic approach to poverty reduction. It underlines the shared responsibility of all states and relevant regional and global actors to finance what the agenda calls "public goods."[6] According to traditional economic theory, public goods—for example, street lighting—are defined as both non-rival and non-excludable. Public goods are available to everyone, and no one can be excluded from sharing the benefits of public goods. The danger is that individual actors might take advantage of the efforts of others to supply public goods, which would inevitably lead to the underprovision of these public goods. The notion of "global public goods," in turn, finds its origins in three books edited by Inge Kaul, former director of the Office of Development Studies at the United Nations Development Programme (UNDP).[7] Kaul makes clear that, through globalization and in an increasingly interconnected world, more and more policy issues possess

---

4 UNGA Resolution A/RES/70/1, 2.

5 Ibid., 26.

6 Ibid., para. 41.

7 Inge Kaul et al., eds., *Global Public Goods: International Cooperation in the 21st Century* (New York: Oxford University Press, 1999); Inge Kaul et al., eds., *Providing Global Public Goods: Managing Globalization* (New York: Oxford University Press, 2003); and Inge Kaul et al., eds., *The New Public Finance: Responding to Global Challenges* (New York: Oxford University Press, 2006). See also Scott Barrett, *Why Cooperate? The Incentive to Supply Global Public Goods* (New York: Oxford University Press, 2007); and Todd Sandler, *Global Collective Action* (Cambridge: Cambridge University Press, 2004).

exactly the same characteristics and face the same risks that national public goods do. Think of malware programs, epidemics, and nuclear proliferation, which pose threats to rich and poor countries alike. The crux of the problem is that sovereign states behave like individuals at the national level and do not perceive the benefits of contributing to the global public goods supply. Kaul's theories resonate as a powerful call for effective international cooperation and coordination.

Over the past decade, the concept of global public goods has permeated the policy discourse of development actors.[8] In 2006, the International Task Force on Global Public Goods, cochaired by Ernesto Zedillo, former president of Mexico, and Tidjane Thiam, former Ivorian minister of development, called for "significant additional expenditures on global public goods."[9] The task force's message was clear: Because greater financing for global public goods benefits not only developing countries but also donors, global public goods need to be addressed separately from and in addition to official development assistance.[10] Development assistance seen through the lens of global public goods is no longer just a matter of pure altruism or solidarity; it is now considered to be in the self-interest of donor countries to cooperate with each other to combat the negative externalities that could arise in the absence of efforts to mitigate climate change, prevent armed conflicts, protect biodiversity, or eradicate communicable diseases.

In line with this changed paradigm of development, the Addis Ababa Action Agenda stresses that "global partnership should reflect the fact that the post-2015 development agenda, including the sustainable development goals, is global in nature and universally applicable to all countries."[11] SDG 17 represents a shift from the prevailing approach to development "assistance" to a sense of common and shared "responsibility" for enabling sustained poverty reduction at the global level. In its 2013 report *A Renewed Global Partnership for Development*, the UN System Task Team on SDG 17, of which the Bank is a member,[12] unambiguously criticizes MDG 8 for perpetuating the model of "donor-recipient" aid, "rather than calling for collective action at the

---

8 Scott Barrett, "Global Public Goods and International Development," in *Too Global to Fail: The World Bank at the Intersection of National and Global Public Policy in 2025*, ed. Warren Evans and Robin Davies (Washington, DC: World Bank, 2015), 13; Michel Mordasini, "Implementing Global Public Policies: Are the Aid Agencies Walking the Talk?" *International Development Policy* 3 (2012).

9 International Task Force on Global Public Goods, *Meeting Global Challenges: International Cooperation in the National Interest*, Final Report (Stockholm, 2006): 99.

10 Ibid., xxv and 110.

11 Third International Conference on Financing for Development, A/CONF.227/L.1, "Outcome Document of the Third International Conference on Financing for Development: Addis Ababa Action Agenda," para. 10, July 15, 2015. http://www.un.org/ga/search/view_doc.asp?symbol=A/CONF.227/L.1.

12 UN System Task Team on the Post-2015 UN Development Agenda, *A Renewed Global Partnership for Development*, Annex III (March 2013).

multilateral level to achieve a stable global economic environment."[13] The report specifically pleads for the mobilization of additional "resources for global public goods"[14] and for the inclusion of new actors to overcome "the collective action problems in the supply of public goods which require internationally coordinated actions in order to ensure adequate provisioning."[15]

Inge Kaul also concludes that, in comparison with MDG 8, the global partnership for sustainable development in SDG 17 reflects a new awareness of "global public goods."[16] Similarly, the European Commission observes in a communication on the new global partnership that "global public goods also need coordinated international policies and action, including through better implementation of international agreements that play a central role in achieving several SDGs."[17] The commission calls on all countries to "make commitments to mobilise and use domestic public finance effectively, including for global public goods such as climate and biodiversity."[18] The Council of the European Union notes in that regard that international financial institutions such as the Bank represent "critical actors for reaching the SDGs" and for "financing for the provision of global public goods."[19]

Global Public Goods in the Bank's Development Policies

Before we address the legal foundations of the Bank's operations in regard to public goods, consider that the institution has, since 2000, encouraged the supply of global public goods across all its development programs. This was a recurring theme in particular in the meetings of the joint World Bank/International Monetary Fund (IMF) Development Committee, which assists the Bank's Board of Governors with critical development issues.[20] The Bank has commissioned a significant number of studies and convened several workshops on its potential role in financing global public goods.[21] At the request of

---

13 Ibid,. 5.

14 Ibid., 11.

15 Ibid., 18.

16 Inge Kaul, "Global Public Goods: A Concept for Framing the Post-2015 Agenda?" *Discussion Paper/Deutsches Institut für Entwicklungspolitik* (2004): 1–51.

17 European Commission, Communication from the Commission to the European Parliament, the Council, the European Economic and Social Committee and the Committee of the Regions, "A Global Partnership for Poverty Eradication and Sustainable Development after 2015," 6, COM(2015) 44 final, February 5, 2015.

18 Ibid., 7.

19 Council Conclusions, "A New Global Partnership for Poverty Eradication and Sustainable Development after 2015," 9241/15, para. 39, May 26, 2015.

20 The Development Committee consists of a joint meeting of 25 ministers of finance or development and has met twice a year since 1974. See IBRD, Board of Governors, Resolution No. 294, "Establishment of Development Committee," October 2, 1974.

21 See, inter alia, Christopher D. Gerrard et al., eds., *Global Public Policies and Programs: Implications for Financing and Evaluation: Proceedings from a World Bank Workshop* (Washington, DC: World Bank, 2001); Marco Ferroni and Ashoka Mody, eds., *International Public Goods:*

the Bank's Board of Executive Directors, the Independent Evaluation Group (IEG)[22] conducted reviews of the Bank's global public goods strategy in various partnership programs.[23]

Although outlining the same characteristics and challenges as identified by Kaul, a staff report prepared for the Development Committee in 2000 redefines global public goods in the context of the Bank's policies as "commodities, resources, services—and also systems of rules or policy regimes with substantial cross-border externalities that are important for development and poverty-reduction, and that can be produced in sufficient supply only through cooperation and collective action by developed and developing countries."[24] In 2001, the committee issued a progress report called "Poverty Reduction and Global Public Goods."[25] At its 2006 annual meeting, the committee again asked the Bank "within its overall strategy, to develop a framework for its role in providing global and regional public goods."[26] In response, a 2007 staff report titled "Global Public Goods: A Framework for the Role of the World

Incentives, Measurement, and Financing (Washington, DC: World Bank, 2002); Anders Hjorth Agerskov, "Global Public Goods and Development: A Guide for Policy Makers," World Bank Seminar Series at Kobe and Hiroshima Universities, Seminar no. 6, May 12, 2005; Randall Purcell, "Delivering Global Public Goods Locally: Lessons Learned and Successful Approaches," The World Bank Development Grant Facility (DGF) Technical Note, February 2003; and J. Warren Evans and Robin Davies, eds., *Too Global to Fail: The World Bank at the Intersection of National and Global Public Policy in 2025* (Washington, DC: World Bank, 2015). See also World Bank, "Collective Solutions 2025: Collaboration to Help Solve Future Sustainable Development Challenges," http://web.worldbank.org/WBSITE/EXTERNAL/TOPICS/EXTSDNET/0,,contentMDK:23310120~pagePK:64885161~piPK:64884432~theSitePK:5929282,00.html.

22 Formerly known as the Operations Evaluation Department.

23 See, inter alia, Operations Evaluation Department, "The World Bank's Approach to Global Programs: An Independent Evaluation," Phase 1 Report, August 1, 2002; Operations Evaluation Department, *The Global Development Network: Addressing Challenges of Globalization: An Independent Evaluation of the World Bank's Approach to Global Programs* (Washington, DC: World Bank, 2004); Operations Evaluation Department, *Strengthening the World Bank's Role in Global Programs and Partnerships* (Washington, DC: World Bank, 2006); Independent Evaluation Group, "Global Program Review: Consultative Group to Assist the Poor," vol. 3, no. 1, October 26, 2008; Independent Evaluation Group, *The World Bank's Involvement in Global and Regional Partnership Programs: An Independent Assessment* (Washington, DC: World Bank, 2010); Independent Evaluation Group, "Global Program Review: The Global Fund to Fight AIDS, Tuberculosis, and Malaria, and the World Bank's Engagement with the Global Fund," vol. 6, no. 1, February 8, 2011; and Independent Evaluation Group, "Results and Performance of the World Bank Group 2014: An Independent Evaluation," vol. 1, Main Report, vii. See also Uma Lele and Christopher Gerrard, "Global Public Goods, Global Programs, and Global Policies: Some Initial Findings from a World Bank Evaluation," *American Journal of Agricultural Economics* 85 (2003): 686.

24 Development Committee, "Poverty Reduction and Global Public Goods: Issues for the World Bank in Supporting Global Collective Action," DC/2000-16, September 6, 2000, 2. See also Development Committee, "Communiqué," para. 3, September 25, 2000.

25 Development Committee, "Poverty Reduction and Global Public Goods: A Progress Report," DC2001-0007, April 13, 2001.

26 Development Committee, "Communiqué," September 18, 2006, para. 3.

Bank" outlines criteria for the Bank's involvement and financing modalities in promoting global public goods.[27]

The staff report describes five global public goods priority areas for the Bank that were endorsed by the Bank's management in a strategic directions paper.[28] Bank initiatives in these five sectors include the following:

- "Protect environmental commons": Since 2000, the Bank has considerably increased its financing for climate change mitigation, waste management, forestry, and biodiversity. Since its inception in 1991, the Global Environment Facility (GEF) has provided US$13.5 billion in grants to support environmental projects in more than 165 developing countries, the largest single source of development assistance related to environmental issues.[29] The GEF is now the financial mechanism for five international environmental agreements.[30]
- "Prevent the spread of communicable diseases": The Bank combats devastating diseases such as HIV/AIDS, tuberculosis, and avian influenza by establishing multidonor partnerships with specialized agencies. For example, the Bank coordinates with the World Health Organization (WHO) and the International Health Partnership (IHP+) which supports more coherent and harmonized national health strategies in developing countries with other agencies and private charities such as the Bill and Melinda Gates Foundation.[31] Since 2002, the Bank has acted as a trustee (and nonvoting member of the board) for the Global Fund to Fight AIDS, Tuberculosis, and Malaria.[32] The IEG describes the Global Fund as "an ambitious attempt by the international community to use a global partnership program to deliver the global public good of controlling HIV/AIDS, tuberculosis, and malaria in high-burden countries, with a particular focus on low-income countries."[33]

---

27 Development Committee, "Global Public Goods: A Framework for the Role of the World Bank," DC2007-0020, September 28, 2007, 13. See also Development Committee, "Communiqué," para. 4, October 21, 2007.

28 World Bank, "Strategic Directions Paper for FY2002–2004: Implementing the World Bank's Strategic Framework," SecM2001-0211, March 29, 2001.

29 See GEF, "What Is the GEF?," https://www.thegef.org/gef/whatisgef.

30 The Convention on Biological Diversity, the UN Framework Convention on Climate Change, the Stockholm Convention on Persistent Organic Pollutants, the UN Convention to Combat Desertification, and the Minamata Convention on Mercury.

31 International Health Partnership, "A Global 'Compact' for Achieving the Health Millennium Development Goals," May 27, 2015, http://www.internationalhealthpartnership.net/fileadmin/uploads/ihp/Documents/Tools/Global_Compact/IHP__global_compact_signatories_65_May_2015.pdf.

32 Global Fund to Fight AIDS, Tuberculosis, and Malaria, "The Framework Document," 2001, Section B, http://www.theglobalfund.org/en/documents/governance/.

33 IEG, "Global Fund," 27. See also David Freestone, *The World Bank and Sustainable Development: Legal Essays* (Leiden: Brill, 2013), 25.

- "Strengthen the international financial architecture": With the IMF, which retains the leading role in the financial sector, the Bank "supported surveillance and capacity building to help countries enhance their resilience to crises."[34] A joint initiative with the IMF that responds to this challenge is the Financial Sector Assessment Program (FSAP). Launched in 1999, the FSAP introduced joint IMF–World Bank assessments and stress tests of the financial health of developing and emerging economies to prevent financial crises.[35] Among other examples, the Consultative Group to Assist the Poor (CGAP) is a consortium of public and private agencies housed within the Bank that helps make microfinance available to the poorest.[36] According to the IEG, "there is no other global program/entity competing with CGAP at the present time in terms of providing global public goods."[37]
- "Strengthen the global trade system": The Bank has advocated additional funding to help developing countries adjust to a multilateral trading system. One prominent example is the Enhanced Integrated Framework for Trade-Related Assistance for the Least Developed Countries (EIF), established in 2007 as a successor to the Integrated Framework (IF), which had existed since 1997. The EIF is a multidonor program that helps some of the 49 poorest countries worldwide integrate into the global trading system. The Bank contributes to the EIF with five other partner agencies, including the IMF, the UNDP, and the World Trade Organization (WTO).[38]
- "Disseminate knowledge for development": The Bank has expanded its nonlending projects to disseminate knowledge in the form of technical assistance and policy analysis.[39] For instance, the Program on Forests (PROFOR) is a multidonor partnership managed by a secretariat at the Bank that supports knowledge-sharing in the field of forest management.[40] The Consultative Group on International Agriculture and Research (CGIAR) is a more informal network of developing agencies, cosponsored by the Bank, whose executive secretariat the Bank hosts without serving as its implementing agency. According to the Bank, the CGIAR serves "to promote agricultural research as a global public good and fill the gaps that could not be met through country-level programs alone."[41]

---

34 Development Committee, "Global Public Goods," 13.

35 IMF, "Factsheet: The Financial Sector Assessment Program (FSAP)," http://www.imf.org/external/np/exr/facts/fsap.htm.

36 CGAP, "Advancing Financial Inclusion to Improve the Lives of the Poor," http://www.cgap.org.

37 IEG, "Consultative Group to Assist the Poor," xiii.

38 WTO, "Enhanced Integrated Framework," https://www.wto.org/english/tratop_e/devel_e/teccop_e/it_e.htm.

39 Development Committee, "A Framework for the Role of the World Bank," v. See also Joseph E. Stiglitz, "Knowledge as a Global Public Good," in *Global Public Goods,* 208.

40 PROFOR, "Our Mission," http://www.profor.info/node/2041.

41 Concessional Finance and Global Partnerships, "Management Framework for World Bank Partnership Programs and Financial Intermediary Funds: Strategic Engagement, Oversight,

In recent years, global public goods have become an important concept in the policy discourse of the Bank's management. In his speech at the annual meeting in October 2007, Bank president Robert Zoellick outlined six themes for the future strategic direction of the World Bank Group, including the need "to play a more active role in fostering regional and global public goods that transcend national boundaries and benefit multiple countries and citizens."[42] At the annual meeting in October 2012, the Development Committee supported the vision of the new president, Dr. Jim Yong Kim, "of a [World Bank Group] that . . . promotes global public goods."[43] In the 2014 annual review, the IEG concluded that, apart from pursuing MDGs, the Bank took "a broader approach to poverty reduction" and that "there was greater emphasis on . . . global public goods."[44]

Although the Bank's partnership programs have proliferated in recent years,[45] it is important to tread cautiously when considering the role that the concept of global public goods plays in the Bank's policies. First, some of the Bank's partnership programs have longer histories than the UNDP publications edited by Kaul, for example, CGIAR, which was created in 1971. Second, although the 2007 staff report notes that the five global public goods are "anchored in international consensus for action,"[46] it is not obvious why these five specific issues rank as priorities over other global public goods that could also be relevant to the Bank's missions, such as postconflict reconstruction or the fight against malnutrition. Third, other Bank reports mention other priorities, a fact that seems to suggest that the aforementioned list is not a closed one.[47] Last but not least, the use of the concept by the Bank is not without critics. According to Devesh Kapur, "seeking to reinvent the Bank's public image, its management and staff may tend to label all kinds of activities or 'networks' as [global public goods], meriting involvement on the basis of the moral claims that public goods invoke, and their ready slogan-appeal for Northern taxpayers."[48] Another commentator notes that "the risk is to create a *catch-all*

---

and Management," Documents of the World Bank, June 12, 2013, 4.

42 Robert B. Zoellick, "An Inclusive and Sustainable Globalization," October 10, 2007, http://web.worldbank.org/WBSITE/EXTERNAL/NEWS/0,,contentMDK:21504730~pagePK:34370~piPK:42770~theSitePK:4607,00.html.

43 Development Committee, "Communiqué," para. 9, October 13, 2012.

44 IEG, "Results and Performance of the World Bank Group 2014," vii.

45 See Concessional Finance and Global Partnerships, *2013 Trust Fund Annual Report* (Washington, DC: World Bank, 2013), 7.

46 Development Committee, "A Framework for the Role of the World Bank," 4.

47 For example, the 2014 report on financial intermediary funds mentions only three global public goods: "preventing communicable diseases," "responding to climate change," and "ensuring food security." See World Bank Group, "Financial Intermediary Funds in the World Bank Group," 2014, 5. The *2013 Trust Fund Annual Report* highlights "the areas of global knowledge sharing, climate change, and access to water and sanitation." See Concessional Finance and Global Partnerships, *2013 Trust Fund Annual Report*, 19.

48 Devesh Kapur, "The Common Pool Dilemma of Global Public Goods: Lessons from the World Bank's Net Income and Reserves," *World Development* 30, no. 3 (2002): 349.

to which people can attach anything they want."[49] It is true that the Bank does not provide comprehensive or systematic data on the funds or exact programs it dedicates specifically to what it now refers to as "global public goods."[50]

Global public goods as referred to in the Bank's policies have thus evolved from a narrow economic concept into a flexible rhetorical tool. The Bank's strategic priorities do not qualify as pure public goods deemed to be inherently non-rival and non-excludable; rather, they should be seen as social constructs, policy choices of the Bank. As such, the concept of global public goods is a malleable one, subject to change, that determines an important strategic reorientation of the Bank's mission toward partnership programs to tackle cross-border development issues.[51]

The Bank's Legal Framework for Providing Global Public Goods

Global public goods have been at the center of the Bank's policy discourse for years. Yet until recently, the Bank's global public goods activities did not attract attention in international legal scholarship.[52] It is with regard to the legal underpinnings of the Bank's global public goods rhetoric that this chapter contributes to the debate. The basic assumption is that the Bank's global public goods agenda does not operate in a legal vacuum. More specifically, the Bank's global public goods strategy must be anchored in its legal mandate in the IBRD Articles of Agreement; the aforementioned financing vehicles to supply global public goods remain subject to legal rules and procedures. As the Bank searches to reorient its programs toward the provision of global public goods, particularly in the context of the global partnership for sustainable development called for by SDG 17, it is important to explore the scope and limits of the Bank's legal mandate, as well as the legal features of the financial mechanisms needed to respond to these challenges.

---

49 Maurizio Carbone, "Supporting or Resisting Global Public Goods? The Policy Dimension of a Contested Concept," *Global Governance* 13 (2007): 185.

50 Nancy Birdsall and Anna Diofasi, "Global Public Goods for Development: How Much and What For," *Center for Global Development* (2015): 5, http://www.cgdev.org/sites/default/files/CGD-Note-Birdsall-Diofasi-Global-Public-Goods-How-Much.pdf.

51 See Samuel Cogolati, Linda Hamid, and Nils Vanstappen, "Global Public Goods and Democracy in International Legal Discourse," *Cambridge Journal of International and Comparative Law* (in press).

52 This is not to say, however, that there is not a burgeoning body of literature on the broader global public goods discourse in international law. See, for example, Daniel Bodansky, "What's in a Concept? Global Public Goods, International Law, and Legitimacy," *European Journal of International Law* 23, no. 3 (2012): 651; Nico Krisch, "The Decay of Consent: International Law in an Age of Global Public Goods," *American Journal of International Law* 108, no. 1 (2014): 1; Ernst-Ulrich Petersmann, ed., *Multilevel Governance of Interdependent Public Goods: Theories, Rules and Institutions for the Central Policy Challenge in the 21st Century*, EUI Working Papers, RSCAS 2012/23, http://cadmus.eui.eu/bitstream/handle/1814/22275/RSCAS_2012_23final.pdf?sequence=2.

The Bank's Legal Mandate to Supply Global Public Goods

In the aforementioned 2007 staff report, one of the five criteria for setting global public goods priorities is that the "Bank['s] engagement should be consistent with its . . . overall mandate to assist countries in achieving sustainable development and poverty reduction."[53] Indeed, as is true of any other international organization, the Bank does not possess a general competence and is governed by the "principle of speciality."[54] But, when the Bank was created at the 1944 Bretton Woods Conference, its founding document was not linked to global public goods. Based on a literal reading of the Bank's founding charter, there is no explicit provision for global public goods.[55] Initially, the Bank was thought of as a "brick-and-mortar financier"[56] to provide loans to post–World War II countries in Europe and, later, developing countries. Article I of the IBRD Articles of Agreement requires that all its investments be, in principle, "for a productive purpose."[57] The general rule on which the Bank may guarantee or make loans in the IBRD Articles is that, "except in special circumstances," the Bank shall finance only "*specific* projects of reconstruction or development" (Article III, Section 4 [viii] IBRD Articles of Agreement)[58]

---

53 Development Committee, "Framework for the Role of the World Bank," 3.

54 See ICJ, *Legality of the Use by a State of Nuclear Weapons in Armed Conflict, Advisory Opinion, International Court of Justice (ICJ) Reports 1996*, 66, para. 25 [hereinafter WHO Opinion]. See also Daniel D. Bradlow and Claudio Grossman, "Limited Mandates and Intertwined Problems: A New Challenge for the World Bank and the IMF," *Human Rights Quarterly* 17 (1995): 411.

55 Nancy Birdsall, "A New Mission for the World Bank," *Project Syndicate*, June 30, 2015, http://www.project-syndicate.org/commentary/world-bank-global-public-goods-cgiar-by-nancy-birdsall-2015-06.

56 Sabine Schlemmer-Schulte, "World Bank," in *Encyclopedia of Intergovernmental Organizations*, ed. Jan Wouters (Deventer, The Netherlands: Kluwer Law International, 2015), 50.

57 IBRD Articles of Agreement, Article I, reads as follows: "The purposes of the Bank are:

(i) To assist in the reconstruction and development of territories of members by facilitating the investment of capital for productive purposes [...].

(ii) To promote private foreign investment by means of guarantees of participations in loans and other investments made by private investors; and when private capital is not available on reasonable terms, to supplement private investment by providing, on suitable conditions, finance for productive purposes out of its own capital, funds raised by it and its other resources.

(iii) To promote the long-range balanced growth of international trade and the maintenance of equilibrium in balances of payments by encouraging international investment for the development of the productive resources of members, thereby assisting in raising productivity, the standard of living and conditions of labor in their territories.

(iv) To arrange the loans made or guaranteed by it in relation to international loans through other channels so that the more useful and urgent projects, large and small alike, will be dealt with first.

(v) To conduct its operations with due regard to the effect of international investment on business conditions in the territories of members and, in the immediate postwar years, to assist in bringing about a smooth transition from a wartime to a peacetime economy."

58 See IDA Articles of Agreement, Article V, Section 1(b).

(emphasis added). The Bank's purposes have remained basically unchanged. The Articles of Agreement have been amended three times (in 1965, 1989, and 2012), and none of these amendments has indicated global public goods as a specific purpose to be served by the institution.

The Bank's evolution from a specific lender/guarantor into a global public goods supplier is the result of a broad and purposive interpretation of its founding document. Since the Bank's creation in 1944, economic and development challenges have changed considerably. As Ibrahim Shihata, former general counsel of the Bank, observes, "the Bank has continuously developed its *functions* beyond the literal provisions of its Articles of Agreement while respecting the overall *purposes* stipulated in these Articles."[59] This evolution has allowed the Bank to gradually cover more diverse policy issues in its operations—issues such as health, gender, social development, education, equity, and social security—and the same could be said of the Bank's increasing coverage of global public goods challenges. As Roberto Dañino, another former general counsel, notes, "globalization has forced us to broaden the range of issues that are of global concern."[60] More recently, Anne-Marie Leroy, the current general counsel, explicitly considered that the "protection of global public goods" was now part of the Bank's mission and of the broader concept of development as it has evolved over the past 60 years.[61]

Treaty provisions are never carved in stone in international law. Article 31(3)(b) of the 1969 Vienna Convention on the Law of Treaties, which forms part of customary international law,[62] provides that in interpreting a treaty, including the founding charter of an international organization,[63] there shall be taken into account, together with the context, "any subsequent practice in the application of the treaty which establishes the agreement of the parties regarding its interpretation." Thus, in delineating the area of competence

59 See Ibrahim F. I. Shihata, "Democracy and Development," *International and Comparative Law Quarterly* 46 (1997): 639–640. See also Ibrahim F. I. Shihata, "Techniques to Avoid Proliferation of International Organizations: The Experience of the World Bank," in *Proliferation of International Organizations: Legal Issues*, ed. Niels M. Blokker and Henry G. Schermers (The Hague: Kluwer Law International, 2001), 120.

60 Roberto Dañino, "The Legal Aspects of the World Bank's Work on Human Rights," *International Lawyer* 41 (2007): 24.

61 Anne-Marie Leroy, "Legal Note on Bank Involvement in the Criminal Justice Sector," February 9, 2012, http://documents.worldbank.org/curated/en/2012/02/15889342/legal-note-bank-involvement-criminal-justice-sector, para. 10.

62 As a treaty, the Vienna Convention is not applicable to the Bank's Articles of Agreement, which preceded the former. Like many of the Vienna Convention's provisions, Article 31 is considered to be part of customary international law. See WHO Opinion, para. 19.

63 The Vienna Convention is applicable to "any treaty which is the constituent instrument of an international organization and to any treaty adopted within an international organization without prejudice to any relevant rules of the organization" (Article 5). The specification at the end of this provision makes clear, though, that the Vienna Convention's application is of a subsidiary nature; see Kirsten Schmalenbach, "Article 5," in *Vienna Convention on the Law of Treaties: A Commentary*, ed. Oliver Dörr and Kirsten Schmalenbach (Heidelberg: Springer, 2012), 89.

of an international organization, the International Court of Justice (ICJ) has inter alia devoted "special attention" to the organization's "own practice" as a means of interpretation.[64] The ICJ has also held that "each organ must, in the first place at least, determine its own jurisdiction."[65] According to the International Law Commission (ILC) special rapporteur's "Third Report on Subsequent Agreements and Subsequent Practice in Relation to the Interpretation of Treaties," this interpretation reflects a general principle of the law of international organizations.[66]

More specifically in the case of the Bank, the IBRD Articles of Agreement vest all powers of authoritative interpretation in the Board of Executive Directors, chaired by the President (IBRD Article IX).[67] Thus, it is for the Bank's own organs to decide whether its global public goods policies come within the confines of the Bank's purposes as stated in its Articles of Agreement. For instance, by virtue of its interpretive powers under Article IX and by reference to the implied powers doctrine, the Bank's Board of Executive Directors gradually expanded the role of the Bank to take up a fiduciary role in trust funds charged with the supply of global public goods.[68] The Development Committee,[69] the Board of Executive Directors, and the Bank President have urged the Bank to adapt its strategy to provide global public goods. In the case of the protection of environmental commons, the 2007 staff report suggests that "supply of this [global public good] has become so critical that it can no longer be kept separate from . . . the Bank's mandate to fight poverty and bring about sustainable development."[70] In short, the Bank's engagement with global public goods is a demonstration that the Articles of Agreement should be seen as dynamic and living instruments.

Yet the Bank's legal mandate is not unlimited. The Bank faces legal constraints as it searches to reorient its development programs toward the provision of global public goods. Any kind of "political" activity is in principle ultra vires. IBRD Articles of Agreement Article IV, Section 10, states that

---

64 WHO Opinion, para. 19.

65 ICJ, *Certain Expenses of the United Nations (Article 17, paragraph 2, of the Charter), Advisory Opinion, ICJ Reports 1962*, 151, 168.

66 ILC, Georg Nolte, Special Rapporteur, "Third Report on Subsequent Agreements and Subsequent Practice in Relation to the Interpretation of Treaties," para. 48, A/CN.4/683, April 7, 2015.

67 See IDA Articles of Agreement, Article X. See also Chittharanjan Felix Amerasinghe, *Principles of the Institutional Law of International Organizations*, 2nd ed. (Cambridge: Cambridge University Press, 2005), 34–35.

68 Shihata, "Techniques to Avoid Proliferation of International Organizations," 124; Schlemmer-Schulte, "World Bank," 21.

69 The legal status of staff papers prepared for the Development Committee should not be overestimated. See Ibrahim F. I. Shihata, "Development Committee Issues," chap. 35 in *The World Bank Legal Papers* (The Hague: Martinus Nijhoff, 2000), 835: "the papers present technical analyses of the issues covered, with the understanding that such issues are 'reviewed and sharpened' through discussions with the Executive Directors."

70 Development Committee, "Framework for the Role of the World Bank," 9.

"only economic considerations shall be relevant to [its] decisions."[71] Article III, Section 5(b), of the IBRD Articles of Agreements adds that the Bank's funds shall be used "with due attention to considerations of economy and efficiency and without regard to political or other non-economic influences or considerations." [72] This interpretation is also recalled in specific legal instruments establishing partnership programs, for example, the GEF: In acting as a trustee, the Bank "shall apply such considerations of economy and efficiency as may be required for the investment and disbursement of funds from the Fund."[73] Thus, when the Development Committee proposed the global public goods strategy of the Bank in 2000, the five priority areas did not cover all kinds of "cross border externalities that call for collective action, notably terrorism, narcotics trafficking, and arms proliferation."[74] The reason, according to the staff report, was that "the political dimensions of addressing these problems [would] directly extend well beyond the Bank's mandate."[75]

However, the line between political intrusion and permissible action on the part of the Bank is increasingly blurry. Although the report prepared for the Development Committee is correct in stating that the fight against terrorism and arms proliferation involves other factors other than purely economic ones, this truth does not explain why global public goods, such as postconflict reconstruction or the fight against malnutrition, are not mentioned as priorities. Given the "artificiality and falsity of the supposed divisions between 'economic' (as defined from time to time) and 'political' and other factors," this limitation has caused much ink to flow in the academic literature.[76] Yet the prevailing view of what amounts to political interference has also evolved within the institution, and a more permissive interpretation has been adopted over time.[77] As Roberto Dañino, former general counsel, opines, "it is consistent

---

71 See IDA Articles of Agreement, Article V, Section 6.

72 See ibid., Section 1(g).

73 GEF, "Instrument for the Establishment of the Restructured GEF," para. 5 of Annex B, March 2015, https://www.thegef.org/gef/sites/thegef.org/files/publication/GEF_Instrument-Interior-March23.2015.pdf.

74 Development Committee, "Issues for the World Bank in Supporting Global Collective Action," 3.

75 Ibid.

76 Mac Darrow, *Between Light and Shadow: The World Bank, the International Monetary Fund, and International Human Rights Law* (Oxford: Hart Publishing, 2003), 192. See also Daniel D. Bradlow, "The World Bank, the IMF, and Human Rights," *Transnational Law and Contemporary Problems* 6 (1996): 47; John D. Ciorciari, "A Prospective Enlargement of the Roles of the Bretton Woods Financial Institutions in International Peace Operations," *Fordham International Law Journal* 22 (1998): 22; Mac Darrow, "World Bank and International Monetary Fund," in *Encyclopedia of Human Rights*, ed. David P. Forsythe (Oxford: Oxford University Press, 2009), 378–379; Galit A. Sarfaty, "Why Culture Matters in International Institutions: The Marginality of Human Rights at the World Bank," *American Journal of International Law* 103 (2009): 647; and Willem van Genugten, "The World Bank Group, the IMF and Human Rights," in *Challenging Territoriality in Human Rights Law: Building Blocks for a Plural and Diverse Duty-Bearer Regime*, ed. Wouter Vandenhole, (Oxford: Routledge, 2015), 48–52.

77 See Hassane Cissé, "Should the Political Prohibition in Charters of International Financial Institutions Be Revisited? The Case of the World Bank," in *The World Bank Legal Review*, vol.

with the Articles that the decision making processes of the Bank incorporate social, political, and any other relevant input that may have an impact on its economic decisions."[78] Under this broader understanding, it is likely that more and more global public goods challenges will be considered to constitute a legitimate area of competence of the Bank, just as environmental considerations (in the 1980s)[79] and governance issues (by the early 1990s)[80] have gradually become part of its mandate.

The Bank's Legal Mechanisms to Supply Global Public Goods

Within the broad confines of its legal mandate, the Bank has increasingly devised innovative legal mechanisms, as a former legal adviser observes, "to fund . . . global public goods such as health, environment, and microfinance."[81] One of the characteristics of global public goods is that they require concerted collective action among various development actors with overlapping legal mandates. To coordinate responses to global public goods challenges, the Bank has entered into partnership programs with other international organizations, national governments, civil society, and the corporate sector.[82] Partnership programs can be funded through three different channels: via grants from the Bank's administrative budget, generally the Development Grant Facility (DGF); via trust funds; and via financial intermediary funds for larger financing projects carried out by external partners and implementing agencies, including CGIAR, GEF, and the Global Fund to Fight AIDS, Tuberculosis, and Malaria. In the latter two options, the Bank acts as a trustee, meaning that it receives, holds, and disburses contributions on behalf of other donors. Among other advantages, such trust funds provide the Bank with a legal tool to "crowd in" and leverage new funds from private charities, NGOs, and businesses—even if sovereign development funders still account for 80 percent of total cash contributions.[83] In its *2013 Trust Fund Annual Report*, the Bank mentions "support to global public goods" as one of the overarching goals of

---

3 (Washington, DC: World Bank, 2011), 59; Ibrahim F. I. Shihata, "Political Activity Prohibited," chap. 9 in *The World Bank Legal Papers* (The Hague: Martinus Nijhoff, 2000), 219.

78 Dañino, "Legal Aspects of the World Bank's Work on Human Rights," 23.

79 See Operational Manual Statement 2.36, *Environmental Aspects of Bank Work,* May 1984. See also Ibrahim F. I. Shihata, "The World Bank and the Environment: A Legal Perspective," *Maryland Journal of International Law* 16 (1992): 42.

80 See World Bank, *Governance and Development* (Washington, DC: World Bank, 1992); and World Bank, *Governance: The World Bank's Experience* (Washington, DC: World Bank, 1994).

81 Anna F. Triponel, "Global Fund to Fight Aids, Tuberculosis, and Malaria: A New Legal and Conceptual Framework for Providing International Development Aid," *North Carolina Journal of International Law & Commercial Regulation* 35 (2009): 173.

82 Concessional Finance and Global Partnerships, "Management Framework," 1. See also J. Warren Evans et al., "Shifting Priorities: Re-envisioning World Bank Partnerships for Transformational Impact," in *Too Global to Fail: The World Bank at the Intersection of National and Global Public Policy in 2025,* ed. J. Warren Evans and Robin Davies (Washington, DC: World Bank, 2015), 189.

83 Concessional Finance and Global Partnerships, *2013 Trust Fund Annual Report,* 7 and 26.

its trust funds.[84] At the end of fiscal year (FY) 2013, the total number of trust fund accounts in the World Bank Group amounted to 1,030 and represented US$28.9 billion.[85]

From a legal perspective, these collaborations are remarkable because they often fall beyond the scope of any one organization's charter, but cut across the legal mandates of individual partners. Yet, most often, such cooperation arrangements do not result in the creation of a legal entity distinct from the Bank.[86] The establishment of a trust fund requires a resolution of the Board of Executive Directors and, when it involves a cooperation arrangement with other international organizations (other than informal arrangements of a temporary and administrative character) and/or decisions on the distribution of the net income of the Bank, a resolution of the Board of Governors as well.[87] The GEF, for example, was established in the IBRD by resolutions of both the Executive Directors[88] and the Board of Governors.[89]

Trust funds may involve legal obligations for the Bank, depending on the needs of the partnership, the trusteeship model, and the content of the specific trust agreement concluded with the Bank. It is impossible to outline all kinds of financial services and corresponding legal responsibilities in this chapter. Here it suffices to note that the Bank's operational role in these trust funds may vary from mere "fiscal agent"[90] to "convener, financial contributor, trustee, member of the governing body, chair, host of the secretariat, administrative support, and implementing agency" (possibly alongside other organizations).[91]

On the one hand, the legal responsibilities of the Bank as a trustee may be extremely limited. For instance, in the Global Fund to Fight AIDS, Tuberculosis, and Malaria, which is the Bank's largest financial intermediary fund (29 percent of the Bank's financial intermediary funds portfolio), the Bank lacks voting powers on the board and is not responsible for monitoring the recipients' use of the assets distributed by the fund. The Bank's role is strictly limited to collecting the funds received from donors; investing all assets to

---

84 Ibid., 19.

85 Ibid., 25.

86 Ilias Bantekas, "Trust Funds," *Max Planck Encyclopedia of Public International Law* (2010): para. 8, http://opil.ouplaw.com/view/10.1093/law:epil/9780199231690/law-9780199231690-e1122?prd=OPIL.

87 Both latter competencies are listed as nondelegable powers of the Board of Governors under IBRD Articles of Agreement, Article V, Sections 2(b)(v) and (viii).

88 IBRD, Executive Directors, Resolution No. 94-2, "Global Environment Facility Trust Fund: Restructuring and First Replenishment of the Global Environment Facility," May 24, 1994.

89 IBRD, Board of Governors, Resolution No. 487, "Protection of the Global Environment," July 7, 1994.

90 Triponel, "Global Fund to Fight Aids," 210.

91 J. Warren Evans et al., "Shifting Priorities," 190.

maximize returns on capital; and reporting to the board.[92] The advantage for the Global Fund of having the Bank as a fiscal agent is that it can benefit from all privileges and immunities from taxation and seizure that the Bank enjoys by virtue of Article VII of the IBRD Articles of Agreement[93] (Article 4 of the Trustee Agreement).[94] Yet the Global Fund's legal status differs from that of other trust funds in which the Bank plays a more active role and that have no separate legal personality. The Global Fund is incorporated as a private foundation under Swiss law, with privileges, exemptions, and immunities granted through a headquarters agreement.[95]

On the other hand, the Bank may not only serve as a trustee but also play additional roles, notably by acting as an implementing agency, which is the case in 17 out of the 21 financial intermediary funds. For each arrangement, a specific instrument sets out the various legal responsibilities of the Bank. For example, the Instrument for the Establishment of the Restructured GEF, which represents the second largest trust-funded program (26 percent of the funds held in trust for financial intermediary funds), charges the Bank with three major tasks. First, the Instrument declares that "the World Bank shall be invited to serve as the Trustee of the Fund."[96] Second, the instrument designates the Bank as an implementing agency, together with the UNDP and the United Nations Environment Programme. In that capacity, the Bank must "prepare cost effective GEF projects" and "implement them in accordance with the operational policies, strategies and decisions of the Council."[97] Third, the Instrument provides that the secretariat "shall be supported

---

92 Global Fund to Fight AIDS, Tuberculosis, and Malaria, Governance Handbook, "Section 9: Financial Resources," May 2014.

93 See IDA Articles of Agreement, Article VIII.

94 Global Fund to Fight AIDS, Tuberculosis, and Malaria, Report of the Governance and Partnership Committee, Annex 6, "Update on Legal Status for the Global Fund," June 5–6, 2003, 9.

95 Global Fund to Fight AIDS, Tuberculosis, and Malaria, "Update on Legal Status for the Global Fund." See also Gülen Atay Newton, "The Global Fund to Fight AIDS, Tuberculosis, and Malaria: An Innovation in the Form of International Organization," *IRPA GAL Working Paper 2012/3*, December 31, 2011; Triponel, "Global Fund to Fight AIDS," 182–193.

96 GEF, "Instrument for the Establishment of the Restructured GEF," para. 8. Annex B provides more specifically that "[t]he responsibilities of the Trustee shall include in particular: (a) the mobilization of resources for the Fund and the preparation of such studies and arrangements as may be required for this purpose; (b) the financial management of the Fund, including the investment of its liquid assets, the disbursement of funds of the implementing and other executing agencies as well as the preparation of the financial reports regarding the investment and use of the Fund's resources; (c) the maintenance of appropriate records and accounts of the Fund, and providing for their audit, in accordance with the rules of the Trustee; and (d) the monitoring of the application of budgetary and projects funds [...] to ensure that the resources of the Fund are being used in accordance with the Instrument and the decisions taken by the Council, including the regular reporting to the Council on the status of the Fund's resources."

97 Ibid., para. 22. Annex D specifies that the Bank "will play the primary role in ensuring the development and management of investment projects" and "draw upon its investment experience in eligible countries to promote investment opportunities and to mobilize private sector resources that are consistent with GEF objectives and national sustainable development strategies."

administratively by the World Bank," even though it "shall operate in a functionally independent and effective manner."[98] By serving in these capacities, the Bank is accountable to the council of the GEF. Paragraph 8 of the Instrument stresses that the Bank remains "bound by its Articles of Agreement, bylaws, rules and decisions, as specified in Annex B."[99] In other words, all the operations related to the fund are subject to the legal rules and procedures governing the Bank. For instance, people and communities adversely affected by a GEF-funded project could lodge a claim with the Bank's Inspection Panel.[100] The Bank's mandate as a trustee in the supply of global public goods may therefore come with a broad scope of legal obligations regarding the implementation of projects, the oversight of the recipients' use of the assets distributed by the fund, and the need to report to the governing body of the fund.

Conclusion

This chapter shows that the Bank's global public goods agenda does not operate in a legal vacuum. The Bank's legal mandate is not unlimited, and its financing vehicles to supply global public goods are subject to legal rules and procedures. The peculiar legal nature of partnership programs used to supply global public goods demonstrates that the Bank has been able to respond to new challenges by implementing creative legal practice. In the future, the legal parameters of the arrangements needed within the Bank to provide global public goods should be explored in order to implement the revitalized global partnership for sustainable development called for in SDG 17. This includes a more thorough analysis of the legal constraints, obligations, and responsibilities the Bank faces in engaging with global public goods issues and in developing new forms of partnership programs, such as complex multistakeholder trust funds. Indeed, as the Development Committee noted in April 2015, one of the main challenges for the Bank in achieving the SDGs will be to coordinate "action on global issues" and "continue to work in partnerships with governments, the UN, multilateral institutions, bilateral agencies, civil society and the private sector, as well as with the new development institutions, within their respective mandates."[101]

98 Ibid., para. 21.

99 Ibid., para. 8.

100 Schlemmer-Schulte, "World Bank," 194.

101 Development Committee, "Communiqué," para. 5, April 18, 2015.

10
The Role of Law in Improving the Livelihoods of Indigenous Peoples under REDD+

JULIUS THALER

Deforestation and forest degradation brought on by the advancement of the agricultural frontier, logging, infrastructure projects, and other activities account for 15 to 20 percent of global greenhouse gas emissions. Indigenous and other forest-dependent communities are especially vulnerable to such pressures, because their livelihoods depend heavily on the forests and their services. As a result, addressing deforestation and forest degradation has become a central issue on the climate change agenda, and bilateral and multilateral initiatives have sprung up to provide incentives to avoid deforestation and forest degradation.

This chapter focuses on the REDD+ initiative. *REDD+* stands for efforts to *r*educe *e*missions from *d*eforestation and forest *d*egradation, and to foster conservation, sustainable management of forests, and enhancement of forest carbon stocks. REDD+ is not a single mechanism; it consists of several bilateral and multilateral initiatives, such as the UN-REDD Programme, the Forest Investment Program, and the Forest Carbon Partnership Facility (FCPF), administered by the World Bank.[1] The FCPF, in recognizing the importance of forests to the livelihoods of forest-dependent indigenous communities and the communities' vital role in the fight against deforestation and forest degradation, has proclaimed as one of its objectives to foster partnerships with "forest-dependent indigenous peoples and forest dwellers to prepare for possible future systems of positive incentives for REDD."[2] Furthermore, the FCPF charter establishes that the operations of the facility should "comply with the World Bank's Operational Policies and Procedures, taking into account the need for effective participation of Forest-Dependent Indigenous Peoples and Forest Dwellers in decisions that may affect them, respecting their rights under national law and applicable international obligations."[3] The chapter discusses two key aspects of the FCPF: providing incentives for REDD+, and

1 For a more detailed overview, see the websites at http://www.un-redd.org/aboutredd and https://www.forestcarbonpartnership.org/what-redd.

2 See International Bank of Reconstruction and Development (IBRD), Charter Establishing the Forest Carbon Partnership Facility (Washington, DC: IRBD, August 8, 2013), Recitals (B), https://www.forestcarbonpartnership.org/sites/fcp/files/2013/August2013/FCPF%20Charter%20-%208-8-13%20clean.pdf.

3 See Section 3.1(d) of the charter.

ensuring that forest-dependent indigenous peoples and forest dwellers are prepared to benefit from any such incentives.

The first aspect, future positive incentives for REDD+, consists of two categories: direct benefits and indirect benefits. Direct benefits are those in the form of payments for emission reductions. The chapter focuses on the kind of preparatory activities that are necessary to ensure that forest-dependent indigenous communities will duly benefit from such future payments, drawing on the World Bank's work with governments and indigenous peoples in Latin America. Indirect benefits, touched on only peripherally, include conserving ecosystems, promoting biodiversity, and improving livelihoods of forest-dependent communities.

The second key aspect, the emphasis the FCPF charter places on indigenous peoples and other forest dwellers and their rights under domestic and international law, is outlined to show how that emphasis accords both with the special legal status assigned to indigenous peoples under international and domestic law and with the World Bank's operational policies, which are referenced in the charter. The uniqueness of the body of law applicable to indigenous peoples is the main reason for focusing on indigenous peoples and not on other forest dwellers. It is important to note, however, that the World Bank has involved nonindigenous forest dwellers, such as *campesino* (small farmer) communities, in its work to ensure their inclusion and participation with respect to future benefits.

The scope of the subject matter covered does not allow for a comprehensive review of all the existing bilateral and multilateral initiatives and the literature on indigenous peoples' rights and REDD+. The chapter instead is devoted to examining the past and ongoing activities, conducted by the World Bank in collaboration with numerous Latin American countries under the FCPF, that are related to safeguarding the rights of indigenous peoples and to providing an overview of the most important legal aspects that should be in place to make REDD+ work for indigenous communities, based on the World Bank's work in Latin America and the Caribbean. The chapter thus demonstrates how international and domestic legal frameworks and jurisprudence can be harnessed to make a meaningful contribution to furthering the livelihoods of indigenous peoples in two principal ways: directly, in their capacity as beneficiaries of payments for emission reductions; and indirectly, by bringing longstanding and unresolved land tenure disputes to the fore and providing an incentive for all parties involved to clarify collective indigenous rights.

The chapter also demonstrates that indigenous communities will benefit from properly implemented REDD+ initiatives while recognizing the undeniable risks—such as land grabs and fraudulent carbon transactions—that indigenous communities could face as a result of an inadequate analysis or application of the legal frameworks applicable to indigenous peoples. Such risks only reinforce the urgency and necessity of a thorough analysis of the legal framework applicable to indigenous peoples in the context of REDD+.

Focus on Indigenous Peoples

REDD+ affects or may affect a wide range of sectors of society because of its ambitious national or otherwise jurisdictional scale. Relatedly, the importance of land tenure makes it almost inevitable that the rights of a wide range of stakeholders need to be considered. Therefore, the focus of this chapter on indigenous peoples should not be misconstrued as meaning that other sectors or segments of society do not have an important role to play. A brief explanation of the reasons for focusing on indigenous peoples is warranted. Historical, environmental, and legal reasons justify, and in the case of legal reasons even mandate, special attention to indigenous peoples.

Basic concerns of equity and fairness mandate that indigenous peoples need to be at the center of any forestry initiative, given that traditionally, and to the present day, they have inhabited large swathes of forested areas in Latin America. Moreover, what has been assumed for quite some time, based on anecdotal evidence, has been confirmed empirically in recent years: community forests boast of the lowest deforestation rates, often displaying a rate of zero or even a negative rate.[4] However, indigenous communities are among the most vulnerable groups in regard to experiencing increased pressure from advancing agricultural frontiers (e.g., cattle, soybean oil, and palm oil farming) and logging activities in and around their forests.

In addition, a proper and separate body of law on indigenous peoples has emerged at the global, regional, and national scales. The recognition of indigenous peoples' collective rights over traditional land and natural resources has been codified under both international and domestic law. As a result, the World Bank, like many other international organizations, has introduced specific policy requirements, in line with developments under international law, for projects affecting indigenous peoples.[5] Not least for these reasons, the course and scope of this chapter are also guided by the requirements of the World Bank's policy on indigenous peoples.

Although there is no universally binding definition of the term "indigenous peoples," the World Bank's Operational Policy (OP) 4.10 provides criteria that guide the Bank in determining the existence of "Indigenous Peoples" as

> a distinct, vulnerable, social and cultural group possessing the following characteristics in varying degrees: (a) self-identification as members of a distinct indigenous cultural group and recognition of this identity by others; (b) collective attachment to geographically distinct habitats or ancestral territories in the project area and to the natural resources in these habitats and territories; (c) customary

---

4 Luciana Porter-Bolland et al., "Community Managed forests and Forest Protected Areas: An Assessment of Their Conservation Effectiveness across the Tropics," *Forest Ecology and Management* 268 (2012): 6–17.

5 See the World Bank's operational policy OP 4.10, "Indigenous Peoples," http://web.worldbank.org/WBSITE/EXTERNAL/PROJECTS/EXTPOLICIES/EXTOPMANUAL/0,,contentMDK:20553653~menuPK:4564185~pagePK:64709096~piPK:64709108~theSitePK:502184,00.html.

cultural, economic, social, or political institutions that are separate from those of the dominant society and culture; and (d) an indigenous language, often different from the official language of the country or region.[6]

It is worth noting that communities of Afro-descendants (e.g., the *comunidades negras* in Colombia and *comunidades etnicas* in Nicaragua) also fit the definition of indigenous peoples under OP 4.10, and some countries, including Colombia and Nicaragua, grant a comparable or similar level of legal status and protection to Afro-descendant communities.[7] Hence, the term "indigenous peoples" in this chapter includes Afro-descendants, unless specified otherwise.

Under international law, International Labour Organization (ILO) Convention 169—a legally binding international instrument that has been ratified by the majority of Latin American countries and transposed into domestic law—is the key legal instrument recognizing indigenous peoples as distinct subjects of international law.[8] Similar to the World Bank's policy, the convention, in Article 1, Section 2, assigns special importance to the criterion of self-identification of indigenous peoples. In addition to ILO Convention 169 and corresponding domestic laws, the inter-American human rights system has given increasingly clear contours to the body of law applicable to indigenous peoples.[9] This body of law addresses a wide range of rights, but the focus here is on the treatment under both international and domestic law in the areas most relevant to REDD+, namely, indigenous peoples' rights to land and natural resources.

The Importance of Land Tenure in the Context of REDD+

Before examining indigenous peoples' rights to land and natural resources, a brief contextualization of the importance of land tenure in the context of REDD+ is in order. Understanding the land tenure situation in potential REDD+ program areas is a sine qua non for making any kind of REDD+ program work. Land tenure is commonly defined as the right that determines who can hold and use land and natural resources.[10] Land tenure rights come in many different shapes and sizes, such as individual landownership ("fee simple" under common law), modes of collective ownership, different forms of user rights, and—often overlooked—customary rights.

---

6 Ibid.

7 See Law 70 of Colombia and Law 445 of Nicaragua.

8 For a detailed discussion of ILO Convention 169, see James Anaya, *Indigenous Peoples in International Law* (Oxford: Oxford University Press, 1996). See especially the full text of ILO Convention 169, available at http://www.ilo.org/dyn/normlex/en/f?p=NORMLEXPUB:12100:0::NO::P12100_ILO_CODE:C169.

9 For a detailed discussion, see Anaya, *Indigenous Peoples in International Law*.

10 Esteve Corbera et al., "Rights to Land, Forests and Carbon in REDD+: Insights from Mexico, Brazil, and Costa Rica," *Forests* (2011): 303.

A thorough analysis of the land tenure situation is a requirement under REDD+ programs for two reasons. The first reason is that a land tenure assessment is not an objective in itself, but rather a necessary prerequisite and the essential first step in the three-step process of determining who the ultimate beneficiaries of emission reduction payments should be. The second step is determining the ownership of the stored carbon and the corresponding emission reductions. The third and last step is designing a fair and transparent benefit-sharing mechanism. The immediate significance of the assessment is that it informs the questions pertaining to carbon rights and stakeholders' shares or entitlement to benefits under future benefit-sharing mechanisms. In other words, current land tenure arrangements serve as a starting point for any analysis of a fair and equitable distribution of future REDD+ benefits.

The second and more indirect reason for conducting a thorough land tenure assessment is that REDD+ has the potential to serve as a catalyst to initiate or revive processes of recognizing, titling, or demarcating indigenous peoples' land rights.

The following sections provide an overview of legal and factual aspects of land tenure that are relevant to REDD+, demonstrating the need to go beyond merely reviewing the existence of formal legal title. Any complete and comprehensive analysis has to factor in less obvious aspects, such as jurisprudence, customary rights, and, perhaps most important, the application and implementation of laws and court decisions in the field.

Indigenous Land Tenure: De Jure and De Facto

De Jure

Any land tenure assessment in the context of REDD+ has to address many categories of land tenure rights, ranging from public lands, such as national parks and other protected areas, to private land holdings. The focus here again is on the essential elements of indigenous peoples' land rights. The key characteristic, and difference, of land tenure rights enjoyed by nonindigenous landowners or landholders is their collective nature. The existence of collective legal rights to indigenous territories held by the community as a whole is a common feature of the vast majority of indigenous communities. This is not to say, however, that individual indigenous communities do not display unique tenure regimes with respect to how user rights are assigned to families and individuals within each community.[11] International law has long recognized the customary nature of indigenous peoples' right to the lands on which they have lived and depended. In essence, the customary land tenure rights of indigenous peoples predate colonial invasions and displacement, and have not been made extinct by the conquering nations' land tenure regimes. In

11 For a more detailed discussion, see S. James Anaya and Robert A. Williams, "The Protection of Indigenous Peoples' Rights over Lands and Natural Resources under the Inter-American Human Rights System," *Harvard Human Rights Journal* 14 (spring 2001): 43–44.

addition, a separate body of law on indigenous land rights has emerged under both international and domestic law. As already noted, the most important body of law applicable to indigenous peoples is ILO Convention 169, which is binding in nature for all states that have ratified it. Most countries in Latin America have ratified the convention and are therefore bound by it. Article14 of ILO Convention 169 mandates that indigenous peoples' "rights of ownership and possession . . . over the lands which they traditionally occupy shall be recognized," and that states "shall take steps as necessary to identify" these lands and to "guarantee effective protection of rights of ownership and possession." Article 13(1) of ILO Convention 169 makes it clear that these rights are collective in nature.

ILO 169 has been transposed into domestic law in many countries where constitutions and statutory law spell out the special body of law applicable to indigenous peoples. At the constitutional level, indigenous collective land rights are often recognized in principle and declared inalienable.[12] More detailed provisions can be found in statutes that specifically address the subject matter of indigenous peoples' rights.[13] It is important to note, however, that such a special body of domestic law does not exist in all Latin American countries where indigenous peoples are present (e.g., Belize and El Salvador), and even in countries where it exists, implementation of the law has been uneven or laws may not grant the same level of protection as ILO Convention 169 does.[14] Given that the lack of a domestic legal regime tends to coincide with not ratifying ILO Convention 169, the regional body of law developed under the inter-American human rights system gains even greater importance in this subset of countries.

In a landmark decision, the Inter-American Court of Human Rights found that the collective land rights of the Mayagna of Awas Tingni constitute property as defined and protected by the Inter-American Convention on Human Rights, and that Nicaragua had failed to protect those rights.[15] Again, familiarity with such domestic or regional jurisprudence should be an essential part of a comprehensive land tenure review.

Domestic jurisprudence has played an equally fundamental role in countries that do not have any specific laws on the land rights of indigenous peoples. Instructive examples are the decisions by the Supreme Court and the Court of Appeals of Belize on the issue of customary land rights in the Maya communities in southern Belize. Both courts confirmed that Maya customary land tenure is tantamount to property rights within the meaning of the

---

12 See the constitutions of Argentina, Colombia, Costa Rica, and Nicaragua.

13 See Law 70 of Colombia, the Indigenous Peoples Law of Costa Rica, and Law 445 of Nicaragua. For a more detailed account of domestic law applicable to indigenous peoples, see Anaya and Williams, "Protection of Indigenous Peoples' Rights," 58 et seq.

14 In Chile, for example, the exact nature, extent, and constitutional rank of indigenous peoples' collective land rights under the Indigenous Law (Law No. 19.253) are subject to debate.

15 For a detailed discussion of the Awas Tingni case, see Anaya, *Indigenous Peoples in International Law.*

constitution of Belize. The highest appellate court for Belize, the Caribbean Court of Justice, is expected to pronounce itself on the two decisions after appeals from both the government of Belize and the Maya communities.

In light of the many different sources of law, not least international and domestic jurisprudence, it is imperative for any REDD+ project or program to conduct a land tenure assessment that goes well beyond a desk review, which essentially consists of a "title check."

De Facto

As a next step, any land tenure review would be well advised to analyze how collective legal title to indigenous community land has been implemented in practice. The following quotation from a United Nations indigenous land rights study illustrates this point:

> In terms of frequency and scope of complaints, the greatest single problem today for indigenous peoples is the failure of States to demarcate indigenous lands. Demarcation of lands is the formal process of identifying the actual locations and boundaries of indigenous lands or territories and physically marking those boundaries on the ground. Purely abstract or legal recognition of indigenous lands, territories or resources can be practically meaningless unless the physical identity of the property is determined and marked.[16]

A common thread for the majority of Latin American countries is the legal recognition of indigenous collective land rights at the levels of constitutional and statutory law, while implementation of those rights in terms of titling and demarcation tends to lag behind. However, for the purposes of REDD+ programs, knowing the exact limits of indigenous lands is just as important as the existence of a formal or customary legal right thereto in order to be in a position to determine the extent of an indigenous community's territory.

Regrettably, land tenure assessments often do not go beyond a desk review of existing legislation coupled with a spot check of land titles at the local cadastre. Some de facto challenges to indigenous land tenure are therefore highlighted below.

As emphasized in the preceding quotation, unclear or no demarcation of indigenous communities' territories is a recurring phenomenon. The most extreme case of a total lack of demarcation occurs less frequently thanks to demarcation efforts across Latin America; however, the lack of demarcation still poses a formidable challenge and needs to be investigated on a case-by-case basis. A prime example is the often unclear demarcation of indigenous territories from protected public areas, resulting in an overlap of the predominantly public protected areas and the lands of indigenous communities. Another challenge is the presence of nonindigenous individuals in indigenous territories. Although the vast majority of such occupants are there illegally,

16 Anaya and Williams, "Protection of Indigenous Peoples' Rights," 75.

some actually have formal rights predating the granting of formal legal title to an indigenous territory. In the latter case, a comprehensive land tenure review should analyze pending or potential expropriation proceedings to ensure that all stakeholders' rights are taken into consideration. In Costa Rica, for example, indigenous communities enjoy legal title to their territories but are confronted by nonindigenous occupants, both with and without formal title to their lands, resulting in de facto access restrictions for indigenous peoples in their own territories. In Nicaragua, the situation is somewhat similar for indigenous peoples in the two autonomous regions in the north and south. However, indigenous peoples in the region of the Pacific north do not enjoy the same level of legal protection as those in the south, because their collective land rights have not yet been formally recognized. Similarly, in Belize, the Maya communities of the Toledo district and in some other parts of the country do not enjoy any statutory rights to their territories. However, recent jurisprudence from the Supreme Court and the Court of Appeals of Belize have recognized Maya land tenure as property protected by the constitution of Belize and mandate legislative and administrative action to implement those rights.

This overview of the land tenure situation in various Latin American countries shows that, notwithstanding the recent progress made in advancing the collective rights of indigenous peoples, the picture is still uneven. Consequently, making payments for reducing emissions solely based on the existence of formal legal title for properly demarcated territories would prevent indigenous communities that find themselves in unclear land tenure situations from benefiting from such payments. Such outcomes would run counter to basic principles of fairness and equity, and would have to be corrected. (See the later section "Benefit-Sharing Mechanisms.")

The Link between Land Tenure and Carbon Rights

As mentioned above, the land tenure assessment is not a goal in itself, other than serving as a catalyst to reignite land tenure discussions as a co-benefit of REDD+. Instead, it is primarily a means to finding an answer to the question of who holds title to carbon rights and to influencing the design of benefit-sharing mechanisms or other subarrangements to ensure a fair and transparent distribution of the revenue emanating from the sale of emission reductions (discussed below).[17]

---

17 It is by no means the intention to "rank" the objective of promoting land tenure discussions as "secondary." Categorizing such important discussions as a co-benefit simply means that it is not the objective per se of the FCPF or other similar REDD+ initiatives to resolve long-standing land tenure disputes as a necessary prerequisite to making payments for emission reductions. Rather, the objective is twofold: (1) working to the extent possible within the existing legal framework while making necessary adjustments (e.g., under a benefit-sharing mechanism); and (2) starting or reinitiating a debate on land tenure as a co-benefit in the sense that such a discussion would be led by the interested parties in parallel with designing an emission reduction program for a specific jurisdiction, given that future payments for emissions reductions should serve as an incentive for governments and indigenous peoples alike to promote land tenure security for indigenous peoples.

It is important to note that there is no universal definition for the term "carbon rights." Nor do the vast majority of domestic legal frameworks define the term.[18] Under the methodological framework of the carbon fund of the FCPF, carbon credits are understood as "emission reductions."[19] Accordingly, any entity wishing to sell emission reductions to the FCPF has to demonstrate the ability to transfer legal title to those emission reductions. Thus, in the present context, carbon rights are understood as title to emission reductions.

The transfer of emission reductions is a contractual transaction under which one party agrees to purchase emission reductions from another party. The question of who should be the beneficiary of such payments for emission reductions can be approached from different angles. Generally, some kind of environmental service needs to be performed to achieve a reduction in emissions. In a first step, under the methodological framework of the FCPF, the selling entity has to demonstrate its ability to transfer title to the emission reductions to the buyer, the FCPF. The seller, usually the government at a jurisdictional scale, therefore must demonstrate that it either is the generic rights holder to the emission reductions or that it has entered into a contractual arrangement with the original rights holder to transfer the emission reductions to the FCPF. The question of who holds the rights to emission reductions, and needs to be compensated accordingly, depends on the domestic legal framework.

Emission reductions are intimately linked to the forests they originate from. Therefore, it seems quite natural to treat the emission reductions as a fruit of the land on which the tree stands, and legal discussions in many countries appear to be moving in this direction. However, a serious analysis should not overlook the points that emission reductions can be traded separately from the forested land or any other fruits of the land and that carbon transactions may affect different categories of rights, such as management and alienation rights, thereby impacting different categories of rights holders ("bundle of rights").[20]

Suffice it to say that there is no one definitive answer to the question of who is the holder of the title to emission reductions. In large part, this uncertainty only reflects and perpetuates the uncertainty of land tenure rights held by indigenous communities. In the end, the answer to this question is determined

---

18 For a broader discussion of the concept of "carbon rights," see Anna Knox, Darrel Vhugen, Soldedad Aguilar, Leo Peskett, and Jonathan Miner, *Forest Carbon Rights Guidebook* (Washington, DC: United States Agency for International Development, May 2012), http://theredddesk.org/sites/default/files/resources/pdf/usaid_land_tenure_prrgp_forest_carbon_rights_guidebook_011314.pdf.

19 The methodological framework of the carbon fund of the FCPF is available at https://www.forestcarbonpartnership.org/sites/fcp/files/2014/MArch/March/FCPF%20Carbon%20Fund%20Methodological%20Framework%20Final%20Dec%2020%202013.pdf.

20 For a comprehensive discussion of the "bundle of rights" and an attempted definition, see Rights and Resources Initiative, *What Rights? A Comparative Analysis of Developing Countries' National Legislation on Community and Indigenous Peoples' Forest Tenure Rights* (Washington, DC: Rights and Resources Initiative, 2012).

by legislators and judicial interpretation in each jurisdiction. Wherever such legislative measures are contemplated, lawmakers should try not to answer this question in isolation but pay due attention to the overall legal framework in their respective jurisdictions in areas such as land tenure rights.

This section demonstrates that indigenous communities in Latin America, regrettably, still have a long way to go to secure their collective land rights over their territories and to see those rights implemented and protected. Therefore, the answer to the question Who holds title to emission reductions? must go beyond simply concluding that the forest owner should also be the original title holder to avoid the pitfall of making payments only to those communities with secure legal title to their land but leaving out the most vulnerable communities that have not yet succeeded in having their collective land rights formally recognized. Such outcomes would only perpetuate existing patterns of inequality and discrimination and run counter to the World Bank's mission to reduce poverty.

As outlined above, the title to emission reductions can be transferred, like most other rights, such that the seller of the title of emission reductions under an emission reductions purchase agreement does not necessarily have to be the original title holder. Nonetheless, any analysis would be best served by taking as a starting point the question Who is the original title holder in a given jurisdiction?

The majority of countries in Latin America, and around the world, do not have specific legislation explicitly addressing the question of who the original holder of the title to emission reductions is. Such absence of specific legislation does not mean, however, that we are operating in a complete vacuum. Even in countries that do not have specific legislation on carbon rights, existing legislation, jurisprudence, or contractual arrangements may be able to provide some helpful guidance and serve as a starting point in determining who the title holders to emission reductions in a specific jurisdiction are.

The following text discusses three categories of countries in Latin America that have begun to look into the issue of title to carbon credits. These ongoing efforts, as well as similar initiatives in other parts of the world, can serve as a useful starting point for countries designing emission reductions programs in the context of REDD+.

In the first category are countries in which legislation addresses the question of who holds title to carbon credits. Such legislation can take different forms. In one scenario, carbon rights are tied to the land, and the title holder to the land also holds the title to the carbon credits. Another scenario is to treat carbon like natural resources in the ground, which belong to the state rather than the landowner. A third scenario is to focus on the "who conserves is paid" principle to ensure that those who provide an environmental service are the recipients of payments. Mexico, for example, has opted for a combination of the first and third scenarios; only those landowners and landholders who have made an effort to render environmental services emanating from the forests by engaging in sustainable forest management practices are entitled to payments.[21]

Similarly, Costa Rica may be able to benefit from its experience in the context of comparable programs at a jurisdictional scale. Costa Rica has pioneered a program at the national level, the National Forestry Financing Fund (FONAFIFO), that enables payments for environmental services, and has passed legislation outlining the beneficiaries of payments for the environmental services provided. Here, the contractual counterparts of Costa Rica's FONAFIFO are the owners of the land, because the environmental service is considered to be rendered by the land.[22] The Constitutional Court of Costa Rica ruled that the environmental service is a right directly derived from the property (i.e., the land) and therefore belongs to the landowner.

The second category consists of countries with experience under the Clean Development Mechanism in the context of individual projects. Depending on the circumstances, landowners, investors, and project developers enter into contractual arrangements to ensure an uninterrupted chain of title transfer to the buyer of the emission reductions.

The third category consists of countries with no legislation or any kind of experience in terms of payments for environmental services or carbon finance projects under the Clean Development Mechanism. Notwithstanding the lack of specific legislation or jurisprudence, the governments in some of these countries are confident that existing legal doctrine mandates that carbon rights belong to the owner of the land. In at least one country, however, the government is currently in the process of discussing the option of decoupling carbon rights from landownership and treating them more like natural resources in the ground, which in many countries belong to the state. The underlying idea is to decouple the rights to emission reductions from existing land tenure rights to ensure a more equitable distribution of the revenue from the sale of emission reductions by allowing the state to claim title to all emission reductions while simultaneously designing a benefit-sharing mechanism to ensure that all forest-dependent communities will benefit from such payments.

The bandwidth of the different examples above serves as a reminder that the issue of carbon rights cannot be answered in a vacuum, that is, without paying due attention to the specific context of each country. Although there may be little bandwidth in terms of legislation specifically addressing the issue of who holds the title to emission reductions, most of the countries surveyed have had to grapple with this issue in one way or another. In countries where there is specific legislation, the situation is generally clearer in terms of legal certainty. However, even in jurisdictions where there appears to be legal certainty with respect to emission reductions, an evaluation of the composition of the eventual beneficiaries from a fairness-and-equity angle would still be

21 See Article 134 of the General Law on Sustainable Forest Development of Mexico.

22 See Law 7575 (1996) of Costa Rica.

warranted to ensure that indigenous and other forest-dependent communities are among the ultimate beneficiaries of the payments for emission reductions (see the following section on benefit-sharing mechanisms).

In countries where carbon rights have yet to be defined legally, it is perhaps even more important to factor in the country context. For example, in Costa Rica, which boasts of a comparatively well-defined land tenure regime and has long-standing experience with payments for environmental services to forest owners (including indigenous communities), the current thinking of primarily tying carbon rights to landownership may be a viable option and, potentially, remaining fairness-and-equity concerns could still be addressed under a benefit-sharing arrangement. In other scenarios, in which land tenure is poorly defined or disadvantages indigenous communities, tying carbon rights to landownership without any corrective measures would only exacerbate existing inequalities and injustices. Decoupling carbon rights from landownership—by declaring state ownership over carbon rights, for example—in conjunction with establishing a fair and equitable benefit-sharing mechanism could be beneficial in scenarios in which indigenous communities do not enjoy secure land tenure rights. However, the same solution could impose restrictions on existing formal or customary collective rights in scenarios in which well-defined or recognized indigenous land rights existed and state ownership could thus be used—in much the same way as natural resources—to exclude indigenous peoples from benefiting to the fullest extent from future payments for emission reductions. Once again, it is important to refrain from pursuing a one-size-fits-all solution. Instead, base any recommendations on the de jure and de facto situations of the jurisdiction in question.

The answer to the question of who is or ought to be the title holder to emission reductions is highly casuistic and contextual. The key lesson to be learned, therefore, is not to make any premature assumptions (e.g., "all carbon belongs to state" or "the owner of the forest must be the owner of the carbon"), jumping to conclusions based on preconceived notions, but instead to engage in an unbiased analysis of the legal framework of each and every jurisdiction. Once the findings are in, they can be analyzed from a fairness-and-equity angle and, if needed, fine-tuned by means of a benefit-sharing arrangement, which would adjust for any shortcomings and ensure that indigenous communities would indeed be among the ultimate beneficiaries of future payments for emission reductions. This is precisely the point where fair and equitable benefit-sharing arrangements come into play.

Benefit-Sharing Mechanisms

With a better understanding of the scope of existing legislation and legal thinking pertaining to indigenous peoples' land tenure and carbon rights, we can turn our focus to the design of benefit-sharing mechanisms. As outlined above, there are many different scenarios in the field that provide indigenous peoples with varying degrees of certainty regarding their land tenure and carbon rights. A quick survey of REDD+ countries in Latin America and the Caribbean yields the result that, as of this writing, not a single country has introduced specific laws or regulations on the creation or design of benefit-sharing mechanisms. Similarly, there is no direct mention of or reference to benefit-sharing mechanisms under international law. However, given the similarities between emission reductions and natural resources, the treatment of the latter under domestic and international law may yield some useful insights for the purposes of this analysis. For instance, ILO Convention 169 requires that "the peoples concerned shall wherever possible participate in the benefits of [resource exploitation], and shall receive fair compensation for any damages which they may sustain as a result of such activities."[23] Drawing an analogy to ILO Convention 169 does not fully answer the question of how to design a fair and equitable benefit-sharing mechanism. It does, however, provide some useful direction in that it provides a guiding principle for allowing indigenous peoples to benefit from the revenue derived from the sale of emission reductions.

Before delving into a more detailed discussion of some of the key aspects of a fair and equitable benefit-sharing mechanism, it is useful to draw a distinction between two different types of mechanisms that are both commonly referred to by the term "benefit-sharing mechanism." The first such mechanism aims to ensure that the payments for emission reductions reach the intended categories of beneficiaries (e.g., private landowners and indigenous communities) in a transparent, fair, and equitable manner. It is referred to here as an emission reductions "program-scale benefit-sharing mechanism." The second type of mechanism, which distributes benefits within a specific community, is here called an "intra-community benefit-sharing mechanism" and becomes relevant after a specific community has been identified as a beneficiary of a share of the payments for emission reductions, and serves the purpose of determining how the benefits will be used and distributed within the community. These two mechanisms are obviously linked, because decisions under the latter can be made only after benefits have been allocated to the community in accordance with the terms of the former.

This section focuses on the program-scale benefit-sharing mechanism for two reasons. First, given that the program-scale benefit-sharing mechanism is not just part of the program but also the final step in the three-step analysis outlined earlier in the chapter, it is an integral part of the program design. Second, the intra-community benefit-sharing mechanism is an internal decision-making process for individual communities that touches on the very essence of indigenous peoples' autonomy and self-governance and should therefore avoid outside interference in the form of prescriptive requirements as part of the program design.

The program-scale benefit-sharing mechanism should ensure a transparent, fair, and equitable distribution of the benefits derived from the sale and

23 Article XX of ILO Convention 169.

purchase of emission reductions among the different categories of beneficiaries. To be able to identify all relevant beneficiary groups, the findings of the land tenure and carbon rights assessments, based on a comprehensive stakeholder engagement process, should serve as the starting point to determine the different categories of beneficiaries under any benefit-sharing mechanism. Depending on the specifics of the land tenure and carbon rights assessments, a benefit-sharing mechanism should be designed in a way that enables indigenous communities without recognized rights to the forests on which they depend to remedy any shortcomings they might encounter, so they can still benefit from future payments for emission reductions.

As a first step, all rights holders should be included in the group of eventual beneficiaries, not least indigenous peoples with recognized formal or customary land tenure rights. Extreme care needs to be exercised not to use a benefit-sharing mechanism in a way that takes away or dilutes indigenous peoples' existing rights. In fact, in scenarios in which the land tenure and carbon rights assessments conclude that indigenous communities are the rightful title holders to both land and emission reductions, a benefit-sharing mechanism should not have to go beyond asserting just those findings. An independent and remedial benefit-sharing mechanism would be needed, however, in cases in which the land tenure and carbon rights assessments concluded that the land tenure or carbon rights of indigenous communities were unrecognized or uncertain in any other way. The latter may be especially relevant in cases of customary land tenure rights, the exact nature of which and extent are often subject to debate. In such a scenario, a benefit-sharing mechanism would have a genuine and independent function to fulfill by ensuring that indigenous forest-dependent communities are able to benefit from the payments made for emission reductions with respect to forests they live in or depend on.

Another important aspect of any benefit-sharing mechanism is procedural. For the mechanism to be accepted by indigenous peoples—and as a requirement of international law and the policies and procedures of international organizations such as the World Bank—the design process has to be participatory and inclusive. Any proposed benefit-sharing mechanism should be discussed with indigenous peoples in a manner that is free, prior, and informed, and should have the objective of securing the broad support of the relevant community. Indigenous peoples therefore need to be actively involved in the design of the mechanism from the beginning, as opposed to merely being presented by the government or another entity entrusted with the task of selling emission reductions with an already designed mechanism to which they can only say either yea or nay. The design of any benefit-sharing mechanism has to respect the applicable domestic and international legal obligations and can do so only by respecting the rights of indigenous peoples with regard to land and natural resources under instruments such as ILO Convention 169 or the extensive inter-American human rights jurisprudence.

It is worth reiterating here that a benefit-sharing mechanism is much more than a negotiated contractual arrangement, in the sense that it is a meeting of the minds of all parties interested in a legal transaction that distributes the payments received from the sale of emission reductions. In other words, the design of a benefit-sharing mechanism is not just a technocratic legal exercise requiring only the input from the legal profession; it also, and more important, requires skill sets—such as intercultural communications skills and an in-depth understanding of local indigenous communities and how to engage with them—that legal professionals do not necessarily have. That is to say, interdisciplinary skills are needed to devise an inclusive, fair, and equitable benefit-sharing mechanism. Only when all relevant stakeholders have been identified, adequately consulted, and given a seat at the table can the negotiation of the actual legal agreement begin in earnest.

The process of designing a fair and equitable distribution needs to take into account numerous factors, many of which are likely to be country specific. As mentioned previously, formal and customary rights are crucial criteria. In addition, factors such as the proximity of certain stakeholder groups (e.g., indigenous communities) to the forests included in the program area, dependence on those forests for their livelihoods, and their contributions to management and conservation should be factored in from an indigenous perspective. There are numerous other aspects to be considered from all stakeholders' perspectives that go beyond the scope of this chapter.[24]

As mentioned above, the intra-community benefit-sharing mechanism is primarily an internal affair of each affected community, given that, pursuant to international law, indigenous peoples have the right to their own institutions and to make their own decisions within their communities. But autonomous decision making and self-governance is possible only if neither the legal framework of a country nor any de facto interference prevents indigenous peoples from making such decisions free of undue outside meddling. In this sense, such benefit-sharing mechanisms truly give weight and meaning to customary or traditional governance systems. Therefore, an analysis of the applicable domestic legal framework is in order to determine the existence of any legal norms that may have such an effect. Again, a thorough analysis of the laws, regulations, and jurisprudence is necessary, as there may well be contradictory norms within the same jurisdiction. For instance, in one of the countries surveyed, the indigenous peoples' law guarantees indigenous peoples the right to create their own institutions and to self-governance. However, later administrative measures would restrict this right by mandating that indigenous communities need to organize following the general model of association under general administrative law without due regard for the rights of indigenous peoples to self-governance under international and domestic law. As a result, the domestic agency leading the REDD+ process in the country agreed to involve not only the associations but also the traditional authorities and institutions in the decision-making process. A decision on

---

24 For example, to determine a government's share, if any, the level of involvement in forest conservation, management efforts, and up-front program financing would have to be taken into account.

representativeness and appropriateness needs to be made by each indigenous community, so the outcome will depend on such factors as the level of acceptance of the "formal" versus the traditional institutions.

Conclusions

This chapter introduces the primary opportunities and challenges of forest-dependent indigenous communities inherent in the REDD+ initiative. It shows that only if a specific REDD+ program is designed in a participatory way—while also reflecting an understanding of the formal and customary rights of indigenous peoples and the proper application of those rights in the context of the program—can indigenous peoples be assured of being among the key beneficiaries. Although the ultimate transaction involves the sale and purchase of emission reductions, the starting point for every analysis should be the land and natural resource tenure rights enjoyed by indigenous peoples, because the question of who has a right to the emission reductions cannot be completely decoupled from the question of who holds rights both to the land on which the trees stand and to the natural resources found on the land. Even if a particular legal framework assigns the right to enter into carbon transactions dealing with the emission reductions to the state, the outcome of a land and natural resource tenure assessment must be the starting point in determining the ultimate beneficiaries of such payments for avoided deforestation and forest degradation. In other words, only a thorough tenure assessment can answer the question of who should ultimately benefit from the payments. Where land and resource tenure is unambiguous and indigenous communities enjoy secure tenure rights, the land tenure assessment answers the question of who should benefit from the payments for emission reductions.

The need for a comprehensive land and resource tenure assessment cannot be overemphasized. In particular, the often propagated solution of a contractual arrangement involving all stakeholders with a (potential) claim to receiving a portion of the payments is not an appropriate solution in a situation in which indigenous peoples enjoy clearly defined tenure rights and therefore must be the key beneficiaries without "having to share the pie" with anyone else. Such a contractual arrangement would, however, be appropriate in a scenario in which tenure rights are poorly defined and a contractual solution would offer the possibility to all parties with a legitimate claim to come to a mutually agreeable solution. Again, a thorough land tenure assessment would be necessary to determine that tenure rights are unclear but that indigenous communities may have a legitimate claim under formal or customary law to some or all of the land or resources. In cases in which indigenous peoples do not have any such rights or claim thereto, a fair and equitable benefit-sharing mechanism would be the proper instrument to ensure that forest-dependent indigenous communities would be able to benefit from payments for emission reductions.

In sum, the three-step process outlined in the chapter ensures that indigenous peoples are rewarded for their centuries-old efforts to avoid deforestation and forest degradation by ensuring that they will receive their due share of the payments for emission reductions. Concomitantly, a properly conducted land and resource tenure assessment brings to the fore the degree of uncertainty of tenure regimes with respect to indigenous peoples and can serve as a catalyst and an incentive to renew ongoing efforts or start new endeavors to address unresolved land tenure issues. Also, such processes must be conducted in a multidisciplinary way, through a combination of legal analyses and social and anthropological skills. Perhaps even more important, and crucial for the success of any REDD+ program, is the active involvement of indigenous communities themselves in the program design. Only when indigenous peoples are in the driver's seat with respect to key design features, such as land tenure and benefit-sharing arrangements, will a REDD+ program have a chance to succeed.

11
Shifting the Paradigm
Rule of Law and the 2030 Agenda for Sustainable Development

IRENE KHAN

The relationship between rule of law and sustainable development was among the most controversial and hotly debated topics during the United Nations consultations on the post-2015 development agenda.[1] Although Organisation for Economic Co-operation and Development (OECD) countries argued for the inclusion of rule of law as a concrete development goal, many developing countries feared that the close links between rule of law and human rights would encourage aid conditionality. Other countries felt that mixing rule of law issues with social and economic development priorities might impinge on national security and undermine national sovereignty. Some UN member-states argued that rule of law was more properly understood as a peace-and-security agenda item for the UN Security Council, not UN development forums. Others believed that rule of law should follow development, rather than be a part of it. Still others maintained that rule of law was not measurable and therefore not appropriate for inclusion as a Sustainable Development Goal (SDG).[2]

---

1 This debate occurred despite the specific and explicit affirmation of the links between rule of law and sustainable development in previous UN conferences. At the 2005 World Summit, member-states noted that "good governance and the rule of law at the national and international levels are essential for sustained economic growth, sustainable development and the eradication of poverty and hunger." See UN General Assembly (UNGA), 2005 World Summit Outcome, A/RES/60/1, October 24, 2005, para. 11. The High-Level Meeting of the General Assembly on the Rule of Law in September 2012 stated that the "advancement of the rule of law at the national and international levels is essential for sustained and inclusive economic growth, sustainable development, the eradication of poverty and hunger and the full realization of all human rights and fundamental freedoms including the right to development, all of which in turn reinforce the rule of law." It went on to state that "the rule of law and development are strongly interrelated and mutually reinforcing" and "should be considered in the post-2015 international development agenda." See UNGA, Declaration of the High-Level Meeting of the General Assembly on the Rule of Law at the National and International Levels, A/RES/67/1, September 24, 2012. Furthermore, the outcome document adopted at the Rio+20 Conference in 2012 noted that rule of law was essential for inclusive economic development, social development, and environmental protection. See UNGA, "The Future We Want," A/RES/66/288, September 11, 2012, para. 10.

2 "Rule of law at the national level is in essence a matter of internal affairs. There is no 'one-size-fits-all' model for rule of law and it is hardly goal-able and properly measured." See "Statement by Dr. Endah Murniningtyas, Deputy Minister for Natural Resources and Environment of the National Development Planning Agency, Indonesia, on behalf of China, Indonesia, and Kazakhstan, Eighth Meeting of the OWG on SDGs, 3–7 February 2014," https://sustainabledevelopment.un.org/content/documents/6340indonesia3.pdf.

Eventually, a combination of broad consultations, tough political negotiations, strong civil society pressure, and persuasive research and advocacy helped to shift the debate.[3] As the pursuit of equality, equity, and social justice gained prominence in the emerging development agenda, so did the realization that without rule of law, development cannot be sustained, nor can wealth and progress be shared in a fair and balanced way.

On September 25, 2015, world leaders adopted what is arguably the most ambitious global development program ever: the 2030 Agenda for Sustainable Development.[4] "People-centered" and focused on the "needs of the poorest and most vulnerable," the 2030 Agenda seeks to align the objectives of eradicating poverty and reducing inequality among present generations with the objective of preserving fragile ecosystems and limited natural resources for future generations. The 2030 Agenda sets out 17 universally applicable SDGs, covering a comprehensive list of economic, social, and environmental priorities.[5]

A distinct feature of the 2030 Agenda is its acknowledgment of rule of law and access to justice as integral parts of development and key drivers of the process of making socioeconomic progress sustainable. That understanding is made explicit in SDG 16 and embedded implicitly in various other goals and targets across the entire agenda—in references to equality, inclusion and equity, rights, legal frameworks, and accountable institutions.[6] Furthermore, the outcome document states that "democracy, good governance and the rule of law, as well as an enabling environment at national and international levels, are essential for sustainable development, including sustained and inclusive economic growth, social development, environmental protection and the eradication of poverty and hunger."[7] The centrality and importance of rule of law for all 17 SDGs is fully apparent.

The adoption of the 2030 Agenda has settled the political and ideological debate, but the challenge now is to ensure that rule of law is translated into results in the field. Achieving these requires a thorough understanding of the role and relevance of rule of law in promoting sustainable development across a range of complex political and social environments and diverse legal systems.

---

3 See, for example, International Development Law Organization (IDLO), "Doing Justice to Sustainable Development: Integrating the Rule of Law into the Post-2015 Development Agenda" (IDLO, Rome, 2014).

4 UNGA, "Transforming Our World: The 2030 Agenda for Sustainable Development," A/70/L.1, September 18, 2015, 21.

5 Sustainable development is often described in terms of three integrated pillars: economic, social, and environmental. See, for example, UNGA, "The Future We Want," A/RES/66/288, September 11, 2012, para. 3: "We therefore acknowledge the need to further mainstream sustainable development at all levels, integrating economic, social and environmental aspects and recognizing their interlinkages, so as to achieve sustainable development in all its dimensions."

6 See, for example, SDGs 4, 5, 8, 10, 11, and 16.

7 UNGA, "Transforming Our World," para. 9.

This chapter contributes to building that understanding. It begins by analyzing the concept of rule of law as an instrument of legal and social justice, focusing on the relationship between rule of law and human rights from the perspective of development. It then highlights the place of rule of law in the 2030 Agenda. Next, drawing on lessons learned from decades of development practice, it explains how rule of law, properly understood and implemented, advances the three pillars of sustainable development—economic, social, and environmental—and reinforces their interlinkage through legal and institutional reforms, protection of rights, access to justice, and legal empowerment strategies.

Rule of Law: A Concept of Justice

The idea of justice is deeply embedded in the notion of sustainable development, which is, after all, "a moral concept that seeks to define a 'fair and just' development."[8] Sustainable development is driven by the conviction that the goals of the present generation must be met without compromising the ability of future generations to meet their own requirements.[9] By acknowledging the need to eradicate poverty and reduce inequalities in the world today, as well as to preserve a viable planet in the interest of future generations, sustainable development provides "an ethical framework that could enable national societies, and indeed the global human society, to respond to emerging environmental and developmental problems in an equitable manner."[10]

The balancing of competing intergenerational and intragenerational interests requires transparent, rule-based processes and mechanisms that can ensure appropriate, inclusive, and equitable arrangements acceptable to all. Broadly speaking, that is what rule of law offers to sustainable development.

The UN secretary-general has referred to rule of law as

> a principle of governance in which all persons, institutions and entities, public and private, including the State itself, are accountable to laws that are publically promulgated, equally enforced and independently adjudicated, and which are consistent with international human rights norms and standards. It requires, as well, measures to ensure adherence to the principles of supremacy of law, equality before the law, accountability to the law, fairness in the application

---

8 Richard Welford and Richard Starkey, *The Earthscan Reader in Business and Sustainable Development* (London: Earthscan, 2001), cited in Jennifer Elliot, *An Introduction to Sustainable Development* (Oxon: Routledge, 2013), 24.

9 World Commission on Environment and Development, *Our Common Future* (Oxford: Oxford University Press, 1987). In "Human Development and Economic Sustainability," *World Development* 28, no. 12 (2000): 2038, Sudhir Anand and Amartya Sen state that "it would be a gross violation of the universalist principle . . . if we were to be obsessed about intergenerational equity without at the same time seizing the problem of intra-generational equity."

10 Oluf Langhelle, "Sustainable Development and Social Justice: Expanding the Rawlsian Framework of Global Justice," *Environmental Values* 9, no. 3 (2000): 296.

> of the law, separation of powers, participation in decision-making, legal certainty, avoidance of arbitrariness and procedural and legal transparency.[11]

At the heart of rule of law lies the notion of equal protection: All persons are equal in the eyes of the law and equally accountable under the law. Rule of law provides for procedural justice, or due process, and for substantive justice, or the pursuit of equitable outcomes, based on human rights. This understanding of rule of law contrasts sharply with the notion of rule *by* law, where the formality, legality, consistency, and efficiency of the law are used as tools to oppress people.[12]

Predictability, clarity, legality, and due process guarantees are the most commonly understood and widely used concepts in the interpretation of rule of law. But rule of law is more than that. It embodies—very importantly—the notion of justice, which has been defined in a variety of ways, including as an absence of bias and discrimination, as the pursuit and realization of equality, and as a norm or virtue that permeates institutions of governance.[13] The UN secretary-general has referred to justice as "an ideal of accountability and fairness in the protection and vindication of rights and the prevention and punishment of wrongs."[14]

From the perspective of development, justice needs to be as preoccupied with fair outcomes as it is with effective and efficient rules and institutions. In the words of Amartya Sen: "The question to ask is whether the demands of justice must be only about getting the institutions and rules right? Should we not also have to examine what does emerge in the society, the kinds of lives that people actually lead?" "Justice," he emphasizes, "cannot be indifferent to the lives of people."[15]

Rule of law, properly understood as an instrument and concept of justice, encompasses human rights, including political and civil rights, as well as economic, social, and cultural rights.

---

11 United Nations, "The Rule of Law and Transitional Justice in Conflict and Post-Conflict Societies," S/2004/616, August 23, 2004, para. 6

12 Although there is no universally acceptable definition of rule of law, interpretations of the concept fall broadly into two categories. The "thin definition" of rule of law refers to formal decision making, with emphasis on consistency, efficiency, and universality in the application of the laws, rules, and regulations. The "thick definition" of rule of law places equal importance on substantive outcomes and procedural fairness, and seeks to protect rights through legal norms, including human rights, as well as due process.

13 See, for example, Eric Heinze, *The Concept of Injustice* (London: Routledge, 2013); John Rawls, *A Theory of Justice*, rev. ed. (Oxford: Oxford University Press, 1999), 3; and Plato, *The Republic*, trans. Robin Waterfield, Oxford World Classics (Oxford: Oxford University Press, 1984).

14 United Nations, "Rule of Law and Transitional Justice," para. 7.

15 Amartya Sen has emphasized the "need to focus on actual realizations and accomplishments, rather than only on the establishment of what are identified as the right institutions and rules," and called for a "realization-focused understanding of justice." See Amartya Sen, *The Idea of Justice* (Cambridge, MA: Harvard University Press, 2009), 10, 18.

Human rights are constraints on state power (e.g., by prohibiting torture and restrictions on free speech) and enablers for state action (e.g., by providing access to education, health care, and housing). They empower and confer dignity on the poor and marginalized. They are claims that the weak advance to hold the powerful to account.[16]

By encouraging participation, accountability, transparency, equality and protection of fundamental freedoms, and fulfillment of basic needs, human rights help to address the deprivation, exclusion, and discrimination that lock people in poverty. Human rights are operationalized by rule of law through constitutional and legal protections, effective institutions for implementation and accountability, judicial and administrative remedies, and the legal empowerment of people to access justice and rights.

SDGs and Rule of Law

The 2030 Agenda acknowledges the significance of rule of law to sustainable development in several distinct ways: by reducing crime and violence, advancing equality and eradicating discrimination, strengthening laws and institutions at the national and international levels, and empowering people.

SDG 16 is the most visible acknowledgment of rule of law in the 2030 Agenda. It calls on states to "promote peaceful and inclusive societies for sustainable development, provide access to justice for all and build effective, accountable and inclusive institutions at all levels."[17] It is explicit in committing states to "promote the rule of law at the national and international levels and ensure equal access to justice for all."[18] It seeks implementation through the strengthening of national institutions, laws, and policies.[19] The targets of SDG 16[20] cover a wide spectrum, from reducing violence, corruption, and bribery, to providing legal identity and public access to information, to ensuring participatory decision making and protecting fundamental freedoms. The strong language on good governance and inclusive societies in SDG 16 gives it a cross-cutting value and makes it a major enabler for the effective implementation of all SDGs.

---

16 Irene Khan, *The Unheard Truth: Poverty and Human Rights* (New York: W.W. Norton, 2009), 21.

17 SDG 16: "Promote peaceful and inclusive societies for sustainable development, provide access to justice for all and build effective, accountable and inclusive institutions at all levels."

18 SDG 16.3: "Promote the rule of law at the national and international levels, and ensure equal access to justice for all."

19 SDG 16.a: "Strengthen relevant national institutions, including through international cooperation, for building capacities at all levels, in particular in developing countries, for preventing violence and combating terrorism and crime."

20 A "goal" for the purposes of the SDGs, is defined as an ambitious commitment to address a single challenge. A "target" is an action that leads to a specific, measurable, and time-bound outcome directly related to the achievement of a goal. "Indicators" are used to measure progress toward a target, and often involve quantitative data.

Three of the ten targets of SDG 16 focus on fighting organized crime and violence.[21] That crime, violence, and insecurity are major impediments to sustainable development is a well-known fact. High levels of organized crime and urban violence can deter investment and economic activity and impede economic growth and employment.[22] Where organized crime is linked to natural resources, it degrades the environment. Gender-based violence is a major obstacle to the advancement of women and girls. Studies have shown that crime has a greater impact on poor and vulnerable groups because redress is harder for them to obtain.[23] Protection from crime and violence ranks among the top development priorities of poor people in all regions of the world.[24]

Organized crime and violence flourish in settings where public institutions are weak or corrupt. By prioritizing the reduction of corruption and bribery, SDG 16 underlines the importance of clean government to sustainable development.

SDG 16 calls for the strengthening of the relevant national institutions to prevent violence, terrorism, and crime. Criminal justice reforms are a key feature of international efforts to strengthen rule of law at the national level. Such reforms are often treated as a priority intervention in postconflict and transitional settings.[25]

SDG 16 is not the only goal in the 2030 Agenda that is relevant to rule of law. The essence of rule of law is captured in a number of other places in the 2030 Agenda, especially in the calls for the reduction of inequality and the promotion of social inclusion. SDGs 5 and 10 are devoted to the advancement of gender equality and equality, respectively.[26] A number of other SDGs also make clear references to equality and nondiscrimination, and to an inclusive

---

21 This is not the only reference to the eradication of violence in the 2030 Agenda. SDG 5.2 calls for the elimination of all forms of violence against women and girls.

22 World Bank, "Violence in the City: Understanding and Supporting Community Responses to Urban Violence" (World Bank, Washington, DC, 2010).

23 See, for example, David Verala and Annette Pearson, "Institutional Responses to Social Demands: Enhancing Access to Justice in Colombia," in *The World Bank Legal Review*, vol. 5, *Fostering Development through Opportunity, Inclusion, and Equity*, ed. Hassane Cissé, N. R. Madhava Menon, Marie-Claire Cordonier Segger, and Vincent O. Nmehielle (Washington, DC: World Bank, 2014); Leonard Maveneka and Zebedee Ruramira, "Final End of the Programme Evaluation of the Support to Access to Justice for All, the Foundation for Good Governance and Poverty Reduction, Rwanda (2008–2013)" (evaluation report, United Nations Development Programme [UNDP], New York, 2013), 23; UNDP, "Programming for Justice: Access for All: A Practitioner's Guide to a Human Rights–Based Approach to Access to Justice" (UNDP, New York, 2005), 3, www.unrol.org/files/Justice_Guides_ProgrammingForJustice-Access-ForAll.pdf.

24 Deepa Narayan et al., *Voices of the Poor: Can Anyone Hear Us?* (Oxford: Oxford University Press, 2000).

25 See Louise Arbour, "Economic and Social Justice for Societies in Transition," *International Law and Politics* 40, no. 1 (Fall 2007–2008): 4–6.

26 SDG 5: "Achieve gender equality and empower all women and girls"; and SDG 10: "Reduce inequality within and among countries."

approach to development.[27] These issues cannot be tackled without rule of law; therefore, implicitly, rule of law is of great significance to these goals.

Extreme inequality has been described by leading human rights proponents as "the defining issue of our time."[28] Inequality—including of income and access to resources, services, and opportunities—has grown steadily in nearly all countries, as well as among countries, over the past two decades.[29] It retards economic growth, generating political protests and social discontent.[30] It hinders political participation, weakening democracy. The failure to address inequalities and the systematic discrimination that underlie them have become drivers of violent conflict and an impediment to recovery in post-conflict countries.[31] Inequality is becoming a multigenerational phenomenon, and experience shows that it cannot be reversed over time without targeted efforts through litigation, legislation, or sweeping policy changes.[32]

Rule of law and human rights provide a strong basis for fighting inequality and discrimination.[33] In the context of human rights, equality is understood as the equality of opportunity, without discriminatory outcomes.[34] The fundamental principle of equal protection inherent in the concept of rule of law helps to reduce inequality and promote social inclusion. Several SDGs refer to laws and regulations as important means of eradicating discrimination and promoting equal access and opportunity.

---

27 See, for example, SDGs 8, 9, 11, and 16.

28 Office of the UN High Commissioner for Human Rights, "Integrating Human Rights into the Post-2015 Development Agenda: Addressing Inequalities and Discrimination in the SDGs," http://www.ohchr.org/Documents/Issues/MDGs/Post2015/EqualityAndNonDiscrimination.pdf.

29 UNDP, "Humanity Divided: Confronting Inequality in Developing Countries" (UNDP, New York, November 2013).

30 Jonathan Ostry et al, "Redistribution, Inequality, and Growth," IMF staff discussion note (International Monetary Fund, Washington, DC, 2014), http://www.imf.org/external/pubs/ft/sdn/2014/sdn1402.pdf.

31 World Bank, *World Development Report 2011: Conflict, Security and Development* (Washington, DC: World Bank, 2011), http://siteresources.worldbank.org/INTWDRS/Resources/WDR2011_Full_Text.pdf.

32 World Bank, *World Development Report 2006: Equity and Development* (Washington, DC: World Bank, 2006), 5, www-wds.worldbank.org/servlet/WDSContentServer/WDSP/IB/2005/09/20/000112742_20050920110826/Rendered/PDF/322040World0Development0Report02006.pdf.

33 "Among the principles that have direct operational implications for development policy and programming, revealing the strongest elements of convergence between development and human rights, are nondiscrimination and equality." See Axel Marx et al., "Human Rights and Service Delivery: A Review of Current Policies, Practices, and Challenges," in *The World Bank Legal Review*, vol. 6, *Improving Delivery in Development: The Role of Voice, Social Contract, and Accountability*, ed. Jan Wouters, Alberto Ninio, Teresa Doherty, and Hassane Cissé (Washington, DC: World Bank, 2015), 45.

34 Evadre Grant, "Dignity and Equality," *Human Rights Law Review* 7, no. 2 (2007): 300; and Radhika Balakrishnan et al., "What Does Inequality Have to Do with Human Rights?" Working Paper 392 (Political Economic Research Institute, University of Massachusetts Amherst, August 2015). See also United Nations, "Report of the Special Rapporteur on Extreme Poverty and Human Rights, Philip Alston," A/HRC/29/31, May, 17, 2015.

Delivering the ambitions of the 2030 Agenda for Sustainable Development will require significantly overhauling laws and policies; building the capacity of institutions, including in the justice sector; and strengthening access to justice. The following sections describe the role that laws, institutions, and legal empowerment can play in the implementation of sustainable development.

Strengthening Laws

Laws reflect society's priorities in the economic, social, and environmental spheres. For many countries, the reformed laws serve as historic milestones, charting progress toward greater freedoms. In apartheid South Africa, for example, laws institutionalized and legitimized racism. Today, South Africa's constitution is considered one of the most progressive in the world. In the United States, the passage of same-sex marriage legislation is upending years of discriminatory practices, much as civil rights legislation targeted discrimination against African Americans 50 years ago.

Laws can magnify or sustain inequality when they allow violence against less powerful groups to go unpunished, or legislate discriminatory policies and practices. This is particularly true for women and girls.[35] Equally, laws can shift norms and practices, thereby countering discrimination and enabling the poor and the marginalized to realize their rights and gain equitable access to essential services, such as health care and education, and to resources, such as land and water.

Antidiscrimination and equal opportunity laws have been used as tools to address inequitable practices that were systemic and historically ingrained. For example, reforming family and inheritance laws to provide women with more equitable access to land can transform women's lives in a host of ways, leading to greater levels of gender equality and food security.[36]

Recognizing the transformative power of laws in the context of equality, the 2030 Agenda calls for efforts to be made toward "eliminating discriminatory laws, policies and practices and promoting appropriate legislation, policies and action in this regard."[37]

Laws are also implicated in the privatization of key services, such as water, sanitation, and energy. Successful privatization can provide for more efficient delivery, lowering the costs to consumers. However, privatization can also lead to the transfer of public assets at fire sale prices or to cuts in services that adversely affect poor people. Effective privatization laws and

---

35 See IDLO, "Accessing Justice: Models, Strategies and Best Practices on Women's Empowerment" (IDLO, Rome, 2013).

36 See Asian Development Bank, "Gender Equality and Food Security: Women's Empowerment as a Tool for Food Security" (Asian Development Bank, Mandaluyong, Philippines, 2013), 24–28.

37 SDG 10.3: "Ensure equal opportunity and reduce inequalities of outcome, including through eliminating discriminatory laws, policies and practices and promoting appropriate legislation, policies and actions in this regard."

postprivatization regulatory capacity, including strong accountability mechanisms, are critical to maintaining the accessibility of high-quality services to all groups. Clear laws and regulations can help to set sectorwide standards. To be effective, however, regulatory frameworks must be backed up by credible enforcement powers, including mechanisms to ensure compliance. The law is indispensable for ensuring that the government remains responsible for holding third parties accountable for their failings.[38]

Effective legal frameworks are also essential for trade, investment, and economic growth. Frequently, developing countries do not have laws that protect their interests in complex, technology-related areas, such as water management and sanitation, or energy generation and distribution. Legal frameworks for taxation, employment, and investment may be outdated. Intellectual property and technology legislation may fail to take advantage of the flexibility or exceptions available under international agreements. Very often, governments of developing countries lack the capacity and skills to negotiate, draft, and apply laws. Developing capacity and improving laws for economic growth are recognized as high priorities by the 2030 Agenda.[39]

Building Institutions

Developing effective, accountable, and transparent institutions at all levels is recognized as a priority in the 2030 Agenda—explicitly in SDG 16.6, and implicitly in other SDGs.[40]

Institutions play an important role in defining the relationship between the state and citizens, and in cementing development gains. Institutions, in their broadest sense, include rules, regulations, laws, government entities, and informal codes of social conduct. In the rule of law sector, the key institutions are courts, ministries of law and justice, police and correctional facilities, and other structures created to resolve disputes and ensure accountability. Through their oversight role, judicial, quasi-judicial, and administrative institutions play an important role not only in resolving disputes but also in ensuring equitable access to and quality of social services, transparency, accountability in the procurement and delivery of development projects, and proper enforcement of environmental laws and regulations.

The judiciary plays a primary role in ensuring that the state and third parties respect legal rights, and in providing remedies when such rights are violated. Sustainable development priorities in areas such as education, social

---

38 United Nations, "The Addis Ababa Action Agenda of the Third International Conference on Financing for Development," A/CONF.227/L.1, July 15, 2015, para. 36.

39 Examples include SDG 17.9, on capacity building: "Enhance international support for implementing effective and targeted capacity building in developing countries to support national plans to implement all sustainable development goals, including through North-South, South-South, and triangular cooperation"; and SDG 16.b: "Promote and enforce nondiscriminatory laws and policies for sustainable development."

40 For example, SDG 1.3 refers to social protection systems. Other examples can be found in SDGs 10.3, 11.3, and 13.b.

protection, adequate housing, and health care are increasingly the subject of economic and social rights litigation.[41] Constitutional courts in particular are at the forefront of securing rights for impoverished groups, including the rights of indigenous communities.

Administrative courts are the subject of increased attention because they are mechanisms critical to the protection of citizens against arbitrary uses of state power. They ensure that state authorities act in accordance with state laws and regulations. They also aim to enhance citizen participation in public policy formulation and oversight.[42] Administrative courts, tribunals, and institutions such as land commissions play an important role in protecting property rights and providing for unbiased dispute resolution mechanisms that attract investment and promote sustained and inclusive economic growth.[43]

National human rights institutions, ombudsmen, and supervisory councils can also be important means of ensuring accountability, transparency, and responsiveness of decision makers, and providing opportunities for citizens to participate in discussions about development.

Effective institutions can do much to eradicate poverty and reduce inequalities, but they themselves need to be transparent and subject to scrutiny. Institutions can be vulnerable to elite capture, when resources designated for the benefit of poorer populations are usurped by a few powerful individuals or groups,[44] leading to increased levels of inequality. To guard against this, financial and technical legal support for rule of law assistance must be accompanied by efforts to build political will in support of new reform agendas.[45]

An important strategy for resisting elite capture of institutions is the empowerment of civil society and rights holders, including through greater access to information.

Accessing Justice

Access to justice has been defined as a condition in which all people are able to resolve conflicts, claim their rights, and seek and obtain remedies for grievances, through formal or informal institutions of justice, in compliance with human

---

41 OECD and World Bank, "Integrating HR into the Post-2015 Development Agenda" (2013), xiv; and Jane Weru et al., "Confronting Complexity: Using Action-Research to Build Voice, Accountability, and Justice in Nairobi's Mukuru Informal Settlements," in *The World Bank Legal Review*, vol. 6, *Improving Delivery in Development*, 248.

42 See *World Development Report 2006*, 157. See also Folke Bernadotte Academy, *Handbook for Monitoring Administrative Justice* (Stockholm: Folke Bernadotte Academy, 2013).

43 SDG 8: "Promote sustained, inclusive and sustainable economic growth, full and productive employment and decent work for all."

44 Diya Dutta, "Elite Capture and Corruption: Concepts and Definitions" (National Council of Applied Economic Research, New Delhi).

45 Urban Jonsson, *Human Rights Approach to Development Programming* (New York: UNICEF, 2003), 22; and Homi Kharas, "The Post-2015 Agenda and the Evolution of the World Bank Group," Global Economy and Development Working Paper 92 (Brookings Institution, Washington, DC, 2015), 3.

rights standards.[46] As noted by the United Nations Development Programme (UNDP), "the attainment of human rights enhances a key capacity needed by the poor to overcome poverty—the capacity to demand accountability."[47] This capacity is critical to leveling the playing field between the vulnerable and the powerful by, for example, deterring corruption, impunity, and other such ills that disempower the poor and trap them in cycles of poverty.

"Accessibility," according to the World Bank, "depends on how compatible laws are with the norms and understandings that shape people's lives. Legal institutions need to be physically and economically accessible and people need to have the knowledge and capacity to claim their rights."[48] Access to justice may also require engaging with traditional justice systems, which are more accessible to and affordable for poor people, but which may reinforce discriminatory practices or existing inequalities through their judgments.

Access to justice can help to improve access to public services and resources, thereby reducing discrimination and social exclusion. In Uganda, for example, formal and informal justice systems in rural areas are largely ill equipped to handle land-related matters, with significant implications for women. In 2012, the organization Uganda Land Alliance trained traditional leaders in equitable dispute resolution techniques, leading to more effective identification and demarcation of land boundaries. These efforts reportedly led to more favorable division of land for widows and children.[49] Interventions such as these could be particularly powerful in shaping land rights in favor of poor and marginalized groups in furtherance of SDGs 2, 5, and 10.[50]

Related to access to justice, awareness of rights and access to information are also critical for empowering people to claim their rights and to hold authorities to account.[51] Access to information ensures transparency of government processes, including budgetary and procurement processes, and allows

---

46 UNDP, *Programming for Justice: Access for All* (New York: UNDP, 2005), 4.

47 Ibid., 3.

48 See *World Development Report 2006*, 157.

49 Maggi Carfield, "Land Justice in Uganda: Preserving Peace, Promoting Integration" (IDLO, Rome, 2011), as cited in IDLO, "Doing Justice to Sustainable Development: Integrating the Rule of Law in the Post 2015 Development Agenda" (IDLO, Rome, 2014).

50 SDG 2.3: "By 2030, double the agricultural productivity and incomes of small-scale food producers, in particular women, indigenous peoples, family farmers, pastoralists and fishers, including through secure and equal access to land, other productive resources and inputs, knowledge, financial services, markets and opportunities for value addition and non-farm employment"; SDG 5a: "Undertake reforms to give women equal rights to economic resources, as well as access to ownership and control over land and other forms of property, financial services, inheritance and natural resources, in accordance with national laws"; SDG 10.3: "Ensure equal opportunity and reduce inequalities of outcome, including by eliminating discriminatory laws, policies and practices and promoting appropriate legislation, policies and action in this regard."

51 One of the main reasons for the failure to capitalize on development initiatives is "due to the inefficient flow of information regarding the activities of public officials." See Sean Fraser, "The Role of Access to Information in Promoting Development," in *The World Bank Legal Review*, vol. 5, *Fostering Development*, 189.

for the monitoring of progress. It encourages public participation, promotes good governance, and protects human rights. Information creates opportunities to discuss a range of available options, to vote in accordance with one's best interests, and to take part in meaningful public policy discussions. SDG 16.10 calls for public access to information.[52]

Studies have shown that providing parents with better information on school budgets, resource inflows, and procedures for appointing teachers and school administrators strongly correlates with higher child literacy rates and improved teacher performance.[53]

In South Africa, the Open Democracy Advice Centre assisted villagers in Kwazulu-Natal to use the Freedom of Information Law to obtain the minutes from council meetings on water use. The information clearly showed that municipal authorities were not acting on the decisions made at a meeting to alleviate drought conditions. After publicizing the issue, water tanks were installed and municipal contracts with service providers were held to greater scrutiny.[54]

In South Africa and elsewhere, rights awareness and information sharing efforts are proven ways to activate communities to realize their rights relating to food security, health care, drinking water, and sanitation—issues relevant to SDGs 2, 3, and 6, among other goals.[55]

From Principles to Practice

As described in the preceding paragraphs, rule of law, when understood as encompassing both substantive and procedural justice, promotes progressive legal reforms and effective, accountable institutions that in turn empower citizens and enable accountable, transparent, and participatory development processes. These elements are crucial and relevant to each of the three dimensions of sustainable development: economic, social, and environmental.

Economic Growth

Stable, transparent legal regimes are key to economic development.[56] Rule of law brings clarity, certainty, and predictability to business transactions and

---

52 SDG 16.10: "Ensure public access to information and protect fundamental freedoms, in accordance with national legislation and international agreements."

53 Transparency International, "The Anti-Corruption Catalyst: Realizing the MDGs by 2015" (Transparency International, Berlin, 2010), 5.

54 Anupama Dokeniya, "The Right to Information as a Tool for Community Empowerment," in *The World Bank Legal Review*, vol. 5.

55 See, for example, SDG 2.5: "By 2020 . . . ensure access to and fair and equitable sharing of benefits arising from the utilization of genetic resources and associated traditional knowledge, as internationally agreed"; SDG 3.7: "By 2030 ensure universal access to sexual and reproductive health-care services, including for family planning, information and education, and the integration of reproductive health into national strategies and programs"; and SDG 6.1: "By 2030, achieve universal and equitable access to safe and affordable drinking water for all."

56 See, for example, Thomas Carothers, "The Rule of Law Revival," *Foreign Affairs* 77, no. 2 (1998).

provides recourse in cases of commercial and civil disputes. By publicly disclosing and enforcing the rights to property and contractual obligations, rule of law creates stability for investment and commercial activities and fosters economic growth. Effective laws and institutions check coercion and predatory behavior, enhance competition, level the playing field for economic actors, support entrepreneurship and innovation, and bolster small and medium enterprises.

In Kyrgyzstan, the European Bank of Reconstruction and Development partnered with the International Development Law Organization (IDLO) and the Kyrgyz judiciary to strengthen the latter's commercial law capacity through, for example, training, institution building, and regional cooperation. A related program, also implemented by IDLO, sought to strengthen the independence and the integrity of the courts, and to bring greater transparency and accountability to commercial dispute resolution. A recent program evaluation revealed significant improvements in the processing of commercial cases by the courts and in public confidence in the courts.[57] Complementing this finding, the World Bank's *Doing Business 2014* indicated that the ease of doing business in Kyrgyzstan had markedly improved since 2005. The Kyrgyz judicial reforms are an example of how improvements in rule of law, as required by SDGs 16.5 and 16.6, can enhance the climate for economic development.

The 2030 Agenda for Sustainable Development calls for equitable and inclusive economic growth to eradicate poverty and reduce inequalities. That means ensuring safe and secure conditions for workers, including migrant workers. It means ensuring that poor people have access to land, property, and financial services and markets. Achieving these changes is heavily dependent on introducing appropriate laws and institutions as well as empowering the poor.

Legal reform is often necessary to ensure that the poor and marginalized have access to markets and financial services. Legal awareness can better enable the poor to protect their assets and scale up their capacity for commercial transactions.

For example, in Ecuador, IDLO promoted access to fair trade markets for two indigenous rural communities by training community members on legal aspects of forming and running microenterprises and on their constitutionally protected rights as indigenous people. Two years later, the groups reported that the interventions had provided them with substantial leverage in entering new markets and accessing new income streams. Also in Ecuador, IDLO partnered with the International Fund for Agricultural Development to build local communities' awareness of agricultural cooperatives. With the added

57 Michael Nussbaumer and Irina Rabinovich, "Raising the Bar for Judges in Central Asia: Five Years of Judicial Capacity Building in the Kyrgyz Republic," in *Law in Transition 2011*, ed. Gerard Sanders and Michael Nussbaumer (London: European Bank for Reconstruction and Development, 2011); and World Bank, *Doing Business 2014: Understanding Regulations for Small and Medium-Size Enterprises* (Washington, DC: World Bank, 2013).

leverage that this knowledge provided, indigenous women were able to make significant gains in accessing fair trade markets.[58]

Establishing secure land rights for the poor significantly boosts economic activity, increases the value of the land as well as its capacity for food production, and contributes to better preservation of the land.[59] The 2030 Agenda recognizes the equal rights to land and property of all men and women, in particular the poor and the vulnerable, as an important means of ending poverty.[60]

In many countries, customary rules regarding land ownership provide insufficient protection for the poor; customary lands may be converted to government or private use without due process or adequate compensation.[61] Land surveys, awareness of the legal aspects of the land titling processes, and greater access to administrative authorities can help rural communities improve their security of land tenure.

In Liberia and Uganda, civil society organizations are expanding the knowledge of traditional dispute resolution actors regarding land issues, national land laws, and especially women's rights.[62] Strong property rights protection is required to ensure that women can engage as productive agents of economic growth and avoid destitution in case of widowhood or divorce.[63] Where land is securely held by women, they are better able to support themselves and improve their families' access to health care, education, and means of survival.[64]

Social Development

To be sustainable, social development efforts must be inclusive, eliminating all forms of discrimination and ensuring access for all to the resources, benefits, and opportunities of development. Strong legal frameworks, coupled with state capacity to implement related laws, regulations, and policies, and

---

58 IDLO, "Legal Empowerment for Fair Trade, Food Security and Natural Resources Management in Ecuador" (Final Report, IDLO, Rome, 2013).

59 IDLO and Namati, "Protecting Community Lands and Resources: Evidence from Liberia, Mozambique and Uganda" (IDLO, Rome; Namati, Washington, DC, 2012).

60 SDG Goal 1.4: "By 2030 ensure that all men and women, particularly the poor and the vulnerable, have equal rights to economic resources, as well as access to basic services, ownership, and control over land and other forms of property, inheritance, natural resources, appropriate new technology, and financial services including microfinance."

61 Jeffrey Hatcher, Lucia Palombi, and Paul Mathieu, "Securing the Land Rights of the Rural Poor: Experiences in Legal Empowerment" (Legal Empowerment: Practitioners' Perspectives, IDLO, Rome, 2010), 7.

62 IDLO, "HIV and Law Project Papua New Guinea: Evaluation Report" (IDLO, Rome, 2012).

63 Nina Berg, Haley Horan, and Deena Patel, "Women's Inheritance and Property Rights: A Vehicle to Accelerate Progress towards the Achievement of the Millennium Development Goals" (Legal Empowerment: Practitioners' Perspectives, IDLO, Rome, 2010), 205.

64 Ana Palacio, "Legal Empowerment of the Poor: An Action Agenda for the World Bank" (World Bank, Washington, DC, 2005), 7.

accompanied by effective legal empowerment strategies, are key to fighting discrimination and marginalization.

Rule of law can facilitate social development by eliminating discrimination and promoting inclusion; giving legal protections to economic, social, and cultural rights; and ensuring acess to justice to seek remedies through administrative and legal redress mechanisms.

To take the example of health care, SDG 3 seeks to "ensure healthy lives and promote well-being for all at all ages." Rule of law is critical to ensuring the highest attainable standards of physical and mental health and social well-being. Constitutions and laws help to respect, protect, and fulfill the right to health. They do this by, among other means, regulating the health sector and other sectors that affect the social determinants of health.

Access to justice and legal empowerment strategies can be an important means of fighting discrimination and ensuring health care, as in the case of people living with HIV. Papua New Guinea has the highest rates of HIV/AIDS in the Pacific region. People living with HIV face various forms of stigma and discrimination, including mistreatment by health and law enforcement agencies and legal barriers to social services. IDLO launched a program in Papua New Guinea focused on providing legal aid, training, and counseling services, and on increasing rights awareness among key constituencies, including law and justice sector professionals, parliamentarians, civil society actors, and the affected communities. An evaluation of the project showed that empowerment of people living with HIV had improved their ability to claim their rights, including better access to health services.[65]

Rule of law plays a particularly important role in fighting gender discrimination, especially given the persistence of legal discrimination against women and girls in many parts of the world. At the global level, young women and girls are "less educated, less healthy and less free" than their male counterparts.[66]

Strengthening the political participation of women can lead to development dividends for them. In Rwanda, 64 percent of the parliamentarians elected in 2013 were women. Increased women's participation over the past decade has led to gender-sensitive lawmaking and policy making, including on controversial issues, such as polygamy and marital rape. The higher number of women in Parliament is the result of a combination of changing gender roles following the 1994 genocide and proactive laws and policies that promote women's political participation and leadership, including through provisions in the 2003 constitution.[67]

65 IDLO, "HIV and Law Project Papua New Guinea."

66 Beyond 2015, "A Holistic and Human Rights–Based Approach for Addressing Inequalities in the Post-2015 Development Agenda" (Beyond 2015, Pretoria, South Africa, 2012), 6.

67 Jennie Burnet, "Gender Balance and the Meanings of Women in Government in Post-Genocide Rwanda," *African Affairs* 107, no. 428 (2008): 361–386.

Legal identity is important for accessing social rights, finding work, establishing a business, owning land, or obtaining a loan. It is necessary for freedom of movement and for accessing justice. Legal identity and birth registration have been specifically recognized in Target 9 of SDG 16.[68]

In Morocco, women's rights NGOs carried out legal rights education and piloted the Court Accompanying program, which enabled unwed mothers to obtain legal identity documents for their children. These women suffered from social stigma and discrimination, and without legal identity papers they could not access social services. Thanks to the legal empowerment efforts, attitudes and behavior among local authorities shifted to some extent, enabling the women to obtain identity papers and access social services.[69]

Environmental Sustainability

Meaningful environmental protection that balances human needs with those of ecosystems and wildlife requires robust legal frameworks, aligned with international standards and enforced through strong mechanisms and institutions.[70] Responsible environmental stewardship also requires that institutions be held accountable through legal mechanisms and with the aid of civil society. The poor and marginalized, especially indigenous groups, must be empowered to demand action if their environment is spoiled, their livelihoods are destroyed, or their water or land rights are violated.

Legal empowerment and accountability for enforcement of environmental laws start with public participation, supported by access to information and access to justice. Unfortunately, in many countries, freedom of information laws are lacking or inadequate. Public participation in environmental and sustainability decision making requires legally protected access to information. Access to justice mechanisms, when coupled with enhanced institutional capacity to manage environmental issues and underpinned by laws that balance environmental issues against social and economic imperatives, provide the poor with a powerful tool.

As a positive example of the benefits of legal empowerment, many local communities in South Africa have established community protocols, which are quasi-legal documents that set out the priorities and governance structure of indigenous and local communities. The communities that have drawn up these protocols can now more readily interact with resource extraction companies to ensure better engagement with the decision making (including prior

---

68 SDG 16.9: "By 2030 provide legal identity for all including birth registration."

69 IDLO, "Accessing Justice."

70 There are many varied forms of regulation that can achieve this purpose. For a discussion of options, see Jonathan B. Wiener, "Global Environmental Regulation: Instrument Choice in Legal Context," *Yale Law Journal* 108, no.4 (1999): 677–800; and Robert Percival, Christopher Schroeder, Alan Miller, and James Leape, *Environmental Regulation Law, Science and Policy*, 7th ed. (New York: Wolters Kluwer Law & Business, 2013).

informed consent) and ultimately benefit sharing (through properly negotiated agreements and contracts, avoiding elite capture).[71]

Measuring Justice

A number of overarching challenges and opportunities for measuring rule of law need to be addressed to facilitate reporting by governments to the UN General Assembly on their progress in achieving the 17 SDGs. It is important to acknowledge that particular national circumstances shape the progress of development in rule of law, including institutional capacities, literacy rates, corruption levels, economic development status, and histories of violent conflicts. The laws of each country vary not only by legal system but also by local, customary, and informal practices. Making progress on the SDGs will require tailor-made, context-specific approaches.

States must provide space for civil society organizations to review results, provide feedback, and ensure greater transparency, accountability, and integrity in reporting.

It is important to employ a variety of both quantitative and qualitative indicators that measure institutional capacity, objective change, and public perceptions of change to ensure a complete picture of any progress in any particular area of rule of law.

Normally, the capacity of institutions can be measured through indicators that look at performance, resource inputs, integrity, transparency, accountability, and quality. In the rule of law context, institutional capacity is traditionally measured by the performance of courts, prosecutor's offices, and the police. Data are primarily in the form of administrative statistics, and are mostly concerned with the efficiency of procedures (e.g., the number and types of cases adjudicated or investigated per year). Data can also include inputs such as resource allocations, trainings, and numbers of staff.

It is also important for countries to measure the effectiveness of institutions from the client perspective. User surveys can be employed to measure, among other things, the ease of accessing services for the poor and marginalized groups, whether those groups are accorded fair hearings when using the justice system, and whether they are able to establish legal identity and claim property.

Objective change is usually tracked to measure whether the social environment has been impacted by changes in organizational policies and practices. Objective change indicators employ objects, facts, and direct observation to help analysts draw conclusions. To increase the accuracy of findings, objective change can be measured by data provided from two or more sources of administrative records. For example, hospital records that demonstrate reduced infant mortality and ministry of health statistics that show increased

71 Harry Jonas, Kabir Bavikatte, and Holly Shrumm, "Community Protocols and Access and Benefit Sharing," *Asian Biotechnology and Development Review* 12, no. 3 (2010): 49–76.

access to prenatal health education may indicate improvements in the right to health. Similarly, household surveys that measure the prevalence of domestic violence can be compared with data on rates of reporting to the police, thus providing a better picture of women's willingness to report abuse and trust in justice institutions.

Conclusion

The 2030 Agenda commits states to 15 years of focused political, technical, and financial support in pursuit of 17 development objectives, comprising 169 targets.

Incorporating access to justice and rule of law in the 2030 Agenda reflects a sea change in international development policy and an opportunity to demonstrate the transformative potential of the new agenda.

Rule of law provides a concrete basis on which to eradicate poverty and fight discrimination and exclusion. Through a stable, transparent legal regime, rule of law provides for predictability and certainty, which are key to economic growth. By ensuring the rights of communities as well as business, it engenders sustainability and social acceptance of economic activities. By promoting equal opportunity and equitable access to basic services, it supports social development. By strengthening the legal framework to protect the environment, it advances the sustainability dimension of development.

In short, rule of law establishes an environment conducive to progress for each pillar of sustainable development. By setting the standards and institutions for equitable development, and by creating avenues of redress when rules and regulations are breached or rights are violated, rule of law promotes equality, accountability, and inclusive participation in the development process.

Where rule of law works well, it is not on account of imported foreign norms but because of careful consideration of the local context. Each country has a specific legal system and set of development challenges; in implementing the 2030 Agenda and measuring progress toward its targets, national ownership and understanding of the local context will be fundamental.

Underpinning these development objectives, rule of law empowers people to claim their rights—through information, legal awareness, and legal aid, for example—and to hold institutions accountable. It ensures, very importantly, that there is accountability, access to justice, and the means for resolving disputes and obtaining remedies when rights and entitlements have been denied.

Equity, social justice, human rights, and rule of law considerations have been central to the conceptualization of the 2030 Agenda. They give the new agenda not only greater legitimacy but also a better chance of success. Rooting sustainable development in a culture of justice through rule of law could well be a game changer.

PART IV

Europe

12
Enforcing Court Decisions
The Role of Enforcement Agents

Alan Colman and Marie-Anne Birken

The Legal Transition Programme (LTP) of the European Bank for Reconstruction and Development (EBRD) is an initiative to improve the investment climate in the EBRD's countries of operations by working with governments to enhance commercial laws and institutions. The LTP is implemented by a commercial law reform unit within the Office of the General Counsel. Its work is based partly on an evidentiary platform of analytical assessments that the Bank conducts in various areas of law, including access to finance, insolvency and restructuring, corporate governance, and dispute resolution. Since the commencement of the EBRD's legal reform activities in the early 1990s, the quality of commercial laws in the countries of operations of the EBRD (EBRD region)[1] has improved markedly. However, the implementation of law in many countries remains fraught with difficulties. One area of concern is the enforcement of court decisions. The EBRD's Judicial Decisions Assessment 2011–2012, which studied the quality of court decisions and compliance with court orders, found poor implementation of decisions to be the most troubling of seven areas studied, including corruption.[2] Governments as well as business communities have recognized these concerns and the negative impact of ineffective enforcement of decisions on the investment climate and the rule of law, including the right to a fair trial under international law.[3] The EBRD's legal reform program has therefore focused greater attention on the role of courts and enforcement agents, sometimes called "bailiffs."[4]

---

1 The EBRD's countries of operations are Albania, Armenia, Azerbaijan, Belarus, Bosnia and Herzegovina, Bulgaria, Croatia, Cyprus, the Arab Republic of Egypt, Estonia, Georgia, Greece, Hungary, Jordan, Kazakhstan, Kosovo, Kyrgyz Republic, Latvia, Lithuania, the former Yugoslav Republic of (FYR) Macedonia, Moldova, Mongolia, Montenegro, Morocco, Poland, Romania, the Russian Federation, Serbia, Slovak Republic, Slovenia, Tajikistan, Tunisia, Turkey, Turkmenistan, Ukraine, and Uzbekistan.

2 See Alan Colman, "The EBRD Judicial Decisions Assessment," *Business Law International* 12, no. 2 (May 2011).

3 Article 14 of the International Covenant on Civil and Political Rights (ICCPR) encompasses the right to have civil judgments implemented, as does Article 6 of the European Convention on Human Rights (ECHR). All countries covered by the EBRD assessment are party to the ICCPR, and all European countries except Belarus are party to the ECHR. Of the countries in the ECHR, all have been found in breach of Article 6 by the European Court of Human Rights for failing to guarantee effective enforcement of court judgments. Businesses have been applicants in these proceedings.

4 "Enforcement agent" is used in preference to the term "bailiff," which in some countries has a narrower meaning connected specifically to court-supervised enforcement.

In 2013–14, the EBRD undertook its Enforcement Agents Assessment,[5] a study of the law and its implementation in practice regarding enforcement agents in the EBRD region. The study looked at enforcement in two regions: the Commonwealth of Independent States (CIS)[6] and Georgia and Mongolia (the CIS+ region), and the countries of South East Europe (the SEE region).[7] The study comprised a survey of government agencies responsible for the enforcement of court decisions, as well as law firms in the countries covered by the study. The survey was supplemented by a desktop review of legislation and publicly available information on the enforcement of court decisions, as well as the perspectives of a large number of government officials, lawyers, and businesses with which the EBRD engaged as part of its ongoing policy dialogue efforts. The survey contained 64 questions, directed at the following seven dimensions of the functioning of enforcement agents (some of the key questions in each area are provided):

- *Resources and framework.* What is the structure of the enforcement system? Are agents qualified and trained? What is an enforcement agent's salary as a percentage of the average wage?
- *Searching for assets.* Do enforcement agents have appropriate access to property registries and bank accounts? Are debtors and third parties required to cooperate? How often do agents succeed in finding assets?
- *Seizure of assets.* What protections are provided to debtors? What notice of seizure is provided? Can there be reasonable use of force? How often do agents succeed in seizing assets?
- *Sale of assets.* Are auctions used to good effect? Is property fairly valued? Are sales well advertised? How often is good value obtained?
- *Speed of enforcement.* What is the typical speed of enforcement? Are rights of appeal clearly delineated? Are there penalties for obstruction or non-compliance? What is the average time taken to complete enforcement?
- *Costs and fees.* Are costs borne by the debtor? Are they reasonable? Does interest continue to accrue on judgment debt until payment is made?
- *Supervision and integrity issues.* Is there a supervisory body? Are there professional standards of conduct and complaint mechanisms? Does the government monitor and report on enforcement processes? Can the public gain access to information on enforcement results?

---

5 *EBRD Enforcement Agents Assessment 2013/2014.* The assessment can be viewed on the EBRD website: http://www.ebrd.com/cs/Satellite?c=Content&cid=1395238675306&pagename=EBRD%2FContent%2FContentLayout.

6 CIS member states are Armenia, Azerbaijan, Belarus, Kazakhstan, the Kyrgyz Republic, Moldova, Russia, Tajikistan, Turkmenistan, Ukraine, and Uzbekistan.

7 Albania, Bosnia and Herzegovina, Croatia, Kosovo, FYR Macedonia, Montenegro, Serbia, and Slovenia.

These dimensions were derived in part from European standards, such as the Council of Europe's Recommendation (2003) 17 of the Committee of Ministers[8] on the question of enforcement and the principles of the European Commission for the Efficiency of Justice (CEPEJ), which were developed to assist Council of Europe member states in improving their enforcement systems.[9]

The Enforcement Agents Assessment used a tentative grading system to rate these seven dimensions.[10] The system highlights key reform challenges and emphasizes differences and similarities between countries. The scores do not constitute a definitive grading of the efficiency of the enforcement system in each country; however, the assessment team considers that the scoring provides a good indication of both the general situation in each country and the relativities between countries. Based on the overall results, countries were scored out of a possible total of 100 points and put into one of four brackets:

- 80+: Slovenia
- 71–80: Albania, Armenia, Georgia, Kosovo, the former Yugoslav Republic of (FYR) Macedonia, Moldova, Montenegro, the Russian Federation
- 65–70: Belarus, Croatia, Kazakhstan, Serbia, Ukraine, Uzbekistan
- 50–65: Azerbaijan, Bosnia and Herzegovina, the Kyrgyz Republic, Mongolia, Tajikistan, Turkmenistan

The most positive picture emerges in Slovenia, where a well-functioning private enforcement system is in place. Next in the rankings is Georgia, which has a state enforcement service running alongside a private system, both of which enjoy broad public confidence. The private enforcement systems in FYR Macedonia and Moldova, and the hybrid public–private system in Albania, all presented well, generating competition between agents for new cases, which appears to drive better performance. State enforcement systems in Armenia and Russia showed good results, particularly in the use of innovations in access to information. At the other end of the spectrum are Bosnia and Herzegovina, where the court-based enforcement process requires claimants themselves to lead the search for assets, and Turkmenistan and Tajikistan, where lack of transparency and limited resources are major concerns. Following are some of the principal thematic issues arising within each of the seven dimensions of enforcement studied in the assessment, and some concluding observations.

---

8 Adopted September 9, 2003, at the 851st meeting of the Ministers' Deputies. Available at https://wcd.coe.int/ViewDoc.jsp?Ref=Rec(2003)17&Sector=secCM&Language=lanEnglish&Ver=original.

9 European Commission on the Efficiency of Justice (CEPEJ), "Guidelines for a Better Implementation of the Existing Council of Europe's Recommendation on Enforcement" (adopted by the CEPEJ at its 14th plenary meeting, Strasbourg, December 9–10, 2009), https://wcd.coe.int/ViewDoc.jsp?Ref=CEPEJ(2009)11&Language=lanEnglish&Ver=original&BackColorInternet=eff2fa&BackColorIntranet=eff2fa&BackColorLogged=c1cbe6.

10 The first dimension, "resources and framework," was not scored.

Enforcement Frameworks

The most significant structural distinction between the various enforcement systems, and between the two regions studied in the assessment, is the role played by the private sector. Perhaps the question of greatest policy relevance to governments considering reforms to their enforcement systems is whether the private sector can deliver better results. The short answer appears to be yes.

Three broad types of enforcement systems exist in the regions surveyed:

- Public systems, in which enforcement agents are employees of the state
- Private systems, in which agents are employed by private sector entities vested with statutory powers
- Hybrid systems, in which public and private agents coexist, with their functions delineated by jurisdictional criteria, such as the type or amount of claim, or the identity of the judgment debtor

In the CIS+ region, most countries have public enforcement systems, with only three countries recognizing private enforcement agents: Moldova, which has an exclusively private system, and Georgia and Kazakhstan, which have hybrid systems. In the SEE region, only two countries have purely public systems (Bosnia and Herzegovina and Croatia); two have hybrid enforcement systems (Albania and Serbia); and four countries have private systems (FYR Macedonia, Montenegro, Kosovo, and Slovenia).

In some CIS+ countries, the private sector plays an indirect role in the enforcement of judgments, but private enforcement agents are not formally recognized. For example, in Russia, judgment debt can be transferred in a manner akin to factoring; it is sold at a discount to private firms, which are then responsible for collecting the debt. In Uzbekistan, private firms often assist state enforcement agents in the performance of their duties.

In the SEE region, there has been a clear trend toward the adoption of private enforcement systems over the past 10 years, either to replace or to complement the state system. The prevalence of private systems in these countries can be linked with various factors: the apparent success of the Slovenian private system, significant European support for the reform of the enforcement sectors, close professional affiliations between the countries in the region, and a common legal heritage in states of the former Yugoslavia. There has also been a broader European trend toward affording the private sector a role in enforcement. In the Council of Europe, there are 32 states with wholly or partly private enforcement systems, and only 15 with purely public systems.[11]

There is no consensus as to which model of enforcement framework is best. The assessment does not make any assumptions about this question; it was designed to explore the relative merits of state and private systems. On the basis of the evidence gathered, it appears that the private systems in the

---

11 Evaluation report of European judicial systems, 2014, CEPEJ, 407, http://coe.int/t/dghl/cooperation/cepej/evaluation/2014/Rapport_en.pdf.

region are working well. They outscore the public systems in relation to each of the seven dimensions with the exception of costs. The state systems, as one might expect, are cheaper from a user perspective. The SEE region, where private systems are common, scored higher than the CIS+ region, where they are not. The two highest-ranked countries from the CIS+ region are Georgia and Moldova, which have private enforcement agents. Commentary from all of the jurisdictions in which private operators are present indicates that public confidence in the enforcement process increased with the introduction of private enforcement agents. Features of the private systems that appear to be contributing to their success include the ability of judgment creditors to choose enforcement agents, better financial rewards and incentives, greater competition among enforcement agents, more rigorous training, tailored codes of conduct, and peer supervision.

Although recognizing the potential benefits that the private sector can bring to the enforcement process, there are important counterconsiderations that must be weighed in the balance. One is the concern of putting coercive state power into private hands. Another relates to the potential cost increases that might be associated with a private system (i.e., cost increases from the perspective of the judgment creditor seeking to use an enforcement agent). A third concern is whether private operators will provide adequate services to the public in relation to potentially less lucrative enforcement cases. These are all significant considerations with which policy makers need to contend. Although greater efficiencies might be expected to result from deregulation and greater competition, the public must be persuaded that adequate safeguards will be put in place, particularly in relation to supervision and transparency. It is interesting to note that proposals to introduce private enforcement systems were developed in both Bosnia and Herzegovina and Croatia, but were ultimately dropped, in part because of concerns relating to the policy considerations mentioned above.

Searching for Assets

Of the various stages in the enforcement process, asset discovery appears to present the greatest difficulties in the countries assessed, particularly in the CIS+ region and the two state systems in the SEE region. In only three countries do lawyers consider that enforcement agents "usually" succeed in finding assets (Georgia, Moldova, and Kosovo).

Noncooperation of Debtors

The law typically imposes obligations on judgment debtors to cooperate with enforcement officers and to provide information on personal assets; however, these rules are frequently ignored in practice. Judgment debtors are able to frustrate the enforcement process with relative impunity, moving or hiding property, or siphoning money out of bank accounts, especially in the CIS+ region. One problem is the ease with which debtors can use different names to open new accounts into which they transfer funds. Another is tunneling, whereby a judgment debtor transfers assets to a third party after legal proceedings are initiated but before enforcement proceedings are initiated. The law does not always provide for "claw back"; claimants must seek to obtain freeze orders from courts at the start of litigation to secure their potential judgment moneys. Moreover, such orders are not always possible or readily granted; judges are reluctant to deprive a person of use of his or her funds or property before the merits of the case are determined. Further, although concealing assets or resisting an enforcement agent is usually a criminal or administrative offense, sanctions are rarely applied. This may be because of the relatively high standard of proof required for convictions. In some cases, as reported in Ukraine, the amount of the fine is so insignificant that it is not a deterrent. The assessment points clearly to a policy need in the region for stiffer penalties, which are enforced and publicized, to deter and punish noncompliance with court judgments.

In the state systems in Bosnia Herzegovina and Croatia, a procedural problem contributes to the difficulties in locating assets. Primary responsibility for identifying assets lies with the claimant, who must submit a request for enforcement to the court and indicate in it the particular assets to be seized. Clearly, this is beyond the capacity of many claimants. In Slovenia, for example, concerns were raised about judgment debtors keeping funds in accounts overseas. However, from 2017 onward, an EU regulation will facilitate cross-border debt recovery in civil and commercial matters, and permit queries to foreign banks concerning debtors' finances, which may address such concerns.[12]

Access to Property Registries and Bank Accounts

An enforcement agent searching for assets usually makes inquiries of banks and state registries of land, securities, movable property (usually vehicles), and collateral. Agents have access to relevant registries in all countries, but with varying degrees of ease and efficiency. In the CIS+ region, some countries' enforcement systems are not at all calibrated with the regulation of property registries, leaving agents in the same position as the general public in seeking information. For example, in Mongolia, enforcement agents have no special rights to information from the General Authority for State Registration, the Land Registration Office, or the Mineral Resources Authority. Enforcement agents have to file a formal, written application in the same manner as any private citizen. Other countries afford enforcement agents somewhat enhanced access rights, but many still impose a system of official paper-based requests, which can create delays (e.g., Azerbaijan, Belarus, the Kyrgyz Republic, and Tajikistan). In Armenia, however, an automated e-tool has been created through which enforcement officers can send requests for information to all state property registers. In the SEE region, there are fewer problems associated with access to databases and registries. The law typically

12 Regulation (EU) No. 655/2014 of the European Parliament and of the Council, May 15, 2014, http://eur-lex.europa.eu/legal-content/EN/TXT/?uri=CELEX:32014R0655.

requires those responsible for registries and official databases to cooperate with the enforcement agents. Further, there are fewer databases that need to be searched, because of the existence of more comprehensive registries, for example, of movable property.

In regard to bank accounts, the assessment found that most countries in the SEE region have dedicated systems for tracking and seizing debtors' bank accounts, either through the country's central bank (Bosnia and Herzegovina, Montenegro, and Serbia) or a specialized agency (Croatia and Slovenia). In Croatia, a claimant submits a request for enforcement to the state Financial Agency (FINA) and pays a fee, whereupon the agency verifies the claim and seizes funds from an account. The situation is different in the CIS+ region, where in most countries banks cannot disclose any information about account holders until ordered to do so by a court. One exception is Russia, where enforcement agents can obtain access to information on private bank accounts through a system of inquiry connected with the tax authorities. Another exception is Armenia, where enforcement agents can send a request to all commercial banks and deposit-taking institutions through a special electronic channel provided by the Central Bank, and operated jointly by the Central Bank and the Ministry of Justice. As a matter of public policy, there is merit in having an efficient, secure, and regulated mechanism that allows enforcement agents to identify whether a debtor has an account and whether sufficient funds exist in the account to cover the debt. Electronic request systems can greatly facilitate efficient access to bank accounts and can increase the efficiency of enforcement work.

Seizure of Assets

The assessment reveals that, once assets are found, their seizure does not present major difficulties, with success achieved "often" in most countries. However, one area of concern is the enforcement of court decisions against government bodies. One might expect this to be easier than enforcement against private parties, as the state ought to comply expeditiously with orders from its own courts. In some countries, such as Belarus, this is the case; however, in many countries, enforcement against the state is more difficult than against private parties, particularly in the CIS+ region. Some of the difficulties in this area are associated with public sector budget legislation that regulates the kinds of payments that can be made. In some instances, no provision is made for payments in satisfaction of judgment debt, such that a state body is, in effect, prohibited from complying with the court's judgment. For example, in Mongolia, if the funds available in the account of the particular debtor agency are insufficient, there is simply no mechanism for another state body or department, such as the treasury, to pay the debt. The debtor agency is responsible, rather than the state itself, and that agency must seek an additional allocation from the state budget, which is often not forthcoming until the following year, if at all. Armenia has found an interesting solution to these problems. If a state agency is a judgment debtor, and the relevant debt cannot be paid from the agency's budget, the debt obligation is substituted for an interest-bearing bill of exchange. In Russia, where budgetary problems have posed significant barriers to enforcement against the state in the past, treasury officials are now in charge of overseeing enforcement against state agencies; requests for payment can be sent to the Ministry of Finance, or to treasury departments of relevant municipalities. To create a compliance culture, it is critical that the state lead by example and satisfy its own judgment debts on time.

Sale of Assets

Rules regarding the sale of seized property are generally complex and comprise elements relating to valuation, advertisement, the sale process, and the transfer of funds to the claimant. The objectives of these rules are to liquidate assets, realize high value, satisfy the judgment debt, and return the excess to the debtor. Yet there is tension between the interest of debtors, which is to achieve the highest possible sale price for the asset, and the interest of creditors, which is simply to have the sale price cover the debt. There is also particular scope for abuse and corruption if the process is not properly regulated and supervised. Enforcement agents' effectiveness in realizing value through the sale of seized property in the region is widely perceived to be low, with respondents in all countries indicating that agents only "sometimes" or "rarely" obtain good value.

Most of the jurisdictions surveyed require the valuation of seized property, which is then the reference point for the reserve price, below which the property generally cannot be sold. Typically, the price is set at a discount against market value (e.g., 80 percent in Moldova, 75 percent in Armenia). In the CIS+ region, the lowest reserve price—50 percent of the valuation price—is in Kazakhstan and Tajikistan; in the SEE region, the lowest initial reserve price is also 50 percent (Bosnia and Herzegovina); and in most of these countries, the initial reserve price is reducible, in subsequent attempts at sale, to around 30 percent. Too high a reserve price can be an impediment to sale, particularly in depressed markets. In Mongolia, for example, property cannot be sold at auction unless the reserve price is reached; a bid fractionally lower than the reserve mark cannot be accepted, and a new auction has to be held. It is reasonable that a reserve price should offer some form of discount against what might be the market price for the item. Assets that have been seized are frequently impaired or impugned in some way, whether physically (such as vehicles sold without keys or papers) or socially (in some countries seized goods have a stigma associated with them).

Across the region, immovable property must generally be sold at auction, which must be advertised. It is important that auction rules be transparent, as auctions are vulnerable to rigging through collusion between the enforcement agent, the auctioneer, and the purchaser, resulting in property being sold at an undervalued price. Advertising widely and requiring inspections of auction procedures, together with strong complaint mechanisms, are critical components in minimizing such abuse. Online auctions have proved very effective in this regard. In Armenia, all auctions take place on the website of a private company, which has detailed descriptions and photographs of the property to be sold. The process has minimized bidder contact with auctioneers and reduced the incidence of corruption while facilitating involvement of bidders from outside the capital. Systems similar to this exist in Russia and Kazakhstan. Croatia introduced online auctions in early 2015. Elsewhere in the SEE region, however, little use appears to be made of online platforms to sell seized property.

Speed of Enforcement

The time required to enforce a court judgment is a major concern for businesses and court users in the EBRD region. In the CIS+ region, procedural legislation in most countries imposes time limits on various stages in the enforcement process, as well as the overall time frame, which is often two months (e.g., in Azerbaijan, Kazakhstan, the Kyrgyz Republic, Russia, and Tajikistan). However, there are few if any consequences for such time limits being exceeded, which they frequently are. In survey responses, the typical average speed of enforcement from date of court judgment to final recovery ranged from four months in Georgia to one year in Ukraine. A typical enforcement time frame in most countries in the SEE region is about four months. The exceptions are Bosnia and Herzegovina and Slovenia, where over six months is common; in extreme cases the process could last up to two years.

One factor affecting the length of enforcement proceedings is the extent to which judgment debtors are able to file appeals against the various stages in the process. Administrative and procedural law often grants wide rights of appeal, allowing any stage in the enforcement process to be challenged. This is particularly the case in the CIS+ region, where appeals can take months to resolve. The apparent ease of obtaining adjournments without a sound reason is a problem that affects civil litigation generally in the region,[13] and also presents difficulties in enforcement. In Armenia, for example, there are a large number of applications seeking court interpretations of enforcement orders, allegedly as a tactic to delay the enforcement process. In Russia, an incredible two hundred thousand appeals were filed in relation to enforcement actions in 2012. Another important element affecting the speed of enforcement is whether appeals by judgment debtors against actions taken by enforcement agents suspend the enforcement process, pending a final determination by a court. In the SEE region, appeals do not suspend the enforcement proceedings; in Albania and FYR Macedonia, such appeals must be determined within a week. By contrast, in the majority of countries in the CIS+ region, an appeal will suspend the enforcement process.[14] In countries where there is no

13 See Colman, "EBRD Judicial Decisions Assessment."

14 Appeals do not suspend enforcement in Armenia, Georgia, Moldova, Russia, or Ukraine.

automatic suspension of the enforcement process, the court has the power to suspend the proceedings if it deems the suspension appropriate for a particular case. This seems a prudent and balanced approach.

Costs and Fees

In most countries surveyed, enforcement costs are borne by the debtor, and are reimbursable from proceeds of the sale of seized property. Costs are regulated in both the private and the state systems, and in the latter they usually form part of the court fee, as determined by court rules. The formulas governing fees can be quite complex. In Slovenia, for example, fees are calculated on the basis of points assigned to various possible components of an enforcement action. The cost regime must be seen in the context of the need to provide adequate incentives for enforcement agents to perform to a high standard. The private systems generally provide greater incentives for agents to seek higher sale prices by basing fees on a percentage of the actual sale price rather than on the debt owed. For private enforcement agents in Kazakhstan, this can be up to 10 percent of the recovered debt or sale price, which appears to account for a notable difference in the perceived success of private and public agents in that country. In the view of one leading Kazakh bank, the major problem affecting the public enforcement system is the absence of incentives for government enforcement agents, whose pay is not linked to their output. However, lawyers noted that private agents in Kazakhstan tend not to be as interested in smaller matters, as they do not consider the returns (even at 10 percent) to be worthwhile. A role for state enforcement agents must always be considered in relation to cases that may not be attractive to private operators.

Cost should also be viewed in terms of the overall burden it imposes on the judgment debtor, who, after all, has put the other party and the state to the cost and effort of enforcement. The overall financial burden on the debtor for willful noncompliance with court orders should be significant enough to affect debtors' behavior and to encourage compliance in the first instance. As well as paying enforcement fees and fines in appropriate cases, a debtor should be liable to pay the creditor interest on judgment debt until the debtor is actually paid. However, in most countries in the CIS+ region, interest ceases to accrue when the decision of the court is handed down; the only exceptions are Armenia, Georgia, and Moldova. In some countries, separate legal proceedings must be brought in order to recover interest in respect of the enforcement period; in practice, this hardly every occurs because the costs of such proceedings will be more than the interest recovered. The position in all of the countries in the SEE region is based on the principle that the debtor pays interest, at commercial rates, until the debt is extinguished.

Supervision and Integrity Issues

All countries studied in the assessment have in place systems to regulate, monitor, and control the work of enforcement agents, and each system provides for administrative and court-based complaint mechanisms. Data from all jurisdictions reveal that these systems are widely used. For example, in Kazakhstan, some four thousand appeals were brought against state enforcement agents in 2012, of which just over three thousand were upheld (only about fifty were brought against private enforcement agents). The majority of these claims were from judgment creditors concerning inaction on the part of enforcement agents. Major grounds for complaints in the region surveyed include breaches of the enforcement procedure, such as failure to provide adequate notice or issues related to the valuation of property (e.g., Mongolia); challenges to the evaluation of assets (FYR Macedonia); breach of professional ethics, including self-dealing (Bosnia and Herzegovina); and unreasonably long enforcement proceedings (Albania).

Providing the public with access to information on the enforcement system is an important component of an effective supervisory framework. Few countries, however, publish detailed reports on the work of their enforcement agencies. In the SEE region, only FYR Macedonia and Slovenia provide clear and detailed information to the public on enforcement agents' activities, through the websites of the Chamber of Enforcement Agents in FYR Macedonia and the Ministry of Justice in Slovenia. In the CIS+ region, agencies in Armenia, Georgia, Russia, and Ukraine publish quarterly reports online. However, Russia is the only country to publish extensive and detailed information on the number of complaints brought against enforcement agents, prosecutions for criminal conduct, and the overall success rate of court decision enforcements. Another positive feature in Russia is its online register of all current enforcement cases, which is available to the public. Information in this register includes the name of the debtor, the number of the enforcement case, the type of enforcement title, the amount and type of debt, the responsible enforcement department, and the enforcement officer.[15] The website also makes it possible to pay debts through various payment services, to search for information about individual debtors by name (including names of legal entities), and to search more generally by reference to various key words. These data are of particular interest to credit rating agencies, creating an additional incentive for debtor compliance.

The authors consider that, at a minimum, governments should publish, or require private enforcement agencies to publish, data relating to the number of pending, incoming, and completed cases; average time taken to complete enforcement; success rates in terms of recovery of full judgment debt; types of services rendered in the course of enforcement; costs incurred in the course of enforcement; and number and nature of complaints against enforcement agents and remedies for problems found.

In many countries surveyed, corruption is perceived to be a problem affecting the entire justice sector, including the enforcement system. The assessment sought to glean some insights into the methods of corruption. One such

15 The Russian online database is available at http://www.fssprus.ru/iss/ip/.

method was said to be for enforcement agents to delay, or temporarily suspend, the arrest of property, so as to allow the debtor to hide the property or otherwise frustrate the enforcement process. Another method was for enforcement agents to delay enforcement to compel the creditor to offer a bribe. In Belarus, Turkmenistan, and Uzbekistan, there were said to be no significant corruption issues. Perhaps fear of government authority is a deterrent to bribe taking (or to the reporting of bribe taking). Thorough supervision, investigation, and publication of reports on alleged corruption must be stepped up to create a climate of accountability that forces potential bribe takers and their clients to think twice. Georgia's statewide anticorruption efforts have touched the enforcement agency. A new case management scheme envisages that different stages of the enforcement process should be under the control of different enforcement agents, lessening the opportunity for aberrant behavior and increasing the likelihood of it being detected. Only the enforcement agency's mediation team have direct contact with the judgment debtor and creditor, reducing potential avenues for improper influence.

In the SEE region, reports of corruption are far fewer. The ability of judgment creditors to choose an enforcement agent appears to limit the likelihood of corrupt practices by agents against creditors in the private systems of that region, although presumably, the position of the judgment debtor is not necessarily assisted by this dynamic. The practice of agents selling seized property at a discount to an associate, for example, remains a threat.

Conclusion

The enforcement of court judgments is a serious challenge across the countries surveyed, and governments have been developing responses to it. The experience of the SEE region provides an insight into the potential benefits of affording the private sector a role in the enforcement process. Overall, the private enforcement systems in both the SEE region and the CIS+ region appear to be performing well, thanks to increased competition and incentives. Yet public concerns about the transfer of coercive state power to private operators, and the potentially higher costs involved in doing so, need to be taken into account, as demonstrated by the policy reversals in Bosnia and Herzegovina and Croatia. Further, the state must be prepared to step in and offer services to cover segments of enforcement work that might not be attractive to private operators (e.g., in very sparsely populated and remote regions). Clearly, a private system will need to remain subject to state monitoring and regulation, including in regard to fees. The challenge is to ensure that these arrangements are understood by the public and will be well maintained.

Governments must collect more and better data on the workings of their enforcement systems to identify relevant problems and to afford greater transparency. The institutional capacity of enforcement agencies must also be improved, as the need for systematic professional training for enforcement agents exemplifies. On the procedural side, limiting the scope for spurious appeals and penalizing those who do not comply with court judgments or the enforcement process need more attention. Governments should pursue policies that promote compliance; the need for coercive enforcement of judgments should be the exception rather than the rule. It is very important that there be a credible prospect of effective enforcement of decisions, as well as the threat of adverse financial consequences for those who do not play by the rules. These consequences should include continuing interest on unpaid judgment debt, costs, and more significant fines. By supporting government reforms in the area of enforcement, international organizations can make a significant contribution to justice sector reform, improving both the investment climate and the rule of law.

13
Judicial Landmarks and Their Making at the Court of Justice of the European Union

SINIŠA RODIN

In 1788, writing in *Federalist Paper* No. 78, Alexander Hamilton described the judiciary as the least dangerous branch of government. The judiciary, he wrote, "has no influence over either the sword or the purse; no direction either of the strength or of the wealth of the society; and can take no active resolution whatever. It may truly be said to have neither force nor will, but merely judgment; and must ultimately depend upon the aid of the executive arm even for the efficacy of its judgments." Yet for all Hamilton's eloquence, certain judicial decisions, no matter which jurisdiction one talks about, clearly do have influence and direction. Such judicial decisions become widely debated, objects of public controversy; they impose limits on other branches of government; and, ultimately, they become symbols. Such judicial decisions are said to be "landmarks."

This chapter discusses four aspects of judicial landmarks. The chapter begins by suggesting what qualities make a certain judicial decision a landmark. The second section asks to what extent the capacity to make a landmark depends on the court that decides a case. The third section singles out a few cases decided by the Court of Justice of the European Union (CJEU) that have acquired iconic status and are generally considered to be landmarks. The chapter concludes by discussing whether the landmark-making capacity of the CJEU has changed over time.

What Makes a Judicial Decision a Landmark?

Judicial decisions are artifacts. They are a design of a subject. But once created, they assume a life independent of their creator. Nothing explains this process better than Jean de La Fontaine's fable about a statue of Jupiter (brought to my attention by French philosopher Bruno Latour):[1]

> A block of marble was so fine,
> To buy it did a sculptor hasten.
> "What shall my chisel, now It's mine—

Opinions expressed in this paper are the author's personal views and do not represent positions of the Court of Justice of the European Union.

1 Bruno Latour, *On the Modern Cult of Factish Gods* (Durham, NC: Duke University Press, 2010), viii.

A god, a table, or a basin?"
"A god," said he, "the thing shall be;
I'll arm it, too, with thunder.
Let people quake, and bow the knee
With reverential wonder."[2]

In my reading, La Fontaine's verses suggest the following. First, just like a sculptor carves a statue from a piece of marble, a court creates an artifact, a judicial decision. Second, the decision emancipates itself from its creator and becomes an object of public debate and critique for future audiences. Judicial decisions, forged in the judicial proceedings and coined in the minds of their authors, once pronounced and published, start to live their independent lives through the agency of future subjects. Gradually, a judgment can transform into a landmark.[3] This happens regardless of the differences between the legal systems of common law and civil law. Although they have different methodologies, the systems share two basic assumptions that make the emergence of landmarks possible: one is the stability of legal reasoning, which enables parties to rely on landmark judgments in future pleadings; the other is the publication of judicial decisions so that they are accessible to professional and general audiences.[4]

Notice that the very word "landmark" implies an objectification. A judgment can become a landmark only by the joint agency of a court and the public. Although the potential of a case to become a landmark is often recognized by a court in advance, there are still no guarantees that it will indeed be recognized as such by others, just as there are no guarantees that the statue of Jupiter will inspire admiration or fear in the eyes of those who see it. To take another example: the Empire State Building was surely conceived by its architects to be a landmark at the time of its construction; however, it became a landmark not only because it was meant to be one, but also because future observers recognized its distinctive features. Today the building is surrounded by a forest of similar ones, and its distinctiveness has been amalgamated into a pattern. Nevertheless, future architects took the building as a model for subsequent construction, and in recognition of its historical distinctiveness, visitors flock to the Empire State Building. Like the Empire State Building, a judicial case is often followed by its progeny. If it is widely accepted, its distinctiveness becomes accepted as a model for future deliberations, and the rule of law it encapsulates enters the judicial mainstream. And it is precisely because of these subsequent cases that a landmark case remains a landmark. A case that is quickly overruled does not become one.

---

2 Jean de La Fontaine, *Le Statuaire et la Statue de Jupiter,* 2nd collection, Book 9, Fable 6.

3 For recent empirical research, see Urska Sadl and Yannis Panagis, "What Is a Leading Case in EU Law? An Empirical Analysis," *European Law Review* 40, no. 1 (2015): 15–34.

4 For a more elaborate analysis, see Siniša Rodin, "Functions of Judicial Opinions and the New Member States in the Legitimacy of Highest Courts' Rulings," in *Judicial Deliberations and Beyond,* ed. Nick Hulls, Maurice Adams, and Jacco Bomhoff (The Hague: Asser Press, 2009).

Are Some Courts More Likely Than Others to Produce Landmarks?

As just noted, landmark judgments cannot be produced exclusively by the actions and intentions of a court; they can be created only in synergy with their future users and other external actors. Nonetheless, do some courts, by their design, possesses a capacity to create landmarks?

The first step in the process of creating a landmark is recognizing the potential of a case to stand out. Certainly, from the perspective of a judge, most cases do *not* qualify as being landmark building material. A judge may well want to create a landmark but, obviously, not every judgment will become one. Furthermore, some courts are better designed to produce them than others. The ability of a court to have a landmark-making capacity depends on three factors:

- The independence of its judges and of the court itself from other branches of government and political bias
- The court's internal structure and decision-making practices
- The mission of the court and the self-awareness of its judges about that mission

Let us briefly examine each of these three factors in the context of the CJEU.

Independence

Creating a judicial landmark is not merely an act of adjudication but a socially relevant fact. Judicial decisions that are narrowly tailored to settle a dispute between the parties rarely have wider social consequences. Also, judgments that merely reproduce law established by other branches of government do not qualify for the status of a landmark. In order to make socially relevant decisions, a judge needs to match legal analysis and reasoning with the wider social context from which the dispute originates and to which its resolution caters. Only an independent court is in a position to be socially relevant beyond a dispute at hand.

There are more ways than one to ensure judicial independence. When compared with courts in some other high jurisdictions, including the Supreme Court of the United States, the CJEU differs with respect to the renewability of judicial office, the lack of dissenting opinions, and the absence of formal docket control. Yet because of the CJEU 's structured appointment procedure, internal organization, and decision-making practices, the CJEU has no less judicial independence than the U.S. Supreme Court.

Stability of judicial office ranks high among the guarantees of judicial independence.[5] Although some observers would suggest that only an appointment for life is a sufficient guarantee, according to Article 253 of the Treaty on the Functioning of the European Union (TFEU), judges of the CJEU (there

---

5 Michal Bobek, ed., *Selecting Europe's Judges: A Critical Review of the Appointment Procedures to the European Courts* (Oxford: Oxford University Press, 2015).

are 28 of them) are appointed for a renewable term of six years. [6] Following national nomination, a judge is screened by an independent panel established under the treaty and known as the 255 Committee. Since March 1, 2010, when it started to operate, the 255 Committee has fulfilled its duty to "give an opinion on candidates' suitability to perform the duties of Judge and Advocate-General of the Court of Justice and the General Court before the governments of the Member States make the appointments." Judges who pass this screening are then appointed by common accord of the governments of the member states. In light of the fact that judicial appointments and reappointments depend on national nomination and, keeping in mind that the CJEU can rule against the member states for violations of EU law, judicial deliberations are protected by secrecy. No dissenting opinions are issued, and, on entry into office, every judge has to swear an oath to protect the confidentiality of deliberations.

Although the relatively short six-year term of office raises some concerns about the judge's independence and gives the member states the power of reappointment, [7] the procedural rules help to stabilize the court. Judges are ranked in order of seniority, which is omnipresent in the protocol that the court follows. Judges who were appointed most recently take the last seat around the table, they enter the *grande salle d'audience* last, they are last to ask questions at the hearing, and they do not have priority for election to administrative functions. The protocol demands that judges who become presidents of the CJEU's chambers have reached a certain level of seniority—a level that is very hard to attain within a judge's first six-year term. The offices of president and vice president of the CJEU can be taken only by senior judges with long experience at the court. Given these rules, a member state has no reason to erode its credibility by replacing a prospering judge.

Internal Structure and Decision-Making Practices

The second guarantee of independence is the CJEU's internal structure and its decision-making routine. The CJEU's 28 judges operate in chambers of 3, 5, or 15 (a "grand chamber") judges or, on rare occasions, in a plenary session.[8] They are assisted by 11 advocates general, who have the same status as judges.

---

6 Article 253 of the TFEU provides as follows: "The Judges and Advocates-General of the Court of Justice shall be chosen from persons whose independence is beyond doubt and who possess the qualifications required for appointment to the highest judicial offices in their respective countries or who are jurisconsults of recognized competence; they shall be appointed by common accord of the governments of the Member States for a term of six years, after consultation of the panel provided for in Article 255."

7 Joseph Weiler, "Epilogue: Judging the Judges—Apology and Critique," in *Judging Europe's Judges: The Legitimacy of the Case Law of the European Court of Justice*, ed. Maurice Adams, Henri de Waele, Johan Meeusen, and Gert Straetmans (Oxford: Hart, 2013), 251–252.

8 The most recent time that the CJEU reached a decision in a plenary session was in December 2014 (Opinion 2/13 pursuant to Article 218[11] TFEU—Draft international agreement—Accession of the European Union to the European Convention for the Protection of Human Rights and Fundamental Freedoms—Compatibility of the draft agreement with the EU and TFEU Treaties of December 18, 2014, EU:C: 2014:2454).

An incoming case is first allocated to a reporting judge by the president of the court, who is required to write a preliminary report and, in agreement with an advocate general allocated to the case by the first advocate general, present it to the *réunion générale* (the RG)—the plenum of the court comprising all judges and advocates general, which meets once a week. The RG decides on the number of judges who will hear a case (i.e., decides on the "formation" of the court), and proposes whether a judgment is needed or whether the case can be decided in a summary way by an order. The reporting judge may propose that a hearing be held, as well as specifying the issues of law and fact that need to be addressed in a hearing in order to restrict the scope of the hearing. There will also be a proposal regarding whether an opinion of an advocate general is indicated and, if it is, which legal issues the opinion should address. Finally, a report will be issued that describes the agreement (or absence of it) between the reporting judge and the advocate general on all mentioned points.

The allocation of a case to a chamber is an element of docket control and has a significant effect on landmark-making capacity. If any formation of the court finds a case to be manifestly inadmissible or manifestly unfounded, it may decide the case by an order instead of delivering a judgment.

The decision to have a case be heard by a chamber of three judges indicates that the law governing the case is clear and that the case will be handled according to the existing case law. In a chamber of three, an opinion of an advocate general is not always needed.

Chambers of five judges decide cases that require more reflection because either the facts are complex or the legal issues are. Five-judge chambers can be said to be the "default" formation of the court. A chamber of five can follow the existing law and extend the scope of the existing case law to new situations. It can clarify previously decided cases, and harmonize case law decided by the General Court or, sometimes, by chambers of three judges. Hearings are the rule rather than the exception, because cases involving complex facts and law may require oral explanations from the parties. The parties will often request a hearing themselves, although such requests are not binding on the court.

A grand chamber of 15 judges is convened to decide about major legal issues that require intervention into existing case law either to develop new law, to overrule the existing law, or to extend its scope to new areas. A grand chamber will also be indicated when the court has not previously expressed itself on a certain legal rule or a point of law. According to the CJEU's rules of procedure, a grand chamber will have to decide on a request of a member state and in disputes between institutions of the European Union. A grand chamber can reach a decision with or without an opinion of an advocate general and with or without a hearing. In this respect, all considerations previously mentioned with regard to a chamber of five apply. The grand chamber seldom reaches a decision without a hearing and an opinion.

The full court (i.e., a formation of all 28 judges) decides only in exceptional situations. According to statute, the CJEU shall sit as a full court when it decides on the dismissal of the ombudsman, on compulsory retirement of a member of the European Commission or a member of the Court of Auditors, or when it considers that a case before it is of exceptional importance. Full court judgments are also usually given in cases regarding requests for opinions pursuant to Article 218(11) of the TFEU, in which the court is called to rule whether an international treaty to which the European Union plans to commit itself is compatible with the treaties.

To the extent that the landmark-making potential of a case can be identified in advance, it is for the reporting judge to recognize it and, in agreement with the advocate general, to bring it to the attention of the RG. The anatomy of the court and the structure of the decision-making process clearly show that the court can assess the landmark potential of each case it decides. However, allocating a case to a grand chamber does not in itself generate a landmark. The full scale of the effect of a judicial decision may be anticipated, but it will rarely be fully envisaged by the court, because the impact depends not only on the court's own reading of the case but also on the reception by the audience to which it is addressed. For a case to become a landmark, its professional utility and social acceptance appear to be at least as relevant as the intentions of the court itself. The court seems to recognize as much in cases in which the court restricts the scope or effects of a judgment to the case at hand. But even a judgment that is restricted to the circumstances of a case may get pleaded in the future and commented on by observers. Generally speaking, two additional factors contribute to the likeliness of a case becoming a landmark. One factor is the relevance of the legal contents of the case and the extent to which a judgment may become a standard part of the repertoire of the future pleadings of the parties; the other factor is the broad social acceptance or at least awareness of the case, usually accompanied by academic commentary on the case.

The Mission of the Court

The third ingredient of judicial independence and, accordingly, of landmark-making capacity is the self-awareness of judges about the mission of the court on which they sit. As far as the CJEU is concerned, the basic mission is laid down in Article 19 of the TFEU, which vests the court with power to ensure "that in the interpretation and application of the Treaties the law is observed." Although it is possible to understand the phrase "the law" as indicating a static role for the CJEU, a closer look reveals that, it is the court itself that defines what the law is. Over the course of its history, the CJEU has contributed to the development of the institutional and legal framework of the European Union, particularly in times of institutional standstill, such as occurred in the 1970s. At that time, the CJEU was subject to both academic and public criticism for venturing into the waters of judicial activism, yet the fact remains that decisions adopted in the formative years of Europe's constitutional law today stand as widely recognized landmarks, created by the court and subsequently generally accepted.

In any case, the role of the court as one of the institutional pillars of the European Union enables it to be an active element in a system of supranational checks and balances. In exercising its jurisdiction, the CJEU acts not only as a supreme court in matters of secondary EU law (i.e., as an interpreter of EU legislation) but also as a constitutional umpire, having the final say in horizontal institutional disputes, such as disputes between institutions of the European Union, as well as in vertical disputes between the European Commission and individual member states. This broad role empowers the court to decide on constitutional issues and to shape the development of integration. That said, the development of judicial landmarks is not purely incidental to the CJEU's adjudicative role. It is also a matter of conscious deliberation and choice. Indeed, in recognition of the court's constitutional role, the rules of procedure make it possible for the institutions of the European Union to demand that a case be decided by a grand chamber, and the court itself is prepared to form a grand chamber whenever a treaty rule requires additional interpretation, regardless of whether a party has asked for it.

The Landmarks

When one contemplates historical landmark cases heard by the CJEU, one immediately thinks of the judgment of the CJEU in the case *Van Gend en Loos*.[9] Decided in 1963, the case is in many ways a European version of *Marbury v. Madison*.[10] It is a starting point of analysis for every scholar of EU law. Interestingly, the judgment itself had to resolve only a limited controversy regarding customs classification; were it not for other reasons, the case would have been forgotten long ago. The question presented to the court in the form of preliminary reference from a Dutch administrative court in customs matters concerned interpretation of the stand-still clause of the treaty. The response of the court changed the shape of what is today the European Union. The case introduced into the legal order of the European Union the concept of direct effect—the legal principle according to which EU law creates individual rights that national courts must protect.

In 1981, Professor Eric Stein noticed that jurisprudence of the CJEU had helped EU law evolve in terms of its effects on national legal orders in three dimensions: from negative to positive obligations; from vertical to horizontal effects, that is, from relationships between individuals and state authorities to relationships between individuals; and from primary to secondary EU law.[11] Those developments were and still are closely connected with the question of the allocation and exercise of regulatory competences within the European Union insofar as the interpretation of direct effect and supremacy of EU law

---

9 Case 26/62, NV Algemene Transport—en Expeditie *Onderneming Van Gend en Loos v. Netherlands Inland Revenue Administration*, EU:C:1963:1.

10 5 U.S. 137 (1803).

11 Eric Stein, "Lawyers, Judges and the Making of a Transnational Constitution," *American Journal of International Law* 75, no. 1 (1981): 1–27.

have enabled the CJEU to fine-tune the relationship between national and European regulatory institutions, as well as between its own jurisdiction and the jurisdiction of the national courts. *Van Gend en Loos* became not only universally recognized as a landmark but also the basis for the functioning of the legal order of the European Union until today.

Some years later, in 1978, in its decision in the case of *Cassis de Dijon*,[12] the CJEU transformed the face of the internal market. Confronted with a stay in the economic integration process, the court introduced the principle of mutual recognition, according to which products manufactured and placed on the market of one member state should have access to markets of all other member states. Today, the principle of mutual recognition has developed into a broadly applied principle. It extends well beyond internal market law in the strict sense, and has become a leading principle in certain areas of social regulation, such as higher education, and, no less important, a cornerstone of judicial cooperation in both civil and criminal matters.

In 1991, in joined cases *Francovich and Bonifaci*,[13] the court clarified that individuals can successfully claim damages against member states when they have failed to fulfill an obligation under EU law. Such claims can be brought before national courts. This principle was subsequently extended to include the responsibility of the member states for their national courts' failure to apply EU law correctly.[14]

A more recent example of landmark-building is provided by a 2014 case, *Digital Rights Ireland*,[15] in which the court was invited to annul the Data Retention Directive for being contrary to Articles 7, 8, and 11 of the EU Charter of Rights. The case was decided by a grand chamber and introduced an important method of interpretation that restricts regulatory discretion beyond the plain wording of the charter, the crucial phrase in the judgment being "strictly necessary."[16] The landmark potential of the case lies in the possibility of drawing parallels with the strict scrutiny test as applied in the United States.

---

12 *Rewe-Zentral AG v. Bundesmonopolverwaltung für Branntwein*, Case 120/78, EU:C:1979:42.

13 *Andrea Francovich v. Italian Republic* and *Danila Bonifaci v. Italian Republic*, joined cases C-6/90 and C-9/90, EU:C:1991:428.

14 Gerhard K*öbler v. Republik Österreich*, Case C-224/01, EU:C:2003:513.

15 Joined cases *Digital Rights Ireland Ltd (C-293/12) v. Minister for Communications, Marine and Natural Resources and Others and Kärntner Landesregierung (C-594/12) and Others*, EU:C:2014:238.

16 In paragraph 48 of the judgment, the court held that "in view of the important role played by the protection of personal data in the light of the fundamental right to respect for private life and the extent and seriousness of the interference with that right caused by Directive 2006/24, the EU legislature's discretion is reduced, with the result that review of that discretion should be strict." And in paragraph 52, the court continued, "So far as concerns the right to respect for private life, the protection of that fundamental right requires, according to the Court's settled case-law, in any event, that derogations and limitations in relation to the protection of personal data must apply only in so far as it is strictly necessary."

The Court's Enduring Landmark-Making Capacity

The CJEU clearly demonstrated its landmark-making capacity in the formative period of the European Union, but has that capacity diminished over time? The answer seems to be that although the court and the constitutional environment in which it operates have changed, the court's capacity to deliver decisions with significant social impact has not faded. Six reasons explain this enduring capacity.

First, the court of 28 judges is a significantly different institution than the court of 9 or 12. The sheer size of the court dictates its internal structure. Therefore, it is not surprising that significant evolution of EU law today takes place primarily in chambers of 15 judges while more straightforward cases are allocated to smaller formations. This by itself requires a certain degree of reflection about which cases may have broader legal and social impact, a task that is entrusted to the college of all judges and advocates general sitting in the RG. In other words, the significance of a case is typically recognized at an early stage of the procedure, putting the judges on notice that an important legal controversy is being decided.

Second, the original design of the court did not provide for docket control in the form of certiorari. This has been remedied by the chamber allocation system, which effectively serves as a system of selecting cases. However, another phenomenon has emerged during the same period. Unlike the Supreme Court of the United States, which selects cases at an early stage, the CJEU has to decide every admissible case within its jurisdiction. This obligation has contributed to the emergence of a specific judicial economy, which drives the court to adopt decisions that will minimize the need for future litigation. In such instances, the court speaks in general language and addresses general audiences, thereby enhancing the likelihood that its decisions will generate social debate and crystallize into landmarks.

Third, the European Union today comprises 28 member states, and so 28 legal systems are represented at the CJEU. This diversity makes the court different from national jurisdictions, because there is a constant need to find legal concepts that are workable in all member states. Inevitably, not all member states will feel comfortable with certain legal developments, and it is possible that EU law will develop an entirely European concept that will have to fit into all national legal systems.[17] In such circumstances, a clearly formulated concept of EU law that is broad enough to accommodate a variety of solutions existing in national law may be a basis for the emergence of a landmark.

---

17 The CJEU described the meaning of a "concept of EU law" in Gaetano Mantello, Case C-261/09, EU:C:2010:683, at point 38: "The concept of 'same acts' in Article 3(2) of the Framework Decision cannot be left to the discretion of the judicial authorities of each Member State on the basis of their national law. It follows from the need for uniform application of European Union law that, since that provision makes no reference to the law of the Member States with regard to that concept, the latter must be given an autonomous and uniform interpretation throughout the European Union."

Fourth, EU law has spread to areas of law far beyond those that it covered in the European Union's formative period. The scope for landmark making has been widened by increasing judicial cooperation in civil and criminal matters, and by the inclusion of the Charter of Fundamental Rights in the primary law of the European Union. Rules of EU law that have not yet been interpreted by the CJEU typically get allocated to the grand chamber, the formation that is best equipped to identify and forge landmark cases.

Fifth, unlike the Supreme Court of the United States, which is often reluctant to decide political questions,[18] the CJEU has explicit constitutional jurisdiction under the Founding Treaties to decide disputes between the institutions concerning the legality of their acts under Article 263 of the TFEU. A recent example involved deciding on a challenge by the Council of Europe to the power of the European Commission to withdraw a legislative proposal from the procedure.[19] No less important, in the area of human rights, which is an area of a constitutional nature for both the European Union and its member states, the pressure applied by the member states and the European Court of Human Rights creates an additional incentive for the CJEU to express itself in a stable and general way in order to forge a meaningful coexistence among the rights enshrined in different legal systems.[20] In other words, institutional balance, both horizontal and vertical, as well as constitutional cases involving human rights protection, add to the pressure for the CJEU to speak in clear, general, and authoritative language about legal issues that have the potential to become the subjects of landmark decisions.

Sixth and last, as the CJEU itself commented in the previously mentioned *Van Gend en Loos* case, decided in 1963, the vigilance of individuals striving to protect their individual rights is an essential element of legal protection within the European Union. That legal protection is channeled largely through cooperation between national courts and the CJEU. Furthermore, the enlargement of the European Union to 28 member states has increased the number of national courts involved in and affected by the application of EU law. The audience for CJEU decisions is much wider today than before, and so is the CJEU's landmark-making potential. In order to unleash that potential, the CJEU needs not only independence and vision in its judges, but also vigilance in the individuals seeking legal protection.

---

18 *Baker v. Carr* (No. 6), 369 U.S. 186 at 179: "In determining whether a question falls within [the political question] category, the appropriateness under our system of government of attributing finality to the action of the political departments and also the lack of satisfactory criteria for a judicial determination are dominant considerations."

19 *Council v. Commission*, Case C 409/13, judgment of April 14, 2015, EU:C: 2015:217.

20 For the relationship between EU law and law of the European Convention on Human Rights and Fundamental Freedoms, see Opinion 2/13, pt. 37 et seq.

14

The New Pillars of the EU Financial Architecture and the Single Supervisory Mechanism

MARINO PERASSI

Integrated supervision is essential to ensure the effective application of prudential rules, risk control and crisis prevention throughout the EU. The current architecture should evolve as soon as possible towards a single European banking supervision system with a European and a national level. The European level would have ultimate responsibility.

Such a system would ensure that the supervision of banks in all EU Member States is equally effective in reducing the probability of bank failures and preventing the need for intervention by joint deposit guarantees or resolution funds. To this end, the European level would be given supervisory authority and pre-emptive intervention powers applicable to all banks. Its direct involvement would vary depending on the size and nature of banks.

The possibilities foreseen under Article 127(6) TFEU regarding the conferral upon the European Central Bank of powers of supervision over banks in the euro area would be fully explored.

—Herman Van Rompuy, President of the European Council, "Towards a Genuine Economic and Monetary Union"

In the aftermath of the worst financial crisis suffered by Europe since World War II, the report issued in June 2012 by EC president Herman Van Rompuy marked the beginning of a process that would lead to the consolidation of the Banking Union.

The report presented a series of proposals for progress "towards a stronger EMU [Economic and Monetary Union] architecture, based on integrated frameworks for the financial sector, for budgetary matters and for economic policy."[1] Since the launch of the single currency in 1999, the financial architecture in the "Euro Area" (i.e., those countries that adopted the single currency)

This topic was discussed on Europe Day, October 22, 2014, at the Law, Justice and Development Week conference held at the World Bank in Washington, DC.

1 Herman Van Rompuy, "Towards a Genuine Economic and Monetary Union" (Report 120/12, European Council, Brussels, Belgium, June, 26 2012), 1. The report—prepared in close cooperation with the presidents of the European Commission, the Eurogroup, and the European Central Bank—set out a vision for the future of the EMU and how it can best contribute to growth, jobs, and stability.

had experienced a trend toward harmonization. But the degree of harmony the Euro Area had achieved proved to be inadequate when the banking system encountered the financial crisis.

The rate of convergence between the rules and the exercise of banking supervision had not kept pace with the increasing integration of banking business in the Euro Area. Differences in supervisory frameworks had been used to attract banking and financial business—a form of competition in laxity.

The distress in the banking sector evidenced the close link between the stability of credit institutions and the member states in which those institutions were established.[2] Because the public sector was considered the last source of support for banks, the loss of confidence in the sovereign debt of a member state could generate mistrust in the banking sector of that country. Moreover, ailing banks held large amounts of sovereign debt, creating a vicious cycle among sovereign debtors and commercial banks, a situation considered unsafe by European institutions.[3] In Greece, concerns over a sovereign default led to the distress of Greek banks in 2009. In Ireland, the crisis originated, conversely, in the banking sector and spilled over to the sovereign debt market in 2010.[4]

The response to the crisis by many EU countries revealed the shortcomings of a fragmented system of financial regulators in a single economic and currency area.

For the European institutions, entrusting an institution with the task of supervising the entire banking system in the Euro Area was the main part of the ambitious project to establish the Banking Union. However, in the aftermath of the financial crisis, it became clear that an effective supervisory system also required adopting a harmonized approach to managing banks and protecting depositors. As a consequence, the Banking Union was made more elaborate by adding two more pillars to the supervisory pillar.

The Three Pillars of the Banking Union and the Establishment of the Single Supervisory Mechanism

Supervisory tasks are an essential component of any system to ensure financial stability. By themselves, however, they are inadequate to that task.

---

2 Council Regulation (EU) No. 1024/2013 of October 15, 2013 (hereinafter SSM [for Single Supervisory Mechanism] Regulation), which assigns specific tasks to the European Central Bank (ECB) concerning policies relating to the prudential supervision of credit institutions; see SSM Regulation, whereas clause 6.

3 And, in fact, breaking the links between states and banks was among the objectives and basic principles of the legal framework for crisis management and resolution of banks of the European Union, the second pillar of the Banking Union, as highlighted by Karl-Philipp Wojcik, a member of the European Commission's Legal Service, in his presentation on Europe Day at the World Bank.

4 See Marco Pagano, "Lessons from the European Financial Crisis," in *Financial Regulation: A Transatlantic Perspective*, ed. Ester Faia et al. (Cambridge: Cambridge University Press, 2015), 24.

Financial stability depends on a tripartite system, which is why, as of this writing (winter 2015–16), the Banking Union has two pillars—the Single Supervisory Mechanism (SSM) and the Single Resolution Mechanism (SRM)—and is in the process of acquiring a third—the European Deposit Insurance Scheme (EDIS) to complement the Common Deposit Guarantee Scheme (CDGS), already in place.

The SSM, which came into force on November 4, 2014,[5] creates a single rulebook, which provides common rules for banks in all 28 member states.

The SRM, which is also based on a single set of rules and which came into force on January 1, 2016,[6] ensures the use of an integrated approach to crisis management and resolution in the banking sector, preventing divergences between, on the one hand, national resolution rules and, on the other hand, practices in the member states of the Euro Area. The European mechanism plays a pivotal role in this field by preventing national interests from interfering with the management of any future banking crisis. This preventive measure helps to break the link between sovereign issuers and banks and helps to foster financial stability.[7]

The SRM Regulation[8] and the EU Bank Recovery and Resolution Directive (BRRD)[9] contain a wide range of provisions concerning the recovery and resolution of credit institutions, and create various tools for use in early intervention or management by competent authorities in resolution proceedings.

When the third pillar is completed, it will establish harmonized and effective rules to protect depositors and enhance their confidence in the banking system. Completion of this pillar will occur when the EDIS is launched to complement the CDGS, which protects bank deposits up to €100,000.[10] The need to add this third pillar to the Banking Union was emphasized in a report issued in June 2015 by the presidents of the five European institutions in charge of the overall stability of the financial and banking system.[11]

---

5 SSM Regulation, art. 34.

6 Regulation (EU) No. 806/2014 of the European Parliament and of the Council of July 15, 2014, establishing uniform rules and a uniform procedure for the resolution of credit institutions and certain investment firms in the framework of a Single Resolution Mechanism and a Single Resolution Fund, in O.J. L 225, 30.7.2014, 1–90 (hereinafter SRM Regulation), art. 99.2.

7 Regarding the vicious links among banks and states in the case of a financial crisis, see the introduction, discussing the Herman Van Rompuy report.

8 Regulation (EU) No. 806/2014, SRM Regulation.

9 Directive 2014/59/EU of the European Parliament and of the Council of May 15, 2014, establishing a framework for the recovery and resolution of credit institutions and investment firms, in O.J. L 173, 12.6.2014, 190–348.

10 Directive 2014/49/EU of the European Parliament and of the Council of April 16, 2014, on Deposit Guarantee Schemes (O.J. L173/149 12.6.2014).

11 Jean-Claude Juncker, with Donald Tusk, Jeroen Dijsselbloem, Mario Draghi, and Martin Schulz, "Completing Europe's Economic and Monetary Union" (European Commission, Brussels, June 22, 2015), para. 3.1. Juncker is the president of the European Commission, Tusk the president of the Euro Summit, Dijsselbloem the president of the Eurogroup,

The three pillars will form a comprehensive set of rules and tools that are closely interrelated and that will work in a coordinated manner.

The legal underpinnings consist of the Maastricht Treaty of 1992, which provides detailed rules for governing the single currency, the euro, while the Treaty on European Union (TEU) and the Treaty on the Functioning of the European Union (TFEU) lay down detailed provisions concerning the European Central Bank (ECB), the Eurosystem, and the European System of Central Banks (ESCB), the bodies charged with the tasks of managing currency and defining and implementing monetary policy in the Euro Area.

Although the governance of the ECB is laid down in detail in its statute, no provision concerning supervisory tasks or supervisory authority was inserted in the treaties. The ECB's legal basis is narrowly limited to the enabling clause in Article 127.6 of the TFEU.[12]

Establishing the SSM was thus a legal challenge; the adoption of a regulation followed the special legislative procedure laid down in Article 127.6, which provides for the adoption of this regulation by the Council of the European Union (the Council), after consulting with the ECB and the European Parliament. This route is quicker than the process of amending the treaties, which is lengthy at the EU level and requires ratification by the member states in accordance with their constitutional rules (Article 48 of the TEU). However, the rules laid down in a regulation are secondary legislation, and must accord with the primary rules in the treaties.

Under the provision of the enabling clause, a Council Regulation was adopted on October 15, 2013,[13] laying down the rules governing the competences and the functioning of the SSM.

The SSM is composed of the ECB and the national competent authorities (NCAs) of the participating member states within the Euro Area; the NCA of a country not in the Euro Area may take part in the mechanism by way of an agreement between that state and the ECB (with a member state in close cooperation).[14] In the absence of such agreements, the European financial and banking sector would be deeply divided into two zones: the Euro Area, with a single currency and a unified system of banking supervision; and the

---

Draghi the president of the European Central Bank, and Schulz the president of the European Parliament.

12 Art. 127.6 of the TFEU reads as follows: "The Council, acting by means of regulations in accordance with a special legislative procedure, may unanimously, and after consulting the European Parliament and the European Central Bank, confer specific tasks upon the European Central Bank concerning policies relating to the prudential supervision of credit institutions and other financial institutions with the exception of insurance."

13 SSM Regulation.

14 In the absence of this agreement, cooperation among the ECB and the supervisory authorities located outside the Euro Area shall be based upon a memorandum of understanding. See SSM Regulation, whereas clause 14.

remainder of the European Union, relying on common rules but having different authorities and supervisory practices.

The single rulebook for banking activity in the European Union ensures a unified set of norms concerning the credit business, but the implementation of those rules is not entrusted to a single supervisory institution.

One weakness of the current system is that, because not all the members (only 19 out of 28) of the European Union have adopted the single currency, banking supervision is the responsibility of the ECB within the Euro Area only. Even though the tasks are allocated to the NCAs and the ECB in accordance with specific criteria (see the section that follows, "The ECB's Supervisory Powers"), the ECB is to be responsible "for the effective and consistent functioning of the SSM."[15]

Even with the close cooperation of competent authorities, member states outside the Euro Area may implement and enforce the rules only by way of indirect supervision of the ECB, because the latter can act only with the necessary intervention of the supervisory authorities of the member state concerned.[16]

The tasks allocated to the SSM are linked to the supervision of banking activities concerning microprudential and macroprudential tasks. No responsibilities in the fields of investment services, consumer protection, or prevention of monetary laundering are assigned, because of the limitations of the secondary legislation adopted to establish the SSM, which must be in line with the treaty. The relevant provision in the treaty, which dates back to the Maastricht Treaty, refers to policies relating to prudential supervision only.

One could reasonably ask whether this limitation might hinder the effectiveness of the action of the SSM, but answering such a question is difficult in the early days of the new system.

The allocation of tasks between the ECB and the NCAs is based on the classification of banks into two groups: significant and less significant. The significant criteria for classification are size (the total value of the bank's assets must exceed €30 billion); economic importance (for either the specific country or the EU economy as a whole); cross-border activity (the total value of the bank's assets must exceed €5 billion, and the ratio of cross-border assets and liabilities in more than one participating member state to total assets and liabilities must be greater than 20 percent); and direct public financial assistance (the bank has requested or received funding from the European Stability Mechanism or the European Financial Stability Facility).[17]

The ECB directly supervises the 123 significant banks in the participating countries. These banks hold almost 82 percent of banking assets in the Euro

15 SSM Regulation, art. 6.1.

16 SSM Regulation, art. 7.

17 SSM Regulation, art. 6.

Area. The remaining credit institutions, classified as less significant, are supervised by the NCAs.

The division of competences follows two principles: the subsidiarity rule (Article 5.3 of the TEU),[18] which contributes to decisions by public authorities being made as closely to the citizen as possible; and the principle of overall responsibility of the ECB over the entire supervised banking system. In other words, the ECB is in charge of indirect supervision of the less significant credit institutions and may decide at any time to take direct responsibility over a less significant bank; the ECB may also issue instructions to the NCAs.[19]

A significant derogation from the general rule concerning the division of competences is provided for the authorization of credit institutions or the withdrawal of the authorization, and for the assessment of the acquisition and disposal of qualifying holdings in credit institutions.[20] These cases are linked to the right to access the banking activity and the market of corporate control of credit institutions; as a consequence, the EU Regulation provides for the competence of the ECB, with the strict cooperation of NCAs in all circumstances, including in the case of less significant banks, in order to ensure a level playing field in the granting of banking licenses and in the market of corporate control of credit institutions, irrespective of their economic importance.

Prior authorization is a key prudential technique to ensure that only adequate undertakings may have access to the credit market; the assessment of the suitability of any new owner of qualifying holdings in banks is a competence of the ECB, which, as an EU institution, is well placed to carry out such an assessment without imposing undue restrictions on the internal market.[21] In these cases, the ECB measures are taken in cooperation with the relevant NCAs (Articles 14 and 15 of the SSM Regulation).

With this framework in mind, the supervisory competence may be divided into three categories: ECB competence, NCA competence, and ECB-NCA shared competence (e.g., the authorization of credit institutions).

This approach, however, is not adequate to describe the inner nature of the new mechanism. The key is the cooperation duty expressly laid down in

---

18 "Under the principle of subsidiarity, in areas which do not fall within its exclusive competence, the Union shall act only if and in so far as the objectives of the proposed action cannot be sufficiently achieved by the member states, either at the central level or at regional and local levels, but can, by reason of the scale or effects of the proposed action, be better achieved at Union level . . . ."

19 On the allocation of tasks, powers, and liability among the ECB and the NCAs within the SSM, see Raffaele D'Ambrosio, "The ECB and NCA Liability within the Single Supervisory Mechanism," *Quaderni di ricerca giuridica della Consulenza Legale, Banca d'Italia, Roma* 78 (2015): 78, 91–116.

20 SSM Regulation, art. 4.1 (a) and (c), and art. 6.4.

21 See SSM Regulation, whereas clauses 20, 21, and 22.

Article 6 of the SSM Regulation,[22] which mirrors the principle of sincere cooperation of the Union and the member states provided in Article 4 of the TEU, a fundamental rule of the European Union.

Despite any misleading interpretation of the division of competences among the ECB and the NCAs, the SSM's structure and functioning are aimed at ensuring the singleness of supervision throughout the Euro Area; distinguishing between significant and less significant has proven to be immaterial because all the banks in the Euro Area are subject to the same legal framework, and the ECB is responsible for the effective and consistent functioning of the SSM (SSM Regulation, Article 6.1), acting as a guarantor of the singleness of the supervisory action.

The ECB is also entitled to adopt a framework to organize the practical arrangements for the implementation of the supervisory tasks, which ensures coordination between the ECB and the NCAs in the SSM.[23]

Important Principles of the Banking Union

Two important aspects of the Banking Union deserve mention: the separation between the regulatory function and the supervisory tasks, and the separation of monetary policy from banking supervision in ECB governance.

In regard to the first aspect, since the start of the SSM, European banking law has relied on a multilayered legal framework, which includes EU regulations, EU directives and the implementation of national laws, delegated acts adopted by the European Commission (the Commission), decisions adopted by the European Banking Authority (EBA), and decisions made by the ECB. This complex picture should be viewed while keeping in mind the principle of the allocation of regulatory powers to bodies not in charge of adopting supervisory measures. The separation of competences implies that the rules will be adopted in general by the Commission, the EBA, and the national competent bodies, and that ECB powers will be limited to the adoption of supervisory measures. According to this view, the ECB's regulatory powers should be restricted to the organizational arrangements in the SSM for carrying out tasks conferred under the SSM Regulation.[24] But a different view is admissible, and the granting of regulatory powers to the ECB, to the extent necessary to complete the set of rules adopted by the previously mentioned authorities, is still

---

22 Ibid., art. 6.2. Both the ECB and national competent authorities shall be subject to a duty of cooperation in good faith and an obligation to exchange information.

23 ECB, Regulation of April 16, 2014, establishing the framework for cooperation within the Single Supervisory Mechanism between the ECB and national competent authorities and with national designated authorities (SSM Framework Regulation) (ECB/2014/17), in O.J. L 141, 14.5.2014, p. 51, adopted by the ECB under the provision in art. 6.7 of the SSM Regulation.

24 Guido Ferrarini and Fabio Recine, "The Single Rulebook and the Single Supervisory Mechanism: Should the ECB Have More Say in Prudential Rule Making?" in *European Banking Union*, ed. Guido Ferrarini and Danny Bush (Oxford: Oxford University Press, 2015), 145.

under scrutiny because of the ambiguity of the SSM Regulation on this matter. In any event, these regulatory powers should be hierarchical and subject to primary and secondary Union law.[25]

The second aspect is extremely important in the architecture of the SSM, and shows how strictly the boundaries of the secondary legislation adopted to establish the system were drawn.

According to the ESCB/ECB Statute (Article 12), the ECB Governing Council is the body responsible for decision making and for defining and implementing Euro Area monetary policy, the primary objective of which is to maintain price stability. Once the supervisory powers have been assigned to the ECB under the applicable enabling clause of the treaty, the Governing Council will also be the body responsible for making supervisory decisions.

In the European landscape, many central banks are also national supervisors (e.g., in Italy, the Netherlands, and Spain), but in some countries the responsibilities of monetary policy and banking supervision are assigned to different authorities (e.g., in France and Germany). During the constitutional phase of the SSM, some countries supported the adoption of the separation model for political reasons. But the main challenge was related to the wording of the ESCB/ECB Statute, which defines monetary stability as the primary objective of the ECB (Article 2); this mandate could be put at risk by the possible conflict of interests between monetary policy functions and supervisory decisions, which in some circumstances might concern the banking/financial system of an entire country.

The primacy of the monetary policy mandate does not seem to be challenged by the supervisory tasks of the ECB; Article 3.3 of the ESCB/ECB Statute (which is primary law) refers to the prudential supervision of credit institutions and the stability of the financial system as a task that, in the hierarchy of tasks, is placed at a lower level than supervising price stability. This interpretation of the provision could be reinforced by the fact that the regulation that entrusted the ECB with supervisory power is secondary legislation (under Article 127.6 of the TFEU), which cannot supersede primary rules.[26]

However, this interpretation is misleading to the extent that it subordinates supervisory decisions to monetary policy considerations, ranking monetary policy above supervisory action and financial stability. The best way to approach this issue is with the principle of separation of monetary policy and banking supervision, which was adopted by the SSM Regulation and clearly

---

25 Concetta Brescia Morra, "From the Single Supervisory Mechanism to the Banking Union: The Role of the ECB and the EBA" (Working Paper, 15-16, LUISS Guido Carli, Rome, 2014). See also Marco Lamandini, David Ramos Muñoz, and Javier Solana Alvarez, "Depicting the Limits to the SSM's Supervisory Powers: The Role of Constitutional Mandates and of Fundamental Rights' Protection" (unpublished draft, ECB Legal Research Programme, July 20, 2015), 26–35.

26 Lamandini, Muñoz, and Alvarez, "Depicting the Limits to the SSM's Supervisory Powers," 42–45.

provides for these functions to be carried out separately to avoid conflicts of interest and to ensure that each function is exercised in accordance with the applicable objectives.[27] It should be remembered that the SSM governance was designed for the express purpose of implementing the principle of separation.

Supervisory measures are adopted by the Supervisory Board of the ESB, as established by the SSM Regulation. The Supervisory Board is composed of a chair and a vice chair, both of whom are appointed by the Council upon the proposal of the ECB, and approved by the European Parliament; four representatives of the ECB; and one NCA representative of each Euro Area member state. The separation at ECB staff levels mirrors the separation of the governing bodies.

The decisions of the Supervisory Board, made by a simple majority, are submitted to the Governing Council for adoption; again, the strict limits of the ESCB/ECB Statute apply, and the Governing Council is the only body that can issue ECB legal acts.

In this case, the principle of separation, which is a pillar of the supervisory mechanism,[28] comes into play again; the SSM Regulation provides for the approval of the draft decision of the Supervisory Board, unless the Governing Council objects by stating its reasons in writing, "in particular stating monetary policy concerns."[29] The provision laid down in Article 26.8 of the SSM Regulation is aimed at limiting the objections that can be raised by the Governing Council, specifying that only monetary policy concerns may be opposed in a draft supervisory decision; however, the wording of the sentence ("*in particular* stating monetary policy concerns"—emphasis added) and the governance of the ECB, in which the Governing Council retains full power of decision, supports a different reading.

However, the SSM Regulation establishes a mediation panel, as seen in Article 25.5: "With a view to ensuring separation between monetary policy and supervisory tasks, the ECB shall create a mediation panel. This panel shall resolve differences of views expressed by the competent authorities of participating Member States concerned regarding an objection of the Governing Council to a draft decision by the Supervisory Board." The wording of this provision supports the strict interpretation of the power of the Governing Council to raise only objections that are based on monetary policy concerns.

The Supervisory Board and the NCAs, when carrying out the functions conferred on them by the new framework, are required to act independently and to neither seek nor take instructions from the institutions or bodies of the Union, from any government of a member state, or from any other public or private body.[30] This provision is aimed at preventing political pressure on the

27 See SSM Regulation, whereas clause 65.

28 Ibid.

29 SSM Regulation, art. 26.8.

30 SSM Regulation, art. 19.1.

governing bodies of the SSM, irrespective of the source, whether European or national. This principle was laid down in the Maastricht Treaty and enshrined in Article 7 of the ESCB/ECB Statute to ensure that the implementation of monetary policy in the Euro Area is in line with the principle of price stability. The principle is now a significant feature of the framework on EU supervision.

The ECB's Supervisory Powers

The SSM Regulation assigns the ECB both microsupervisory and macrosupervisory tasks. The former are provided for under Article 4 and are aimed at ensuring the safety and soundness of credit institutions; the latter are referred to under Article 5, with a view to contributing to financial stability within the European Union and each member state. The corresponding micro- and macroprudential tools are separately singled out in Article 16 of the SSM Regulation and in Articles 130ff. of the so-called CRD IV Directive, respectively.[31]

Despite the effort to separate the micro- and macroprudential tools, the distinction is not always clear. To counter macroprudential risks, supervisors may also adopt (besides the instruments under Articles 130ff. of the CRD IV Directive) the measures under Article 16.2 of the SSM Regulation. Indeed, these latter measures may be adopted for the purposes of Article 9.1, which include, in turn, both micro- and macroprudential purposes, because it refers to Articles 4 and 5 of the SSM Regulation. The still-uncertain nature of the ECB's practice on the topic suggests that the interpreter should be cautious. The further ECB application of Article 16 of the SSM Regulation will clarify the scope of the provisions therein.

Although expressly enumerated in Article 16.2 of the SSM Regulation, the microprudential tools available to the ECB are basically the same as those specified in Article 104 of the CRD IV (the so-called Pillar 2 measures), the only difference being that Article 16 gives the ECB the further power—expressly mentioned in Article 16.2(m)—to "remove at any time members from the management body of credit institutions who do not fulfil the requirements set out in the acts referred to in the first subparagraph of Article 4.3."[32]

In addition to the removal clause, Article 16.2 provides the ECB with the following powers:

(a) to require institutions to hold own funds in excess of the capital requirements laid down in Union Law related to elements of risks and risks not covered by the relevant Union acts;

(b) to require the reinforcement of the arrangements, processes, mechanisms and strategies;

---

31 Directive 2013/36/EU of the European Parliament and of the Council, June 26, 2013, on access to the activity of credit institutions and the prudential supervision of credit institutions and investment firms, in O.J. L 176, 27.6.2013, 338–436.

32 SSM Regulation, art. 16.2(m).

(c) to require institutions to present a plan to restore compliance with supervisory requirements pursuant to Union Law and set a deadline for its implementation, including improvements to that plan regarding scope and deadline;

(d) to require institutions to apply a specific provisioning policy or treatment of assets in terms of own funds requirements;

(e) to restrict or limit the business, operations or network of institutions or to request the divestment of activities that pose excessive risks to the soundness of an institution;

(f) to require the reduction of the risk inherent in the activities, products and systems of institutions;

(g) to require institutions to limit variable remuneration as a percentage of net revenues when it is inconsistent with the maintenance of a sound capital base;

(h) to require institutions to use net profits to strengthen own funds;

(i) to restrict or prohibit distributions by the institution to shareholders, members or holders of Additional Tier 1 instruments where the prohibition does not constitute an event of default of the institution;

(j) to impose additional or more frequent reporting requirements, including reporting on capital and liquidity positions;

(k) to impose specific liquidity requirements, including restrictions on maturity mismatches between assets and liabilities;

(l) to require additional disclosures.[33]

All these powers may also be employed as measures at an early stage under the conditions laid down in Article 16.1 of the SSM Regulation and need to be coordinated with the relevant measures provided in the second pillar of the Banking Union concerning, for example, the recovery and resolution of credit institutions (Article 13 of the SRM Regulation[34] and Article 2.1 of the BRRD Directive[35]); early intervention (Article 27.1 of the BRRD Directive); the removal of senior management or management body (Article 28 of the BRRD Directive); and the appointment of a temporary administrator (Article 29 of the BRRD Directive).

---

33 SSM Regulation, art. 16.2.

34 Regulation (EU) No. 806/2014.

35 Directive 2014/59/EU. Under art. 2(1), point 21, of the directive, "'competent authority' means a competent authority as defined in Point 40 of art. 4(1) of Regulation (EU) No. 575/2013, including the European Central Bank with regard to specific tasks conferred on it by Council Regulation (EU) No. 1024/2013." In light of this, the ECB will enjoy all the powers NCAs are vested with under the relevant provisions of the BRRD.

The addressees of the ECB powers under Article 16 of the SSM Regulation are significant credit institutions. With regard to the less significant credit institutions not falling under these regulations, the NCAs may avail themselves of the powers provided for under the national laws transposing Article 104 of the CRD IV Directive.

The macroprudential tools available to both the ECB and the NCAs and national designated authorities (NDAs), per Article 5 of the SSM Regulation and singled out under Articles 130ff. of the CRD IV Directive, are the following:

- The countercyclical buffer (introduced by the CRD IV in order to counteract the effects of an economic cycle on banks' lending activity. It works as follows: when an economy experiences good credit growth, banks are required to have an additional amount of capital; when the economy cycle turns, the buffer can be released).
- The global systemic institution buffer (a mandatory systemic risk buffer of common equity tier 1 [CET 1] capital for banks identified by the relevant authority as being of global systemic importance);
- The other systemically important institution buffer (a buffer on other systemically important institutions, both at the domestic and the EU level);
- The systemic risk buffer (a buffer of CET 1 capital for the financial sector, aimed at preventing and mitigating long-term non-cyclical macroprudential risks with the potential of serious negative consequences to the financial system and the real economy of a specific member state).

In addition to using these buffers, the ECB may also apply to domestically authorized credit institutions the national macroprudential measures referred to under the so-called flexibility clause, provided for under Article 458 of the Capital Requirements Regulation (CRR).[36] The NCAs and NDAs will continue to be vested with the power to apply any macroprudential tool that is not provided for in the relevant Union law.

Both the national authorities and the ECB may apply the macroprudential tools provided for under the CRD IV Directive/CRR Regulation package in relation to all credit institutions, irrespective of their significant or less significant status.

The initiative in applying the tools is taken by the national authorities. Nevertheless, the ECB may apply higher buffers or take stricter measures than those of the national authorities. Despite the less than perfectly clear wording

36 Regulation (EU) No. 575/2013 of the European Parliament and of the Council of June 26, 2013, on prudential requirements for credit institutions and investment firms, in O.J. L 176, 27.6.2013, 1–337.

of Article 5.2 of the SSM Regulation, the ECB should apply these tools even where the national authorities do not apply them at all.

Compliance with macroprudential instruments should be supervised by the relevant competent authority—namely, the ECB for significant credit institutions and the NCAs for the less significant ones.

Supervisory Decisions and Judicial Review

The measures taken by the ECB are subject to judicial review under the rules of the European Treaties. A challenge in court of a monetary policy decision is extremely unlikely, because courts do not dictate economic policy, and according to the guidance coming from the European Court of Justice, the implementation of monetary policy is an area subject to much discretion.[37]

Nonetheless, legal actions are likely to occur in the supervisory area. The SSM Regulation provides for a preliminary examination of the decisions by the Administrative Board of Review (ABoR), which does not preclude a direct challenge before the EU courts. The ABoR is composed of five permanent and two alternate members—from different countries and different backgrounds and with experience in central banking, banking supervision, and banking law—who are appointed for five-year terms by the Governing Council of the ECB.[38]

Any natural or legal person may request a review of a supervisory decision of the ECB that is addressed to that person or is of a direct and individual concern to that person. Upon receiving such a request, the ABoR will carry out an internal administrative review of the ECB decision and provide an opinion based on the expertise and the judgment of its members. The opinion is not binding. It is up to the Supervisory Board to follow it or not, and to propose to the Governing Council to alter or confirm its initial decision. The Governing Council has the right to follow it or not.

If the governing bodies of the SSM decide not to act on the opinion of the ABoR, the interested persons can then challenge the decision before the EU courts, and in that proceeding the acts of the ABoR will be open to those persons and the court will decide if a recommended course of action has not been followed by the Supervisory Board or the Governing Council. In other words, a supervisory decision dissenting from the ABoR opinion without an adequate motivation is exposed to a significant legal risk in the court proceeding.

---

37 Lamandini, Muñoz, and Alvarez, "Depicting the Limits to the SSM's Supervisory Powers," 48–49. See also European Court of Justice, Case C-62/14, *Peter Gauweiler and others v. Deutsche Bundestag*, June 16, 2015.

38 ECB, "Decision Concerning the Establishment of the Administrative Board of Review and Its Operating Rules" (ECB/2014/16), OJ L 175, 14.6.2014, p. 47.

This system is quite different from the redress mechanism established in cases of the decisions made by the European regulatory authorities.[39] A measure adopted by the EBA may be challenged before the Joint Board of Appeal, an independent body that has the power to issue a decision that is binding for the EBA, which subsequently will adopt an amended decision on the case concerned.[40] In addition, the pronouncements of the Joint Board of Appeal may be brought before EU courts. The binding effect of the decisions of the Joint Board of Appeal offers protection of the rights of the parties affected by the measures taken by the authorities.

The judicial review of the supervisory acts adopted by the governing bodies of the ECB and the NCAs in a multilayered system raises a number of issues. The acts of the ECB are subject to review by the EU courts; in the case of common procedures, where the preliminary phase of the proceeding is carried out by an NCA at national level, a part of the proceeding may not be in line with a national rule. The challenge before the EU court will also bring to the attention of the judge the violation of the national rules.

Should a decision of an NCA be appealed before a national judge, the proceeding will also focus on the possible breach of the European law applied by the NCA. In some cases, the NCAs have to adopt decisions upon instructions of the ECB; the decisions are binding, in accordance with the principle of the supremacy of EU law over the national legal framework. In these cases, the judicial review will also take place at the national level; however, the court could raise the preliminary question of the validity and interpretation of acts of the ECB, an EU institution, before the European Court of Justice, in accordance with Article 267(b) of the TFEU. Here again is a situation in which the interplay between EU law and a national legal framework will be essential in the functioning of the SSM.

A number of problematic issues regarding Euro Area supervision remain unsettled. The mechanism was established by adopting legal acts concerning the governance of the system and the supervisory functions, and by relying on the single EU rulebook; the process developed rapidly and was implemented by way of secondary legislation.

The shortcomings of this approach may be seen in the lack of harmonization of the rules that are necessarily involved in the exercise of supervisory powers: company law, insolvency rules, and taxation. The legislative process in the last decade of the 20th century to adopt the single currency, the euro, was more prudent; based on new treaty provisions, a legal convergence of the national legislation process was put in place before the start of the monetary

---

39 The EBA, the European Insurance and Occupational Pensions Authority (EIOPA), the European Securities and Market Authority (ESMA), and the European Supervisory Authorities.

40 Regulation (EU) No. 1093/2010 of the European Parliament and of the Council, November 24, 2010, establishing a European Supervisory Authority (European Banking Authority), art. 60.5.

union (Article 131 of the TFEU) and enforced through an in-depth method of verification.

A new challenge for the European institutions is to ensure the harmonization of the full legal framework concerning banking and financial activity in the Euro Area. Tackling this challenge will probably require further specific intervention by the European institutions in the years to come.

Recent history suggests that the unification of rules can have a powerful impact over the long term. Launched in 1999, the single currency eventually led to a thorough harmonization in the field of monetary law, payment systems, and payment means, a situation that had been inconceivable in the early days of the euro. In the same vein, the SSM will generate growing pressure to establish common rules for banking activities.

Corporate law concerning the governance of banking institutions still relies on principles that differ from one country to another, and the rules concerning stakeholders' rights laid down in private law may not be in line with the mandatory provision of the prudential regulation of the SSM. This situation may well provoke legal disputes.

Furthermore, the tax treatment of financial activities still reveals many areas of inadequate harmonization. The legal framework in this field is strictly linked to sovereign powers, and EU member states are traditionally very cautious in launching reforms that affect fiscal revenues or limit their sovereign powers.

Progress toward convergence of widely shared legal principles could be achieved through corporate law, which offers the suitable tools of civil law and would rely on the court system to settle disputes over stakeholders' rights. For such a convergence to occur, pressure from the market would be extremely important.

Despite the legal complexities of the system and the national political interests that may hamper the development of that system,[41] the new pillars of the EU financial architecture constitute a major step forward in the construction of the European Union.

---

41 Elis Ferran, "European Banking Union: Imperfect But It Can Work," in *European Banking Union*, ed. Ferrarini and Bush, 56.

Index

Page numbers in italics refer to figures.

ECO-AUDIT

Environmental Benefits Statement

The World Bank Group is committed to reducing its environmental footprint. In support of this commitment, the Publishing and Knowledge Division leverages electronic publishing options and print-on-demand technology, which is located in regional hubs worldwide. Together, these initiatives enable print runs to be lowered and shipping distances decreased, resulting in reduced paper consumption, chemical use, greenhouse gas emissions, and waste.

The World Bank Group follows the recommended standards for paper use set by the Green Press Initiative. The majority of our books are printed on Forest Stewardship Council (FSC)–certified paper, with nearly all containing 50–100 percent recycled content. The recycled fiber in our book paper is either unbleached or bleached using totally chlorine-free (TCF), processed chlorine-free (PCF), or enhanced elemental chlorine-free (EECF) processes.

More information about the Bank's environmental philosophy can be found at http://www.worldbank.org/corporateresponsibility.

green press INITIATIVE